SOLVED!
THE MYSTERIES
OF
SPACE, TIME
AND UFOS

Inner Light - Global Communications
PO Box 753
New Brunswick, NJ 08903
MRUFO8@HOTMAIL.COM

Solved! The Mysteries of Space, Time and UFOs

By Dakini

With additional material by Timothy Green Beckley, Sean Casteel, Diane Tessman, Tim R. Swartz

Copyright © 2021 by Timothy Green Beckley

dba Inner Light/Global Communications

All Rights Reserved

No part of these manuscripts may be copied or reproduced by any mechanical or digital methods and no excerpts or quotes may be used in any other book or manuscript without permission in writing by the Publisher, Inner Light/Global Communications, except by a reviewer who may quote brief passages in a review.

Timothy Green Beckley: Editorial Director
Carol Rodriguez: Publishers Assistant
Editor and Layout: Tim R. Swartz
Sean Casteel: Associate Editor
William Kern: Editorial Assistant
Michelle Sweatt: YouTube and Media Director

Published in the United States of America By

Inner Light/Global Communications

Box 753, New Brunswick, NJ 08903

www.ConspiracyJournal.com

Email: mrufo8@hotmail.com

Contents

A Dakini – Or "Space Goer" – Penned This Volume From Another Dimension 5

An Introduction To Exploring the Univese With The Space Gods 9

1. T. Lobsang Rampa Visits Venus 15

2. Creative Space 23

3. Phenomena of Space 45

4. Gods and Men Out of Space 75

5. Fear of Inner and Outer Space 98

6. The Enigma of Matter 111

7. Thought 131

8. The Self – Its Relation to Space and Matter 159

9. The Reality and Illusion of Death 197

10. Ghosts 229

11. Problems of Illusion 242

12. Omniscience, Omipotence and Omnipresence 261

13. Sound and Silence 274

14. Psychic Phenomena and the UFO Mystery 296

15. Practical Mediumship 326

16. Energizing Your Thoughts Into Reality 342

Conclusion 354

A DAKINI – OR "SPACE GOER" – PENNED THIS VOLUME FROM ANOTHER DIMENSION
By Timothy Green Beckley

This wonderful book was written using telepathy as the medium of communications.

This is NOT your ordinary channeled book! Though you can believe it is if you so desire and don't wish to "go all the way," and believe that a Sky God put these words onto paper.

For you see, these in depth transmissions, these remarkable essays, were bought into our space and time – our world as it were – by an advanced entity known as a Dakini.

Dakini means "She Who Can Fly".

A Dakini is a Sky God, a Space Goer, or Space Dancer who guides humans along the path to enlightenment, most often in regard to the exact nature of the universe and its vast domains. She is most often pictured with exquisite jewelry and long flowing hair and in the nude, to symbolize the clarity of thought and truth as all is revealed a Dakini has the ability to move freely in space beyond thoughts and beyond fabrications.

The world's she inhabits includes parallel dimensions and all individual universal time zones and curves and dilations.

She is furthermore, a female spirit messenger of wisdom that can sometimes take on human form. It is understood by many that women make superior spiritual practitioners. Dakinis are often connected to the phenomena of synchronicity. "Coincidences" as we have seen run rampant throughout the body of works on UFOs and the paranormal, dealing a erratic hand to those involved as field investigators of the strange and unknown.

A Dakini can move about in the heavens like Luke Skywalker and thus transport themselves at the speed of light from one place to another. Though most frequently associated with **Buddhism,** belief in this entity has been widespread throughout the Himalayas for centuries and has been recognized by the local shamans.

While connected with elements of both white and black magic, on the positive side this powerful spirit can remove physical hindrances and spiritual obstacles such as those associated with pride and ego. When she is portrayed alone, she dances gracefully; her right leg is raised and bent, and her left leg would usually be planted on a prostrate figure. Originally, for ritualistic purposes, she would have held a curved, chopping knife in her right hand and a bowl made from a skull in her left that is filled with minstrel blood.

THE MYSTERIES OF SPACE AND TIME

Though the words in this volume were transmitted rather quickly (just as they would have been in "sacred books" like *"Oahspe"* which was written on the earliest of typewriters, circa 1860, yet at a phenomenal speed, which no human could possibly have accomplished at that time) it took several years to assemble the book by John Hay and the Light of the Freedom Institute.

The final product is phenomenal just like the phenomenal **topics that are discussed and explained.**

"The Magic of Space, Time and UFOs," covers such subjects as Flying Saucers, (now known as UAPs) Angels (without wings), Demons and other Occult subjects. The supernatural being only the unknown sciences yet to be rationalized by the academic communities because of "unclear thinking."

This book contains facts about the secrecy and suppression of such subjects as religion, psychiatry, physics and outer and inner space.

As a text book on life and death in the universe it will bring release from fear.

It will answer such questions as –

* *What is Atomic Fusion?*

SOLVED! THE MYSTERIES OF SPACE, TIME AND UFOS

* What is an apport?

* Who is responsible for the use of drugs? Wars? Civil unrest? Prejudice?

* What really happened to the early space contactees who were so popular in the Fifties and Sixties and went out on a limp to tell their intriguing stories of communicating with extraterrestrials?

The entity that is Dakini says it is time we knew the truth about Inner Space and the Divine Intelligence which will ultimately enable humans to abandon any hatred they may harbor toward one another.

This work constitutes a feverish attempt – before it is too late – to explore and explain the cosmic laws to men and women of all faiths living in all nations around our planet.

"The dakini is a messenger of spaciousness and a force of truth, presiding over the funeral of self-deception."

Lama Tsultrim Allione, from her book *Wisdom Rising: Journey into the Mandala of the Empowered Feminine*

Diane Tessman in meditative stage as she ponders the secrets of time and space. She has maintained contact with her own "star person" since an early age and continues to speak with her "Special One."

AN INTRODUCTION TO EXPLORING THE UNIVERSE WITH THE SKY GODS
By Diane Tessman

When publisher and author Timothy Green Beckley asked me to write the Forward for this unique book, I became fascinated with the Dakini. I had heard of them and knew their roots to be Tibetan. I thought of them as part of the mystical aspect of Buddhism, which they are, but their legend began long before Buddhism.

Every belief system maintained by early humans on Planet Earth seems to have "sky people," or "visitors from the stars," or "space gods" as part of their heritage and cultural background. The pre-Celts told of the Tuatha De Danann who came from the stars, settled on Earth as one of the early tribes in Ireland, but then "turned sideways to the sun," when they could no longer endure human ignorance and cruelty.

Native Americans from the east coast to the west coast of the Americas (and in the middle of the continent as well), all have myths and legends of sky gods. During their ceremonies they even dress up like the spiritual beings who frequently visited them. They are known among the Hopi and other tribes as the Kachina, and miniature replicas can be purchased at any gift shop in the South West.

Anu was the Mesopotamiasky sky god and a member of the triad of deities completed by Enlil and Enki. Like most sky gods, Anu, although theoretically the highest god, remained aloof from the Mesopotamian people but his power was great.

There is a strong argument for the possibility that the Greek gods were actually travelers of space-time who settled on Mount Olympus, possibly in an effort to begin to organize civilization for humankind.

The list of "sky entities" that were a part of either history or myth in ancient civilizations, is a long one. Some of these entities, like the Dakini of Tibet, still play a powerful role in the spiritual life of the people. Belief systems and religions spring out of the needs, trials, and tribulations of the people of Earth.

As I delved into the Dakini in depth, I realized that not only did they wield legendary power and give the Tibetan people help and guidance, they also fit into the worldwide legends of beings from the stars with their many fantastic abilities.

Yet, the Dakini are seldom mentioned. Who are the Dakini, do we have specifics?

Among the ancient Tibetan people of the Himalayan foothills and mountains, long before The Buddha was born, there were accounts of the Dakini, a sky tribe of spirit women who possess great wisdom. I found one mention of males called Daka, but it is clear, in this legend, the females hold all the power. In several tales, it tells of how the dakas became extinct.

It is said that dakini entities traverse both space and time, and yet, they care for Mother Earth and her life-forms; in particular, they care for the humans of the mighty Himalayan Mountains.

Dakinis are not perceived as all-benevolent on every occasion. As with Hindu legends of the Bhagavata Purana and Brahma Purana, an angry Dakini can bring great harm to an individual who has wronged her or wronged someone she protects. Some illustrations, cherished by her followers, show the mystical Dakini as an angry, vengeful goddess.

Dakinis' insistence on being illustrated in the nude except for their jewelry, indicates their vicious love of freedom and also, their raw power. They are indeed powerful spirits according to all who know them and have experienced them.

These traits of the Dakini had manifested before Buddhism embraced them as part of the mystical aspect of that belief system. As time passed, Vajrayana Buddhism became the preferred spirituality of Tibet, and these sky goddesses fit into the belief system perfectly.

The Tibetan people know the Dakini very well. For instance, there is a diva Dakini who is particularly loved, and she is summoned when help is needed. Her name is Kurukulla, the Diva Dakini of Enlightened Magic; she is the enchantress who transforms seduction into "the cause of wisdom and knowledge." And so, she is seductive and sensual for the good cause of gaining wisdom to bring about a good result to the problem.

Tibetan Buddhist priests make the point that dakinis are not gods as the western world thinks of Greek gods or Nordic gods. Dakinis are not even exotic sky women, enticingly nude except for their jewelry. In truth, they are advanced entities composed of cosmic energy which take the form of the Dakini.

I am reminded of the communication I received from the God Cloud, a cloud of super-intelligent particles on a level of advanced evolution which I could not even fully grasp. Dakinis are not of that level, as I see it, they feel emotions which humans feel, such as anger and the need for vengeance. The extremes of emotion within dakinis perhaps are caused because humans can only relate to entities that do have these extreme emotions. So, humans must make them something like embodied gods or spirits. This is what we can comprehend at this level of our evolution.

The elusive, powerful, mystical, exotic Dakini is today still a part of the Tibetan people's spiritual lives. The mighty Himalayan Mountains are home to both humans and their ancient spirits. Come along and learn more about these fascinating spirits of deep space-time, and see what one such entity has to say on a variety of topics that have long been dear to our western souls. It's a entirely different concept, but it is one worth of delving into.

This book holds many truths.

Learn from it.

* * * * * * * *

PUBLISHER'S NOTE: Most of our readers know of my involvement with Diane going back to the early 1980s when she was participating in investigating UFO reports for the Aerial Phenomena Research Organization (APRO), as well as the Mutual UFO Network (MUFON). Strange events were transpiring in her own life, including a series of unexplainable beeps in her home which seemed to correspond with a major tragic event in which many died. Diane Tessman has contributed her fair share of material to the various volumes we have published. Her most recent books are – *"The Real Life UFO Transformation of Diane Tessman: A Continuous Close Encounter with Future Man - Space Man,"* and *"Future Humans and the UFOs."* She can be reached at—

UFO News, Earth Change, Predictions, Diane Tessman, UFOs ...

www.earthchangepredictions.com

Diane does spiritual work with powerful Kilkenny white quartz.

Diane Tessman's book, "*The Real Life UFO Transformation of Diane Tessman,*" offers personal, never-before documented, alien and paranormal experiences leading her to wisdom about the very nature of the universe.

T. Lobsang Rampa was the author of such books as "*Beyond The Tenth*," published by Inner Light/Global Communications.

1

T. LOBSANG RAMPA VISITS VENUS
By Sean Casteel and Timothy Green Beckley

As we shall see, our renowned teacher on the mystic path most certainly has been influenced – "chatted with" most likely – a mighty Dakini. It shows in the nature of his wisdom of the cosmos and in all things space related.

For those who do not know, T. Lobsang Rampa is a legendary spiritual leader whose gifts to humanity have continued to offer his readers a true and trustworthy vision of the wondrous worlds that lie just within reach of our own.

More than 25 years after his death, Rampa's writings still manage to touch the heart with their uncannily realistic stories about the astral plane, the existence of people from other worlds, an underground civilization, the marvels of outer space, and the beauty of the Tibet he loved so much.

A diminutive tome which was omitted by his publisher from his first book "*The Third Eye*," because they felt it would be too controversial in nature, has continued to fascinate Rampa's millions of fans.

"*My Visit To Venus*" is an excellent example of Rampa's unique genius. First published in the British "*Flying Saucer Review*," this masterpiece has been reissued several times in the States, along with an edition by our own publishing company. This particular version includes commentary by well-known researcher and author John Keel. Keel who gives the reader a short course in Rampa's life story, including the engrossing tale of how Rampa became what may have been the first modern case of the Walk-In phenomenon. How a struggling British writer was transformed into a venerated New Age teacher and spiritual adventurer is beautifully told by Keel in his customary wonderful prose. A general history of the abduction phenomenon through the millennia is also included, which helps put Rampa's experiences in the context of mankind's age-old hand-in-hand stroll with the unknown.

Next comes an introduction by Gray Barker, one of the early pioneers of UFO research. Barker discusses his decision to publish some of Rampa's earliest work and gives a detailed account of the controversy that accompanied the publication of *"The Third Eye,"* Rampa's first book. Both Tibetans and the British media were up in arms about it, calling it a fraudulent piece of work and claiming that Rampa had never been to Tibet at all. Rampa answered his critics by saying that while he had never been there in his present body, the spirit of a Tibetan lama had entered his body under unusual circumstances. Barker's introduction also includes testimony from Rampa's wife as to the reality of the extreme personality changes in Rampa after the lama had moved in.

From that fascinating beginning, the book moves on to Rampa's own telling of the tale, which this time around features a journey to Venus, as the title implies. Rampa is on a journey, accompanied by a few fellow lamas, to meet with the beings that are telepathically leading them on. After a freezing trek through a Tibetan mountain range, they come to a warm and blissful garden called The Hidden Land. There they encounter a deserted flying saucer sitting on the ground, which they enter and explore. Soon they meet an alien Rampa calls The Tall One, who briefs them on their coming tour through outer space, the real purpose of their journey. Instead of describing the experience as warm and fuzzy, sweetness and light, Rampa talks frankly about the terror he feels as he is surrounded on all sides by such "high strangeness." That is another aspect of the abduction experience he shares with the more recent spate of modern abductees--one's initial reaction to the alien presence is nearly always one of fear. But after those first moments of fright, Rampa and his friends traverse the heavens on a flying saucer and witness all the beauty of an alien paradise on Venus. In all fairness to Rampa, it isn't really necessary that the location is literally the planet Venus. It could be anywhere in any universe and the message would still be the same--heaven is waiting for those who are ready to go there. You can read *"My Visit To Venus"* in one sitting, but its positive effects may last you a lifetime.

* * * * * * * * *

RAMPA – THE WALK IN
By T. Lobsang Rampa
With Editorial Comments And Structuring By Sean Casteel

There remains a considerable controversy over exactly who Rampa was. There are some Nay Sayers who insist that Tuesday was nothing more than a British plumber who one day cracked his head in an accident and came to thinking he was a gentleman – a lama – from Tibet with mystical powers.

Others see beyond this facade and consider him one of the greatest sagest of all times. They realize that he is more than just a mortal man, that he was what we in modern terms would call a "Walk In." This does NOT mean Rampa is possessed, but that he either shares his soul with another individual or has taken over a body for the purpose of disseminating important information to all of humankind.

From his humble origins as a "pipe fitter" in 1950s England, he claimed to have taken on the soul of a young Buddhist monk who lived in Tibet and studied with innumerable wise masters. His implanted soul remembered a lecture by an elderly lama who explained the concept of "transmigration" in a fascinating bit of historical mythology.

There can be little doubt that he has mastered and integrated the cosmology of the universe which he has mixed into his inspirational words.

THE GARDENERS OF THE EARTH

"Long before recorded history began," the lama said, "giants walked up on the Earth. They were the Gardeners of the Earth, those who came here to supervise the development of life on this planet. The Race of Giants was not very suitable for life on Earth, and so by magical means the Race of Giants shrank until they were the same size as humans. Thus they were able to mingle with humans without being recognized as the Gardeners.

"But it was often necessary for a different senior Gardener to come and carry out special tasks. It took too long to have a boy born to a woman and then wait out the years of his babyhood and childhood and adolescence. So the science of the Gardeners of the Earth had a different system: they grew certain bodies and made sure that those bodies would be compatible with the spirit who would later inhabit them.

"But the Gardeners of the Earth permitted certain men and women to mate so that a child was born to each, and the growth of that child would be most carefully supervised throughout, perhaps, the first fifteen or twenty or thirty years of life. Then there would come a time when a highly placed Gardener would need to come to Earth within a matter of hours, so helpers would place the trained body into a trance, into stasis, or, if you like, into a state of suspended animation.

"Helpers in the astral world would come to the living body, together with the entity who wanted to go to Earth, and with their special knowledge they could detach the Silver Cord and connect in its place the Silver Cord of the entity who was the Gardener of the Earth coming to the Earth. The host would then become the vehicle of the Gardener of the Earth, and the astral body of the host would go away to the astral world just as he would do in the case of a person who had died.

In Tibet, legends state that Mount Kailash is the home of an ancient race of extraterrestrials whose spaceships are kept in caves that are hidden around the sacred mountain.

THE TRANSMIGRATION

"This is called 'transmigration,' the migration of one entity into the body of another. The body taken over is known as the host, and it has been known throughout history. It was practiced extensively in Egypt and it gave rise to what is known as embalming, because in those days in Egypt there were quite a number of bodies kept in a state of suspended animation. They were living but unmoving. They were ready for occupancy by higher entities just as we keep ponies waiting for a monk or lama to mount the animal and ride off somewhere."

"Oh, my!" exclaimed one boy listening to the lama's lecture. "I expect friends of the host were mightily surprised when the body awakened and the one they had thought of as their friend in the past was possessed of all knowledge. My! I wouldn't like to be a host. It must be a terrible feeling to have someone else take over one's body."

The teacher laughed and said, "It would certainly be a unique experience. People still do it. Bodies are still prepared, specially raised so that, if the need arises, a different entity can take over a fresh body – if it becomes necessary for the good of the world as a whole."

RAMPA'S THOUGHTS ON THE UFO PHENOMENA

Much of the foregoing statements by Rampa's lama have their echoes in the UFO and abduction literature that came later. For instance, New England housewife and abductee Betty Luca Andreasson said that the familiar gray aliens called themselves "the Watchers," and compared themselves to "Gardeners of the Earth." Abductee Whitley Strieber was shown an alien standing in front of a dresser drawer full of "bodies" that the aliens put on and took off like clothes. So the idea of inserting a different soul or consciousness into an otherwise empty body is part of the same continuum that Rampa's lecturing lama describes. At another point in his abduction history, Strieber is told by the aliens that they "recycle souls," which could mean either reincarnation or is perhaps another way of referring to the Walk-In phenomenon.

THE LAMA, THE HERMIT AND THE ALIENS

Meanwhile, Rampa was no stranger to direct contact with the alien presence. In the last book Rampa authored, called *"Tibetan Sage,"* he encounters a UFO while on a mission with his mentor, the Lama Mingyar Dondup, to rescue a hermit overseeing a small hermitage in the mountains of Tibet. A sudden earthquake topples the hermit to his death and does serious injury to the Lama Mingyar Dondup's legs, who finds himself trapped under a boulder.

In the process of freeing his mentor, the young Rampa stumbles onto a secret compartment in the mountainside and carries the Lama inside. The compartment houses a flying saucer, which Rampa explores with the Lama and which will come to be the primary setting for the rest of the book.

Much to Rampa's surprise, the Lama is already familiar with the aliens and the languages they use and even with much of their technology. The ship has lain dormant for a million years, yet everything is still pristinely clean and functional. Some alien occupants are discovered frozen at their control consoles in a state of suspended animation.

There is often a dramatic shift of consciousness associated with a human being actually boarding a UFO called "the Oz Effect." It is given that name because the extreme contrast between the two environments resembles that moment in the film *"The Wizard of Oz"* when Dorothy crosses over from the black and white world of Kansas to the Technicolor Land of Oz This is certainly applicable to the changes Rampa undergoes in "Tibetan Sage," as he views holographic recordings of the formation of the Earth up through the Second World War, all stored in the mythic Hall of Records and accessed onboard the flying saucer. Rampa feels as though he is living and breathing in those previous and even future times, a degree of realism still not attainable by our own current technology. Sadly, most of what he sees involves bloody warfare both among people and between the gods themselves, another testimony to alien truthfulness, with no attempt to paint a rosy picture for Rampa's benefit.

MOSES – AND THE SKY GODS

In a new reprint of Rampa's book *"Beyond The Tenth,"* published by Timothy Green Beckley at Global Communications, Rampa deals with the UFO controversy from another angle.

"Moses was found in the bulrushes," Rampa writes. "But he was placed there by the Gardeners of the Earth, that is, the people who are known as UFO people, to be found. And later in life, Moses ascended into the mountain; Moses did a lot of strange things. But if you reread the relevant chapters, you will find that Moses stepped on a terraced floor. Did he do that on a mountain, or did he step into a flying ship, a UFO? Moses had the Rod of Power. It wasn't made on Earth, you know, it was made on another world. Moses was in fact another spaceman specially planted on Earth."

Solved! The Mysteries of Space, Time and UFOs

It's so interesting to see Rampa speaking out for the ancient astronauts' theory of UFOs and the Bible, many years before the idea was popularized by researchers who came later, like Erich Von Daniken and Zechariah Sitchin.

A few pages further along, Rampa again discusses UFOs.

"There are people in spaceships," he writes, "who are watching this world. Watching to see what happens. 'Well, why do they not come and talk to us like sensible people would?' you may ask, but the only reply is that they ARE being sensible. Humans try to shoot them and try in any way to harm these UFOs, and if UFOs, or rather the people within them, have the intelligence to cross space, then they have the intelligence to make an apparatus which can listen to Earth radio and Earth television. And if they watch Earth television – well, then they will think they have come to some vast mental home, because what could be more insane than the television programs which are foisted on a suffering public? Television programs which glorify the unclean, which glorify the criminal, which teach sex in the wrong way, in the worst possible way, which teach people that only self-gain and sex matter.

THE PEOPLE OF SPACE AND WHAT TO EXPECT FROM THEM

"Rampa compares people's expectation that the aliens would come and speak to humanity openly as being as silly as asking one of us to dive into a fish tank to discuss things with some worms at the bottom of the tank, or going into a hothouse and speaking to the plants and saying, "Take me to your leader."

"So the people of space," he says, "whose one-year-old children would know more than the wisest man on Earth, just watch over this colony."

Rampa also writes about UFO sightings of his own. While living in Montevideo, the capital of Uruguay, he was able to see, from his ninth floor apartment, across the river and out to the South Atlantic with no obstacles or obstructions to his view.

"Night after night, my family and I used to watch UFOs coming from the direction of the South Pole straight over our apartment building, and coming lower so that they could alight in the Matto Grosso of Brazil. Night after night, with unvarying regularity, these UFOs came. They were seen not just by us, but by a multitude of people, and in Argentina they are officially recognized as Unknown Flying Objects. The Argentine government is well aware that these things are not the product of hysteria or a fevered imagination. They are aware that UFOs are of surpassing reality."

With his combined expertise in Eastern mysticism and occult practices, with the additional factor in the mix of his fervent belief in the UFO and alien phenomena, Rampa's many books make for interesting reading indeed. While they are to say the least entertaining as a peculiar kind of science fiction, Rampa himself would bristle at the term. In spite of the fantastic nature of what he writes about, Rampa insisted to his dying day it was all hardcore fact, etched in the stone of time to endure forever. And the point of origin for Rampa's legacy of wisdom is traced back to when the soul of the sincerest of Buddhist monks replaced the soul of an English plumber and took the reading public on an epic journey that has no end, even in the decades since Rampa's passing.

And no doubt he had the assistance of a Dakini or two in his universal quest to "tell it like it is!"

SOURCES

www.chinabuddhismencyclopedia.com/en/index.php?title=Dakini

www.chinabuddhismencyclopedia.com/en/index.php/Dakinis:_Sky_Dancers

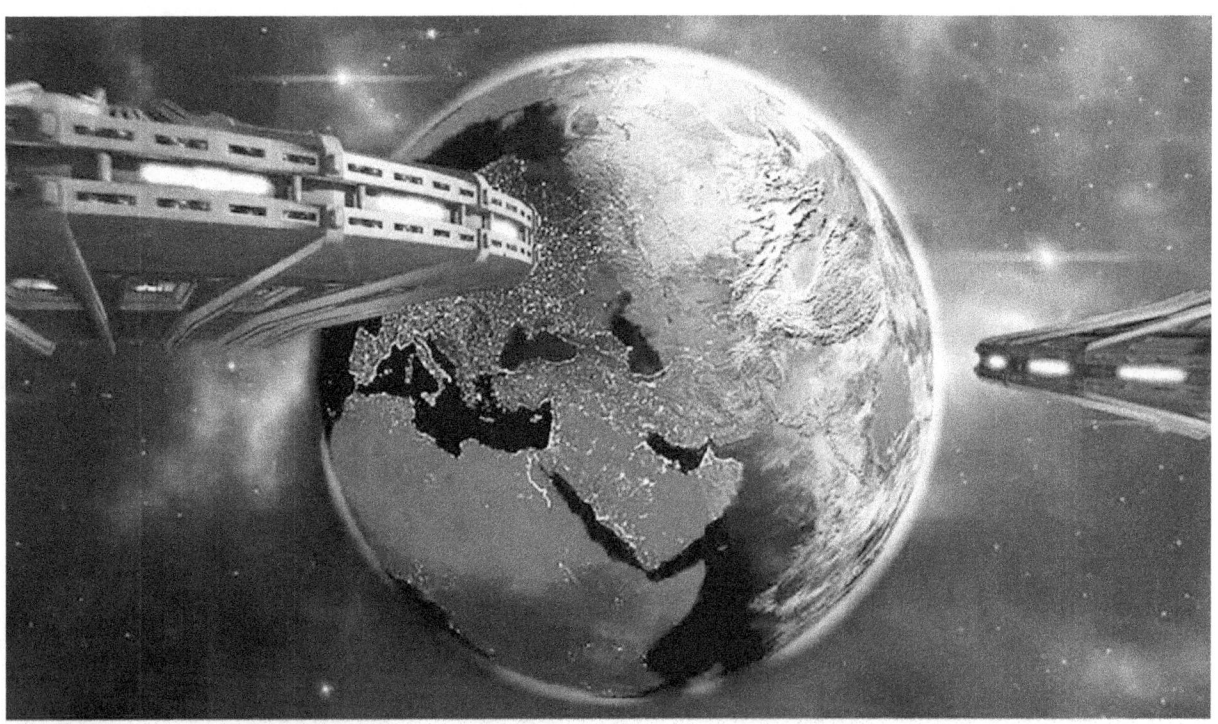

Have beings from other worlds been secretly observing planet Earth for thousands of years? If so, for what purpose?

2

CREATIVE SPACE

This chapter is of special interest to everyone intrigued with the possibilities of outer space travel. Although barely covering the subject of cosmological beginnings, it does, in a very concise way, present the Greek speculations on the subject of the atom. We must remember that Greek civilization, although we term it "ancient," is relatively modern as compared to those civilizations that transmitted to the Greeks their world of culture which eventually spread through the civilized world via the Roman Empire and its force of arms. Today's ideological battles seem to be based upon the superiority of atomic weapons.

Because of the nature of the subject matter which we wish to present to the public, this book contains little or no reference to the ancients' discoveries about outer space. Although Sanskrit literature has many references to outer space vehicles and atomic weapons, all that the Greeks have bequeathed to us is the study of the microcosm and the alchemists' speculations on matter. For this reason there is no subject matter in this book covering the so-called Gentile or Pagan world knowledge of astrology which, in pre-Christian times, was used as a method of worship.

It is not by coincidence that modern astronomy still retains the names used by the ancients to designate what we consider to be planetary intelligences. The modern world has completely ignored the ancients' knowledge of "space." With this in mind, this chapter uses John Dalton as the jumping-off point for modern physical investigation. Without involving ourselves in the Baconian-Shakespeare controversy, we ask the reader to consider that much of Shakespeare's wisdom, presented through the medium of his plays for public consumption, was contemporary with Sir Francis Bacon's "*Novum Organum*," which all agree changed the tide of scientific physical investigation.

Until 1875 man and his inner psychic potentialities were relegated to the realm of ancient superstitions and legend. In 1886, the well-known scientists of the day, including Sir William Crookes, Sir Humphrey Davy, Professor Corson, Flammarion of Paris, and others of equal rank, were actively interested in psychic phenomena. Societies for Psychical Research were established, and much that was discovered never became public knowledge. Physical research has moved rapidly forward to the point where the abstract scientist, Albert Einstein, was able to prove that (tall is one"; namely, that matter is energy, energy is space, and that release of energy from matter gives us unbelievable power to eliminate space as an obstacle to physical travel. Parallel with this has come the fear of self-destruction, and practically no research by modern man on his true relationship with space.

Such knowledge as did exist comes to us only through legend and fantasy, except from those people who, by their very natures, are able to contact centers of consciousness existing in space. These people have had extreme difficulty in communicating their experiences to the general public only because we have at best a very poor means of correlating what they see and experience with technical knowledge that should have developed prior to this time. We hope this book serves the purpose of making their position a little easier in society.

Cosmologists interested in the birth of the world seem today to have been overshadowed by the strident scientists of interplanetary travel; and our dull old planet appears to be interesting only as a take-off ramp for a flight to Venus. Yet man, from his very beginning, has had an insatiable curiosity concerning the creation of the earth, and the subject has rivaled the creation of life itself as a prolific source of myth, miracle and invention.

Man's speculation concerning world origins was recorded some 4,000 years ago for the first time by Akkadian scribes, who presented the following explanation. Before the world existed there was Chaos, which was a shapeless mass of ocean, fresh water and fog. In this Chaos there were two gods, Apsu (the fresh waters), and Ti'amat (the sea), who lived and loved. From their love union sprang Lahmu and Lahamu, who fashioned the earth from sedimentary silts. And later we find that Semitic scribes adapted this myth to the monotheistic concepts which finally produced the biblical Book of Genesis.

In ancient Phoenicia, God lay in an egg (the World Egg), which he broke at birth, and made its silver bottom into the world and its golden top into the sky. For the Hindu, the cosmos is eternal and does not have an origin. It constantly dies and is reborn out of a lotus blossom growing from Brahma's navel. The Zuni believed that a Creator had used mystical thought powers in order to become the Sun-Father. Rubbing his hands together he made balls from the sloughed skin. He cast these into the waters, from which came the stars and the earth.

To those who are interested, we refer the Canadian Department of Mines, National Museum of Canada, for Bulletin No. 61, compiled by our friend, Marius Barbeau, entitled, *"Totem Poles of the Gitksan, Upper Skeena River, British Columbia."* We know of no more complete record of American Indian knowledge of the occult. Logical Greek thinkers, debating over two contradictory cosmologies, finally endorsed the clockwork universe of Plato and Aristotle, ignoring Democritus' infinite and eternal atoms from which he taught that the earth was created.

During the last decade, man's field of knowledge has expanded in two directions; cosmically into outer space, and microcosmically into the primary elements of life. Greatly improved biochemical techniques have knocked down the barrier between organic and inorganic chemistry, and have brought closer the alchemist's dream of creating life in a laboratory. The notion of the spontaneous generation of living organisms has haunted men's minds ever since the dawn of civilization. We find that the ancient Chinese were convinced that insects grew spontaneously on bamboo shoots, while the Egyptians had no doubt that frogs, toads, snakes and mice sprang from the Nile silt when it was warmed by the sun.

All of the Greek philosophers seemed to accept spontaneous generation as a basic fact, although they differed considerably on its modus operandi. Democritus held that life appeared as the result of a mechanical combination of particles (atoms)-although without any divine or supernatural intervention, while Epicurus taught a similar mechanistic view, which a multitude of creatures could arise from earth or manure merely as a result of moist heat or decay.

Aristotle not only accepted the theory of spontaneous generation of numerous organisms, but in addition theorized on the nature of life itself, stating that living things were created by the conjunction of the passive principle, or matter, with an active principle, or form, and that the form of living things could be seen in the soul of the body, which infuses matter and gives it motion.

The later Stoics taught that life was originated by an "engendering force" contained in the pneuma, while in the third century, Plotinus explained the creation of life as the animation of matter by a living spirit, or "life force" concept. Medieval Europe, steeped in demon- ology and mysticism, merrily created frogs from the dews of May, geese and ducks from barnacles (or else grown on trees), and sheep from melons. A favorite "creation" was the "homunculus," a tiny, fully-formed human being, which creatures Paracelsus taught could be manufactured by placing human sperm in a sealed gourd inside a horse's stomach and effecting various other fantastic manipulations.

The old controversy between the vitalists and the mechanists on the nature of life is by no means dead today, and we still hear the mechanistic theory that life can be explained in physico-chemical terms without the need of the metaphysical entity, or soul, of the vitalists. But this still leaves unresolved a clear definition of life itself, and still entirely speculative, except to students of occultism, is the question of how life actually originated on our earth. It is the occult explanation which we shall now present for your consideration.

THE REALITY OF CONSCIOUSNESS

Divine Consciousness, being Universal, necessarily manifests everywhere. Looking at it from the objective side, and in the mineral kingdom, we speak of the cohesion of minerals. Minerals cannot be cohesive, we find, unless there is a certain amount of consciousness to hold them together. If we examine what we call the "transition" states, or if we go back of the mineral kingdom to the gases which chemicalized to produce the minerals, we find something we call chemical affinity, which is a certain form of consciousness. And in the case of boiling water, if the fire and the water were but inert matter acting upon inert matter, and there were no consciousness, the vibrations could not be raised and the water be made to boil. It is the conscious side of the atoms composing the fire, acting upon the conscious side of the atoms composing the water, which raises those lower vibrations of the water and makes it boil.

Now in the vegetable kingdom we find pine, hemlock and spruce trees growing side by side, each taking from the earth only such particles as it needs to sustain its individual life, thus showing that here is a conscious selection of elements being made by each tree. In the animal kingdom, this consciousness becomes so distinctly individualized that in order to distinguish its higher form from the lower, or vegetable kingdom, we call it something more than consciousness – we call it intelligence. In man we find a still higher form of consciousness than in the animal, which we designate as Mind, and this state of development is the highest with which we are familiar. Therefore, when we use the term Universal Consciousness, or Divine Mind, we mean that which comprehends, embodies, and includes all that we call consciousness-individualized or otherwise. We mean all that is visible or invisible, known or unknown; all that can be seen, touched, handled, or sensed. All that can be apprehended – All is God.

The Universal Mind consists of two portions – the manifested, and the unmanifested. The manifested portion can be apprehended by the human mind, but that which is unmanifested cannot be apprehended. There is a "plus" element which is always above and beyond that which is manifested. The manifestation takes place within the unmanifested, and there is always something from within which brings forth the manifested. This "plus" element we shall not attempt to explain, since the greatest occultists have been unable to fathom much of its nature. The two portions of the Universal Mind, in oriental literature, are designated Yang and Yin. This is symbolized by the Korean flag, which is composed of a circle divided by a spiral line, representing Divine Cosmic Energy. It also represents the energy described in the Yoga Upanishads, and in some of the Puranas. Other references may be found in the works of the Mohammedan Sutras; in particular, in the *"RISALA-I-HAQ-NUMA,"* by Prince Mahomed Dara Shikoh.

From man's point of view, the manifested portion of the Universal Mind consists of two parts, the visible and the invisible; and yet each of these is only a condition, a part or diversity, of the complete unity of the Universal Consciousness. Upon the visible plane of manifestation, Divine Mind, or Consciousness, expresses itself in the two great forms which are popularly known as force and matter. While we do know that matter is the hypothetical substance of physical phenomena, physically we can actually know very little of either force or matter, since this objective world is on the plane of effects.

Matter is divided into two great portions, the particled and the unparticled. The particled portion comes forth from the unparticled as a precipitation of it. If you place a pan of water outside your window when the temperature of the atmosphere is below freezing point, you will find that gradually there is a lowering of the rate of the vibrations of the atoms which compose the water, until there comes a crystalline formation within the pan. Most of the water in the pan is still fluidic, but there are now also these crystalline formations, and we have therefore both the particled and the unparticled portions in the pan. In a like manner, these two forms of matter are forever seen throughout Nature during a period of manifestation, or evolution, and it is the particled portion of matter that science has agreed to call atoms. Concerning the nature of the atom, the physicists agree that logically and necessarily there must be an ultimate element, and this produces the phenomenon which we call physical life.

If any generalization is possible in such a constantly expanding micro-universe, it is that the atom is at the origin of all matter – but beyond that lies speculative physics. Our first speculators were two Greek philosophers, Leucippus and Democritus, who came to the conclusion that all things were made of tiny, simple, indivisible and indestructible particles, in perpetual motion in empty space. For them, each substance had its own distinctive atoms, or arrangement of atoms. The smallest, fastest, and most perfectly spherical atoms made up the soul which was in man and in all other matter. Dreams, visions, and hallucinations had their own particular atoms, light and noble, while heavier and coarser particles made up the more material substances.

Universal Consciousness is the medium in which all things are embedded.

Empedocles, also a fifth-century Greek, who was more poetic, taught the exact opposite; that everything was made from one basic, universal material, called hylem. He stated that substances differed from one another because they contained different proportions of the four principal elements; fire, water, air and earth, and that a centripetal force, Love, held cohesive substances together while centrifugal strife dispersed the diffusible ones. During the fourth century, Plato and Aristotle adopted both hylem and Love, and in addition discovered the fifth primary element-heaven. One hundred years later Epicurus endorsed Democritus' atomism, incorporating it into his own teachings. Pronounced a materialist, and the enemy of religion and superstition, Epicurus was declared a subversive-and, guilty by association, atomism went "underground" until the 19th century. During the Middle-Ages the Church declared the atomic theory a "Satanic rebellion" which was designed to undermine the Faith and to "pulverize" Christianity.

Eighteenth Century John Dalton defined the atom as the smallest possible particle of matter; solid, indivisible and unchanging, postulating that there are as many atom types as there are substances, each substance containing only atoms of a single species. The first 20th Century model of an atom showed a central, positively charged nucleus, surrounded by much empty space and a few electrons. Radium finally fell apart in the Curies' laboratory in Paris, producing four surprises – one atom of lead, one of helium (the alpha ray) one electron (the beta ray), and one gamma ray, with radioactivity being the final proof of the atom's complex structure. We know, therefore, that the atom does exist, and that atoms are the building blocks of matter; the bricks with which the world is built. Then comes the question of how the world was created. There are currently three theories as to how the elements were formed, two of which go all the way back to the creation of the universe. All three assume that our universe is expanding.

One theory postulates that all of the matter now in the universe was once collected into a single dense mass – the primeval atom – so compact that a teaspoonful might have weighed a hundred million tons. This atom became "radioactive," and flew apart, and the energies released during this decay forced the densely crowded nucleons to stick together and form the elements. This theory has been criticized because it explains the formation of heavy elements only.

A second theory also concurs that the matter of our universe was once collected into a single blob of hot gas, and adds that so great was the pressure that the electrons were compressed into the protons, and that most of the mass consisted of neutrons, the neutron mass exploding about five billion years ago. Being relieved from the pressure and heat, some of the neutrons decayed into protons, which immediately became glued to other neutrons.

The third theory is that of the "steady state" universe, which shows that three fields of force are known; one in the atom's nucleus, tiny but very powerful; one extending from the atom into stellar space, which is electromagnetic, and the third, gravitation, encompassing clusters of galaxies. Now a fourth is added, the "creation field," which covers the entire universe. Within the field, powered by all the matter in the universe, new matter arises spontaneously, and is created. This is not a transformation of energy, but is a real creation. The newly-made particle joins the interstellar gas, contributing to the pressure which is driving the universe apart. The interstellar gas slowly condenses into blobs which collapse under their own gravity, forming galaxies and stars. As these galaxies are driven outward by the newly-formed matter, they slowly age, die and disappear; however, new galaxies are forming meanwhile, so that the universe remains always the same, adding new matter and losing old.

While the structure of the atom and the origin of matter are still mysteries to science, the answers to these questions may be found in the truth of occult teachings, and we shall endeavor to present here a condensed form of these teachings for your consideration.

The atom is created by the will of Deity. Deity desires to manifest, to raise itself to a higher form of existence, and this desire, going forth within itself, causes the Universe to grow into objectivity. This desire manifests first in the unparticled portion, and is a force which, being sent into the unparticled matter causes a precipitate within itself, which is called "atoms." Everywhere throughout space we find only one basis for the physical universe, which basis we agree to call "matter." Most people, however, are inclined to give to matter qualities that it does not possess, and therefore give it a power over themselves. If we understand the nature of matter, and look at it from the right standpoint, we will be able to control it; however, if we give to it qualities that do not belong to it, then it will control or limit us.

The other great power which is recognized as a factor in building the physical world is force, and we find a limited amount of knowledge concerning it also. Scientists have classified forces as electric force, force of heat, force of steam, etc., but actually we find that all the physicist knows of force is that it is the immediate cause of a change in the velocity or direction of the motion of a body. In other words, it is the proximate cause of the phenomenon of form. When we view the material world as the manifestation of Deity, we know that behind this motion we call force, and behind this form which we call matter, there is a cause which produces them.

DIVINE ESSENCE

All is Deity, or Divine Essence. This Divine Essence, manifesting as motion, is called force by both the occultist and the physicist. The occultist also calls it "thought," because all force in its ultimate is either thought or the result of thought. With the occultist, force and thought are identical, and force is the product of mind. The Divine Essence manifesting as matter is what both the physicists and occultists call substance – substance being the collective name for the atoms; and we call it substance because it is that which stands under, or lies behind, the visible Universe. The physical Universe is, therefore, atoms in motion or vibration, and back of motion and matter is Divine Essence.

The Supreme Universal Divine Essence-Consciousness, or God, manifests in a duality of motion and matter, which gives us the trinity of Consciousness, Force and Substance, each portion of the trinity playing an important part in life. The atom is dual, and has its consciousness aspect and its substance aspect. Its positive aspect is consciousness, and its negative aspect is substance, and these two are inseparable. The physical side of the atom is the vehicle for consciousness, and we find that this duality of the atom is the keynote to occultism. The knowledge of this fact is essential to the conscious production of phenomena.

Understanding this, we can realize how the visible Universe is produced; how forces are controlled, and how cures are performed by mental therapeutics. It all resolves itself into the action of mind upon mind, or upon lesser and other forms of consciousness. Matter is subject to mind when mind controls form through the consciousness side of substance, by making and modifying vibrations, the cause of form. The world of form is merely atoms vibrating at certain established rates. Vibrations which appeal to us as sound actually have no inherent sound, but are due to the rates of vibration that impinge upon the nerves of the ear, and are transmitted as vibrations to the brain, and from the brain to the mind. These vibrations which appeal to the eye as color actually has no light, but are rates of vibration that impinge upon the optic nerves, and are transmitted to the brain as vibration. All is vibration, modified either by Consciousness behind it or by individual consciousness within it. All sensation is only the effect of vibration upon the mind; and it is the relationship of our individual consciousness to the external world of vibrations which makes the world for us.

Now let us consider Divine Mind in its subjective manifestations. The lower portion of the unparticled part of that Consciousness is, in the scientific phraseology of the physicists, the ether. The two are identical. Ether, like the atom, is something that must exist; it is a logical necessity, but no one can see it; we know only that it produces certain phenomena. The ether is a subtle, universal, magnetic, fluidic medium in which all manifested things are imbedded. What Aristotle once conceived of as pure "ether" is now a vast chemical laboratory, the product of which is breathed in by man as his daily ration of atmosphere.

Considering these qualities of the ether from a mental standpoint, first of all we find that the ether is subtle, and interpenetrates all other forms of existence and all other forms of physical life. You see another person because of this subtle essence that is between you. We are talking about an aspect of the Universal Mind, and you must remember that this subtle essence is Consciousness, or Mind. We are permeated with it; the atoms of our bodies are held together in groups by it. This subtle consciousness is in every portion of our being; we swim, live, and exist in a sea of it.

We must understand that the ether is universal, and cannot be excluded from any plane or place. Universal Consciousness is, as its name implies, everywhere. It is important to remember this universality, since in thought transference, or in treating mentally a person at a distance, we must realize that there is no separateness in mind. Thought passes immediately from one to another, upon the plane of Mind; therefore we do not have to make a great effort to reach another mind, but can reach it instantly and easily through the medium of this Mind, since it is universal.

Solved! The Mysteries of Space, Time and UFOs

The ether being magnetic, it attracts all its parts, and since every part and particle of itself is interdependent, none are independent. Every particled part of this sea of magnetism, each individualized part, regardless of whether it is an atom, a man, or a sun, is a magnetic center, and since the whole is magnetic, each part must therefore be magnetic. Evolution can only be carried on by reason of these centers, and it was for this purpose that they were brought into existence. Every center in the Universal Consciousness should be preserved; therefore, your first duty to God and to yourself is to preserve your own magnetic center. This is known to all men as the law of self-preservation-the basis of all common law.

Occultism teaches no sacrifice of self, since evolution would be retarded, rather than aided, by such teaching. This must not be misunderstood as meaning that there should be no self-denial or that there should be no giving up of personal or selfish comforts, but it does mean that the individual center should never be destroyed or depleted until it has become an imperfect medium for Deity to work through. Occultism teaches us that no one should sacrifice his life for another, for every life is important to Deity – and, for all we know, the life to be sacrificed may be the more important center of the two at that particular time. We are not speaking of sentimentality, but merely stating a law.

No person should continue to give of his own spiritual, mental or physical force until he is a bankrupt, for a depleted center is of no use to Deity in the evolutionary struggle. If you will think of your altruistic friends who constantly bear other peoples' burdens, you can easily see how the law has acted in their cases. Many of them are mentally, physically, or financially depleted, and of comparatively little use, because of this conscious or unconscious violation of the law. Altruism is said to have been taught by the occultist Jesus, and, admitting that he has been correctly reported in this respect in the records we now have, then his teachings could only have been intended to neutralize the intense and almost universal selfishness which prevailed at that time.

Altruism and selfishness are both extreme views, while intelligent individualism is the middle ground, and is in accordance with the law. It is fortunate that selfishness is so earnestly condemned, and that altruism is more preached than practiced, or humanity would not be able to go on in compliance with the law as it is doing at present. Your duty to yourself and to Deity is to become a positive center, and the higher your rate of vibration, the more powerful you become. If you have ever stood on the bank of a river and watched the water whirl around a center or vortex in the middle of the stream, you probably observed how that vortex drew to itself everything that floated down the current. That was an active, positive center, distinct from any other center or vortex in that stream – and because of its individualized strength it had the power of attraction; therefore everything was drawn into it. So it is that men become vortices in this great magnetic sea of consciousness, and as they become strong and positive they draw to themselves whatever they desire. But we cannot help others until we have become strong ourselves. We must have force ourselves, before we can impart it to others; and we must know before we can teach.

The ether is fluidic, and this unparticled sea of Divine Consciousness flows according to the impetus given to it both by Deity Itself and by man; and it moves in the direction in which it is sent. This is another important fact to remember, because we will see later on that there are, currents within this fluidic sea, and we shall learn how to attach ourselves to these currents and forces, and to draw what we desire into ourselves. There are currents of Love, and we can attach ourselves to these in order to draw love to us. There are also destructive currents, and we must learn how to avoid attaching ourselves to those.

If you were a thousand miles from home and desired to help some member of your family you could, with your power of thought, make this fluidic force, or Consciousness and life, flow into the person you desired to help. So it is most important that you realize something about the nature of this fluidic Universal Consciousness. It is a wonderful storehouse, in which everything that is conceivable to the mind of man is stored-and his thoughts going forth into it can bring back to him exactly what he desires. Dr. Frederick Gonder, in his, "*The New Curved Light Theory*", states, "Light rays travel from the sun in a curve and, if not obstructed, will continue to make a complete circle."

This Consciousness, the ether, is the medium in which all things are embedded, and through which all things are connected with each other. Since it is a medium, there is no friction between any of its parts; it yields to you, and yet it connects you with any or all of its parts. It does not impair or retard the force you sent out into it, but brings back to you exactly what you send out into it. If you think love to a friend, your love will go to him precisely as you think it, and with no greater nor less intensity than you feel it. If there were any friction in this Universal Ether, or Divine Consciousness, we would not be able to receive the light from the stars, and the worlds would some time stop in their orbits, because no world would be able to revolve for more than a limited time if there were the least resistance to its progress through space.

If you consciously direct your thought into the Ether it is sure to reach the person, place or thing to which you send it. If you wish to give someone a mental treatment, you think kindly and positively of that person, and the thought, going from you into the Ether, makes a little pathway for itself until it reaches the person of whom you are thinking. For the time being there is a magnetic cord established between you and that person, and over that magnetic cord you send your thoughts of health and strength. No wave of thought vibration can ever be impaired. Modern scientists agree that at the same place and at the same time there may be an infinite variety of etheric waves of different lengths, with none of them interfering with each other. We can see waves, which we call light, as they are sent to us from the stars, and if we could translate the messages of those waves of light, or vibrations, which are brought to us, we should be wiser and better than we are. But we do know that the color of a star indicates its state of development, and in this way we are able to determine which of the heavenly bodies are above or below us in their evolution.

Shakespeare once described the sun as an "alchemist," and this was not merely poetic expression. In the earth's atmosphere the solar energy enters into myriad chemical and photoelectric combinations vitally affecting the life on this planet. Ancient man worshipped the sun as the source of the earth's vitality – today's scientists know that every solar event manifests itself in geophysical phenomena on earth; sometimes instantly, and sometimes over eons.

The earth is constantly bathed in a solar "fluid," consisting of waves and particles. Electromagnetic radiation varies between wave lengths of perhaps one angstrom unit (X-ray range) to several hundred kilometers. Electrically charged particles vary between "slow" corpuscles (several hundred miles per second) to cosmic rays traveling at a fraction of light velocity.

Few persons know much about the magnetic power which is daily given to all living creatures by our sun. The sun's energy that warms the Earth, drives the winds and supplies vital force is steady. We do know that the sunshine often dispels the fears which we had during the night, and we know that difficulties which seemed insurmountable at night melt away when the golden rays of the sun shine upon them. We may be courageous, positive and strong while the sun shines, but when it has disappeared below the horizon and night has come, our courage often dwindles and we become weak and negative. History records the fact that frontier warfare with the American Indian terminated at sundown.

More souls pass out of their bodies at night than while the sun is shining, and people who are ill grow worse as night comes on. All of these conditions are governed by the law of vibration. The light waves or vibrations from the sun are the strongest, most powerful, and most magnetic that comes to us from any source. They vibrate at a rate of golden yellow, and therefore there is a continuous flow of force currents to this world and to all other planets close enough to receive their vibrations. When a person-or any other individualized consciousness-concentrates its thoughts upon the sun it receives a mental and a magnetic treatment from that great center, since the concentration of thought opens a direct channel for the great force to flow through to the one concentrating upon it; and the vibrations, both mental and physical, of that person or creature are raised in proportion to the intensity of its powers of concentration.

We find that Divine Mind is precisely analogous to a sensitive plate, and that each human thought makes a picture on that plate. By thought you make the exposure, and the thing pictured will in time become your own, for you are attached to your creations, and time develops the picture for you. If you hold the image you have made long enough, you will get a perfect picture-if you think idly, then you have made what the photographers would call an under-exposure, and the picture is not full, clear and perfect, many details being left out. By holding the picture firmly and strongly you make it a permanency, and then it is yours – for thoughts become "things."

THOUGHTS MADE REAL

Mental pictures are first mental things, but after a time they become physical things, or draw physical things to them, for the great Consciousness gives back to us precisely what we send into it. It gives to us whatever we ask of it, and our ignorance in making demands will be no protection to us. The only way that evolution can go on is by Divine Mind granting every request that we persistently make; it is in this way that we gain wisdom through experience. This automatic action, as it were, of Divine Consciousness, was fully taught by Jesus, but it is as little understood or believed in by his present so-called followers as it was by those whom he originally tried to teach. You will remember that he said, "Judge not, that ye be not judged; for with what judgment ye judge ye shall be judged, and with what measure ye meet it shall be measured to you again." He also said, "Ask, and it shall be given unto you; seek, and ye shall find; knock, and it shall be opened unto you." And when he said these things he was stating what he knew was a Law, which could be put into operation then or at any time afterwards.

Consciousness is limited in its manifestation by the medium or media through which it manifests. For an illustration, let us take the consciousness of a flower, an animal, and a man. There is a limitation of the expression in each of these, by reason of the form in which it manifests. It accentuates that particular portion of the Universe, or planet, or man, in which it manifests. If you will concentrate your consciousness, or mind, on your right foot and hold it there for a time, you will draw the blood from other parts of the body into the foot, until it will become swollen and red. You are thinking of your foot to the exclusion of all the rest of your body. That portion of your consciousness which is functioning in your foot has been accentuated above the consciousness which remains in the rest of the body. If we carry this a step further we will find that the law operates in exactly the same manner with the entire man. Consciousness accentuates that portion of the man in which its greatest expression is. For that reason, ever since the early Christian centuries the body has been mistaken for the man, because it was the last medium through which his consciousness or mind expressed itself – it was that portion of the man which was accentuated by the consciousness.

Very little was known of the real nature of man after the second and third centuries of the Christian era, except that he was a body which was generally regarded as the man. The theologians knew there was a body, and consequently, in their theology, the body was put forth primarily as man. They thought he had a soul, and taught certain doctrines concerning that indefinite something which they designated as his soul. This term "soul" is still somewhat indefinite at the present day. Any of the leading dictionaries will give you a large variety of meanings attached to the word. The theologians could not define nor picture the soul, but they accepted the Jewish conception of the Adamic man, believing that Adam was created out of the dust of the ground, and that afterward God breathed into him the breath of life; therefore they regarded that breath as his "soul."

The exoteric Jews had no conception of a soul as distinct from the Universal Life Principle – and have very little conception of it today. When the Christians rendered in theological language the Jewish thought, they called the life principle of man his soul. Later in the centuries, the "moral philosophers" appeared upon the scene, and were almost as indefinite in their teachings concerning his true nature as were the theologians. These moral philosophers, whom we now call metaphysicians, also taught something about a soul, or mind- but there was a confusion of words (due, of course, to a confusion of thought), and instead of teaching what soul or mind was, they described the phenomena of mind. Actually, all of the occidental ancient moral philosophy concerning the inner mind, soul, or spirit, as they were indefinitely designated, was really what we now call physiological psychology, and pertained entirely to the action of mind upon or through the body.

Since the consciousness manifested chiefly in the external man in those days, and since the body, plus a little indefinite something more, was regarded as the man, it was only natural that the theologians should have taught the doctrine of a physical resurrection. Many of them did not know how to account for immortality, unless there was to be a physical resurrection – at least this was true after the Council of Nice. We find at that time that the Christian and the Jew were the only two religionists in the world who feared dissolution of the physical body – and naturally there arose the barbaric practice of burying dead bodies for the purpose of preserving them. The Egyptians preserved their dead only for the supposed purpose of having their old atoms to use again on their return to Earth.

The majority of people of the present day have not progressed much further than the theologians and the metaphysicians of the early centuries. Ask ten men whom you may meet in everyday life what a man is, and nine of them will describe the physical body. You will be surprised to learn how little is known of anything besides the physiological man. Many of the old paintings represent the soul as a body floating through space with a pair of wings. The body, plus wings, was the artistic conception of the psychic or real man in ancient times. With nine-tenths of the people there is no distinction between themselves and their bodies, for man actually knows very little of himself at the present time.

In the middle of the Nineteenth century, the more adventurous minds commenced to investigate the nature of man, and the fact of whether or not immortality was demonstrable, and there arose what is known as the Spiritualistic movement, or Spiritualism. In England and in France the investigators maintained that there is a persistency or consciousness after the dissolution of the physical body, and that certain phenomena are produced by it.

This was the first general, deliberate attempt in Christian times to discover the soul of man, and the first effort to collect a sufficient amount of scientific data on which to base a philosophy concerning the psychic man. The principal tenet of their belief is that beyond this Earth life there is somewhere an eternal progression for the human soul – which certainly is an improvement on the old orthodox Christian belief in stagnation by reason of the wearing of crowns, waving of palms, and singing of hallelujahs forever and ever.

The next movement along this line commenced in 1875, and was known as the Theosophical movement. This was started for the purpose of studying, among other things, man – and particularly his latent psychic faculties. This movement gave a more exhaustive and complete theory concerning the nature of man than was then to be had in the Occident. Vague it was at times, and the several sections of the movement differed in belief among themselves. Some made man a combination of seven, and others of fourteen, different personalities or principles; but nevertheless it was an attempt to reach something besides the physical.

In 1886 there was another movement along the line of investigation of psychic phenomena. This was called the Society for Psychical Research, and worked along the same general lines which the Spiritualists were investigating. The object to be attained was to establish scientific demonstrations of the persistency of man's consciousness after death, and many scholarly men and women became investigators with this object in view.

Finally there came that body of investigators whose practice is called Hypnotism, and which is actually "Mesmerism," revamped and renamed. Hypnotism had done little good for the world, and will do considerable harm before its investigators, and those who regard it as a "hobby," have finished experimenting with it. However, we wish to call to your attention a few of the facts that Hypnotism has brought forth. It has proved to the minds of many – and has certainly given evidence to the minds of all who have investigated it, that the body of man is not the man. When a person is put into the state of hypnosis, the body is unable to think, feel or function in any way. If the body were the man, sleep could not extinguish entirely his consciousness, and there would be enough left to register sensation.

If you stick a pin into the flesh of a man in ordinary sleep you will get a quick response, and, unless you are very active, you may regret making the investigation. However, if you stick a pin into the flesh of a man who is in a state of complete hypnosis, you will find there is no response at all, which shows that in the one case there is consciousness, and in the other there is none. This evidence is sufficient to prove to the unprejudiced investigator that the body is not the man, but that there is within the body some sort of recording business that is capable to the maximum degree of sensing things which are external to the body. Hypnotism has also shown that the mind is not the product of the molecular vibration of the brain, since during hypnosis, and while the brain is quiescent, the mind continues to be active.

We are not humans experiencing life, but life experiencing being human.

These experiments have been further verified by the use of anesthetics. When a person is under ether, the effect is the same as if he was hypnotized, because in both these cases the mind, or the real man, is forced out of his physical body, which is then incapable of functioning, and remains inert until the reasoning principle returns to its habitation. There are many cases where a subject has been put into hypnosis and the consciousness sent out of the body to a distant place – and it has brought back a correct report of things that were occurring there at that time. Hypnotism, therefore, has done two very good things; it has scientifically proved that man is mind, the thinker, and that mind can persist separate and apart from its vehicle, the body; and if that condition can exist for one moment, then there is no logical reason why it should not exist throughout eternity. And so we have here some scientific data for immortality.

Investigators found that there is a mind capable of experiencing sensations which ordinarily functioned in the human body, but which could be separated from it as has been just described. But they also found that there is a secondary mind in man, and that after the first mind is well under the control of the hypnotist, there is still a secondary mind or intelligence which may act independently of the first. This secondary consciousness they have named the subliminal self. So they have found that man is not only a mind, but that he is two minds. In the course of time, the first consciousness to be reached became known as the objective mind, and the second consciousness as the subjective mind.

If mind is something, and hypnotism has shown us that it is, then mind must have a form and a color. We cannot conceive of anything in the Universe that is without form and color. Individualization, or separateness, requires form and color, or else those conditions could not exist. A great mass of evidence has been collected from various sources on this subject. Spiritualistic Societies, the Society for Psychical Research, and clairvoyants, seers and sensitives all over the world agree upon this one point-that mind has form. They differ somewhat upon the question of whether or not it has color, but that is a logical necessity. They do say that mind has form, and that its form is the same as that of the body which it inhabits, and that the real man is an etherialized prototype of his physical self. In other words, the physical self is but a materialized picture of the inner man or mind.

Regarding color, there is a great difference of opinion, due to the difference in the respective development of the observers. Some persons who ordinarily function solely upon the objective plane of life, under exceptional conditions sometimes see the outlines or the figure of the psychic, or the real man. Other, more careful, observers, having advanced to the point where they can command the higher natural forces, and can function upon the subjective side of life, may not only see the outlines of these mind or soul forms, but see them as plainly as they see physical forms around them in ordinary affairs of life. Then there are others who have advanced so far in their evolution that they can look beneath the form of the man and see the character. These persons are the Seers, or higher Clairvoyants. The last two classes agree with the occultist in making the assertion that the character of mind is always known by its color; and this must be scientifically true, since there could be no differentiation of form except through the vibration which manifests as color. So it is a logical necessity, as well as a matter of testimony, that every human mind or psychic man has form and color.

There is one thing in the world that cannot lie, and that thing is vibration. The vibrations of a man determine his form and his color. And his thought or character is the cause of his vibrations. Now as far as we have gone we have learned that man is identical with mind, and that this mind has form and color; also that man has two consciousnesses, which are called the objective and subjective minds. The normal color of the subjective mind of man-known in the theological parlance as spirit—is blue. It is of the same nature as the Ether, or Divine Consciousness, from which it came. The color of the objective mind of man, called by the theologians the soul, is green; and man's predominating color is always determined by the mind which dominates.

Evolution is not carried on equally throughout all its parts. We find this is true whenever we investigate the operations of this law. But Evolution is carried on by the creation of centers within the Great Consciousness, and by enlarging and preserving these centers. As actual reform is carried on in a great city by the reformation, first, of individuals, and not with trying to reform the whole public at once, so it is with the great law which works through centers or individuals.

Nature, unaided, fails – and there could be no evolution except by working through conscious centers. For instance, our sun is a center purposely formed, and through that center great life force is consciously sent out to smaller, weaker centers, imbuing them with life and promoting other forms of life and growth upon them, as it does upon this planet of ours. It is the same with species and types; it is not a natural selection, in the sense of nature working blindly, that causes evolution, but it is rather an artificial selection, or the raising up of individual parts. This has been demonstrated by Luther Burbank through his work with plant life.

Take man, for instance; the Adept selects such advanced men and women whom he knows are capable of evolving more rapidly than others, and by putting his own force and strength upon them he aids in their development, and in this way these selected individuals are assisted upwards until they become the highest expressions of manhood and womanhood.

In the animal and vegetable kingdom, man takes the highest expression of this or that form or type and through artificial, conscious selection, unites them with other forms, and thus produces a higher type of expression, as in the breeding of animals and the grafting of trees and flowers. The purposiveness of Deity, or Nature, is present in all its individualized parts, but becomes fully manifested only through the conscious cooperation of the more evolved centers of itself.

For Hindus the universe was created by Brahma, the creator who made the universe out of himself. After Brahma created the world, it is the power of Vishnu which preserves the world

3

PHENOMENA OF SPACE

The following chapter can be found mystically explained in the Sanskrit KATHOPANISHAD, and an excellent translation of this Sanskrit work by Swami Yatiswarananda, published by Sri Ramakrishna Math, Mylapore, Madras, India, will give the reader an insight into ancient Indian culture.

George Adamski, in his books and writings, and on the lecture platform, has claimed that this identical information had been given to him previous to the discovery of the Van Allen radiation belt. In his book, "Flying Saucers Have Landed," you will note that coauthor Desmond Leslie has made considerable study and has given credit to the books of A. A. Bailey and the Tibetan, and especially, "*A Treatise On Cosmic Fire.*" All of these books have their foundation in Sanskrit literature. A study of Adamski's book will pose the problem of whether the information contained therein came from "Space People," or is the result of studying ancient Sanskrit literature.

We draw to your attention the work of Mr. George Van Tassel, of Yucca Valley, California. Mr. Van Tassel has been one of the leading lecturers on the subject of outer space contact and UFO activity. Mr. Van Tassel is a serious student of the Bible, and for those who might be termed "anti-religious," he may seem to have mixed fact with fiction; the fiction, of course, being the actuality of "Angels," or Space Beings. Mr. Van Tassel, however, has managed to achieve a practical demonstration of his beliefs in the construction of his apparatus which he calls the "world's first Integratron." Considerable research is being done by

Westinghouse and General Electric into the subject of positive and negative ions, and their relation to healing and health.

Those who are seriously interested in animal evolution are referred to a fairly accurate evolutionary process described by Mr. Max Heindel in his book, *"The Rosicrucian Cosmo-Conception; an Elementary Treatise upon Man's Past Evolution, Present Constitution and Future Development."*

Bible students and all Christians who are firm believers in monogamy will find a clear reference to this particular subject of Ego reunion in the Bible under two separate sections; the first, of course, being in the Book of Genesis, dealing with the "separation" of Eve from Adam, and the second being the re-union as depicted in the Song of Solomon.

With reference to the matriarchal system referred hereto, one has only to study the Koran to realize that the Mohammedan world, although seemingly to place the woman in the inferior position, actually has more laws for the protection of the female than in any other religious system.

The modern State of Israel has had considerable success in developing her mineral wealth by tracing locations as described in the Bible. Daily we find increasing credence given to Bible stories; therefore the reader, with a little initiative, can find references in the Bible – which is, after all, a Judaic and Christian heritage of fact – to most of the information given in this Chapter.

H. P. Blavatsky, in her writings, predicted that the Dead Sea Scrolls, when discovered, would confirm much of the ancient history which she discussed during her lifetime without having tangible proof at that time.

THE COSMIC NIGHT

Before the beginning of our Cosmic Day, and before "God created the heavens and the Earth," the Father-Mother principle, the Positive and Negative, Male and Female aspects of the Universal Principle, existed. While the darkness of the Cosmic Night prevailed throughout the Universe, and while the Elohim, or Planetary Spirits, were subconsciously resting in the bosom of the Infinite, God said, "Let there be Light," and the Positive Divine Force went instantly forth from the great Cosmic Heart into the silent, negative Ether; vibration began, and the first morning of our Cosmic Day was born.

The whole universe is a manifestation of alternate eras of evolution and dissolution. There is no such thing as eternity, as understood by the Western mind, for nothing can go on working forever and forever without rest. Everything moves according to given law, within certain periods, and there are actions and reactions throughout all nature. This same thought is brought out in the Eastern philosophy, and is described as "the days and nights of Brahma." The Great Consciousness manifests itself periodically as the Universe, and after each manifestation there comes a period of rest, a period of night—for even Divine Consciousness must rest.

When the "Night of Brahma" is coming on, gradually the living Universe finds its life pulsations growing slower and slower, and fainter and fainter; and one by one the planets fade from sight. One by one the stars cease to give forth their light, and the suns themselves grow dim. Then men and gods and worlds and suns all sink to sleep – there are no thoughts in the Great Mind. All is silence, rest and a sea of darkness. Reaction has followed action; the day's work has been done throughout all parts of the Supreme, and the Cosmic Night has come.

The night of rest lasts for eons, embracing thousands and untold thousands of years, and then comes creation's dawn. There is a slight pulsation within the Great Consciousness, and there begin to be the rudiments of the Universe. That which was darkness becomes light, and the non-existent exists, and becomes motion. From the innermost heart of the Great Consciousness goes forth the pulsating life, and the Solar Deities, in whom are embodied the greatest power and wisdom that man can conceive, are awakened to take up their part of the work in the new day. A sun springs into existence, and then another, and another, and the whole universe is again brought into activity. These Deities radiate the life force which thrills into activity the Planetary Spirits, who also take up their work, and worlds come forth into space again. And the Planetary Spirits radiate the life force that awakens the minds of men who have slept through the long night of Brahma, and they resume their evolutionary journey. And so the morning of a Cosmic Day has come-Deity has awakened and has planned the day.

The Cosmic Days are more or less alike, as are all the days of men's years alike, except that each Cosmic Day is better than the one preceding it, since each new period of evolution is an advance beyond the one that passed before. Divine Mind images within itself, or pictures the new day, and thus creates the outline of the plan by which all things shall evolve during that period. Then the greatest centers of consciousness take the plan, as imaged by Deity, and carry into execution the idea of the Great Architect. God thinks, and the creative agencies bring into existence the physical worlds according to God's idea, which they see. God wills and divides into two parts, which we have described as the particled and the unparticled portions, and there is the force and matter ensouled by consciousness. Then, by their will power, the great centers of consciousness direct this force and this matter into the different matrices that Deity has planned, and the suns are formed to give forth light, and the worlds are made for men and animals to evolve upon.

During the night of Brahma, all of creation withdraws into an unmanifest state. Souls that were still manifest and not liberated during the day withdraw from outward manifestation but persist in "seed" form. Following the night, they appear in manifest form during the day of Brahma.

RADIATING THE NATURAL LAWS

The plans made by Deity in the dawn of each Cosmic Day are what men call "Natural Laws." They are the ways in which Deity selects to manifest during that particular Cosmic Day. These plans, emanating from the center of the Supreme, radiate throughout every part and portion of It, and the law which governs the visible side of life is the same law which governs the invisible side; therefore, if you find a law operating in the realm of physics, you may know that it also operates in the realm of metaphysics. Now we have seen how Divine Thought has manifested Itself in physical re-embodiment, and how the law of periodicity has once again caused thought to be embodied in form, and how thereafter the law of periodicity makes itself felt everywhere throughout the Cosmic Day.

We find that the sun travels from a given point in space through its orbit, and returns again in about twenty-five thousand, nine hundred years. The law of periodicity has caused the sun to go forth and to return, and a cycle has been made. The moon also has its particular orbit, as has our Earth and all of the planets swinging in space; all are governed by the law of periodicity. Then again we have history repeating itself, and man forming his habits by a repetition of thought. And as it is with the law of periodicity, so it is with all of the other impulses which are sent into the Universe by Deity – they continue to manifest over and over again from the moment they are sent forth until the last throb of the great Deific heart shall be given and the Cosmic Night shall come again. The impulses which form a Universe persist throughout the Universe, and manifest as the Laws of the Universe. And when we find that the Supreme consciousness re-embodies itself for a new Cosmic Day, we know that the law of re-embodiment must apply to every part and portion of the Universe, and that re-embodiment is a Cosmic Law, a law of nature.

Worlds are brought into existence by Planetary Spirits, or Elohim, who see the Divine thought or picture of worlds, and use the images for matrices. They then project their thoughts into these centers, creating vortices which, through the intensity of their vibrations and the tremendous velocity with which they revolve, draw from boundless space the tiny particles we call atoms, and these seething masses of matter become huge balls of flaming gases. This is the principle of the Cyclotron. However, we use this principle negatively; that is to say, for atomic fission, not atomic fusion.

The atoms are brilliant little particles, all whirling and floating in different directions. This "cosmic dust" is formed into great clouds of vibrating atoms, all being drawn into a common center. A group of Elohim focuses their forces upon the mass of vibrating atoms, which will be their creation. As a group they generate the power which they send forth into great streams of brilliant light. When these great streams of light reach the point in space which is the center of the mass, the distance has been so well calculated that if they were not focused to form a center there, they would each form an elliptical circuit and return to the Center from which they emanated. But as they meet at this point, a new center of force is formed, and because of the rapid vibrations of the particles of cosmic dust, and because of the rotary motion given to the entire mass, a vortex is formed which, by its own generating power, will continue to draw to itself more and more of the detached floating atoms within its radius.

The vibrating mass of brilliance seems alive, and as it grows there suddenly come from the mass sharp, red, forked tongues of fire which blaze out and disappear, creating great billowing clouds. Finally, with a terrible shrieking, a brilliant ball of fire rapidly comes towards the mass, throwing off sparks and creating great peals of thunder and flashes of lightning. This is a destructive comet, which seems to fill the whole heavens, causing an intense heat. With a horrible crash the coalescing of the comet takes place with the mass of cosmic dust which eventually will be a world.

The aurora borealis and its southern counterpart, the aurora australis, are caused by solar particles impinging on the upper atmosphere, guided toward the earth's magnetic poles by its magnetic field, and exciting oxygen and nitrogen atoms in order to produce the colored glow. It has now been ascertained by science that auroras occur practically simultaneously in the northern and southern hemispheres, linked by magnetic fields, and that low-energy particles, perhaps X-rays, are produced during the auroral process.

Related to the aurora borealis is what is called by science the "night airglow," a faint radiation often invisible to the naked eye, but perceived by photoelectric photometer telescopes in all latitudes, and traced to the excitation of oxygen, sodium and the hydroxyl radical. *This is similar to Claude Neon's work with electrically excited gases.

Extensive western hemisphere observations have established that the "airglow," once thought to be relatively quiet, actually may become quite agitated, with blobs of faint light wandering about the sky at what seems to be 150 miles per hour. Researchers have also noted that cosmic radiation changes greatly with variations in electromagnetic phenomena originating on the sun. Within a few hours of a magnetic storm, cosmic ray intensity may dip as much as 10 percent, increasing significantly during periods of sunspot minimum. Primary particles streaming earthward tend to curve toward the magnetic poles; relatively low-energy particles tend to cluster at the poles, while the ones entering the equator need a minimum energy of 15 billion electron volts. The drop in cosmic ray intensity after solar flares is due to the fact that, during magnetic storms, the sun sends forth huge clouds of highly charged gases carrying their own magnetic fields, and these form an electronic barrier which deflects the cosmic rays.

Were it not for the ionosphere, the high electrified layer of thin air particles which begins fifty miles overhead, radio waves would go off into space instead of being reflected back to Earth. Using different radio frequencies, scientists have been able to differentiate between various ionospheric layers, the higher ones reflecting higher frequencies. The 108-megacycle transmission set for satellites would be able to pierce the ionosphere and maintain communication with space travelers. Radio probing stations have studied and measured the ionosphere for years; its free electrons, height, changes with time and season, geography, and sunspot cycle. They have studied "whistlers," the chirping radio signals generated by lightning flashes, and found that the energy in the spectrum's very low frequency range travels via the earth's magnetic field far into space, following the magnetic path back to Earth in the opposite hemisphere and then rebounding back and forth. Bursts of solar gas in space create other signals, which enter the magnetic field and behave in the same way.

Ionospheric and other studies provide compelling evidence that interplanetary space is not empty, but that it contains an atmosphere; thin gases and elementary particles such as protons and electrons. Geomagnetists tell us that space is filled with matter having mass and electrical properties, pointing to our own not-too-distant discoveries of magnetic links between space vehicles and the use of space matter for power, braking and steering.

It must be understood that the great Centers of Consciousness, such as the Solar Deities and the Elohim, or the Creative Gods, are the evolutionary products of remote Cosmic Days, having evolved from manhood into godhood, and that on the morning of our first period they were again called into activity, and were not newly created, as was anciently believed. For God did not create the earth and all it contained first, and then made "two great lights; the greater light to rule the day and the lesser light to rule the night: and the stars and set them in the firmament of the heavens to give light upon the Earth," as it is stated in Genesis.

CELESTIAL BEINGS

In accordance with the Divine Law, which is also the law of necessity, the stronger centers of force preceded the weaker, in this Cosmic Day, the same as they did in previous periods, and will forever continue to do; therefore, before the creation of worlds or planetary systems, the suns were created which were to give light and heat and magnetic life to those worlds. These suns were created by the greatest individualized centers of consciousness that exist in the Universe – the Solar Deities, or Lords of the Flame, commonly called Sun Gods by the sun worshiping peoples. After those centers of magnetic force and light had been created and their orbits established, the Elohim or Planetary Spirits brought into materialized form lesser magnetic centers and arranged them into systems of worlds.

Other Celestial Beings, who in our Scriptures were sometimes called the Seraphim and Cherubim, and who had been but waiting for the Divine summons to rouse them to activity, began the work which the All-Father, Divine Mind, desired them to do. Like the Elohim, these great Beings were also centers of individualized consciousness, but differed from them in being the products of the Cosmic Day preceding this. When the last Cosmic Night came on they had, through individualization, evolved to a point beyond the probability of re-absorbment into the Universal Consciousness. And, although they were possessed of lesser power, being smaller centers than the Elohim, still the individual Godhood of each had been established, and they belonged to the "Heavenly Host" who work everlastingly for the up-building of the Universe.

Throughout the Bible these Beings are frequently mentioned, and were called by various names, according to the impression which they made upon the mind of the individual who saw them. They usually appeared singly to persons, as in the case of Saul, who was going to Damascus to persecute the Christians. The description he gave of the Being who stopped him in his mad career was more nearly correct than was usually given in those days. He was impressed with the thought that it was Jesus of Nazareth who spoke to him. It may or may not have been the Being who had been using the body of the humble Nazarene in order to teach humanity how to live up to higher standards of morality; but whether it was He or not, it certainly was a Celestial Being who had been sent to Saul to enlighten him regarding the mistakes he was making in persecuting his fellowmen. And it was not the first nor the last incident of the kind which has occurred among mankind. (*Angel of Mons - World War I.*)

In the first chapter of Ezekiel there is a most graphic description of four of these Beings, who, the prophet declared, had appeared to him. He stated that they looked exactly alike, and had "the appearance of the likeness of the glory of the Lord." And when he heard the voice of the One who spoke, he fell upon his face, and was unable to stand before them. It is not unreasonable to believe that the description of that Celestial Quartet given by Ezekiel was highly colored by his intense emotional condition, as well as by the imperfection of his clairvoyant vision at that time. So far as the details are concerned, his description could not have been correct, since Beings who have reached the point of development which entitles them to the position of Creative Gods have no need for wings; neither do they have animal heads, nor bird faces. Unless we accept the Egyptian legend that the Masters and Adepts could appear in animal or semi-human form by controlling their astral form. This ability is also claimed for Kaballistic Adepts, Tibetan Shamans and other occult Masters.

They are Great Souls who, in their Cosmic Day, were like the men of our present day, but who have now become disembodied, yet have retained every principle except their physical vehicle, for which they have no further need. And, instead of going to some faraway heaven and spending an eternity in selfish bliss, they have chosen to do the work of self-sacrifice which ends only with the Cosmic Day in which that work is undertaken. Combined, they form the invisible "Host" which ever protects and watches over humanity within its karmic limits. The Kumaras of the Buddhist Hierarchy of Gods are the Planetary intelligences.

Singularly, or in pairs, they sometimes visit individuals who have become worthy of their help. They are the protecting, compassionate, Guardian Angels for the struggling, suffering souls of earth. They are the Elder Brothers, the Saviors, and the Avatars for undeveloped men. With their intense and rapid rates of vibration, they sometimes appear to man as great centers of light, or as radiant suns encircled by all of the colors of the rainbow. And if one of these wondrous Beings comes into close proximity with an undeveloped incarnated ego, that person is often unable to bear the Presence and retain his consciousness on the material plane. Sometimes these Beings take physical bodies, to use for the purpose of enabling them to mingle with men, and thus to help a race or a nation by leading it over a difficult place in its evolution. And some take physical bodies and appear among men as Adepts and Masters in order to teach and guide those who have reached the point in their evolution where they are ready for such assistance, for "when the student is ready, the Master will appear."

Those who give a merely passing and superficial attention to the subject of occultism constantly inquire why, if Adepts in life exist, they do not appear to the world, and show their powers. Why do they walk about among men in "disguise," so to speak, and unrecognized? And, if there are Great Masters dwelling upon our earth, whose abode cannot be found by men, is this not proof that they do not exist at all? While there are Adepts and Masters upon the earth, the earth must preserve to them places of seclusion. This is a fact in nature which is only an external expression of a profound fact in super-nature.

Throughout all time, the wise men have lived apart from the masses, and even when one of them walks in the midst of human life, his seclusion and safety are preserved as completely as ever. This is a part of his inheritance, part of his position, and unknown by men all safe occasionally aided by the actual power and presence of the Adept. They are known only as mystics by those who have the power to recognize them – the power given by the conquering of self. Otherwise, they could not exist, even for an hour, in such a mental and psychic atmosphere as is created by the confusion and disorder of a city. Unless protected and made safe, their own growth would be interfered with, and their work injured.

It is possible for a Neophyte to meet an Adept in the flesh – even to live in the same house with him, and yet be unable to recognize him, for no nearness in space, and no closeness of revelations nor daily intimacy can do away with the inexorable laws which give to the Adept his seclusion. Often they are considered by the mass of humanity as "fools" – sometimes they are the subject of ridicule by the lower classes, and looked down upon by those of the upper classes. But whether incarnated or not, and whether ridiculed or not, they continue to inspire and uplift humanity and the leaders of the people, teaching them at all times the highest truths that they are able to understand.

When our World was in a vaporous condition, an irregular shapeless mass of burning gases, the Universal Principle called forth from the Ether, in which all things latently reposed, the different elements which combined and solidified and produced the mineral kingdom of our Earth. And after her creation was completed, and her orbit in the heavens established, for ages she still remained in a negative condition, receptive only to the restless, surging Father Force, the sea, which covered, magnetized, and enriched her, and made it possible for her to "bring forth" the vegetable and the animal creations which she had conceived in the darkness and silence.

When our globe had become surrounded and ensouled with its color currents, about which we will study in a later chapter, it was ready to bring forth into objectivity the various vegetable and animal forms which Divine Mind had created on the mental plane, and in this work the Seraphim and Cherubim, the Lord Gods of the second chapter of Genesis, became the demonstrators. According to the command of God, the Divine Mind, the Elohim had created the Sons of God out of the differentiated part of the Universal Consciousness, and had placed them in a realm of innocence upon another sphere or orb in our planetary chain; and now the Seraphim and Cherubim undertook the work of creating the forms of vegetable and animal life, and the bodies of animal men, out of that part of the differentiated portion of the Universal Consciousness which had been attracted to and had ensouled the earth.

Since Divine Mind had pictured certain portions of the earth covered with grasses, flowers and trees, and had thus formed the matrices for these individualized expressions of itself, seven Seraphs and seven Cherubs, each half-souls of the other, had formed into a group of Creative Beings for the purpose of materializing Divine Mind's creations. It was these Beings who, with their united force, raised continents above the surface of the waters, and caused "the waters under the heaven to be gathered together into one place." *Tibetan Herukkas and Dakinis.*

After the waters had been made to bring forth, these Celestial Beings then began to slowly materialize the insect and animal forms which they had seen pictured in Divine Mind. From the decaying roots of the grasses and the flowers, the life principle was drawn into tiny insect and animal forms (which, of course, did not include the malignant creatures which were subsequently the offspring of men's minds). We see this in the case of the wheat germ giving life to the grub if moisture is allowed in the jar by air induction.

According to Christian tradition, seraphim rank highest among the angels. Jewish tradition holds that seraphim are heavenly beings separate from angels.

THE CREATION OF HIGHER LIFE FORMS

From the decaying roots of shrubs and trees the life principle was drawn into larger animal forms. The soul of the squirrel which now has its home in the hollow of a decaying tree was once the soul of the tree. Then it depended upon the soil and atmosphere for its individual maintenance and its limitations held it firmly attached to the mother earth which bore it. When its experience as a tree had been sufficient, and when its material tree body began to decay, Universal Consciousness, desiring a higher individualization for it, acted as the evolutionary impulse and pushed the tree soul out of its dying vehicle, and the Celestial Beings molded it into the tiny squirrel form which they saw pictured in Divine Mind. Because of its former life as a tree, and because of its past associations with the forest, in its new and more progressed form it loved and made its home among the trees until, after many reincarnations as a squirrel, it outgrew that condition also, and was able to use a larger and a stronger body. And thus the animal kingdom was gradually evolved through the re-embodiment of the life principle, combined with the procreative and individualizing forces, until a form was evolved which stood erect and walked upon two feet. This form the Celestial Beings (The Lord Gods) created or evolved from "the dust of the ground." It was the materialized and mineralized product of the earth. And when they "breathed into his nostrils the breath of life," or drew into his body the combined cosmic life currents (animal), "man became a living (animal) soul," and was ready to receive the divine, immortal principle which was waiting upon another planet to come and immortalize his existence. Darwin's Evolution considers only physical evolution, not the evolving consciousness.

Re-embodiment is a fact in nature, with the indestructibility of matter and force re-embodying themselves for the purpose of evolution. This law of re-embodiment manifests on all planes, and on all worlds or planets. The fact that we do not see the operation of a law is no proof that the law has ceased to act. Nor is the fact that this law manifests differently in different kingdoms of nature, and in different forms, evidence of the limitation or non-existence of the law. Every law manifests in each class or form alike, but differs in its manifestations in different classes of forms because the consciousness within the form restricts but does not prevent the manifestation. For example, the law of gravity manifests the same in all iron, but manifests differently in different kingdoms and substances.

Individualized consciousness not only re-embodies itself constantly during earth life, but it re-embodies itself after it drops its entire physical body. In other words, it reincarnates. During the space of every seven years, man undergoes a complete change of body; therefore he is in the process of re-embodying himself by this constant renewal of his atoms. According to his rates of vibration, or as his thoughts are elevated or debased, does he draw new atoms to himself. And, after he has dropped one physical body, it is certainly not surprising that he should have the power to draw to himself another. The fact that most men do not remember their past lives is no proof that they did not formerly exist. If it were, the majority of men did not exist between the first and third years of their present lives, nor in a pre-natal condition. Man does remember his past lives when his subjective mind controls his objective mind, and can function through it, for in the subjective is stored the memories of past experience. What we call "conscience" is only the memory of past experiences, warning us not to repeat former follies and mistakes.

And when Mother Earth had finally evolved from her animal kingdom a form with a brain of sufficient vibratory power to enable it to receive from the Universal Principle the Divine Spark which would lead and enlighten it throughout the ages to come, and when animal man stood erect and walked upon two feet instead of four, he knew very little about himself, and nothing about his source. After an almost interminable length of time, the law of Evolution, which is God's will operating in every living thing, brought to the Earth and to each of her animal men the subjective minds or souls which had been created, to work out a double purpose; first, to gain for each subjective mind a greater strength and power by contacting with a material world at a lower rate of vibration than its own; and, second, to subject animal man, and raise him to a higher point of development.

THE YING-YANG OF SEX

When these subjective minds or souls first came to Earth, they knew nothing of sex, nor of things sensory or sensual. But each had been created in the image of God, and was a part of the Father-Mother principle; therefore, each of the subjective minds possessed both a positive and a negative side to its nature. In the realm where these minds had dwelt before coming to earth, this complexity in each had caused no inharmonious conditions. Since there had been no trials to endure, and no temptations to resist, existence there had been a blissful, beautiful dream. But when these Sons of God came to this world and saw "the daughters of men," the animal forms which had been raised to receive them as their lords, each mind was found to make its selection. And it was then that the sex question, with all its ramifications and mystifications, arose.

Acting according to its natural tendencies, the positive part of each of these subjective minds was attracted toward the female animal form, while the negative part of each mind, by reason of its nature, was attracted toward the male animal form. This caused dissention through jealousy, and war was declared in the heaven of each individual mind. Then came the first divorce ever granted upon this earth, and God gave one to each of Its Sons. It came through the courts of Evolutionary Law, of which the divorce courts of the present day are but remote ramifications. These first divorces, like those of the present day, were given for the purpose of permitting each Son of God to work out his salvation in his own way; or, in other words, to give him free will. And since there were more animal forms than there were Sons of God to incarnate in them, it was expedient that these incarnating minds should divide into halves, each half taking a body in conformity with its desires, in order that the new evolutionary scheme should be carried out in a shorter time than in former Cosmic Days.

When the war of minds was ended and each subjective mind or soul had become accustomed to the new order of things, it was quite delighted with its conditions, for everything was here that could please the eye and gratifies the senses. Then to each mind came the desire for individual possessions, and a great accumulation of material things. Man's original vibrations began to grow more and more gross, until the beautiful subjective blue and yellow which had characterized his innocence deepened into the darkest shade of selfish myrtle green. The animal nature which he had espoused and had come to rule rose in its desires and ruled him. He sank "lower than the animals," because he had enough of the Divine Principle within him to give him reasoning power, by means of which he could better accomplish his purposes than could the animals.

This was the "Original Sin," or "fall from grace" mentioned in the Scriptures. But Divine Consciousness never goes backward. It is constantly pushing onward and upward; and, although sometimes, from a narrow point of view, it seems that men and things are degenerating and retrograding, this is only seeming, and is not real. Now when the subjective man plunged from his realm of innocence and inexperience into the experiences of this earth, he was negatively good. He had never been tempted, and had never come into contact with anything of a lower rate of vibration than his own. He was pure because his environment had been pure; or, in other words, he was an "infant" mind or soul, entering in upon a new state of existence. Because he had not experienced it, he did not know that indulgence in sexual excesses would ruin his body. Neither did he understand that his generative organs had been made for the purpose of creating new human bodies for other egos to incarnate in.

As it has always been with every race at every great period of time since man came to live upon this planet, the first egos who came to incarnate were the stronger ones, possessing more persistence and endurance than those who arrived later. This was a necessity, in order that each new race should have its pioneers, its strong men, to do the heavy work and to prepare the way for the weaker ones who would follow after them. But as time passed the weaker egos incarnated in greater numbers, and when they could enjoy more comforts and luxuries than their progenitors, without the same efforts to obtain them, the morals of the people became more and more corrupt. Men and women began making the fearful mistake of thinking that their generative organs were created for the sole purpose of gratifying their own sexual animal desires, and for the amusement and entertainment of their friends. They indulged themselves in every sexual excess that the human mind could devise, until the time came to pay the penalty for attempting to break the Law of Being.

Then the physical bodies of the offspring began to manifest weaknesses inherited from their parents, and in the course of a great number of generations the man who originally, in the beginning of his race, had stood ten or twelve feet in height became reduced in stature to six or seven feet, and his physical strength decreased. There came a time with every race when it was almost impossible to find positive virtue in either sex. If a pure ego came to dwell among those people, it received persecution, abuse, and even crucifixion, for attempting to live on a higher plane of morality than that of its time. And when the races became so corrupt that they constantly despised purity and loved impurity, there was nothing that Divine Law could do to help their condition but to permit a cataclysm or a holocaust to sweep them off the earth, in order to begin a new period of evolution.

Ever since the Sons of God separated from their God-Flames and incarnated on earth, each half has been earnestly seeking a reunion with the other part of itself. Subconsciously, each one holds a mental picture of his past happiness when, in the realm of innocence and purity, he was free from the ills and troubles of his present state of existence. And each one longs for a return to the old blissful condition – for happiness is really what every human soul desires more than anything else in the world; and it is happiness for which everyone is striving.

With Divine Man's descent into the material realm, it was, not long before he forgot his origin. But in an inner chamber of each heart, where none can enter or disturb, there is a picture of another face, which looks smilingly out and seems to beckon to the seeker after happiness, saying, "I am your happiness. I am the one that you desire. When you find and possess me you will have your wish." Perhaps Man does not know it, but this picture is of the other half of himself, the only one in the entire Universe whose basic vibrations correspond with his own. He loves it, but he does not know why. Should he be an artist, he tries to reproduce it upon his canvas. If he is a musician, he composes and sings to it; if an actor, he plays his best when he thinks he sees it among his audience. If he is a man of finance, he saves money for it, and dreams of the day when,, in human form, it will sit at his table, wear his jewels, and be his lifelong companion.

Sometimes he has a fancy that he has seen it. A woman whom he meets reminds him of his sacred picture; there is a look or a gesture which he believes he remembers, and he eagerly seeks an introduction. It may or may not be the one for whom he is looking, but if it is, and a marriage is consummated between them, then his longing is satisfied. There will be no other face so dear, and no other form so precious, as hers. If he is a man well on in his development, he will always be true to her-and should she be taken from him by the transition called death, he would never seek to fill with another the place in his heart that she occupied. Should he be an undeveloped man, with animal passions unrestrained, he would, in his brutal way, always love her best – but she might not be his only love.

True cosmic marriage is the reunion of the two halves of an ego, and any other union which in any way imitates it is necessarily an earthly marriage. When two mismated halves attempt to consummate a union, it is but an abortive attempt at marriage, and is never perfectly satisfactory to either. When we stop to consider how many millions of half-souls are living upon this planet today, and when we realize that there are at least half as many more upon the subjective planes surrounding the earth, and that from this vast multitude there are only two whose basic vibrations are the same, and who belong to each other, it is not difficult to understand why Earth marriages are so numerous.

That they are a necessity to a certain point, during the evolutionary work which must be done, no one can deny. At this time they are helpful to those who engage in them, because they bring experiences which are necessary in order that marriage may be understood and appreciated. There is no contract which a man makes that is so far-reaching in its ramifications as the legalized marriage contract. It affects, for good or ill, more persons than does any other contract, and it not only colors the life in which it is made, but often influences following incarnations.

It is a comfort to know that, as the human race evolves; half-souls meet oftener, and enjoy the privilege of each other's society for longer periods of time. And as these unions are made more often, a deeper consciousness comes with each, and the evolution of egos is thereby hastened. It is no longer a disgrace for a woman to go through life alone, if she feels so disposed. The woman who prefers not to wed, but to remain true to her ideal – the sacred picture which she carries in her heart—shows a courage which many unhappily married women wish they had copied. And because a male has not wed, there is no reason to suppose that he does not have his sacred picture in his heart, and that he does not worship at that shrine the same as do all other half-souls.

In the Holy Kabbalah, which dates back into the most obscure past of Judaism, is told of "... spiritual union below for the Sons of the Doctrine, so that they are encompassed by two females; the wife who is on Earth, and the Unseen Helpmate." It is further described that when the master "...of the Law was going by himself upon a journey, and when, technically speaking, the male was to be apart from the female, he was not for that reason in a state of separation from his (Spiritual Companion) ... supposing that he had prayed to the Holy One before starting, in order to maintain the union between male and female abroad as well as at home. Another condition was that he must watch over all his actions in every phase of life; otherwise he might be separated from his Spiritual Companion, putting a stop to the union, and rendering himself an incomplete being."

It is stated also that "...he who abides in the true way will meet in marriage with the woman-soul which was his pre-natal companion. If he has deviated, it may happen that the woman predestined to him is espoused to another; but in the event of his repentance a time will come when the alien male will disappear, thus yielding the woman to her true mate." And further, "...the union between God and the soul is often in the sense of vision, although there are deeper stages. That which is substituted is the union in heaven of souls who have been espoused on earth-being those who were espoused previously* before the world began... for in the heights of heaven there is yet another union of two born in love and forever inseparable."

According to Hindu belief, the creation of the universe is believed to be a product of divine sexual union which reflects upon the sexual nature of all living things.

"And should the twin-souls be of necessity separated; that is, leading separate lives on earth, the soul may leave its body and... when souls leave the lower world they enter into a certain palace which is above, if they carry the proper warrants, and therein those which are male are again united to the female, in which union they radiate light as in sparkles... during the day the females are separated from the males, each living their separate earth life; but the spouses are in union at night, and in their mutual embrace the lights of both dissolve into a single light."

"...the souls born of celestial unions are reserved in a palace, and when a man is converted, his twin-soul takes flight and comes under the wings of Shekinah, who embraces her-because she is the "fruit of the just" in their intercourse – and sends her into the body of the convert where she (or he) remains, and from that moment the convert acquires the title of Just. This is the mystery of the words in the Scriptures, "the fruit of the just is the Tree of Life." There is another sense in which the Holy One affects the union of twin-souls, so that they may engender other souls, themselves animated by those sacred forces which are above them."

"...and so the souls go up, male and female, into the world beyond; if they are prepared souls, they find one another, and the union that is everlasting begins in the Light of God."

And although these statements from the Holy Kaballah appear not to be taking reincarnation into consideration, this is not true. For once the twin-souls have been rejoined, mentally and spiritually, in the sight of God, then they can never again be separated; that is, although separated physically, perhaps, they are in constant mental and spiritual contact throughout their earthly lives* being joined as one Being between lives, and separating again as male and female when they return for re-embodiment.

As evolution goes on and egos increase in strength and positive goodness, the Law of Attraction, acting along the line of least resistance, will bring half-souls together without even the aid of their own conscious, mental demands, while mismated egos will be, by the law of repulsion, separated and swept apart more quickly than before. We often hear ridicule of marriage by unhappily married people, and contemptuous remarks constantly made about it on television and in places of amusement. The supposedly funny men use this subject for the object at which to fire their witticisms, and it is true that the jokes nearly always bring a laugh from the mismated egos that are or have been suffering from the inconveniences or miseries of an earthly marriage. But a laugh is not always an expression of pleasure; sometimes it is only a thin veil for a sob, and very often those who laugh do so because they do not know what else to do.

However, Earth marriage is a necessity at this time in the evolution of the race. It is not only a social and political necessity, but it is a karmic necessity as well – and through it many egos are brought together in the family circle to work out past obligations, and to pay debts which could be paid in no other way. The Law of Justice does rule the world, although the contrary sometimes appears to be true; and it operates in the most infinitesimal affairs and relations of life. If a man and woman have entered into an earth marriage, there was a karmic reason for it. One or the other, or both, perhaps, owe a karmic debt which must be paid, and it could be faithfully and fully done only through the devotion which is demanded and received through a covenant of this kind. If all persons who are chafing under the restraint caused by their matrimonial fetters could but realize that their present condition of unhappiness is but the result of past mistakes, and of unjust treatment which they have given, in some other life, to the very individual with whom they are now joined in wedlock, it would serve to explain many of the mysteries and miseries of wedded life.

As a nation or race advances in evolution, the Divine Law brings reforms, and in spite of the mixed desires of the mass of humanity a way will be found to improve their condition. Every tribe or nation, no matter how gross or how sensual, has its wise men who are stronger than those whom they undertake to teach, and those men who were in advance of the ignorant masses became the spiritual advisers of not only the people, but also of kings and rulers. Many of the wise men, the High Priests of ancient Bible times, were occultists, and understood that true marriage meant the reunion of two half-souls; and when those ancient peoples had evolved to a point where they would listen to, and be influenced by, their wise men on the subject of marriage, the High Priests made the attempt to establish monogamy among them. When the priests were unable to determine whether those who wished to marry really belonged to each other or not, they consulted the stars, which were supposed to indicate at the birth of each individual the exact point of development he had reached during his previous life. If the stars indicated adversely, then the banns were forbidden, and the marriage was not consummated. But if they indicated favorably, the wedding was sanctified by a most solemn sacrament, and during the performance of the religious marriage rites the command was given forth by the officiating priest, "whom God hath joined together let no man put asunder."

It is to this fragment of occult teachings that some Churches of today hold as a reason for their refusal to recognize the union by contract, or the modern divorce. And, although they still attempt to enforce what they believe to be the command of God, and refuse to believe in human power to annul a marriage, still they do not take the trouble to first ascertain whether or not it is the sacred reunion of half-souls which is being consummated, or even if there is a psychic or physical affinity between them. They bestow their blessings freely and indiscriminately upon all alike, and expect, notwithstanding the ignorance of the persons entering into a covenant of this kind, that it shall be maintained until the end of their natural lives. They are quite willing to forgive and absolve from consequences any mistake which man makes except his matrimonial mistakes; but these, which are the most serious of all, and which affect more persons than any others, these Churches do not permit him to correct.

THE REALITY OF REINCARNATION

The Law of Demand and Supply has been operating in the Universe since it was created. And although men have not known how to use that law intelligently and scientifically, nevertheless, whatever a man desires in his heart will come to him sooner or later. After a long period of wishing and waiting, a man's desire for knowledge concerning conception and parental duty was met. Advanced egos, men who had lived through a former period of evolution and gained a knowledge far beyond that of the people whom they came to help, were sent to this earth to incarnate in human form, and to become teachers of the growing races.

These teachers taught men and women that to become the father or mother of a human body was a sacred, divine privilege; that parenthood should always be assumed with deepest reverence, and with an earnest demand for wisdom to train each little personality in a manner that would make it tractable for the incarnating ego to control, so that when the tiny brain should become expanded to the point where the ego could take full possession, it would be a good instrument, instead of a poor one, for it to use.

Before, a woman conceives the embryo which is to become a human body, the Divine Law attracts to her an ego who in a past life has been associated either pleasantly or unpleasantly with her or with the man who will be the father of her child. Sometimes this ego who is about to reincarnate does not leave her for weeks, or perhaps for months, before conception. It is ever present, waiting for the moment to come when copulation will occur and the conditions will be favorable for the conception of its body. And. when the desired conditions are produced, it sends forth from itself into the ovum within the mother, a tiny blue magnetic thread, and fastens it to the life germ which the father has just deposited there.

To the eyes of the clairvoyant, this magnetic thread appears upon the subjective plane as the web thread of the spider appears to the physical eyes upon the material plane. Both seem to be equally fragile and easily broken, but the magnetic thread, when once attached to its embryo, is strengthened in its hold by the reincarnating ego's intense desire for life. The Law of Attraction which brought that ego to that family also gives protection to the embryo through its action upon the uterus containing it. It causes that organ to contract around the tiny life germ for the first few days after it is received, or until a membrane, which will be a further protection to the embryo, is completely formed within the opening of the cervix.

When conception is established, then comes the building of the body which the reincarnating ego will possess. If the ego or builder is an undeveloped mind, and is being forced back without its volition into earth-life by the great Law, then the building of the body is not a conscious creation of its own, but is the result of the physical action of the law and of the mother's mind. But the advanced ego consciously selects from the mother's blood the finest atoms for its embryo, and mentally moulds its vehicle according to its purpose. The reincarnating ego completely envelopes the mother of its embryo at the moment of conception, and continues in that close relationship during the whole period of gestation, and affects more or less her disposition and desires.

If it is of a weaker nature than hers, then its influence is not externally apparent to any large degree; but if it is a stronger, even though more undeveloped, nature than hers, it dominates her in every way. She will no longer have the same likes or dislikes, and will sometimes yield to the most unaccountable tastes. Persons whom she once loved she will now despise, and vice versa. Sometimes she will seem to be obsessed by a demon of animal passion, and during the whole period of gestation her sexual desires will be insatiable. To her friends she becomes a source of sorrow, because they do not understand the cause of the change in her. She, herself, may not understand it, and usually does not even care to know the reason.

Through the intense, and perhaps gross, desires of the reincarnating ego, it may impress the tiny body with impurities. It may poison the blood of the child with its own hatred and anger. Through its un-controlled emotions and passions it often produces an abnormal condition of some of its internal organs, and the body will be born with impure blood and a defective brain, and perhaps with a physical deformity of limb or body. Then it would be said that these misfortunes were inherited from its parents, or that they were birthmarks caused by some fault of the mother, or by some mishap which befell her during the period of gestation.

When the woman is relieved of the burden of carrying the child, and her normal mental condition has reasserted itself, by reason of the reincarnating ego having been removed a step from her aura, she often suffers the deepest remorse because of the unfortunate plight of her child. Her friends and her husband tell her how disgracefully she has misbehaved, and blames her for the condition of her offspring. In reality, however, she neither consciously nor unconsciously produced it, and it may be that the ego of the child was drawn into her family because of its past relationship with her husband, who is now its father. It is true that she was karmically connected with her husband, and that the Law brought them together for that reason. Through her relationship with him she had to participate in his karma, but she may not have had a past association with the particular ego who was now reincarnated as their child, and should not be blamed for its misfortunes.

According to the Divine Law, the union of the sexes should never take place without the desire of both the male and the female who participate in that union, and the desire should never be stimulated by anything except the mutual attraction of each toward the other. During the perfect sex union of normal human bodies there is an exchange of magnetic force which is strengthening both to the physical bodies and to the minds of each. This exchange of magnetic force is due to the fact that the generative organs of the male and female act upon each other as do the opposite poles of an electrical instrument. A perfect circuit is made between the two bodies, and at the point of direct contact, heat, power and life are generated. Then the nerves and blood absorb this electric fluid which flows from one body to another, and they become electrified and strengthened; and with an electrified and strengthened body, the mind gains power.

If a developed or advanced ego is seeking reincarnation in a certain family, it is because of karmic reasons. During some past life there was formed a pleasant relationship between it and some member of that family. Or perhaps it may be that it is the other half of the ego of the mother to whom it has now come in the relationship of child. In a case such as this, the mother will be uplifted during the entire period of gestation, and she will anticipate the coming of her child with the happiness that she would feel at the prospect of a visit from her dearest friend. She will dream of it at night, and plan beautiful things for it by day; and the things happening in her household or among her friends that once disturbed and annoyed her now bring a smile to her face.

If the incarnating ego is not the other half of herself, but is equal to her in development, then she may be contented and pleased with the possibility of becoming a mother. If it should be an ego greatly in advance of her, or should she, by reason of lifetimes of hard work, have evolved to the place where her sincerity and purity of ego make it possible for an Adept seeking embodiment to select her for this purpose, she would be blessed in many ways by the close relationship during gestation, and the impetus which she would receive from the association would carry her a long step in advance of where she was when she conceived the little body.

However, in the case of an Adept wishing to reincarnate, it is not too often possible to find a channel open to sincere and loving parents, and many times Beings wishing to re-embody for particular work at a particular time will avail themselves of the first opportunity presenting itself, which results in separation from the mother at an early age; sometimes by the death of the mother at childbirth, but more often by infant abandonment, especially if there is no karmic tie here which would make it necessary for the Being reincarnating to be raised by that particular mother, or in a particular family. When even this opportunity is not available to an Adept, there are cases where, providing there is found the proper vehicle, the Adept may use the physical body of a small child which has passed through transition, entering the body at the moment the soul of the child leaves it, which results in the seemingly "miraculous recovery" of the child.

Heredity, according to the common acceptance of the term, is impossible. Neither the father nor the mother of a child can give to it its character, or any part of it. It is true that if the reincarnating ego is not as strong as either of its parents the physical body may resemble in appearance one or both of them. This may be due to one of two causes; first, the reincarnating ego may, in a general way, be of a similar character to one or both parents or, second, it may be that it is not a conscious builder of its body, and negatively waits for the Law and for its mother's mind to mold the body for it.

By many physicians and by society in general, it is believed that the father or mother can transmit impurities and disease through their blood to their innocent offspring, and that a child will thus be made to suffer for the sins of its parents. No ego could reincarnate with parents who would transmit poisons or disease to its body unless, by reason of its own past mistakes, that ego deserved to have them. It could never be brought into that family by the Law if it did not belong there, because the Law is Justice. To the mother who finds in her children the taint of a poison she knows she did not give them, but which came from their father, we would tell her to permit no bitterness to live in her heart toward the man to whom she is married, because this is a debt which is being paid, and the child who appears to be an innocent sufferer for another's sins had sins of its own to expiate, and is expiating them now under the right and proper conditions.

By this is not meant that nothing should be done to improve the condition of the child, because improvement is always needed at every moment during the life of a human. But God should not be blamed for the affliction; neither should it be believed that it is a special dispensation of Providence. Force should not be wasted by weeping over the condition, but rather should be used to help that ego live a better life than it did before, in order that it may not suffer again in a like manner. And while the poison is being eliminated from the child's body, the poisonous thoughts which produced the condition should also be eliminated from its mind.

Because of their love for their children, parents often make slaves of themselves and sacrifice much which they need and desire, in order that their children may have more than they can afford to give them. The one object in life is the development and growth of every individual ego, and no one should be retarded in his or her evolution by becoming the slave of another. The mother who works all day in a factory or laundry in order to save her grown daughter from the stains of labor is not only retarding her own growth, but she is at the same time fostering her daughter's character to a degree of selfishness which will retard, instead of advance, her progress in life. If the ego who came to reincarnate as the daughter of the hard-working, self- sacrificing woman had not needed and deserved the lessons in physical labor which Divine Law intended she should get in that environment, then she would not have been brought to that family to incarnate. Because of the many self-imposed tasks the mother cannot take time to read or to think along educational lines; she has very little or no time to spend upon her appearance, and, as a consequence, she appears illiterate, stupid and poorly dressed, and her greatest heartache comes when she finds that the daughter for whom she has toiled so hard is ashamed of her.

It is not infrequent that the father and mother are left unthanked and alone to toil and pay off the mortgage that, while laboring under their mistaken sense of duty, they have put upon their home in order that their boy could go to college and have a sufficient amount of money to spend in company with wealthier men's sons. And it is not infrequent, when the young man returns to his humble home and compares it, and his parents, with the homes and parents of his fashionable friends, that he feels ashamed, and often blames his father and mother for his poverty.

Just as parents should not make slaves of themselves for their children, neither should a husband or wife become a slave for his or her marriage partner, nor a woman support a worthless husband who refuses to work. There is a way to become free from the unpleasant conditions which attend an earth marriage, even though it has been karmically produced. It is the divine right and privilege of every human being to demand of Divine Mind its freedom from unpleasant environment. If the mental demand is made and goes forth into the Great Consciousness with all the earnestness of a suffering soul, the fetters will begin to fall away, and one after another, the limitations will be broken. The liberation will come in the way which Divine Mind wishes, and which, in view of all past mistakes and injustices, is best for the one making the demand.

When the majority of the women of any nation refuse to become mothers, whether it is because of poverty and inability to support children, or because they are too fashionable and have not the time to give to the duties of motherhood, then the world may realize that what is known as "race suicide" has begun in that portion of the globe. For the law of Demand and Supply works along this line as forcefully as along any other, and when women commence to picture themselves as barren, and demand barrenness, they are scientifically creating that condition for themselves and for the nation to which they belong. If artificial means are used to produce this condition, the demise of the nation will be hastened. And if a point has been reached where its limitation of thought, its fixed religious beliefs, and its unprogressive modes of living are causing mental strangulation to the individuals who compose it, then the addition of these various causes to the first cause soon brings national demolition.

Since there are two sides to every subject, there is another side to this one. In opposition to race suicide stands the other extreme, which is parental slavery. Parenthood is a necessary experience in man's evolution, but parental slavery, produced by too much parenthood, is another great mistake. Simply because God said, on the morning of man's creation, "be fruitful and multiply, and replenish the earth and subdue it", many people have believed it to be a duty they owe to God to give birth to as many children as possible and, regardless of health or of financial conditions, have borne children in such numbers that they have been utterly unable to take care of them. This is exhibiting extravagance in the parental privileges of man, and is as much to be deplored as any other extravagance. It is true that there are many egos upon the subjective plane awaiting an opportunity for reincarnation. But so is there an abundance of food that is waiting to be transformed into blood, bone and muscle. A man who constantly overcrowds his stomach in order to accommodate the food that is waiting to be transformed into something higher than food is abusing that organ, and will eventually reach a point where he cannot retain any food, and will shorten his life as a penalty for his extravagance in eating.

There are certain religious groups which encourage, and even command, their female members to give birth to as many children as possible; and priests have been known to advise the sacrifice of the life of a mother for the sake of bringing another child into the world, even though at that moment there was a family of little ones to be left motherless by his decision. Such advice as this, coming from a priest, supposedly a holy man, should be regarded as a crime, and should be made punishable by the State. It is a mistake to allow men to teach ignorant people to commit such wrongs as these, for it is as great a wrong to sacrifice the incarnation of one ego for the sake of giving reincarnation to another as it is to take life in any other way.

It is not necessary that an ego should become a slave to a larger family than it has means to provide for comfortably. It is not right or just for a man and woman to toil early and late and be deprived of the advantages and pleasures of life in order that a number of other egos may have an opportunity to reincarnate. However, every married man and woman should be willing to pay the parental debt they owe to the Divine Law by having some children. In other words, they should be willing and glad to give bodies and to educate at least two other egos in payment for their own birth and education.

We all chose to experience physical reality before we incarnated. Those who chose to live here on planet Earth are brave and strong souls capable of amazing things. We came here to love, learn and expand. We are the Universe experiencing itself in physical form, and we want to expand.

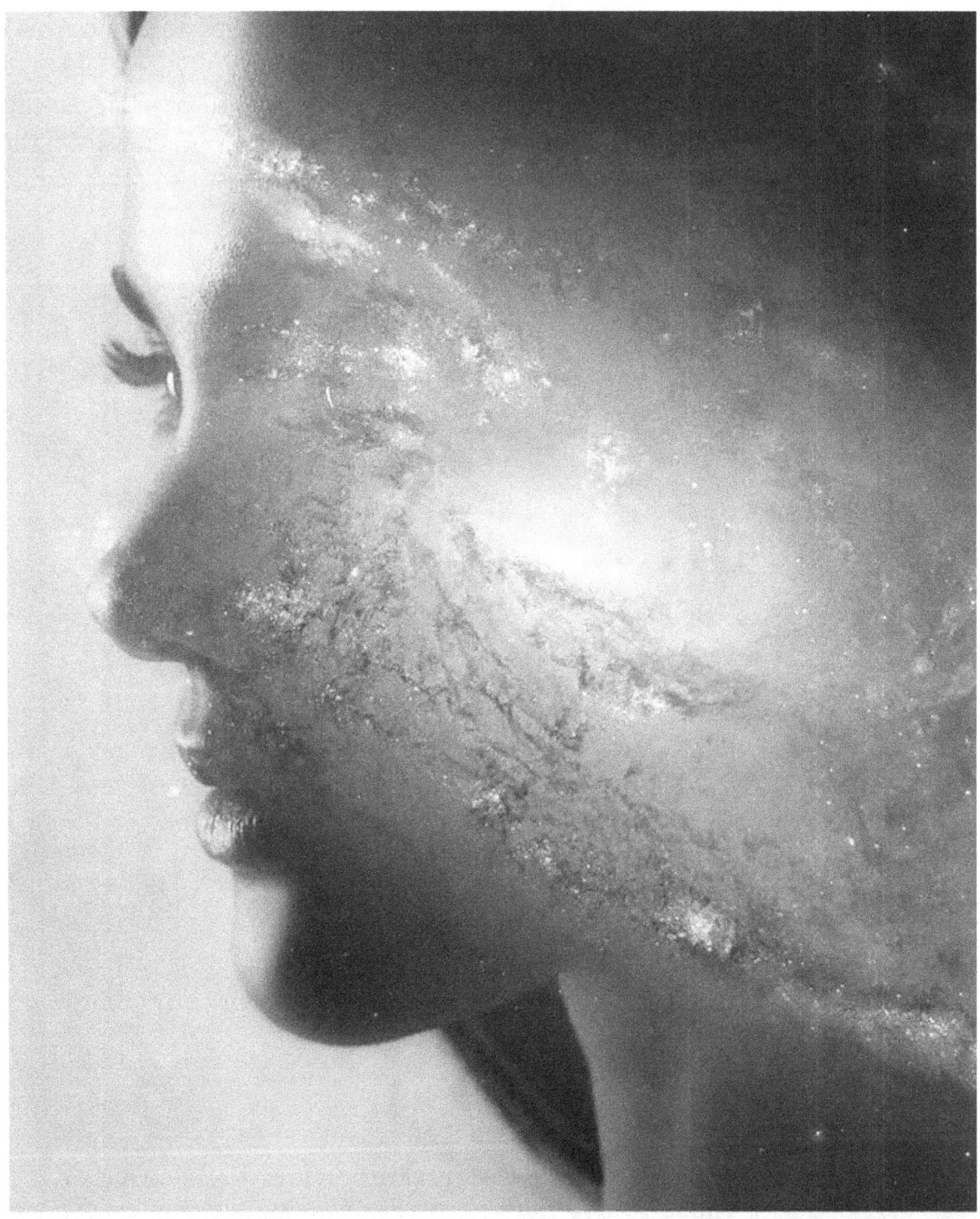

Universal consciousness is the undivided nature of yourself. The aspect of your mind that is not limited by time, space and causation. We are all part of the Universal mind which resides beyond time and space.

4

GODS AND MEN OUT OF SPACE

All those of the Catholic faith will remember the recent Church ruling that it is the Spiritual man who is resurrected, not the physical. This recent ruling by the Church was made to clarify the Catholic position on eye banks and donations of physical organs for medical purposes. The human body is sacred per se as a Temple of the Lord and this ruling obviously violates the ancient conception of the necessity for keeping the corpse inviolate and in sacred ground. Eventually cremation will prove more hygienic and economical. It is stated in this book that "occultism is the science of Divine unfoldment." It is obvious, from the above that also is Catholicism.

While it is true that God created man in His own image, according to the Scripture, man, in his search for the truth concerning his origin and the creation of his world, has also been creating God in man's image. Therefore, when primitive man began to realize the "**I AM I**"; that is, that he was something distinct and apart from everything else, he came to the point where he began to manifest the principle of self-consciousness; he began to think, to analyze, and to worship. The first thing he saw which awakened a feeling of fear or reverence in him was what we call Nature, and natural forces. When he perceived that they were stronger than he was, he began to worship them as his Deity. Next he passed on to the making of an image of the thing he worshiped, such as the totem and idol, and later he worshiped the sun, the moon and the stars. When he had finally learned by experience that fire could destroy both his body and his possessions, he began to worship that also-and thus he continued to live for ages, alternately worshiping and propitiating everything which he did not understand and could not control.

The idea of Deity is first found in individual worship. Each man has his own particular God which is a true one for him, because each person has his own conception of God. But as he becomes stronger he is not satisfied to worship alone, and then he desires to impress his ideas upon those with whom he comes in contact, and we find him in the second stage of his worship, which is tribal. When a certain tribe of men becomes stronger numerically than another, and begins to dominate that other, it immediately forces its own God idea upon the conquered people, as was most excellently illustrated in the primitive Grecian States. There each little state had its own particular God, but as the states became merged, a national God idea gradually took form, by the weaker states accepting the God of the stronger.

But sometimes the tribal or national God of the conquered people appealed to the wants or needs of the conquerors, and was adopted by them, as when Isis became Diana of Ephesus. Christianity has given us another example of this adoption of another nation's God by accepting Judea's God Jah-Hovah and renaming Him Jehovah. Jah-Hovah was nothing more than the Male-Female creative principle united. It was a Planetary Spirit, or one of the Elohim. Christianity adopted Him from Judaism, and improved upon the conception of its votaries by making Him a Universal-personal God. Much of his supposed wrath and vengeance was modified by attributing to Him enough of the element of Love to enable Him to show a leniency toward such of his creatures as he had elected or fore-ordained to be saved.

But now we have passed into a transition state, and man's conception of Deity is broadening from the anthropomorphic to a real Universal God, without modifications or limitations. The anthropomorphic idea means God made in the image of man, or ascribing human attributes to God. In olden times the attributes of human weaknesses and human traits were ascribed to the Jehovic God. But we have now arrived at the point where anthropomorphism is no longer characteristic of most progressive thinkers, and we are now able to conceive of a Universal Deity; one without human weaknesses, one without human limitation. And if there is one thing above all others that this great mental and metaphysical movement stands for, it is the sweeping away of the old anthropomorphic idea and the giving in its place of a Universal Deity.

A NEW CONCEPT OF GOD

"Divine Mind" has been selected for the term to be applied to this new conception of God in order to emphasize this idea of Universal Deity; in order to bring out clearly first the Deific idea, and, second, the fact that it is consciousness-for mind and consciousness are really synonymous terms. We prefer the term "Universal Consciousness," or "Divine Consciousness," and will use these terms interchangeably as we further present the truths of the occult teachings. Professor Shapley, the astronomer, states that by logic alone we must anticipate life on other planets.

Occultism is the science of Divine Unfoldment. The student of occultism regards Deity as the All; and is taught that there is not, nor cannot be, any manifestation outside the Deity. Whether we look at a blade of grass, or a drop of water, or upon our planet with its teeming myriads of men and animals, or look away into space at system after system of worlds, all is Deity in various states of manifestation. The occultist is primarily an evolutionist, and says that all evolution is carried on during vast periods of time which he calls Cosmic Days; that Deity realizes a picture of what It will accomplish during a Cosmic Day, and that the whole impulse of evolution, which is Divine Energy, is onward and upward, striving ever to reach that idealization. Everything in the universe is an unfoldment of Deity Itself, and occultism is the science of that Unfoldment, It teaches the laws under which that Unfoldment takes place – not only upon the objective plane of life, but also upon the subjective plane.

In the middle ages, occultism embraced primarily what is now known as the physical sciences. It was understood to mean those things which were unknown, but which by experimentation might become known. Chemistry, as a branch of Alchemy, was regarded as one of the occult sciences because it was largely unknown, but through investigation and experimentation it constantly became better known. But occultism also had a secondary meaning which was coupled with the first – namely, mysticism, or esotericism. In ancient days people thought it not unwise to attempt the discovery of the unknown through experimentation with the subjective, as well as the objective, side of nature, and the two meanings – that which pertained to the objective, which was unknown but could be ascertained, and that which pertained to the subjective, which was also unknown and could be ascertained, were both included in the term occultism.

Materialism, as it grew in strength, called the unknown, "science," but branded the belief in, or the investigation of, the subjective side of life as "superstition." Most people became very much afraid of that word, and became afraid of being known as superstitious, even more than being known as ignorant; and such persons preferred to remain ignorant of the occult. In time the word occultism grew to mean that which pertained to the subjective, or that which pertained to esotericism, and at present it is defined as esotericism.

As we go back in history we find that esotericism has always played a large part in molding the thoughts of men. There were always the esoteric and the exoteric religions and sciences. There has always been, and there will be for ages yet to come, one religion for the masses and another for the students. There have been for a long time, and will be for some time yet to come, two sciences – one for the materialist, diluted for the masses, and another for the students of occultism. Traces of this duality are found in any religion at any period in history.

The habit of the Nazarene, the inspired leader of the Christians, of speaking in parables, together with his reasons for doing so, are the strongest evidence of his determination to conceal his esoteric doctrines from the masses. When the disciples came and asked him, "why speakest thou unto them in parables?" he said, "Because it is given to you to know the mysteries of the kingdom of heaven – but to them it is not given. Therefore I speak to them in parables because they, seeing, see not – and hearing, they hear not; neither do they understand. For their hearts are waxed gross, and their ears are dull of hearing, and their eyes they have closed." He also said, "...that it might be fulfilled which was spoken by the prophet – I will open my mouth in parables; I will utter things which have been kept secret from the very foundation of the world." This makes it quite clear that he thought it inexpedient to divulge to these people anything more than they could understand or assimilate.

His estimate of men, and his knowledge of their needs, was perfect, and he gave to each class with whom he had to deal just what was necessary to enable them to perform the work assigned to them. He taught the multitude the principles of morality and justice among men, and pointed the way to eternal life – but he did not teach them how to heal the sick. He taught his chosen ones the true method of healing the sick, and divulged the exact conditions of its exercise – but he did not teach them the scientific principles upon which his system of healing was founded. He gave to each his needs, and, true to his spiritual mission, he enjoined upon all men the necessity of first seeking the kingdom of heaven, when all other needful things would be added unto them. It wasn't necessary for his disciples to know the esoteric science of healing, in order to enable them to heal the sick, any more than it is for us today.

Another reason for withholding a statement of the scientific principles involved in his manifestations of power and his spiritual philosophy was that he foresaw the time coming when the world would reason it out for itself; and when that time came, mankind would be prepared to receive it. He foresaw that in the progress of civilization and enlightenment the time would come when the world would not be content to rest its belief upon the doctrine of anyone, whatever his claims to inspiration or authority. In other words, he foresaw the present age of materialism and its tendency towards skepticism regarding everything which cannot be scientifically demonstrated by the inductive processes of reasoning. He also knew that when the time arrived in the history of man's intellectual development, the truth of his doctrines would be all the more forcibly impressed upon mankind – if they could be proved by the rules of logic. Science and inductive reasoning would have been lost upon the people with whom he had to deal. To have attempted to reason with them would have been "casting pearls before swine," and he appealed to them by the only logic they could understand. He gave them the only evidence they could appreciate – the evidence of their senses.

And in all religions, whether it be Egyptian, Buddhism, or Judaism, there are truths which are revealed only to the student. In Judaism there was the Jehovic teaching for the masses, the Kabbalistic for the most secret students, and between these two was a third, the Talmudic, which partook of the nature of both. So the truth reached all grades of society, according to the comprehension of each – a plan that was adopted later by the Church of Rome with great success.

Of course many religionists, especially those calling themselves Christians, will deny that there is any esotericism in their faith. But those who are acquainted with the history of the early Christian Church and the writings of the Fathers, and those who are familiar with the philosophy of The Logos, and the mysticism of Paul as shown in his Epistles, will never attempt to deny it to the educated. But however violent the denial of esotericism may be by the religionist, it will not exceed in violence the denial of the term "science" to anything pertaining to the occult by the majority of physicist; yet scorn, laughter or denial will not blot from the pages of either sacred or profane history the fact that Magic was and is practiced among all people. The existence of magic necessitates the knowledge of certain laws and forces which are as yet unknown to the materialist, although the modem scientist, having gone almost to the limit of the visible, has begun to knock at the door of the occult sciences, and to pry into the invisible.

As materialistic as was the Nineteenth Century, we find that a few men once more began to turn their thoughts toward the realm of the unknown and the unseen in order to discover, if possible, the "why" of existence. And certain scientific men thought it not unreasonable or undignified to investigate the occult, or to organize a society for the purpose of investigating these occult subjects. We have seen the great cult of Spiritualism spread through the world, and witnessed the revival of Palmistry and Astrology, and other quasi-occult sciences. Then, following these, the crowning effort of all, we find that a great psychic wave swept over the world, and man began to realize that he was Mind, and as such was neither bound by time nor space, but could send his thoughts in any given direction, and could communicate without words with distant minds; and that mind could compel matter to obey it. With the awakening of the world the occult sciences have again challenged the attention of the most progressive men of the race.

Man grows tired of externals, and life after life, as he evolves, he studies deeper and deeper into Nature's laws. We do not always accomplish the same amount of study in each life, because we think that we cannot spare the time for study. We believe that we have much else to do that is of much more importance to us. Then there is the external world, with its duties and pleasures and our attention is so deeply engrossed with these things that we have no time left for more serious subjects. But in each life we take up as much of the study of these sciences as we have the time and the inclination for, and gradually, after many ages have passed, we become earnest and devoted students.

A knowledge of occult Law may be gained in two ways; by original research, and by teachers. There are courageous souls who choose to progress along the lines of personal experimentation, instead of taking the easier and perhaps the better way of gaining a knowledge of its principles through the aid of teachers. These strong souls often make the terrible mistakes and sacrifices which are unnecessary, for, after leaving the objective plane, they come upon the hidden, or subjective side, where there are forces and agencies that turn to naught man's thought and efforts unless both be properly directed. But even when knowledge has been gained through teachers it does not put an end to experimentation, because the teacher explains the law and leaves the pupil to make his own verification after having been taught how it should be done. The knowledge comes, as all real knowledge must, by experimentation – and by experience.

The teachers may be grouped into three great classes: Masters, Adepts, and Disciples. The Masters of occultism are those who, in a prior period of Cosmic evolution, passed upward through the human stage until they reached the Divine, and became Gods. When a new Cosmic Day commences, and new planets are formed, and men are brought into existence for the purpose of unfolding more and more of the Deity within themselves, and enlarging their consciousness as individualized parts of nature, the Masters are they who lead and teach the evolving race, usually from the subjective side, but, as we have explained, occasionally taking embodiment. The Adepts are those advanced egos of our own race who are students of the Masters, while at the same time they are teachers of the Disciples. They are those who have perfected themselves among certain lines, but have not reached perfection along all lines. The Disciples are those who are studying under these Adepts; they are persons who desire to know the truth and have devoted themselves to the study of these particular, sciences. They hold the same relation to the Adepts as Adepts hold to the Masters.

There are different grades of Masters, since they who finished their evolution upon their system of worlds earlier in the great Cosmic Day are stronger than they who finished later. And so there are grades of Adepts, and of Disciples. We find that there is everywhere grades of intelligence. There are intelligences in this universe as superior to man as man is superior to a black beetle; yet both are proceeding upward in their evolutionary, career; the one, of course, being far in advance of the other. It does not require much scientific imagination to conceive that there is an infinite gradation of intelligence, because what is true upon the lower plane of our daily experience is also true throughout nature. The Masters and Adepts are the custodians of the Occult Sciences, which are perfected sciences because they cover all departments of nature, both physical and metaphysical, the objective and the subjective.

All of the facts and principles of these sciences must be verified by each person as he progresses along his evolutionary path. Every student of occultism must verify each statement of his teacher in order that he may make it a part of his own being – which he may know that it is true; otherwise it would be a belief, and beliefs do not amount to much, because there are nearly as many beliefs and theories as there are individuals.

In this particular Cosmic Day occultism commenced when the Masters came upon this planet to teach mankind. The evolution on this planet is divided into a certain number of periods, and we are at the present time in what the Occultists know as the fifth period. In the first and second periods very little was accomplished by man. He was, as it were, in a new world, with new sensations and new experiences, and his life was entirely objective and largely animal. The theater of this activity was that continent known to tradition as "The Land of the Gods," Mount Meru, "The Imperishable Isles," or what we would prosaically call the Continent of the North Pole. *Dr. Churchward, of New Rochelle, New York, has written scholarly books on the Continent of "Mu."

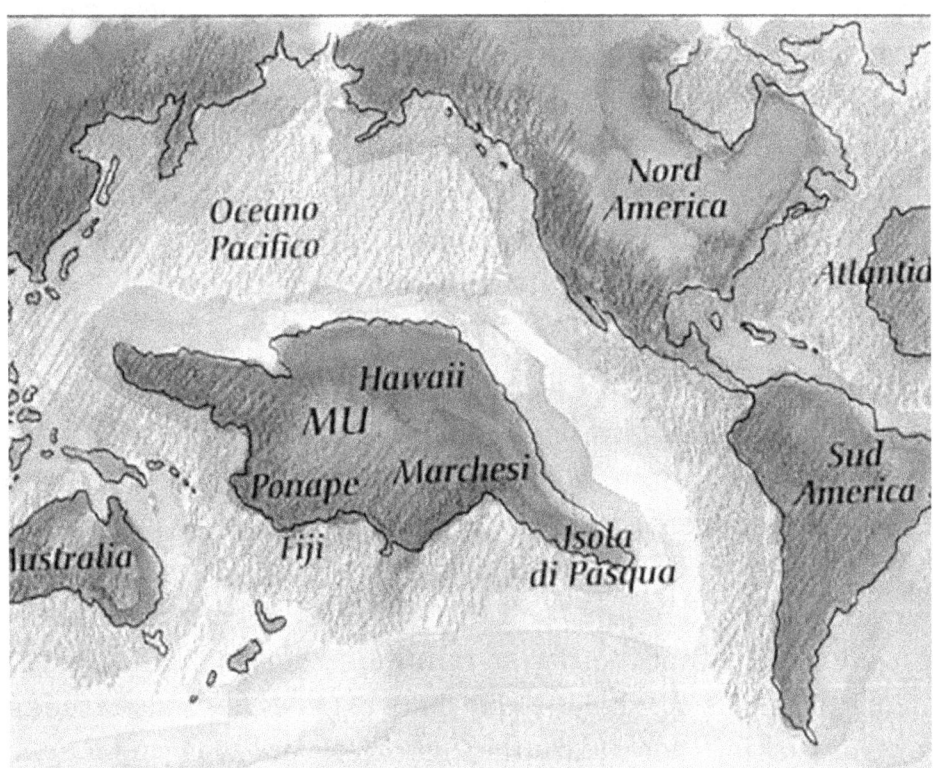

It is thought that there once was a continent named Lemuria that extended from the Indian Ocean into the Pacific. Like Atlantis, parts of Lemuria were destroyed by earthquakes, until only a section in the Pacific remained. Eventually, it too was consumed by the waters.

LEMURIA

During the third period of evolution, man lived upon the continent known as Lemuria, which was a continent lying in the Pacific Ocean, Arabian Sea, and arid Indian Ocean. Its northern portion was very much in the present location of Australia, the Philippines, and the Islands of the Southern Pacific; all of which constitute the remnants of that continent now sunken beneath the seas. That periods occur in which there is a sinking of certain continents, and a rising of others, is well known to geologists as well as to occultists. In Lemuria, man passed from his lowest state of animal existence into what we may call a more rational, or human state. His development during this time is substantially shown in the history of primitive man. Some of the egos, outstripping the others, succeeded in reaching Adeptship along certain lines, but the great mass of the people lived sensuous and sensual lives. There was very little spirituality manifested by the race during this period, and the perversion of natural laws and forces became marked toward its close.

The most notable event which occurred on that continent, immediately prior to the cataclysm which swept it beneath the waters, was the establishment of colonies in India. The colonists consisted of Masters, the Adepts, and the cream of the race. It was these colonists who built the rock temples of Elephanta and the other great temples of India – those temples in which mysticism seems to have had its earlier home; and upon whose walls are painted the strange old symbols, in colors, which indicate the history and the growth of man. Those were the souls who gave to India its riches in literature and philosophy, and established the mighty empires which even tradition had forgotten. But it was the degenerate descendants of these colonists who spread northward and westward, and populated first Asia, and, later, Europe.

ATLANTIS

After the continent of Lemuria had passed away, then came the fourth period, with man's field of activity in Atlantis. Atlantis extended from the West Indies to the coast of Central and Northern Africa, as we know from the investigations of the British Government, which spent many years and large sums of money in determining the extent of the sunken continent – and it was here that civilization proceeded with tremendous strides. All of the accumulated knowledge of the other periods was stored in the minds of those who had been the Lemurians, and were then incarnating as Atlanteans. As they acquired greater and greater knowledge, they not only reached a point in mechanical development far beyond anything that we have reached at the present day, but they also took up the study of occultism, which became common among the people.

By that time the great Masters had retired from physical contact with men, and the Adepts had taken their places as direct teachers of the people. They moved among men, and were the kings and rulers, the lawgivers and inventors; in fact, they were the inspirers of the race up to the time it reached its highest point of development in that period. Then the continent became divided into five great kingdoms, and in each one of these there were lodges of Adepts. At the height of Atlantis' glory, once more the people turned to sensual abandonment, and the Adepts withdrew into Retreats with their pupils, for the people refused to listen to them or to be aided by them any longer. In the course of time, materialism swept over that continent, as it has swept over Europe and America; and occultism was forgotten by the masses and remembered only by the few; and then, gradually, that which was pure occultism became perverted, and men began to use their powers criminally.

Those who remembered or practiced occultism, put into operation mental and certain other forces which enslaved all of those who had forgotten how to use their own forces, or who were not developed to the same point as themselves, and what we call "black magic" swept over Atlantis. Thus it became a continent where a few immensely wealthy, powerful, and strong egos ruled the majority of the people, and made them their slaves. But the misuse of occult forces brought its reaction, as it always does, and as Plato tells us, Atlantis suddenly became submerged. You remember that when he went to Egypt he was informed that the last remnants of Atlantis had disappeared about five years prior to his visit; and also that the priests had records of the old continent, as well as of their own country, which extended back thousands of years. These records were kept by the occultists, who were priests in the time of Plato, and are still kept in triplicate; one copy has been placed in each of the three great repositories situated on separate continents.

Before Atlantis went down, those of the inhabitants who had preserved their purity and who were trying to lead upright lives were taken by the Adepts out of the country. The Priests and Priestesses in the Temples of the Sacred Fire set forth with the chosen ones in one hundred ships of the great Atlantean Fleet, guarding those living Flames with their magnetizing and sustaining Fire. Some went westward and settled in the neighborhood of the Easter Islands, Peru, and Mexico, while others ventured farther across the vast expanse of the Pacific into Asia, but of the one hundred parties which originally set out, only ten arrived at their various destinations. A portion of the actual undying Sacred Fire from the Atlantean Temples carried in the great golden braziers that had hung above the Altars, was established in each of the retreats at Luxor, Peru, and various places which were destined to remain upon the surface of the earth, and there they still remain.

Those living in the Western empires were colonized in Central and South America. In Central America that rare civilization which preceded our own was founded, and was the duplicate in every respect of the one formerly established in India. The degenerate descendants from the Central American civilization emigrated to North and South America, and populated them. The degeneracy of these aboriginal Americans was due to the fact that at this time in that Fourth Period the undeveloped souls of the Atlanteans were incarnating in those bodies, for it was with the Atlanteans as it was with the Lemurians – the strongest souls came first, and became the pioneers. They bore the heaviest burdens, and thus prepared the way for the less developed souls who had not the strength to do the work that their elder brothers had done. And it should not be forgotten that the history of the Lemurians and the Atlanteans is but the history of ourselves. Our strongest and bravest souls came forward to start the Fifth Period onward in its evolution, even as a cursory reading of general history will disclose, and they have, reappeared from time to time to manifest their energies in the several lines of human achievement in order to teach, help, and direct the course of events.

From the Eastern empires of Atlantis the advanced souls went into Africa and laid the foundation of what is now know as the Egyptian empire. And this brings us to the Fifth Period, in which occultism was again taught popularly and openly among the people. A study of Egyptian history reveals that during its entire period there were occultists – Magicians, as they were called– who could produce great phenomena. They were teachers of the people and were the priests and law-givers; they were the friends of the kings, and were consulted whenever there was sickness or national calamity. These teachers were the Adepts who came in contact with the people.

Atlantis had once been a powerful kingdom thanks to their ability to navigate the seas. After the destruction of their homeland, the surviving Atlantean priests took their wisdom to other lands across the globe to help rebuild their civilization.

In the Fifth Period, which is the present one, the descendants of the colony which remained in India, having reached the height of its prosperity and development, passed Westward and founded the Assyrian and Babylonian Empires, and there again the Adepts moved among men. In both the sacred and profane history of those times we find that the Magi were able to cure all manner of diseases, and to manipulate the laws of nature. Babylon became the great metropolis of western Asia, and the peoples of the old world turned to it for their supplies. In the beginning of the nation's career there was much to admire and little to condemn – but as it grew richer and more prosperous, and as the weaker egos of the older races came to incarnate in the Babylonian race, avarice and greed for wealth overcame all the higher principles of the people, and the time came when the domestic virtues were recklessly flung away for further gratification. It became a law that every Babylonian woman once in her life must offer herself to strangers publicly before the temple of Beltis, in order to attract to the city of Babylon the trade of strangers. Babylon became the earthly paradise for gluttony and lust, and whatever ministered to the appetites, and sensuality was eagerly enjoyed without scruple by the people.

Notwithstanding all these things, in no country except Egypt were the ceremonies of religion more carefully preserved. Temples arose on every side, and Priests, engaged in the work peculiar to their supposedly sacred offices, were always to be seen. The dissolute kings were chief worshippers at the holy shrines, and princes went devotedly to the temples. During the early part of the life of Nebuchadnezzar the Babylonian nation reached its zenith of wealth and power, and at that time the vices of the people were greatest. The king himself set the example of cruelty and selfishness to his people, who were delighted to follow his lead. Murder and rape were his chief amusements, and the suffering of his victims seemed to give him the greatest pleasure. However, when well advanced in age this monarch dreamed the prophetic dream which foretold his approaching downfall, and from that day his power and the power of the nation began to wane.

When Belshazzar came to the throne the downfall of the nation was close at hand; but in his contempt for an enemy whom he believed to be powerless to harm him, he recklessly gave himself to the enjoyment of a great annual festival of the Babylonians. While the drunken revel was at its height, the enemy stole silently in and opened the river sluices into the canals, and the river began to sink. There was then nothing to prevent the foe from entering the gates – the city was at its mercy, and the drunken Babylonians received the kind of treatment that they had given to others in the past. Their karma had fallen upon them, and the prophecy of Isaiah was fulfilled.

Passing upward from Babylon and Syria to the Mediterranean, we find that the great remnants of the Third and Fourth periods were merged and blended in the Fifth Period in the Phoenician, the Grecian, the Carthaginian, and the Roman peoples. At the beginning of this Fifth Period, we had, a new burst of occult knowledge and force, because all of the knowledge acquired in the preceding periods by the egos had been brought over in these later incarnations, and in the early history, of each of the nations mentioned, occultism was taught to the people once more. The Adepts, were friends of the people, and were freely consulted by them. But gradually, as materialism advanced and sensuality became the dominant trait of each of these peoples, the Adepts withdrew again from personal contact with the world, just as the great Masters had withdrawn in previous periods of time.

THE RISE OF MATERIALISM

In Greece, materialism in its most artistic form began to stamp itself upon the minds of the people, who turned, from spiritual teachings and caused the Adepts to withdraw entirely from the world of men. And it came to pass that all magic or occultism (for they were identical in those days) was confined to what is known now as temple magic, and was practiced by the priests who were students of the Adepts. In various Grecian temples, mechanical or ceremonial magic was taught; that is, a knowledge of mental forces united with a knowledge of chemistry and alchemy, by the blending of which great phenomena were produced. Some record of this great knowledge is preserved in even the histories which we now have. Before occultism in Greece passed away, one final attempt was made to counteract materialism, and the Eleusinian Mysteries were founded. In these mysteries, the development and evolution of the human soul were taught in symbolic form, and the wisest men of that age thought it a privilege to be initiated into these Mysteries. But even this proved unable to stem the tide of materialism, and therefore the priests ceased to publicly proclaim or exert their occult powers. Occasionally some enthusiastic student came forward and exhibited his knowledge of the occult by the performance of a few miracles and marvelous phenomena; but the people, as a class, were too materialistic to be taught anything better or higher than their own gross beliefs, and soon such students had to retire from public work.

Then Christianity arose, and its doctrines were received by a great many that, after a brief period of genuine revival of spirituality, used them for political purposes. The different orders of the priesthood became the occult bodies within the Christian Church, and up to the middle ages the priests in the Church possessed all the knowledge of occultism that the world had. And the Catholic Church is now the only one that has preserved a trace of this ancient truth. It was during the Middle Ages that the occultists as a class withdrew from the Church of Rome and formed secret bodies and societies, such as the Rosicrucians, in various parts of the world. At the present day, almost all knowledge of the occult is possessed and preserved by only such individuals as have reached a point in their evolution which has made them capable of receiving the higher truth. In this way portions of this secret knowledge are given to the world from time to time as the world becomes able to receive them.

The culmination of what is known as the Dark Ages, in this period of evolution, came in the nineteenth century. *(This is known as "Kali Yuga," or the Dark Age; "Kali," being a destructive symbol.) At that time the world reached its lowest point in materialism, and from now on the tendency will continue to be upward toward spirituality. A few occultists believe that the time has passed when there is a necessity for guarding these secrets with such jealous care, and believe the world is ready to receive more of these truths than formerly. Then too, many persons are making more discoveries along these lines and are ignorantly misusing the forces they are learning to use. So it has been decided to teach the people something about these forces, and how they can and should be used, in the hope of averting, if possible, the fate of the Lemurians and Atlanteans.

TEACHING THE MYSTERIES

Almost every day we see in the newspapers and magazines advertisements in which the offer is made to instruct people concerning personal magnetism and how to use it; how to become successful, how to become popular, and how to dominate other minds until they become enslaved. The people are awakening, and are beginning to feel a great desire to know about these occult forces – and if they do not use them rightly they will surely use them wrongly. At the present time various efforts are being made to give the occult teachings to such persons as are fitted to receive them, but they cannot yet be taught in full to the great mass of people. They should be given only to those who desire to know the Truth, and who wish to ally their forces with those of nature for the good of others, and for the benefit of themselves.

Man returns to Earth many times – just as soon as the fruit he has earned in the physical life has refined in the spirit-world. This does not go on without ending, but he keeps on passing into other forms until he reaches perfection.

One man is born in want and misery, and is endowed with only inferior abilities, and it seems from the beginning that he is destined to a miserable existence. Another is born in the best of surroundings, and is looked after and cherished by loving hands and hearts; he shows signs of valuable talents from the beginning. His career is almost certain to turn out successfully. Those who do not know would say that one man had been "born" fortunate, and the other unfortunate – but anyone who is a student of nature knows that there is nothing that happens by chance; that every effect must have a cause. Man generally thinks that talents and abilities are "inherited" from some branch of the family, and there is enough seeming proof to convince almost anyone that this is a fact. The many books on heredity apparently prove it beyond the shadow of a doubt – yet, in the face of all the seeming proof, we tell you that the events in which man took part formed his talents and abilities, and that he does not owe them to heredity from his ancestors. Man is today the result of what he was and did in the past.

There is something in man himself which determines his birth and certain environments, just the same as certain flowers have to be planted in certain places before they will thrive. Hereditists point to their proofs: "see how certain talents are inherited in families." For two and a half centuries musical talents were inherited by members of the Bach family. From the Bernoulli family, eight great mathematicians were born. Some of these started in very different occupations at the beginning, but the inherited talents always drove them to the family vocation. They point out that by studying the ancestry you can find out the person's natural abilities, as they will have the same as those of their ancestors. They do not stop to consider that inherited talents can, of themselves, no more combine into a complete personality than the parts of an automobile can put themselves together. They may say that the cooperation of the parents will produce the combination of talents, but if you will study any child you will find that he often possesses abilities entirely new and different from those of the parents, so that these could not have come from the parents.

There seems a definite mental aptitude or predisposition inherited in a family, and certain gifts accumulate and combine in a wonderful personality in some descendant, but it is an admitted fact that it is very seldom that a celebrated name stands at the top of the family in the line of descent. A man, as a rule, does show the characteristics of his ancestors, for the spirit-soul, that which starts a new physical existence, at birth draws its bodily substance from that which heredity bestowed on it. But that Being already possesses, in his own nature, the characteristics of this medium, which it uses for its descent.

Instead of inheriting any characteristics and abilities from his ancestors, anyone who will give the subject any thought will see that this would be a great injustice, as it would make a successful life for some – only depending upon their ancestors. But, as has been stated before, the most celebrated name stands at the bottom of a line of family descent, which shows us that the bearer of that name needed that particular ancestry to build the body necessary for the expression of his personality. This does not mean that his actual, personal qualities were inherited. This would be opposed to all sound logic, and the laws of nature. If personal gifts were inherited, they would be found at the beginning of a line of descent, and then transmitted to its descendants. These stand at the end, and show that they were not transmitted.

It seems almost impossible to believe that so many intelligent people can believe solely in physical heredity, and that it should be possible for two tiny germs alone to contain nothing but the inherited forces of their ancestors. On the other hand, if you accept the correct theory that at the time of conception the conditions were right for the "spiritual germ," and for that individual to start a new physical existence, then you must admit that it is possible for our Creator to create life in any way He wishes, and that the physical germs might contain the inherited forces, but it certainly is illogical to believe that He would permit the fate of a child to rest solely with the parents. It is more reasonable to believe that when conception takes place, the child born to that family is not born by chance, but that he enters the world through this physical means because the conditions are just as they should be for his evolution. Man is not built by purely inherited forces from without, for a spiritual Being, individuality exists in the aura or magnetic field of the mother before life, and helps fashion the new body.

If you will study man carefully, you will find that he has an inner life which is continually trying to express itself. This could not come from heredity, but must have been originated in former lives. Parents are not generators in the full sense of the word. They are the means through which the organic substance is supplied. When a soul enters another physical existence here, it is known in advance what the temperament, character, tendencies, etc., of its parents are. This is why the children show the particular combination of the characteristics of the parents. No parents can originate the real ultimate center of a personality. Neither do they possess the power to hinder a personality in its development. Every individual pre-exists, as regards the fundamental form of his spirit, for no individual, from a spiritual point of view, resembles another. The forces shaping a being are the result of causes existing in former lives.

We will now examine the subjective and objective minds of man. The subjective mind of man came direct from the substance of Deity. With the cooperation of the Elohim – those great Ones who said, "let us make man in our own image," the Supreme Consciousness coalesced within itself quantities of the particled portion of itself until mind forms were created. The atoms were drawn together by the power of attraction, and thus it was that the subjective minds were born. For an illustration, look into the atmosphere on a cloudless day, and imagine it to be the Supreme Consciousness. After a while you may see a gradual condensation of some portion of the atmosphere – a center is being formed, and a cloud appears which is of the same nature as a part of the atmosphere, and sufficiently condensed to become visible to you. In this manner individual minds are born out of the Ether, and in the same manner is the substance of Deity condensed.

An immediate condensation of consciousness within the Great Consciousness is caused by the desire of Deity to manifest or express itself in individualized forms, and this expression is brought into actuality through the instrumentality of the Planetary Spirits or Elohim. These great Beings send their thoughts to a designated point in the Ether, form a center, and through the vibrations of their united thought-forces cause an assembling of atoms whose conscious sides respond to these vibration.

With the groupings of atoms into molecular life a new individuality is always created, which is something more than the sum total of its constituent parts. The union of the conscious side of the atoms causes the character or individuality to appear in the group. So, when the many atomic consciousnesses are compressed into an oval form by the Elohim, there comes into being an organized consciousness or mind, which controls its atomic parts. These Ether-born minds thenceforth take up their evolution, and gather and store their experience as they progress, and by such methods become more and more individualized. The evolution of these subjective minds begins upon the subjective side of life, and for ages they continue to progress upon planets which are composed of such tenuous matter that they are invisible to the present sight of men. After these subjective minds have become thoroughly individualized they – or rather, we – for these subjective minds are ourselves – become ready to incarnate into animal forms on this physical world of ours.

There are two classes of subjective minds which always incarnate at the same time on a physical world; those who have been brought into existence in the Cosmic Day, and those who have attempted their evolutionary career one or more times before, in some other Cosmic Day, but who failed and are now making another attempt to go on in their evolution. For a center of consciousness may not be successful in the particular period of evolution in which it is first brought into existence; and salvation is not a mere matter of faith or belief alone. It depends upon one's self entirely whether one reaches God-hood from manhood in the evolutionary period in which one sets out.

Until the half-way point was reached in the evolutionary career of man and this planet, the Universal Consciousness pushed men forward. After the half-way point was passed, and men had reached their mental majority, and should have become individualized, the old order of things was changed. Men must use their own minds now, and must make use of the knowledge they have of Nature's laws, if they expect to go on in their evolution. It is either progress, or fails and returns into space, to remain until another period of evolution shall commence, when souls shall again attempt to perpetuate their individuality. Ultimately, man's destiny is to evolve to something higher than manhood – he needs some time to reach godhood.

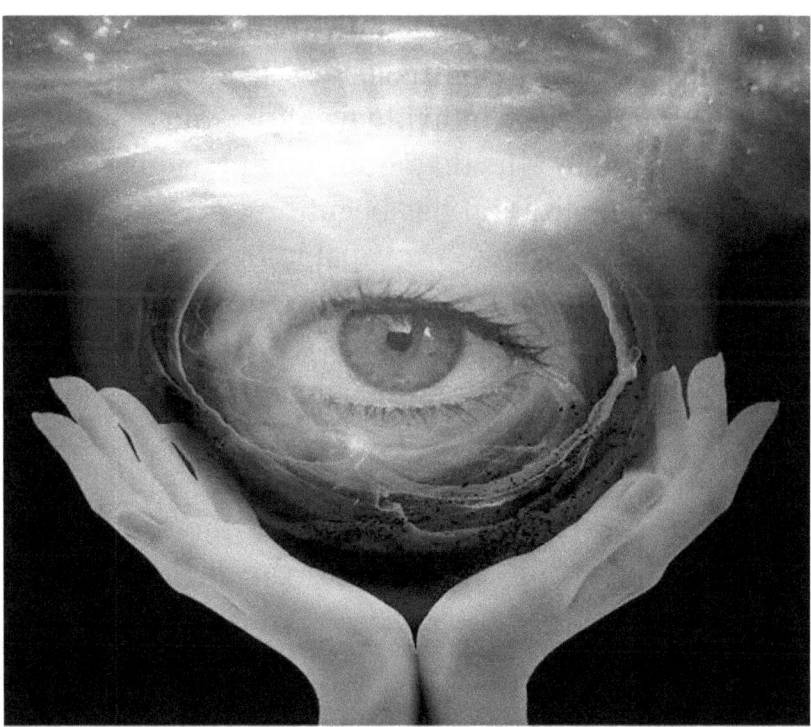

All of us live in a participatory universe. Once you decide that you want to participate fully, with mind, body, and soul, the paradigm shift becomes personal. The reality you inhabit will be yours to either embrace or change.

THE SUBJECTIVE MIND VS. THE OBJECTIVE MIND

The subjective mind is the divine nature, because it comes directly from the Great Universal Consciousness; it is the Logos, or the Word made flesh. It is the highest because it is the first expression of the Universal Consciousness; it is close to the heart of God; it is the first-born, and carries the first impress of Deity. Because its evolution was entirely subjective before it reached this planet and because it now functions normally on the plane of causes – the mental plane – it is the intuitive portion of man. It is that portion which knows without reasoning, which apprehends immediately upon the presentation of a subject; that which sees causes.

The objective mind evolves entirely upon this planet. It is an off-spring of this particular period of evolution, and its nature is the result of its objective growth and physical experiences. Deity settles down as a great mass or cloud of consciousness upon a planet and vitalizes it, gives life and form to it, and gives to the mineral kingdom its form of consciousness by ensouling it. We do not mean that this lower kingdom becomes wholly individualized. For instance, in the vast fields of coal and iron the Great Consciousness has not individualized because that form of expression restricts individualization; but when we examine the higher portion of this kingdom – its diamonds and precious stones – we find that here, in a measure, individualization has begun. A part of the mass, a few of the purest and best atoms, those which are capable of taking a more rapid rate of vibration, have become separated from the others, and have made an attempt at individualization. Then a part of the Great Consciousness passes on to the vegetable kingdom, where we have first the lichens and grasses; each of these is a separate and distinct form, and consciousness is there individualized; but the individualization is not perpetual because of the frailty and lack of persistence of the forms. Thence the consciousness passes into the bush, and afterwards it reaches perfect individualization in the tree, the highest form of life in the vegetable world.

Then a portion of the Great Consciousness sweeps on into the animal kingdom, and ensouls the lowest animal forms, and gradually, as evolution prepares better vehicles, these souls of animals, or individualized intelligences, re-embody themselves in higher physical forms of animals, until we have the elephant, the horse, the dog and the cat. Here individualization becomes not only consciousness, but it becomes mind, and persists as animal mind. It re-embodies itself in one form after another, and the dog, for instance, comes back many times to this material plane a dog, and gains more strength and knowledge by its experiences. Finally these individualized animal minds pass into the ape form, and thence into physical human bodies – and although these bodies disintegrate and pass away, the animal minds persist and reincarnate, and ultimately become the objective minds of men.

When these quasi-human forms have reached the point of development where they are capable of becoming vehicles for the Divine Subjective minds, then the union of the subjective and objective minds takes place. The subjective minds come to earth for the purpose of getting more experience upon this material plane, that they may become wiser, and more strongly individualized; and also that they may raise the animal minds, or objective consciousness, which they ensoul, to a higher and better condition of development; for with the interblending of the Divine subjective mind with the objective or animal mind comes a permanent union, and those "whom God hath joined together" cannot be separated without a tremendous loss to each.

After the union of the subjective and objective minds has taken place, this united entity continues to incarnate and reincarnate as its physical bodies wear out. Understanding this, you will be better able to appreciate the meaning of Chapter Six of Genesis, where it says: "And it came to pass, when (animal) men began to multiply on the face of the earth and daughters were born to them (that is, when sufficient forms were created) that the sons of God (the subjective minds) saw the daughters of men (the objective minds) that they were fair; and they took them wives (blended with them) of all which they chose."

The objective mind, or animal intelligence, is the reasoning or intellectual faculty of man; it is that faculty which becomes educated through external means, and learns from books; and it is that faculty which is taught to reason, and which is the seat of sensation. If it were not for the objective mind we could not feel, as was shown when we cited hypnotism. The objective mind is also sometimes designated as the brain intelligence. Because it gains its knowledge entirely from externals, it is more often wrong than right in relation to true causes. It takes into account only effects or phenomena and then, not having all the facts, in most cases it is incapable alone of deducing a right conclusion.

When the subjective mind has incarnated into the objective mind, we have the real psychic man, the dual man. This interblending of these two consciousnesses makes one form, and in that form it perpetuates itself. Why is a man not as wide as he is long? It is because of the form of the inner man, which is the model for the physical body. The inner man is the magnetic matrix into which the physical particles are built. Thus it is that all form has its mental basis. Before a form can exist on the physical plane it must be created on the mental plane. Since both of these minds are condensations of the Universal Mind, they both have naturally the characteristics of that Mind. The Universal Consciousness brought them into existence through its creative capacity, so both these minds have the power of creating. The great trouble, however, is that the objective mind, through its animal experience, has acquired the animal fears. This is the chief characteristic of the animal mind, and is the mainspring of action; hence most of the creations of the objective mind are either the product of fear, or are colored by fear.

For example, our mothers stamp fear upon us before we are born, and continue to do it after we are born, and until we have grown old enough to fear for ourselves. They create diseases for us through their fears of diseases until we get old enough to create our own diseases. And that wretched fear follows us from the cradle to the grave. We are afraid we shall not succeed in business, and we create our own failures. We are afraid we shall not have the money to pay our bills for the current month, and we generally lack something because we have created that lack. We fear bad luck, disasters, and death, and it is a wonder that man has not swept himself off the face of the earth through his fearful creations. The offspring's of fear are the creatures and creations of this objective mind, and the subjective mind which is within the objective mind accepts the unfortunate creations, believes the misrepresentations, and unites its own forces with those of the objective mind in bringing the pictured calamities into real external existence.

The dominant consciousness always controls the creations; and the environment shows which consciousness controls. Ignorance of the laws of life excuses no one. If you continue to create ignorantly you will suffer the same as though you knew the law, because an unwise use of the law brings unfortunate results, just as the wise use of the law brings good results. God always gives you in time precisely what you create, and if you allow your objective mind to do the creating you must accept its creations; your ignorance will not excuse you. If you should kill a man because you were angry, whether you knew it was against the laws of the State or not, you would be punished. It is the same with moral law. Both of your minds can create good, but the objective mind usually does not do so until it has been properly trained. The subjective mind of man must control the objective mind and its fears before he can make pictures that will bring him pleasant environment.

Every time an unpleasant thought or a fear comes to your mind, banish it. Every time a thought of disease comes, blot it out. You can do it, because you have the divine power, and can control your objective mind, which is your instrument and vehicle. If a mental picture of disease comes into your mind and you let it remain, it will become a physical reality; but if you destroy it the moment you see it, nothing can come from it. In the place of a picture that you do not like, make one that you do like. Make your thought picture and God, in time, will fulfill your desires thus expressed. But you will never be successful, and you will never reach the highest of your possibilities until you control your own objective mind and its forces.

The dual nature of man, or of mind, will explain many of the contradictions of human nature. It will give a full explanation of original sin, which is nothing more or less than the uncontrolled animal nature of the objective mind, which expresses itself whenever and wherever the opportunity is given, until it has been disciplined. The distinction of this dual nature of mind enables us to understand what has paralyzed the force of the Christian Scientists, and has filled them with great terror. They describe a "something" outside of Deity that is not Divine; which creates, but can create only evil. They do not know where it comes from; they merely know it is in man. That cult calls it "malicious animal magnetism," and makes of it a personal devil; but it is nothing but the objective mind of man, uncontrolled. It is a part of the Universal Consciousness, and therefore cannot be devoid of good. It is more ignorant than bad, and makes mistaken creations in its undeveloped state.

Understanding the lower nature of man, you will understand the nature of evil. Evil is but the creations, through ignorance, of this objective mind. It is a misdirection of the creative forces; it is the permitting of the unenlightened animal mind to make creations.

5

FEAR OF INNER AND OUTER SPACE

The following chapter can be summed up in the famous words of the late Franklin Delano Roosevelt: "We have nothing to fear but fear itself." Regardless of the political affiliations of the reader, he will recognize, as all the world does, that this idea embodied in the words of a President of the United States made it possible for the mass of people to respond in a manner required to win a battle against planetary evil. This one statement by Mr. Roosevelt should make it clear that he was an Initiate, regardless of his personal and worldly activities.

There is one thing that every man and woman should and must learn-and that is not to have fear. Fear is a dangerous disease, and likely to spread. Of course, everyone is more or less subject to outside influences; it is only natural to be receptive. If you were not, you would be getting into all kinds of danger. You are constantly receiving warnings, and you would not be able to learn, see or feel anything if you were not receptive. The mind must receive before it can give out- and it must acquire before it can serve.

Do not try to stop the receptive attitude of mind. Work in harmony with nature's forces, and do not antagonize anything. Be the chooser, however, of what you want to receive. You are given the power of intelligence to choose those things to which you wish to respond. Your development will depend a great deal upon how you are able to choose the unseen vibrations. No one is immune to vibrations, whether he is conscious of them or not. The difference between the one who is developed and the one who is not is that the former is conscious of what he sees and therefore knows what is transpiring, while the other does not.

There is nothing to be afraid of in developing the higher senses, except your fears. Set these aside and proceed.

You must cultivate acquaintances that are in harmony with your way of thinking. Do not be selfish as your knowledge increases, but give out some of the truths you discover to others. Help others to grow, if you wish to grow yourself. Resolve to use your power and the higher faculties you develop for constructive and good purposes only. This is very important to your advancement. No matter how good or how evil you have been in the past, be determined that you are going to start a new life with the very best there is in you, and make use of that best to bring out other knowledge.

KNOWING RIGHT FROM WRONG

One of the first things you must learn is Discrimination. In the entire world there are really only two kinds of people; those who know, and those who do not know, and this knowledge is the one thing which matters. What a man's religion is, or to what race he belongs – these things are not important. The really important thing is this knowledge – the knowledge of God's plan for men. When once you have seen this, and you really know it, then you cannot help but work for it and make yourself one with it. And so, because you do know, you will be on God's side, working for evolution rather than for selfishness – standing for Good, and resisting evil.

If you are on God's side then you are one of us, and it does not matter at all whether you call yourself a Hindu, a Buddhist, a Christian, or a Mohammedan – and it does not matter whether you are Indian, English, or Chinese. Those who are on God's side know why they are here, and what they should do, and they are trying to do it. The others do not understand yet what they should do, and they often act foolishly and try to invent ways for themselves which they think will be pleasant for themselves only, not understanding that All are One. They are following the unreal instead of the real. Until they have learned to distinguish between the two they have not ranged themselves upon God's side, and so this discrimination is the first step.

But even when this choice is made, we must still remember that there are many varieties of the real and the unreal; discrimination must be made between the right and the wrong, the important and the unimportant – the useful and the useless, the true and the false, the selfish and the unselfish. It should not be difficult to choose between the right and the wrong, for those who wish to follow the teachings of the Masters have already decided to take the right at all costs. But we must remember that there are two selves – the outer, objective self and the Real person within you, and what your inner self wishes is not always what the body wishes.

When your outer self wishes something, you must stop and think whether you really wish it, for the real you inside your body is God, and of course your will is God's will – but you must dig down deep inside yourself to find the God within you, and listen to His voice. Do not make the mistake of thinking that any of your bodies are yourself-the physical, the astral, nor the mental – for each one of them will pretend to be the Self in order to get what it wants. But you must know them all, and know yourself as their Master.

The outer body must be treated well, and taken good care of; you must not overwork it – you must feed it properly and keep it strictly clean. Without a perfectly clean and healthy body you cannot work properly. Many times students find themselves "out of balance" in one direction or another, and some come to the conclusion that, since the real self is the person within the body, and since we strive for the pure spiritual life and knowledge, then the outer body is a mere "nothing," and should be ignored. But you must have respect for your temple in which the real self dwells. The body is your animal; the horse upon which you ride – and it must always be you who controls that body, not it which controls you.

The astral body also has its desires, for it is a mirror for the objective mind. It would like you to be angry and to say sharp words; it wants you to be jealous, and to be greedy for money, to envy other people for their possessions, and to yield yourself to depression. It wants these things, and many more, not because it wishes to harm you or cause you trouble, but because it likes violent vibrations, and likes to change them constantly. But you do not really want these things, and you must be careful to discriminate between your wants and your body's. *This is the battleground described in the Bhagavad Gita.

Your mental body would like to think of itself as proudly separate – thinking much of itself and little of others. Even when you have turned it away from worldly things it still tries to calculate for self; even to the point of making you think of your own progress, rather than thinking of the work of the Masters, and of helping others. Your mental body is for you to use, not to be your control –

therefore discrimination is necessary here also, and you must guard your thoughts constantly.

Occultism knows no compromise between right and wrong, and no matter what the apparent cost, if you are going to become an occult student you must do what is right and you must under no circumstances do what is wrong, no matter what anyone else may think or say to you. You must always use reason and common sense, for your inner self knows what is right and what is wrong for you. You must discriminate between the important and the unimportant; you must be firm as a rock where right and wrong are concerned, but yield to others in the things which do not matter. You must always be gentle and kind to others, reasonable and accommodating, and thus you leave to others the same full liberty which you need for yourself.

No matter how much you have already learned, you will have much more to learn as you progress with your occult studies, so here again you must use discrimination, and you must consider most carefully what is worth learning. All knowledge is useful, of course, and one day you will have attained all knowledge. But while you have only part of it, be sure that it is the most useful part; in other words, first study that which will help you most to help others. Only a wise man can be wisely helpful – no matter how much you wish to help, if you are ignorant you may do far more harm than good; therefore bear in mind that a little knowledge is a dangerous thing.

You must learn to discriminate between truth and falsehood, and you must learn to be true in thought, and word, and deed. There are many untrue thoughts in the world, and many superstitions, and one who is enslaved by them cannot make progress. Therefore you must not hold a thought simply because many other people hold it, or because it has been believed for centuries, but must think it through for yourself, and judge for yourself whether it is reasonable. Your thought about other people must also be true, and you must never think things of them that you do not really know to be true.

Do not suppose that they are always thinking of you. If someone has done something which you think will harm you, or says something unkind which you think applies to you, do not immediately think, "he meant to injure me." He probably did not think of you at all, for each soul has its own troubles, and its thoughts turn chiefly around itself. If a man has spoken angrily to you, do not think, "He hates me; he wishes to hurt me" – for probably someone or something else made him angry, and simply because he happened to meet you he turned his anger upon you. Of course he is acting foolishly, for all anger is foolish – but simply because of this you must not think untruly of him.

You must be true in your speech, also – accurate, and without exaggeration. Never attribute motives to another person – he may be acting from reasons which have never entered your mind. If you hear a story against anyone, be careful not to repeat it. It may not be true – but even if it is, be careful; it is far kinder to say nothing. Be true in your actions, and never pretend to be other than you are, for all pretenses are a hindrance to the pure light of truth which should shine through you. You must also be discriminate between the selfish and the unselfish, for selfishness has many forms, and when you think you have finally killed it in one form, it arises in another as strongly as ever. You must discriminate in another way, also – learn to distinguish the God in everyone and in everything, no matter how evil he or it may appear on the surface. You can help others through that which you have in common with them. Learn how to arouse the spark of God in them, and learn how to appeal to the Christ in them.

YOUR ACTIONS DETERMINE YOUR FUTURE

You must learn that you do not see with your eyes, but with your mind. To be exact, you see with your attention. Going further, you see just what you are looking for, or choose. The hunter going through the woods sees game; the lumberman sees lumber – the artist sees beauty. Each one sees what he is looking for, and each has trained himself to see certain things. The state of mind gives sight as much as the open eyes. We really see with the mind, and the eye is only the instrument used.

Your personality exists after you. Each error you make is a debt charged against you, which must be acquitted through the suffering of following incarnations. You generate your future by the way you act in the present. A selfish life is a life devoted to yourself, but one who lives an unselfish life takes into consideration the effect his actions have upon the lives of others. This is responsibility. It is only by aiding others that you can assist in evolution, while, if you live solely for yourself, you assist in involution and devolution. You may have a desire to see the result of your work; if you help someone, you want to see how much you have helped him – and perhaps you want him to see it also, and to be grateful. When you pour out your strength to help, there must be a result, whether you can see it or not. If you know the Law, you know that this must be so. But you must do what is right for the sake of the right, and not in the hope of reward – you must work for the sake of the work, and not in the hope of seeing the result-and, above all, you must give yourself to the service of the world because you love it, and cannot help giving yourself to it.

Before speaking, think carefully whether what you are about to say is true, kind and helpful – and if it has not those three qualifications, then do not say it. Learn to listen rather than to talk, and do not offer your opinions unless you are directly asked for them. A common desire which we must learn to repress sternly is the wish to meddle in other men's affairs. What another man does or says or believes is no business of yours, and you must learn to let him absolutely alone. He has a full right to free thought and speech and action, so long as he does not interfere with anyone else. You yourself claim the freedom to do what you think is proper, and you must allow him the same freedom, and when he expresses it you have absolutely no right to interfere with him.

If you think he is doing wrong, and you can find an opportunity of privately and very politely telling him why you think so, it is possible that you may convince him; but there are many cases in which even that would be an improper interference. On no account must you go and gossip to some third person about the matter. If we see a case of cruelty to a child or to an animal, then it is our duty to interfere; if we are placed in charge of another person in order to teach him, it may become our duty to gently point out to him his faults. Except in such cases, however, we must mind our own business and learn the virtue of silence.

He who injures you contracts a moral obligation which at some time he will have to settle. He becomes, by his own actions, your slave. If you look at the hatred of his action, and believe in vengeance, you are egotizing yourself and you involuntarily generate the evil forces which would kill your spirituality. If you forgive him, however, you develop your spirituality, and kill not only the evil which you would otherwise inflict upon yourself, but also the evil which your enemy has done himself. You advance by your actions; by voluntary forgiveness you can make a most wonderful appeal to God for help and guidance.

There are two kinds of cruelty; intentional and unintentional. Intentional cruelty is purposely giving pain to another living being, and that is the greatest of all sins; the work of a devil, rather than a man. You would say that no man could do such a thing, but men with sadistic natures have done it often, and are daily doing it right now. Inquisitors did it; many religious people did it in the name of their religion, and some vivisectionists do it. All of these people try to excuse their brutality by saying that it is expedient or customary – but a crime does not cease to be a crime simply because many commit it.

Karma takes no account of custom, and the karma of cruelty is the most terrible of all. The fate of the cruel must also fall upon those who go out intentionally to kill God's creatures in the name of "sport." But there is a cruelty in speech as well as in act, and a man who says a word with the deliberate intention to wound another is guilty of this crime. Sometimes a careless word may do as much harm as a malicious one, so we must be on guard against unintentional cruelty. It comes usually from thoughtlessness, for much suffering is caused by carelessness – by forgetting to think how an action or a word will affect others. But karma never forgets, and it takes no account of the fact that men forget.

The human race is in varied stages of development. There are persons capable of entering consciously en rapport with the invisible plane. In time you will reach this state of intense development of the transcendental faculties, and you will then be "one who knows." The first contact with the astral plane, on the part of a person on the physical plane, usually will take place either very abruptly, with intense and direct visions, or else very slowly, starting with hearing first, and then gradually developing into visions. The first step mentioned is very rare. It is one which takes place when the invisible acts directly upon the being of its choice, without his request or expectation. After the first experience with the invisible plane, connection between the two planes is accomplished more easily, but always under the direction of the invisible, and without loss of the control of the faculties for even one second.

The other path of communication is easier, and should be conducted alone or under the direction of a living Master. We do not mean to convey that any mystic path is easy to tread, for they are filled with trials, humiliations, and constant sacrifices which are likely to discourage even the most zealous at the beginning. The occult Brotherhoods have certain paths along which to conduct their students. Certain mental training is given, the teacher explaining the danger of the egotism which is liable to lead one to believe himself purer than any other human, and making him unwilling to soil his purity by astral or physical association with evil conditions.

The student is taught that the mental plane is the plane of pride, so that he will not be deceived by the Panthean Serpent during his astral sojourn. To the person who has abandoned the heart plane, the astral is everything – and to the beginner all the aid necessary is given. Not more than one in twenty succeeds in passing the first Initiation – but the one who does, and triumphs over the illusions of the Astral Serpent, is then ready to receive the aid of an invisible Power from the Divine Plane; occultists call it the "Guardian Angel," "Receiver of Light," the "Messenger of the Celestial Virgin," and other appropriate names.

Then the student is impelled no longer to speak evil of his poor brothers, nor judge them; still less to condemn them. This step passed, the inner hearing is developed through the heart and/or direct vision through the Pineal Gland, which we shall discuss a little further on. Or, distant perceptions may be perceived through the centers of the Solar Plexus. The person thus developed does not fear to lose his purity by association with the impure. He may live among the suffering and the humble, and mingle with the sick, the hopeless and the poor. It is by sharing what has been given him with those who have nothing that his aspirations and merits, as well as his faculties, are strengthened. After the student has passed through the above training, the perception of Divine personalities becomes more acute.

KNOWLEDGE THROUGH PSYCHIC DEVELOPMENT

One of the first things the student tries to discover is the change which takes place after death, and why one has come to live upon this earth. He is soon taught the meaning of it all – why the selfish and materialistic forces equilibrate the actions of the altruistic and spiritualistic forces. The man who concentrates all of his terrestrial efforts upon the acquisition of earthly gold passes through a frightful state when "death" approaches. His experience is similar to a rich financier obliged to exchange his mansion and his fine clothing for a prison cell and a convict's uniform. But instead, if a man has concentrated his efforts upon the acquisition of spiritual goods, which are of the domain of the Lord of the World, the vigilant sentinel of the Eternal Christ, then death is looked upon as the desired crowning of a constant effort, and, far from being pitiful, is happiness and joy.

Practically everyone has that "otherworldly sense," intuition, or "gut feeling." We just need help learning how to develop our psychic abilities.

Man gains his greatest knowledge by psychic development. His spirit often visits other worlds in order to be raised by the luminous Guides there into the "higher mansions," and when he returns here below it is only as an actor who plays a part, while his Real Self is elsewhere. As the relations between the two planes become more frequent, the Real Self feels itself near the end, and death is the simplest thing in the world, and also the happiest; it is the definite return to the true native land which it used to visit. The Initiate who dies on earth has, for some moments, the sensation of a delicious soaring; he floats upon a beautiful river, carried in a graceful bark, where he softly sails into the celestial immensity. Death is but the reentrance into another world.

But what of the anguish of those who have constructed their houses only for this world? The spirit, awakening, weeps for earthly riches which have become vain phantoms. Intense grief is produced by the sight of the decomposition of his fleshy body, which he had believed was his real self, and the center of adoration – what good is it now? Why did he not realize that it was worth more to recall the infinite goodness of the Father who has never judged anyone, and who has sent his pacific receivers to draw him from that state of trouble until the moment when the Celestial Virgin shall extend to him the mercy with which her heart is full for all the blind and sinful? Death is dreaded only by those who do not know of the conditions involved; all those who have come from the Divine plane to the earth plane.

Psychologists speak of brain power, but the brain in the human creates nothing-it reflects the living light of the heart. The seeker after occult knowledge will see the dawn of the centers of instruction where each one present pretends himself endowed with deep knowledge and in possession of the total integral truth – when, in fact, he has been disclosed only glimpses of the truth, the real Truth being concealed until he is ready for more clearness. His trials are many. He may hear tirades against God, and especially against Christ. He must be on his guard -- he has penetrated only the veil of the mental path. We can judge others only by our own eyes. They see differently than we do, but some day they will understand their present delusion as we have.

After reaching his ideal development on the mental plane, the seeker is first permitted to see for a minute on the astral plane, and what he sees in this minute is enough to astonish him. Then does he realize the pretense of those who have claimed to be adepts, and see how dangerous it would be to take a stroll in the astral without a guide. But our Father surrounds us with protectors, invisible to us, perhaps, whose object is to guard those who are worthy of being protected. Generally before a person becomes interested in the occult he has seen or heard of some phenomenon. He wants to learn something of the invisible world, and the astral forces. There are many things which the occult student must avoid. He must not believe himself all-powerful, and he must not wish to control the invisible beings. Another error he must avoid is the use of the occult forces in black magic.

The path of spiritual development is simple, and the way is clear – the seeker lives always for others, and never for self (for we must do unto others that which we wish done to ourselves, on all planes); never does he speak evil, and never does he think evil. If you think of the evil in another you are actually doing three harmful things. First, you are filling your neighborhood with evil thought instead of good thought, and thus adding to the sorrow of the world. Second, if there is in that man the evil which you think there is, you are strengthening it and feeding it, and so you are making your brother worse instead of better. And generally the evil is not there, and you have only fancied it – and then your wicked thought tempts your brother to do wrong, for if he is not yet perfect you may make him that which you have thought him.

Third, you are filling your own mind with evil thoughts instead of good ones; and so you hinder your own growth and make yourself, for those who can see an ugly and painful object instead of a beautiful and loveable one. There is a physical purification, such as the meatless diet, which diminishes the intensity of material attraction; but in so purging the body of animal influences, one does not at the same time purge the astral of the selfish influence, and the spirit of the influence of pride is one hundred times more dangerous than the impulses coming from the use of meat. When a man acts as though he knows more than someone else, he actually knows very little. When he shuts himself away from the world and retires, he shuts out much of the knowledge that he would gain by coming in contact more with the world.

The real Adept lives simply, realizing his weaknesses and the value of coming into contact with the Divine Will. He never becomes occupied with his personal purity, and thinks little of his personal wants – but much of the sufferings of others. By his life he is recognized by the Christ, and gradually his powers are unfolded. The seeker gives assistance, and he himself requires assistance at all times. He lives simply, in preference to ostentation, and instructs the men who present themselves to him as perfect. On the physical plane he assists his fellowmen, and as he does, the Masters teach him. All along the route he is given assistance and illumination in the same degree that he assists and illuminates others. His trials are many, but if he has the Peace at heart he will finally reach the spiritual plane, where he will receive assistance from the Guardian spirits maintained to help all. Gradually one veil after another is lifted. In time the curtain will be drawn aside for a few moments, and the divine sensation of accepted prayer fills the heart with courage and love.

The student must bear his karma cheerfully, whatever it may be, taking it as an honor that suffering comes to him, because it shows that the Lords of Karma consider him worth helping. However hard it is, be thankful that it is no worse. Remember that you are of but little use to the Masters until your evil karma is worked out, and you are free. By offering yourself for service to the Masters, you have asked that your karma may be hurried, and so now, in one or two lives, you work through what otherwise might have been spread out over a hundred. But in order to make the best of it you must bear it cheerfully, and gladly. You must give up all feeling of possession. Karma may take from you the things which you like best -- and even the people whom you love most. Even then you must remain cheerful, ready to part with anything and everything. Often the Master needs to pour out His strength upon others through you, as His servant – and He cannot do so if the servant yields to depression.

The large majority who take up the study of occultism try to find some magic key that will open the door to the mysteries. There is no short road. It is a waste of time to try and find one. However, if one studies and takes the time, there is no reason why he should not advance along the mystic path. The door of the path cannot be opened by the aspirant, but must be opened by his invisible guide and the tension of his spiritual body. It is an open path to every human who becomes worthy to tread it. The man who represents himself as being great is only proud, and disqualifies himself. He must become as a little child before the entrance becomes visible to him. Strait is the gate, and narrow is the way; and few there be that find it – but it is wide enough for all humanity.

SUMMARY:

*This chapter has ended with the reference to a magic key. Unfortunately the United States Government itself has participated in this frantic search. Those wishing more information on this subject should read the book entitled, *"The Sacred Mushroom,"* by Dr. Puharich. According to Ruth Montgomery in the *New York Journal* - January 14, 1960, "Washington: The Army Intelligence Service is beginning to delve into an unknown reach of the mind...a number of top intelligence agents are conducting research experiments in mental telepathy...the Intelligence Service hopes to develop enough "sensitive" agents, and to perfect their technique to such an extent that they could actually pick up thought waves emanating from the Cold War 'enemy' camp."

Military intelligence for some time has been delving into the possible utilization of hypnosis in spying. The "magic key" being sought by government agencies to unlock the mysteries revealed in this book is the evil produced by drugs and hypnosis. We cannot stress too strongly the avoidance of hypnosis and the use of drugs.

Franz Anton Mesmer practised and popularised a therapy known as "Animal Magnetism" that is thought to be the precursor to modern hypnotherapy.

6

THE ENIGMA OF MATTER

It has been stated in this chapter that occultism is considered by the average man as a subject for idle dreamers and poets. Sir Humphrey Davy wrote a paper entitled, *"The Dance of Matter"* and one should read it in connection with this chapter, for although speculative and scientific, it propounds perfectly the science of the *"Dance of Shiv."* Poetically, this has been beautifully expounded by Percy Bysshe Shelley in his, *"The Dance of Matter: The Motion of the Spheres."* Artistically we see the same idea expressed in the 13th Century bronze figure of Shri Nataraja (Shiva as Lord of the Dance), in the Museum van Aziatische Kunst, Amsterdam, Holland. Poets and scientists of the creative type are always pointing the way either from imagination or by intuition. Sir John Woodruff's translations from the *"Shata Chakra Nirupana"* and *"Paduka Panchaka"* are two works on Laya Yoga translated from the Sanskrit, but are too erudite except for the most dedicated and determined scholars. However, this entire book makes the "occultism" of such works simple and clear.

Man has the power to raise himself out of his present condition. If he so determines, he can advance, by self-devised efforts, far beyond the point which he would have reached in the present incarnation under ordinary circumstances. By right thought and action, man can so live that the world will be the better for his having lived.

If the windows of perception were cleansed, everything would appear to man as it is – infinite. Man has closed himself up, until he sees everything through the narrow chinks of his cavern-the greater beauties of the universe being shut out from his vision. The person who has never made a study of this subject is convinced that the world he knows requires a single vision only. The world appears to him solid and material. He knows nothing of other planes, and he will, at first, look upon this book as being highly imaginative fiction. However, let him make a careful study of the subject and he will be convinced, and will no longer regard occultism as a subject only for idle dreamers and poets.

All humanity is twofold, and capable of correspondence with two orders of existence. The higher self is always drawn towards union with the reality; the lower self is drawn into the illusion, the visible world. It can be proven to man that behind the visible world there is another – the world invisible, which is hidden from the outer senses; and that it is possible for man to penetrate into that unseen world by developing in himself the psychic powers which lie dormant in everyone. *The dreamer uses these faculties; i.e., the ability to see with the physical eyes closed.

You are not asked to believe a single statement given here until you actually realize that it is true. All you are asked to do is read with an open mind. If you start out with the idea that there is not a hidden world, you will be very likely to shut out a good deal of knowledge that would otherwise flow to you. It is not necessary for you to believe that there is an unseen world behind the visible one. If you are firmly of the opinion that the world perceived by man; through his physical senses is the only one, hold on to this view until you are convinced otherwise. We were all of this opinion at sometime in our evolution.

THE PURPOSE OF CREATION

A survey of the visible world propounds enigmas to man which can never be solved by the facts of that world itself. The visible world is closely interwoven with the invisible world, and therefore, before we can understand the inner nature of the visible world, we must learn something of the hidden world. He who does not realize that this is true, closes his eyes to the problems which obviously spring up everywhere and are deemed unanswerable.

There is no limit to human knowledge, and there are no bounds preventing man from gaining more knowledge of the invisible world – and nothing to stop him from penetrating into the higher existing worlds. Every day more persons endeavor to learn of the visible presence of the "something unseen"; they realize that there is something hidden from their consciousness.

Life is one continued new birth; from one birth we go to another, and from one dream we go to another.

Money cannot buy the higher knowledge, and in order to gain it you must become acquainted with all of the details of the supersensible world. At first a series of communications is made about the invisible nature of man. You must learn what happens when "death" opens the portals; the evolution of man, the earth, and the entire solar system. Not before you know all this can you realize what is within you. Before man's soul can be lifted into the sphere of the divine he must have patience, an open mind, and be ready to assimilate the food given.

Everyone wants to know why man was created. Everyone wants' to know what awaits him after death. We shall not indulge in theories, or assumptions, since we do not believe in making idle statements – this is too important a subject to merely set forth arguments. We shall endeavor to explain the mightiest truths of the universe, so that all may be able to see them as they are, and not as some would prefer to have them.

There is nothing on this Earth which is not unstable and unsubstantial, and from this there must come something that is permanent and fixed. The cry of unending change of which scientists speak refers only to the dream state of humanity. Science proves, itself, that it is a dream state by claiming that life and creation have always come and gone, and will continue to do so, going on aimlessly and hopelessly forever and ever. In spite of all their investigations, this is as close as they have come to a conclusion. The investigations will be continued, but when science has reached its highest knowledge and achieved its greatest triumphs, it will have arrived only at chaos.

You will find the complete evidence of a definite purpose in all creation. There has been a steady, gradual progress from chaos of matter to the perfect order as we find it today. Our Creator has planned a road with a clear and definite goal, and there has been no deviation of this plan since the earth took its shape. The purpose and the goal are revealed to us by the steps which have already been taken. We know that we are getting nearer the Creator from the fact that man has ever been moving along converging lines with his Creator.

Life is but a dream, we are told, but that does not mean that it is not a reality. There cannot be a dream without a dreamer. Man goes to sleep and dreams; he awakens and goes to work, and works out that dream in his discoveries and inventions, by which in turn civilization advances a little nearer to the ultimate goal. It is also true that in the grander and more important dreams of earthly existence, it is possible to solve the future and destiny of the world and man's place in the universe is determined.

Man is made out of matter that is scattered in chaos on earth, and he enters the womb of woman that he may be born; this is the process of life. If the sole purpose of creation were to live and die here, there would have been no need for the waste and pain of going and coming. Man could just as well have been made as he is at maturity, just as man himself makes the automobile and, instead of adding the gasoline before starting it, it would have been necessary only to breathe into man the spirit of life, and set him going.

Life would be useless unless something were to follow. This is a fact which has done more towards keeping men believing in religion than all other influences. As man advances in mental development, the mind raises its standards by which all things are seen and measured from the viewpoint of his existence, and his belief in the Hereafter is either shattered or strengthened. There is nothing that seems real or satisfying that is of human duration.

When we finally realize that we are in a dream state, then we are able to understand better, and we see the harmony between our experiences of Earth and the motive of creation. Life is one continued new birth; from one birth we go to another, and from one dream we go to another. Finally we will reach the awakening state, and then our destiny will really commence. There has always been a connecting link between the present and the past; always the thread of life linking us to the past. We have developed as we proceeded, and it is necessary that we make progress here, so that we may set the thread farther ahead to link us to our future lives.

Humans who are born into this world must take on a new birth for the reason that life has been a dream instead of a reality. All of our transactions and estimates of this world are but fragments of the physical, or objective, mind. Had life here been a reality, then our existence here would have been permanent. There would have been no justice in bringing living beings into the world just as stepping stones, and then sending them to a real grave after they have been compelled to go through untold suffering. And that is why the dream-state was made to take the place of the real, so that we would not suffer from any injustice. If life had been real, it would have been necessary to have given to it stability and substance, and this could not have been done without changing the entire plan, as nothing had been created which was worth being made permanent. You can see, then, that the dream state was the only possible one under the circumstances.

There is not one thing throughout the entire universe that is permanent. Everything is in a transitory state; nothing lasts. Man goes on preparing as if he were going to live forever – and a few days illness ends his physical life. The more material things change continually – matter crumbles, metals rust and tarnish, fortunes vanish. We cannot take one dollar of our wealth from this life into the next. If life were real, not a dream, it would be fixed, certain, and definite forever. We wish you to understand this well. If you do not, you will not understand what is to follow. That which has not yet reached a stage where the best qualities are developed cannot be made permanent; therefore, it must not be given the realities of life, but must take on the substitute of life. All dreaming is a substitute of life. If you do not realize the truth of this statement at present, you will in time.

Civilized man was the first being made by our Creator fit to be reborn spiritually. The forms previous to him were only stepping stones. The object of creation is to produce form out of matter. When there was nothing living on the earth, everything was in a chaotic state everywhere. The matter was controlled by certain Laws to get it ready for the plant life which finally appeared. Higher forms, and, in time, thousands of new species and animals were eventually made; finally man, the highest form of the animal kingdom – and, with the coming of a subjective mind, the beginnings of civilized man evolved from the animal-man. Not until civilized man appeared was there any effort made to produce inanimate forms, or artifacts.

There are two live, creative processes at work; each has a distinct work to do. One is the making of life, and the other is the making of material forms. The Creator is the Great Cause of everything; living and material forms are created according to his plan. Man is taken into partnership with the Creator, and material forms are created by the Power working through him. This shows that man is the highest type of life upon this planet.

Man is not perfect, but is progressing, however slowly. He is in a dream state; and because this dream state we call life is a reflection of the real, everything is reversed to him (as in a mirror). Slowly he has learned to see and feel with his objective mind and physical body. The experiences that are real seem unreal to him, and those which are unreal seem real; this is because the physical brain is not yet able to grasp what is real. But he is fast reaching that stage when he will acquire the faculties necessary to understand the real. Eventually everyone will be born with these powers; then it will be possible to come into direct companionship with the Creator. The veil which separates man from the Creator is wearing very thin. It has been pierced by many at the present time, so it is not elusive. When this stage is reached, the real life commences.

Remember this; whatever you keep your attention upon will accumulate knowledge for your mind. All facts of the intuition come from the Universal thought. All human experience and activities of the earth are connected with our dream life, but they will not furnish us with the facts which are part of our intuition, and are, therefore, not part of the Universal thought. When your mind has become so developed that it is able to receive and absorb knowledge from the Universal Mind, then you will change wonderfully. You will then have the key to other knowledge, and ultimately your higher intuition is developed. You will then know that there is life after death, and life on this earth is a dream.

BECOMING ONE WITH THE CREATOR

Man, although the highest type of living animal upon the Earth, is not yet fit to become the eternal companion of the Creator. Man can become a partner to the

Creator, and is given the power to produce matter from chaos. Man is fast reaching the climax of existence, and needs only one more step in order to reach eternal companionship with his Creator. He must, by his own efforts, emerge from the physical unreality to the non-physical reality. Man has proceeded step by step to a higher state, and has not been hindered in his development by conditions over which he has no control. He has become a partner of the Creator, and is able to produce forms out of matter. Man, therefore, can be a Master, both of matter and of himself. It has taken billions of years for man to pass through the successive stages before he reached his high place. The Creator takes him up to a point where he can get a glimpse of the world of reality, but He leaves to man himself the task of completing the great work which has occupied all the billions of years.

It would seem cruel to produce life, for the most part to be destroyed. And it seems cruel to be born, knowing it will not be many years before we die. But we all know it to be a fact – plants die; animal life does the same, but everything leaves behind its counterpart. The plants and flowers leave seeds, to bring forth others of the same kind. Animals have souls which live after them when their physical bodies are dead. These souls at some future time inhabit other bodies. Man does the same, but he is of higher development, and comes nearer to the point where rebirth on this planet is no longer necessary. There are a very great many civilized humans who are getting very close to the separation from animals. Our Creator could "jump us over" if He wanted to, but there would be too great a separation, too great a change. No person can climb to the top of a ladder and kick the ladder away until a new and safe landing place has been affected. The process of becoming separated from this world must be gradual.

THE NATURE OF FREE WILL

Man is a free agent to do as he pleases – so long as he does not injure anyone else. It is a fixed rule of nature that no one must be forced, solicited, coaxed, or frightened into bettering his life. Men and women must learn from experience what is best for them, and the desire must be born in the individual before he can understand this. Everyone should try to help his fellow-man, but it is never well to take away his privilege of learning by depriving him of experience.

You may say, "suppose I should live again in this world, be born, and grow up to another life – what good would my previous life be to me if both were distinct and separate, as two different beings?" You may not be able to remember any previous lives; there are very few who do – but you are what you are today because of your past experiences. Whatever we build in character that is not of permanent good cannot be transplanted into higher spheres of life, and must be disintegrated before we can pass to a higher plane. All unfit material must be eliminated. This we can plainly see in this life. We should therefore aim to live so as to build up that which lives beyond the grave. When man has cleared away all of his illusions, and separated the real from the unreal, and when all of his obstructive elements have been eliminated, this is done.

One of the most common mistaken conceptions of the average student of the occult sciences, and of so-called "psychic" phenomena, in general, is that which may be expressed by the term "supernatural." This term, as you know, is used to express the idea of "that which is outside of the realm of Nature, and of Nature's laws." As all advanced students and teachers of the occult doctrines know, we have no direct knowledge whatsoever of anything that is "outside the realm of Nature and of Nature's laws." It is true that we may, by an act of faith, according to the manner in which we have been brought up in religion, profess to believe in powers and beings entirely apart from the great realm of nature – in fact, most persons do believe in such powers and beings in connection with their formal religion – but their belief is entirely within the category of Faith, and is not even pretended to be based upon actual experience and phenomenal manifestation.

The moment that there appears any manifestation which is possible of being known to, or experienced by, the human senses, ordinary or extraordinary, that moment the phenomena and the immediate cause thereof must be regarded as being properly classed in the category of "natural." This is not only true of such phenomena as are perceived by means of our ordinary five senses, but also of those which are perceptible to only the highest powers of perception, or higher senses, which are latent in all human beings, but which are unfolded only in the case of a comparatively few individuals of the race.

It should be clearly understood by all students of occultism or psychic phenomena that our knowledge and experience, normal or supernormal, is confined to the realm of Nature. There is a "ring-pass-not" around the boundaries of the Kingdom of Nature which mortals cannot pass; no matter how high may be their degree of development and advancement. Even those great mystics whose writings are filled with the startling revelations of "union with the Divine," and "At-one-ment with Deity," are under no illusion concerning this fact, for they know that only insofar as Deity involves Itself in Nature – wraps itself up in the garments of Nature – can it be directly experienced by man, and thus actually known by him.

Perhaps a clearer understanding of this important subject will be had if we substitute the term "supernormal" for that of "supernatural." The term "supernormal" is not commonly employed, but a study of its meaning, and its adoption in our thinking, will serve to give us a clearer conception of the true nature of many strange phases of experience of which we have become conscious, either by reason of their manifestation by ourselves, or else by the manifestation on the part of others. Supernormal means "beyond, above, or exceeding that which is normal" extraordinary, inexplicable, perhaps, but not supernatural. The term "normal" means, "conforming to a certain standard, rule or type"; hence, anything that is supernormal is something that is above this usual pattern, rule or type. There is an important distinction to be noted here; a thing may be outside of the usual pattern, rule or type in the sense of being inferior to, or under* the ordinary standard – and in this case it is known as "abnormal," the latter term being employed as a term of depreciation. On the other hand, the "outside of the standard" quality may consist of a superiority to the prevailing standard, and accordingly is entitled to be classed in the category of the "supernormal" the prefix "super" meaning above, over, higher, etc.

On our own plane of existence the senses of hearing and sight, respectively, are included in the usual standard pattern and type of sense normality; every normal person possesses these senses in a certain general degree of power. Hence, on this plane of existence, a person born deaf or blind is spoken of as "abnormal," or deficient in regard to the sense powers. On the contrary, let us imagine a plane of existence in which the greater majority of individuals lack the power of sight and hearing. On such a plane of existence, the occasional individual who was born possessed of these powers would be properly regarded as "supernormal," or in other words, such a person would be superior to the ordinary run of individuals. The term "abnormal" means minus the ordinary standard quality, while the term "supernormal" means plus the ordinary standard quality. And yet both the "plus" and the "minus" would be outside the normal type, although there is a difference as wide as that between the two poles in this "outsideness."

Solved! The Mysteries of Space, Time and UFOs

The above important statement is not made merely for the purpose of academic differentiation and classification; on the other hand, it is made because there is a tendency to regard and to classify certain high phases of occult and psychic manifestation of power as "abnormal," or below the standard. Properly speaking, such manifestations of power are far above the standard. This attitude on the part of the public toward this class of phenomena is akin to that of a community of blind and deaf persons, satisfied that their own "three sense" standard is the highest possible one attained by living creatures, and that all variation there from must be considered as "abnormal." In such a community there would occasionally be born certain individuals possessed of the senses of sight and hearing, in addition to the common three senses possessed by the entire community.

Judging by what we know of the tendency of human nature in such cases, we are warranted in suspecting that the average person in such a community would avoid the seeing and hearing individuals as "abnormal," and the possessors of these powers therefore to be pitied, and, perhaps, shunned. Only the intelligent and thoughtful members of such a community would be able to grasp the fact that these exceptional individuals were really not "abnormal," or inferior, but that they were really "supernormal," and superior to type.

Those to whom the above illustration may seem exaggerated are asked to consider the unthinking attitude which the great majority of the people, at least at first, present toward that most wonderful display of supernormal powers known as "occult or psychic," made by the few highly developed individuals of the race who are able to manifest them to some degree. These individuals are regarded as "queer" and "strange"; unnatural and abnormal, by their neighbors and associates, just as the seeing and hearing exceptional individuals were likewise so regarded by their blind and deaf neighbors in the above illustration. And here, as in the illustration, it is only the few individuals of the community who are informed on the subject who recognize that the departure from the standard type is in the direction of advancement and gain, rather of retrogression and loss-a plus attribute, rather than a minus one.

But it would be unjust and unfair to the general public were we to fail to add to the above criticism the fact that there is under way a great change in public opinion regarding this important matter. More and more persons are becoming interested in Nature's finer forces every day; more are becoming familiar with the phenomena manifested by the gifted individuals possessing these wonderful powers; and more are coming to realize that these powers are really latent in all of the members of the human race, although lying dormant in the majority, and may be unfolded and brought into active manifestation by scientific methods of training and development. But even so, the student and teacher of this great subject should bear in mind the important distinction made above between that which is "abnormal" and that which is "supernormal," and such should lose no opportunity in pointing out this important distinction whenever the subject arises in conversation or argument-for the propaganda of truth should be earnestly and vigorously pursued, in order that the world may be liberated from its chains of error.

Returning to the subject considered previously; namely, the naturalness of the occult and psychic higher powers, and the manifestation of them, we strongly advise all students of these subjects to acquire a working knowledge of the place in Nature occupied by these powers and their manifestations. A little scientific information on the subject will render the student better able to teach others intelligently concerning these matters – and also to defend himself successfully when others seek to attack the things which are so dear to his heart, and so real and evident to himself. Many, because of their lack of scientific knowledge on these points, not only fail to make converts to their cause of truth, but often really drive away persons who might otherwise be interested. Many persons are truly interested in and attracted to the manifestations of the higher occult and psychic powers, but are fearful of anything "unnatural" or "supernatural," and are disposed to be frightened off by any suspicion of such qualities becoming evident. These same persons, if shown that the phenomena have a perfectly valid scientific basis in natural forces and laws, will throw aside their fears and become earnest students of this great subject.

OTHER VIBRATIONAL PLANES OF EXISTENCE

Modern science now furnishes abundant testimony to support and substantiate the teachings of the ancient Hindu sages to the effect that everything in the Universe is in constant motion, which manifests by varying rates, degrees, and modes of vibrations. The modern scientists, like the ancient occultists, know that the differences between the things of the Universe arise mainly from the different rates, modes and degrees of the vibrations manifested in the things themselves. If we change the vibration of a thing, we are practically changing the manifested nature of that thing. The difference between solid ice, liquid water, semi-gaseous vapor, and gaseous steam, is simply the difference caused by the various rates of the vibration caused by heat. The difference between red and blue, green and violet, is simply that caused by varying rates of vibration. Light and heat, as well as sound, depend for their differences upon rates of vibration.

As every textbook on science can inform us, there are sounds too low, as well as those too high, for the human ear to register, but which are registered by delicate instruments. And there are colors beyond the place of red, at one end of the visible spectrum, and others beyond the place of violet at the other end of the spectrum, which the human eye is unable to register and detect but which laboratory apparatus plainly registers. The ray of light which registers on a photographic plate, or which causes sunburn to our skin, is too high a rate of vibration for our eyes to see. X-rays and many others of the finer rays of light known to science are also imperceptible to unaided human vision. They are actually "dark rays," so far as the human eye is concerned, although man has devised instruments by which they may be caught and registered.

The vibrations of magnetism and electricity are imperceptible to our sight, although they may be registered by the appropriate apparatus; and if we had the proper sense apparatus to perceive them, these rays of vibratory force would open up a new world to us. Likewise, if we could increase our power of hearing perception, we would seem to be living in a whole new world of sound now closed to us. Reasoning along the same line of thought, many great thinkers have held that there is no reason for doubting the possible existence of other worlds, planes of being, just as real and as actual as the one upon which we live and move and have our being, but which are forever invisible to the ordinary human sight and senses -- the apparent nothingness of these worlds arising solely from the great difference in the rates of vibrations between the two planes of being.

And what of the possibility of entire worlds existing in the same space occupied by us, but of which we are unconscious by reason of our failure to sense their vibrations? All of our sensations are due to the impact upon our sense-organs of vibrations in some form. Variations in the strength and rapidity of these vibrations constitute the difference in our perceptions. Our range of response is but a limited one; some vibrations are too rapid and some are too slow to affect our senses, and therefore we have called to our aid various mechanical contrivances to enable us to recognize existences which would otherwise remain unknown. But it is still conceivable that there may be, and doubtless are, conditions of vibratory energy which escape us and which, if we could develop finer senses, would yield wonderful results and extensions of our power and knowledge. Today we are coming into contact with forces, possibilities, and personalities which amount to a revelation of a whole new universe of things.

It is true that "things are not what they seem," but everything seems to be a certain way to us only because of its particular plane of being, and that plane of being is determined by its vibrations. One plane has a certain vibratory rate or speed; on another plane we find a different one. But a plane is not a place, but a state – and so it is entirely possible that two utterly different planes of being might coexist in the same place and be entirely unknown to one another. That may seem absurd, but it is a scientific truth, and many authorities have endorsed it. Experiments at the Lawrence Radiation Laboratory, U. of C., indicate the theory of antimatter, or the "mirror-type symmetry" known as "conservation of parity."

There may be, right here and now, passing through us and our world, some planet invisible to us – with mountains, oceans, lakes, rivers, cities, and inhabitants; and yet we know absolutely nothing of their existence. Some students find it difficult to grasp the idea of a number of manifestations, each having its own rate of vibration, occupying the same point of space at the same time. A slight consideration of the phenomena of the physical world would perhaps aid such persons in assimilating the concept in question. For instance, as every student of physics can tell you, a single point of space may contain at the same time vibrations of heat, light of many shades, magnetism, electricity, X-rays, etc., each manifesting its own rate of vibration, and yet none interferes with the others. Every beam of sunlight contains many different colors, each with its own degree of vibration, yet none crowds out the others. By the use of the proper forms of laboratory apparatus, each kind of light may be separated from the others, and the ray split up. The difference of colors arises simply from the different rates of etheric vibrations. Again, it is possible to send many telegrams along the same wire, at the same time, by using senders and receivers of different vibratory keynotes. The same thing has its corresponding analogy in the case of the wireless telegraphy. On the physical plane we find many forms of vibratory energy manifesting on, in, and at the same point of space, at the same time-all without interfering with each other.

Your soul, or core consciousness, has a presence in all realities at the same time. Despite this multidimensional presence, we are normally focused on only one dimension, with little awareness of the others.

The ancient occult teachings have always insisted upon the presence of numerous planes of existence, of which our own particular plane is only one. And all of these numerous planes are equally within the realms of Nature – none is supernatural. There exists always a correspondence between these several planes of manifestation, and, under supernormal conditions, a certain degree of communication is possible between them. Each of these planes has numerous subdivisions and sub-planes, the divisions being according to the rule of "sevens." In other words, there are seven grand planes, and each of these is divided into seven secondary planes -- and each of these is subdivided into seven tertiary planes, and so on, until the division has been made seven times.

The student of occultism, particularly at the beginning of his studies, usually has difficulty in understanding just what is meant by the term "plane," as employed in occult teachings. His first impression, usually encouraged by the use of a dictionary, is that each "plane" is one of a series of strata, or layers, above and below which are other layers or strata. Even after the student has progressed in his understanding of the subject, this original picture of material layers and strata seems to persist in his thought on the subject The error, of course, arises from his original conception of the planes, layers or strata being composed of gross material matter, whereas, actually, only one of the many planes is so composed. When one stops to think that even the grossest form of matter is itself composed of vibrations of energy (for science itself teaches us that all matter is energy), and that all other forms of material substance are likewise composed of vibrations of energy, then one is on the road to discovery of the real state of affairs.

He then begins to realize that, instead of the planes of being rising one above the other in the scale of their fineness, they are graded according to their degree of vibration energy, and each may actually occupy the same space as all the others. The "planes," then, are not strata, or layers of matter at all, but are simply different states of vibration or energy, and that which we know as "matter" is simply one (and a very low one, at that) of the many forms of such vibrations. From this it can be seen that the various planes of being are not distinguished by their position in space; they do not lay one superimposed upon the other, like layers of matter. Instead, they interpenetrate each other in the same limits of space.

A single point of space may accommodate the manifestations of each of the seven great planes of being, and all of the subdivisions and sub-planes (seven-fold in division) at the same time. The old occultists impressed this, and the other facts, upon the minds of their pupils by constantly reminding them that a plane is not a place of being, but a state of being. And the "state of being" is simply a certain manifestation of vibratory energy. With these ideas firmly fixed in the mind, the student is less apt to wander astray from the facts.

To those who may be disposed to regard the above statements concerning the "planes of being" as somewhat visionary, imaginary, or theoretical, we can say, "go to modern science for the verification of these statements." We are apt to think that we are familiar with every kind of matter in existence, but such is not the case at all. We are familiar with only a few forms of matter. Spectrum analysis shows us that on certain fixed stars there are forms of matter far different from matter as we know it on this planet. On some stars, this unknown matter appears to be of a much lower form of vibration than that manifested by terrestrial matter; while on others there appears to be a much higher vibratory rate than even that manifested by the most subtle forms of ultra-gaseous matter known to us here. Even on our own planet we can distinguish between several classes of matter. In addition to the forms known as "solid," "liquid," and "gaseous," science now, recognizes a fourth plane of matter known as "ultra-gaseous" matter, and there are indications of several even finer states of matter, known under the general term of "radiant matter." In fact, the radiant matter spoken of now fades away into "radiant energy."

In view of the facts of modern science concerning the different planes of substance, matter and energy, only ignorance of these facts makes questionable the possibility of the existence of a great plane of being and life beyond the range of the ordinary senses of man, or the possibility of planes surrounding us on all sides, occupying the same space as we do. They are unseen by us, and we largely unseen by those dwelling upon such planes. There are many who, while admitting the possibility of other and finer planes of being and life, question the possibility of communication between these planes of existence. With apparently sound logic they wonder how it is possible for a human, with his ordinary senses, to "sense" things or beings dwelling on the finer planes.

Not only may things on the finer planes become perceptible to humans by means of the lowering of the vibrations of these finer vibratory objects in certain ways, but humans may develop and cultivate an increased power in their senses of sight and hearing, and thus raise their vibrations – and, still more, humans may (and often do) develop and cultivate certain latent powers of "sensing" which are inherent in every one of us, and thus directly "sense" the sights and sounds of the higher planes of existence almost, if not quite, as clearly as they can sense the objects and events of their own plane of existence. To understand how this can be, it is necessary to carefully consider the question of "sensing" in general, so as to understand just what it is that enables us to "sense" anything at all. Once understanding this, it is but a step further to understanding the "supernormal" sensing referred to. Let us then examine this matter of "sensing."

The reports of our sense organs are called "sensations." A sensation is defined as "an impression, or the consciousness of an impression, made upon the mind through the medium of a nerve or one of the organs of sense." The term "sense" is defined as a "faculty possessed by animals of perceiving external objects by means of impressions made upon certain organs of the body." Our senses have been well said to constitute the "doors to the outside world." Unless our attention is especially directed to the subject, few of us even begin to realize how completely we are dependent upon these doors to the outside world for our knowledge of that outside world. It is only when we stop to imagine how completely shut in, or shut out, we would be if all of our sense channels should be destroyed, that we can even begin to realize just how dependent we: are upon our senses for our knowledge of the world in which we live and move and have our being.

Psychologists have pointed out to us the fact that if a human were born without sense organs – no matter how perfect a brain he might have – his life would be little more than that of a plant. Such a person would exist in merely a dreamlike state, with only the very faintest manifestations of consciousness. His consciousness would not be able to react in response to the impact of sensation from the outside world, for there would be no such impact. And, as consciousness depends almost entirely upon the impact of, or resistance to, outside impressions, his consciousness would be almost entirely inactive. He would be conscious of his own existence, but would probably never realize the fact fully, for he would have nothing else with which to compare himself, and his self-consciousness would never be aroused by contact with things outside of himself. Such a person would not even have the memories of previous sensations or experiences to arouse or heighten his consciousness or thought, and consequently he would have no imagination to use. In other words he would be, to all intents and purposes, a living corpse.

Science informs us that all of the five senses of man; namely, the respective senses of touch, sight, hearing, taste, and smell, are but modifications of one elementary sense, which is the sense of touch, and that the other senses have been gradually evolved from that one elementary sense. This is seen to be the case when it is realized that the only way we "sense" the presence of an outside object-be that object either a material object, a vibration of the air, or an etheric vibration of light – is by that outside object coming into contact, directly or indirectly, with one or more of our sensory nerves, the latter conveying the report of the contact to the brain, which translates the sensation into what is called a "perception." This is true of the sensations of touch, sight, hearing, taste, and smell, and of the senses higher than these and which are as yet not recognized by science. Consequently the consciousness of the presence of an outside thing arises from contact with that outside thing through the channel of the sense of touch, or of some of its more complex evolved phases.

From what has been said, it is seen that we can know only these things concerning the outside world which are capable of being reported to us by means of sense impressions, simple or complex – all of our thought regarding the world being made up from the raw materials which psychologists have termed "sensations." Consequently, if an individual is deprived of one or more of his ordinary senses, his knowledge of the outside world is decreased to just that extent. And, likewise, if the individual were to be given one or more additional senses, his knowledge of the world would be increased in the same ratio. The same result, at least in a certain degree, would be attained if the existing senses of the individual were to be increased in power so as to register higher rates of vibration than they now consciously register and record.

This subject of increased sense-powers has always been a fascinating one for the psychologists, and much speculation has been indulged in concerning the increased consciousness of mankind, were additional senses opened to it. As a useful exercise for young students, it was once suggested that they make a consideration of the changes which would be worked in our ordinary world if the varied branches of our receiving instruments happened to exchange duties; for instance, if we heard all colors, and saw all sounds. All this is less fantastic than it seems. Music is but the interpretation of certain vibrations undertaken by the ear; and color is but the interpretation of other vibrations undertaken by the eye. Were such an alteration of our senses to take place, the world would still be sending us the same messages, but we should be interpreting them differently. Beauty would still be ours, though speaking in another tongue. The birds' songs would then strike our retina as a pageant of color – we should see all of the magical tones of the wind, and hear as a great concert the repeated and harmonized greens of the forest, and the cadences of stormy skies. Could we realize how slight an adjustment of our own organs is needed to initiate us into such a world, we should perhaps be far less contemptuous of those mystics who tell us in moments of consciousness of a transcendental degree that they "heard flowers that sounded, and saw notes that shone" or that they have experienced rare moments of consciousness in which the senses were organs fused into a single and ineffable act of perception, in which color and sound were known as aspects of the same thing.

In view of the facts and principles above set forth for consideration, we begin to see now that there really is nothing "unnatural" in the hypothesis that there are reports conveyed to the consciousness of man by means of higher vibrations than those of ordinary sound, or ordinary sight – providing that man has either highly developed his ordinary senses of sight, hearing, or touch to a degree sufficiently high to register these higher vibrations, or that he has evolved and unfolded into consciousness certain latent faculties of sense-impression which are lying dormant in the great masses of mankind.

In fact, the thoughtful person will be forced to admit that this new knowledge of the nature of sensations, and of their relation to vibratory motion, renders extremely probable the truth of the great body of reports of such so-called extra-conscious knowledge which the experience of the race has furnished from the beginning of human history down to the present time. Such a person will see that it is not a sign of "credulity" for a person to accept such reports, so universally set forth; but that, rather, it is only a sign of "credulity" for such a person to accept blindly the dogmatic assertions of the materialistic skeptics to the effect that "there is no such thing possible in the natural world, under natural laws, and that the whole thing is delusion or else deliberate fraud." Such persons are usually found to really know much that is not true, and to lack the knowledge of much that is true, regarding Nature, her realm, and her laws.

Ordinary people can and do experience an altered view of reality from time to time. In this unique view, they may perceive things that the mind can't usually comprehend. This could mean that some UFO events show a reality that is separate from our own. Art by Carol Ann Rodriguez.

7

THOUGHT

The following chapter, devoted to the psychic realm, is possibly one of the most important chapters of this book. Modern psychiatry is in the hands of medical men with little or no knowledge of the psychic realm. This is unfortunate because we find, as a result, that many people are being prescribed anti-depressant and anti-psychotic drugs as the result of the indiscreet confessions of their paranormal experiences. The occult law, "to know...and be silent" has been broken. Due to a lack of discrimination, many people with extreme psychic experiences are condemned to the same fate. They are thought to have mental disorders and drugs are brought in to "normalize" them to become useful, non-disruptive consumers. We must not forget that also, due to greed or other selfish reasons, many are over-medicated by those who, under other circumstances, would have had more understanding.

The Kearney incident is typical of what can happen to a private individual in the United States today. Reinhold O. Schmidt, after telling authorities of his experiences with spacecraft, was committed to a mental institution. His release was obtained through the efforts of his family. Every avenue possible was exploited to support the charges of his personal lack of integrity and any personal mistakes he had made in the past, as a basis for discrediting his experiences.

The ability of man to travel psychically through space is described in this chapter, and Orfeo Angelucci has given a perfect description of his experience. Mr. Angelucci and all space fans will find in this chapter a thorough explanation of his experience, and the unexplained phenomena with which he had so many heart-breaking trials in trying to rationalize to the public. The public press has dismissed most of this type of literature as "sensational" and having no more reality than the recordings from a psychiatrist's couch. We hope this chapter will vindicate such courageous people as Orfeo Angelucci.

It is very essential that we should know something about the psychic realm, if for no other reason than that we may be able to avoid it. It is a semi-dark side of nature; nevertheless, it seems desirable for the reader to know the truth, although it may offend – or even frighten – some. The necessity for bringing up the subject is due, first, to the fact that people who take up this line of study are, for this very reason, in a position where they must contact very closely the psychic realm; and second, that humanity as a whole, in its evolutionary career, is now beginning to approach the psychic plane. The psychically advanced members of the human race have contacted it already, much to the detriment of some of them, and for these reasons the facts concerning the psychic realm should be revealed, even though these facts may arouse the enmity of those who have fallen under its deceptive influence.

DWELLERS OF THE THRESHOLD

We all have to face the "dwellers of the threshold" when we contact the psychic realm, and not only do the students of occultism have to meet them, but the whole human race, as it develops, must come in contact with this realm. There are many types of inhabitants on the psychic plane. You will recall that we have discussed how the objective and subjective minds were united and became men. We also saw that a battle has to be waged between the two minds when the subjective awakens and undertakes the control of its affairs. In the course of time the fight between these two minds of man becomes so tremendous that there sometimes comes a cleavage between the two, and the subjective conquers its lower mind, making it a tractable vehicle. But sometimes the objective mind is stronger than the subjective, and refuses to be governed. It is then that a separation comes, and the objective mind, strong in its victory, becomes detached from its subjective. The subjective, being unwilling to remain under the domination of its objective mind, leaves it to its ultimate destruction and goes back into the Infinite, to rest until another Cosmic Day comes and it can start forth with a new objective mind.

You are experiencing the psychic realm all the time. Your body is like an antenna and is constantly picking up signals. The problem is, we fail to notice.

This rebellious objective mind is so strong that it may continue to occupy its physical body for several years after the separation, and goes through the remainder of that life the semblance of a human, but devoid of moral character. When it excarnates and its body is destroyed, it may or may not be strong enough to reincarnate. If it does then it will be of an intellectual animal nature, with no conception of morality or spirituality. In case it is not strong enough to reincarnate, it becomes a "dweller upon the threshold"– an individualized consciousness upon the subjective side of life, invisible to the physical eyes of men but active in its destructive desires and purposes. It becomes one of the many unpleasant forces or entities with which we have to come in contact when we reach the psychic realm.

But there are many other denizens of that plane. Every soul that excarnates, if it is not able to pass into the planes beyond, by reason of its under development and strong animal nature, must remain there and become a dweller on the threshold also. Then there is the third class of dwellers known as "elementals." These centers of consciousness and force have not developed to the point where incarnation is possible for them. They are the fairies, undines, goblins, and brownies. These entities are not fanciful creations of the imagination, as many persons suppose, for they do exist in elemental forms; and when they have been seen and described by persons whose psychic sense made them conscious of them, they were realities. Man cannot imagine that which does not exist, for no one man can make a picture of the non-existent.

Elementals are created by the thoughts of men. As man develops he thinks more and more forcefully, and as he thinks, he creates little centers of consciousness within Divine Mind. These centers of consciousness assume different forms according to the quality of the thoughts which created them. These centers which man creates draw strength and vitality from him, and remain within the photosphere of their creator. But since whatever is created upon the mental plane must, in the course of time, objectivize, or embody itself in a physical form, at some time these elementals must take on material bodies of some kind. There are the so-called good and bad elementals, and when they become embodied in animal or insect form, that form will be assumed which corresponds to the nature of the consciousness seeking embodiment. Should the elemental be of a mischievous, destructive nature, then it was the result of mischievous, destructive thoughts of man, and will take upon itself the form of an animal or insect that will annoy man and destroy his property, because it is a law that whatsoever man sends forth mentally must and will return to him.

THOUGHT-FORMS

We often hear the expression that "thoughts are things," although most people do not realize the truth of this statement. In fact, it is a difficult thing for most of us to have any clear idea as to exactly what kind of a "thing" a thought really is. All students know that what is known as the "aura" of man is the outer part of the cloudlike substance of his higher bodies, interpenetrating each other and extending beyond his physical body, which is the smallest of all, and the subject of auras will be taken up in a later chapter. However, two of these bodies, the mental and desire bodies, are those which are chiefly concerned with the appearance of what we call thought-forms.

The mental body is composed of innumerable combinations of the subtle matter of the mental plane, and this body is more or less refined in its constituents and organized more or less fully for its functions, according to the stage of intellectual development at which the man himself has arrived. The mental body is an object of great beauty, and delicacy and rapid motion of its particles causing it to have the appearance of living iridescent light. Of course, this beauty becomes an extraordinarily radiant and breath-taking loveliness as the intellect becomes more highly evolved, and is employed chiefly on pure and sublime topics.

Now, every thought gives rise to a set of correlated vibrations in the matter of this body, accompanied by a marvelous play of color, such as the spray of a waterfall when the sunlight strikes it- which is only a poor comparison, since there is no way in which to describe the degree of color, or the vivid delicacy. The body, under this impulse, throws off a vibrating portion of itself, shaped by the nature of the vibrations, much in the same way that figures are made by sand on a disc vibrating to a musical note -- and this gathers from the surrounding atmosphere matter like itself in fineness, from the elemental essence of the mental world.

We then have a pure and simple thought-form, and it is a living entity of intense activity animated by the one idea that generated it. If it is made of the finer kinds of matter, it will be of great power and energy, and may be used as a most powerful agent when directed by a strong and steady will. When the man's energy flows outwards toward external objects of desire, or is occupied in passionate and emotional activities, this energy works in a less subtle order of matter than the mental, or in that of the astral world.

What is known as the desire-body is composed of astral matter, and it forms the most prominent part of the aura in the undeveloped man. Where the man is of a gross type, the desire-body is of the denser matter of the astral plane, and is dull in color, consisting mostly of browns, dirty greens and dull reds. Through this flash various characteristic colors, as his passions are excited. A man of a higher type has his desire-body composed of the finer qualities of astral matter, with the colors which ripple over and through it being fine and clear in hue. While it is less delicate and less radiant than the mental body, nevertheless it forms a beautiful object, and as selfishness is eliminated all of the duller and heavier shades disappear.

This desire, or astral, body gives rise to a second class of entities, similar in their general constitution to the thought-forms already described, though limited to the astral plane, and generated by the mind under the dominion of the animal nature. These are caused by the activity of the lower mind throwing itself out through the astral body, or the mind dominated by desire. Vibrations in the body of desire, or astral body, are in this case set up – and under these, this body throws off a vibrating portion of itself, shaped, as in the previous case, by the nature of the vibrations, and this attracts to itself some of the appropriate elemental essence of the astral world.

Such a thought-form has for its body this elemental essence, and for its animating soul the desire or passion which threw it forth; according to the amount of mental energy combined with this desire or passion will be the force of the thought-form. These, like those belonging to the mental plane, are called artificial elementals, and they are by far the most common, as few thoughts of ordinary men and women are un-tinged with desire, passion or emotion.

Each definite thought produces two effects – a radiating vibration and a floating form. The thought itself appears to the person with clairvoyant sight as a vibration in the mental body, and this may be either simple or complex. If the thought itself is absolutely simple, then there is only one rate of vibration, and only one type of mental matter will be strongly affected. The mental body, you see, is composed of matter of several degrees of density, which we can arrange in classes, according to the sub-planes, and each of the sub-planes has many subdivisions.

So you see that there are many varieties of this mental matter, and each one has its own special and appropriate rate of vibration, to which it seems most accustomed, so that it will readily respond to it, and tends to return to it as soon as possible when it has been forced away from it by a strong rush of thought or feeling. When a sudden wave of some emotion sweeps over a man, for example, his astral body is thrown into violent agitation, and the original colors are, for the time, almost obscured by the flush of scarlet or blue or dull green which corresponds with the rate of vibration of that particular emotion. This change is only temporary, of course, and passes off in a few seconds, and the astral body rapidly resumes its usual condition.

However, every rush of feeling such as this produces a permanent effect; it always adds a little of its hue to the normal coloring of the astral body, so that every time the man yields himself to a certain emotion, it becomes easier for him to yield himself to it again, because his astral body is getting into the habit of vibrating at that special rate. The majority of human thoughts are by no means simple. Absolutely pure affection, of course, does exist – but we very often find it tinged with pride, or with selfishness, jealousy, or animal passion. This means that at least two separate vibrations appear both in the mental and astral bodies- and frequently more than two. The radiating vibration, therefore, will be quite complex, and the resultant thought-form will show several colors instead of only one.

These radiating vibrations, like all others in nature, become less powerful according to the distance from their source. And, like other vibrations, they tend to reproduce themselves whenever the opportunity is offered to them, and so whenever they strike upon another mental body they tend to set it off, or charge it, in their own rate of motion. That is, from the point of view of the man whose mental body is touched by these waves, they tend to produce in his mind thoughts of the same type as those which had previously arisen in the mind of the thinker who sent forth the waves.

The distance to which such thought waves penetrate, and the force and persistency with which they are able to strike against the mental bodies of others, depends upon the strength and clearness of the original thought. In this way, the thinker is in the same position as a man who is speaking. The voice of the speaker sets in motion waves of sound in the air, which radiate from him in all directions, carrying his message to all who are within hearing distance, and the distance to which his voice can penetrate depends, of course, upon its power and upon the clearness of his enunciation. Now in just this same way the forceful thought will carry much further than the weak and undecided thought; but clearness and definiteness are of even greater importance here than is strength. And, in addition, just as the speaker's voice may fall upon "deaf" ears, where men are already engaged in business or pleasure, so can a mighty wave of thought sweep past without affecting the mind of the man, if he is already deeply engrossed in some other line of thought.

Another important fact is that this radiating vibration conveys the character of the thought, but not its subject. For instance, if a Hindu is sitting in rapt devotion to Krishna, the waves of feeling which pour forth from him will stimulate devotional feeling in all those who come under their influence – although in the case of someone who follows Islam, the devotion is to Allah, and in the case of a Christian, the devotion is to Jesus. A man thinking keenly upon some high subject pours out from himself vibrations which will stir up thought at a similar level in others, but they in no way suggest to those others the special subject of his thought.

Naturally they act with special force or vigor upon those minds already in the habit of sending out vibrations of a similar character, but they have some effect on every mental body against which they strike, so that their tendency is to awaken the power of higher thought in those to whom it has not yet become a custom. So actually, every man who thinks along high lines is really doing "missionary work," even though he may be entirely unconscious of it.

THE ELEMENTAL ESSENCE

And now we come to the second effect of thought, the creation of a definite form, the discussion of which is the purpose of this particular writing. Most of us are acquainted with the idea of the "elemental essence," that strange, half-intelligent life which surrounds us in all directions, vivifying the matter of the mental and astral planes. This matter, which is animated, responds very readily to the influence of human thought, and every impulse sent out, either from the mental body or from the astral body of a man, immediately clothes itself in a temporary vehicle of this vitalized matter. Therefore, such a thought or impulse becomes, for the time, a kind of living creature, the thought-force being the soul, and the vitalized matter the body. H. P. Blavatsky called this quickened matter, "astral or mental matter ensouled by the monadic essence at the stage of one of the elemental kingdoms"; however, for simplicity's sake we might call it elemental essence, and some students simply refer to the thought-form as "an elemental."

There can be infinite variety in the color and shape of such elementals or thought-forms, for each thought draws around it the matter which is appropriate for its expression, and sets that matter into vibration in harmony with its own, so that the character of the thought decides its color. If a man's thought or feeling is directly connected with someone else, the resultant thought-form moves towards that person and discharges itself upon his astral and mental bodies. If the man's thought is about himself, or is based on a personal feeling, as the vast majority of thoughts are, it hovers around its creator, and is always ready to react upon him whenever he is for a moment in a passive condition.

As an example, a man who yields to thoughts of impurity may forget all about them when he is engaged in the daily routine of his business, even though the resultant forms are hanging around him in a heavy cloud, because his attention is otherwise directed, and his astral body is therefore not capable of being impressed, at the time, by any other rate of vibration than its own. But when the marked vibration slackens, and the man rests after work, and leaves his mind blank as regards definite thought, he more than likely will feel the vibration of impurity stealing upon him. If the consciousness of the man is to any extent awakened he may notice this and, especially if he is a Christian, he will get down on his knees and cry that he is being tempted "by the devil." But the truth is, the temptation comes from outside only in appearance, since it is nothing but the natural reaction upon him of his own thought-forms.

Therefore, each man travels through space enclosed in a cage of his own building, surrounded by a mass of the forms created by his habitual thoughts. Through this medium he looks out upon the world, and naturally he sees everything tinged with its predominant colors, and all the rates of vibration which reach him from without are more or less modified by its rate. In other words, he sees in others the things which are in his own mind; for instance, if he is overly suspicious of others, he feels, of course, that everyone is suspicious of him; if he is constantly thinking of ways to cheat others, he sees all others in that light, and feels that everyone he knows has an ulterior motive in being friendly with him, and that is, of course, to either steal from him outright or to cheat him out of something. And so until the man learns complete control of thought and feeling, he sees nothing as it really is, since all of his observations must be made through this medium, which distorts and colors everything, like badly made glass.

If the thought-form is neither definitely personal nor especially aimed at someone else, it simply floats, detached, in the atmosphere, all the time radiating vibrations similar to those originally sent forth by its creator. If it does not come into contact with any other mental body, this radiation gradually exhausts its store of energy, and in that case the form falls to pieces. But if it succeeds in awakening sympathetic vibration in any mental body near at hand, an attraction is set up, and the thought-form is usually absorbed by that mental body. Thus we see that the influence of the thought-form is by no means as far-reaching as that of the original vibration, but insofar as it acts, it acts with much greater precision.

THE COLORS OF THOUGHT-FORMS

What it produces in the mind-body which it influences is not merely a thought of an order similar to that which gave it birth, but it actually is the same thought. The radiation may affect thousands, and stir up in them thoughts on the same level as the original (such as Hitler's fanatic speeches) and yet it may happen that no one of them will be identical with that original. The thought-form can affect only a few, but in those few cases it will reproduce exactly the initiatory idea. And so we come to the conclusions, both from reasoning out and from the clairvoyant observation, that it is the quality of the thought which determines the color of the thought-form; it is the nature of the thought which determines the form itself, and the definiteness of the thought determines the clearness of the outline.

Red, of all shades from lurid brick-red to brilliant scarlet, indicates anger; brutal anger will show as flashes of lurid red from dark brown clouds, while the anger of righteous indignation is a vivid scarlet, by no means unbeautiful, although it gives an unpleasant thrill. The dark and unpleasant red of the color known as "dragon's blood," shows animal passion and sensual desire of various kinds. Clear brown (almost a burnt sienna) shows avarice; hard, dull brown-grey is a sign of selfishness, a color which is very common. Deep heavy grey shows depression, while a livid pale grey is associated with fear; grey-green is a sign of deceit, while brownish-green (usually flecked with points and flashes of scarlet) shows jealousy.

Green seems to always denote adaptability; in the lowest case, when mingled with selfishness, this adaptability becomes deceit. At a later stage, when the color becomes purer as the person becomes individualized, it can mean the wish to be all things to all men, even though it may be solely for the sake of becoming popular and having a "good reputation" with them. In its still higher, more delicate and more luminous aspect, it shows the divine power of sympathy, or compassion. Affection always expresses itself in shades of crimson and rose; a full, clear carmine shows a strong, healthy affection of normal type. If stained heavily with brown-grey, a selfish and grasping feeling is indicated, while pure rose shows that absolutely unselfish love which is possible only to higher natures. It passes from the dull crimson of animal-love to the most exquisite shades of lovely delicate rose, as the love becomes purified from all selfish elements and flows out in wider and wider circles of generous, impersonal tenderness and compassion to all who are in need. With a touch of the blue of devotion in it, this can express a strong realization of the universal Brotherhood of humanity.

Deep orange signifies pride or ambition, and the various shades of yellow denote intellect or intellectual gratification, dull yellow ochre implying selfish purposes, a clear gamboge showing a distinctly higher type, and the pale luminous primrose yellow being a sign of the highest and most unselfish use of intellectual power, the pure reason directed to spiritual ends. The different shades of blue all indicate religious feeling, and range through all hues, from the dark brown-blue of selfish devotion, the pallid grey-blue of fetish worship tinged with fear, up to the rich, deep, clear color of heart-felt adoration, and the beautiful pale azure of the highest form, which implies self-renunciation and union with the Divine. The devotional thought of an unselfish heart is very lovely, like the deep blue of a summer sky. Through such clouds of blue will often shine out golden stars of great brilliancy, darting upwards like a shower of sparks. A mixture of affection and devotion is manifested by a tint of violet, and the more delicate shades of this show the capacity of absorbing and responding to a high and beautiful ideal. The brilliancy and depth of the colors are usually a measure of the strength and the activity of the feeling.

We will now consider the matter in which these forms are generated. For example, if a thought is purely intellectual and impersonal, such as a thinker attempting to solve a problem in algebra or geometry, then the thought-form and the wave of vibration will be confined entirely to the mental plane. If, however, the thought be of a spiritual nature, if it is tinged with love and aspiration, and a deep unselfish feeling, it will rise upwards from the mental plane, and will borrow much of the splendor and glory of the spiritual level. In such a case its influence is exceedingly powerful, and every such thought is a mighty force for good, which cannot but produce a decided effect upon all mental bodies within reach, if they contain any quality at all which is capable of response. On the other hand, if the thought has in it something of self, or of personal desire, then its vibration at once turns downward, and it draws around itself a body of astral matter in addition to its clothing of mental matter. Such a thought-form is capable of acting upon the astral bodies of other men, as well as their minds, so that it not only raises thought within them, but can also stir up their feelings.

Thought-forms can be grouped into three classes, the first of which is that which takes the image of the thinker. For instance, when a man thinks of himself as in some distant place, or wishes earnestly to be in that place, he makes a thought-form in his own image which appears there. Such a form is sometimes seen by others, and is sometimes taken for the astral body, or "apparition" of the man himself. *There are many historically recorded facts about apparitions. Some of the famous ones are, of course, legendary – such as The Flying Dutchman, a sailing ship – but the poet Goethe's vision of a horseman is well recorded. The Baroness Lotte von Strahl saw the "ghosts" of Rockingham Castle, namely Lord Watson and his daughter. The first United States citizen to be on active service in World War II, Commander Charles M. Cree, later British Vice

Consul at Houston, Texas, states that his father and mother, separated for the moment due to family illness, saw the same apparition at approximately the same time.

In such cases, either the person seeing this must have enough clairvoyance, for the time, to be able to observe the astral shape, or the thought-form must have sufficient strength to materialize itself; that is, to draw around itself temporarily a certain amount of physical matter. The thoughts which generate such forms must be very strong ones, and they employ a larger proportion of the matter of the mental body, so that although the form is small and compressed when it leaves the thinker, it draws around itself a considerable amount of astral matter, and usually expands to life-size before it appears at its destination. This, however, is not the same thing as projecting the consciousness, and accounts for the many times in which the person will say, "I saw you quite clearly," while the person addressed is quite surprised, since he was not in the least aware of having "projected" the image.

The second class of thought-forms is those which take the image of some material object. When a man thinks of his friend, he forms within his mental body a minute image of that friend, which often passes outward and usually floats suspended in the air before him. In the same way, if he thinks of a room, a house, or a landscape, tiny images of these things are formed within the mental body, and afterwards externalized. This, then, is the principle of the crystal ball, and, in addition, people are capable of "seeing" their past incarnations because something has unlocked the door to their memory; the mental body forms the image and projects it, like a moving picture on a screen.

The third class is the thought-form which takes a form entirely its own, expressing its inherent qualities in the matter which it draws around it. Only thought-forms of this class can be usefully described for the purpose we wish, since everyone knows what a house or a landscape looks like. In this third group are the forms natural to the mental or astral planes, and they usually manifest themselves upon the astral plane, as the vast majority of them are expressions of feeling, as well as of thought. Beautiful thought-forms can be created in definite meditation by those who, through long practice, have learned how to think.

Thought-forms directed toward individuals produce definitely marked effects, these effects being either partially reproduced in the aura of the recipient, and so increasing the total result, or else repelled from it. A thought of love and of desire to protect, directed strongly towards some beloved object, creates a form which goes to the person thought of, and remains in his aura as a shielding and protecting agent; it will seek all opportunities to serve, and all opportunities to defend – not by a conscious and deliberate action, but by a blind following out of the impulse impressed upon it, and it will strengthen friendly forces that come into contact with the aura, and weaken the unfriendly ones. In group healing, the thoughts sent by a well-organized group of metaphysical healers can often produce amazing results.

In cases in which good or evil thoughts are projected at individuals, those thoughts, if they are to directly fulfill their mission, must find in the aura of the object to which they are sent the materials capable of responding sympathetically to their vibrations. Any combination of matter can only vibrate within certain definite limits, and if the thought-forms be outside the limits within which the aura is capable of vibrating, it cannot affect that aura at all. It consequently rebounds from it, and does this with a force proportionate to the energy with which it struck against it. This is why it is said that a "pure heart and mind" are the best protectors against any assault, for such a pure heart and mind will construct an astral and mental body of fine and subtle materials, and these bodies cannot respond to the vibrations which demand coarse and dense matter. If an evil thought, then, projected with malefic intent, strikes such a body, it can only rebound from it, and is flung back with all its own energy. It then flies backwards along the magnetic line of least resistance, that over which it has just come, and strikes its projector, who has matter in his astral and mental bodies similar to that of the thought-form he has generated. It is then thrown into responding vibrations, and he suffers the destructive effects he had intended to cause to another.

This is the meaning of the expression that "curses (and blessings) come home to roost." And we can also see the very serious effects of hating and suspecting a good and highly advanced man; the thought-forms sent against him cannot injure him, and they rebound against their projectors, shattering them mentally, morally and physically. As long as any of the coarser kinds of matter connected with evil and selfish thoughts remain in a person's body, he is open to attack from those who wish him evil. But when he has perfectly eliminated these by self-purification, his haters cannot injure him.

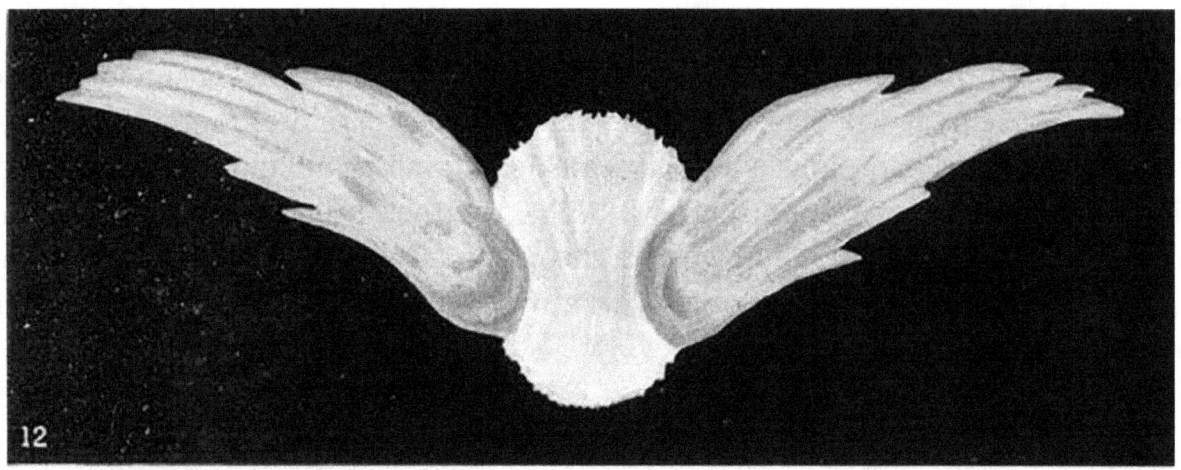

Thought-Form named "Peace and Protection." This is a thought of love and peace, protection and benediction, sent forth by one who has the power and has earned the right to bless. From the 1901 book *Thought-Forms* **by Annie Besant and C.W. Leadbeater.**

We will now attempt to describe some of the various thought-forms which have been seen by a clairvoyant. There are the vague and undirected thought-forms which are rather like small clouds, shapeless and formless, which come from people like small colored puffs of smoke. We have often observed this type coming from the family cat. When she has been sufficiently fed and petted and loved, and is at peace with her cat-sized world, we have observed small rose-colored puffs, rather like gradually enlarging shells, radiating slowly outward from her body as she purrs with contentment, feeling her animal pleasure and, to her, what is affection. These puffs fade into invisibility at the distance of a few feet from their small creator.

There are many types of emotion, and many colors of these cloud-shaped vague thought-forms, but they are for the most part not especially keen or strong feelings. We may see one which has the carmine color of love (not the evolved rose-color, but nevertheless what is termed as love or affection at that stage of evolution) – but it will be tinged with the dull, hard brown-grey of selfishness. Then we see that the affection which is indicated is closely connected with satisfaction at favors already received, and there is a lively anticipation of others to come in the near future. In the case of definite affection, for instance, which is truly meant, instead of the vague cloud we will see more of a definite shape. There seems to take place the formation within the astral body of large crimson coils or vortices, lined with living light. These thought-forms of intense affection are almost immediately ejected toward the object of the feeling.

The clearness of the color shows the purity of the emotion. The precision of the outline shows the evidence of power, and vigorous purpose. To intentionally radiate or generate affection, to make an effort to pour oneself forth in love to all beings, can produce a beautiful radiating form. All of these thought-forms are constantly in motion. They are exceedingly hard to describe, and the definite and intentional ones from a highly evolved nature widen out like ripples when a pebble drops into a pool, seeming to have an inexhaustible fountain welling from the center. Now usually there does not exist in the mind of the creator the exact shape that this thought will take, although some subconscious thought may determine this. A thought of love, peace and protection may appear in this manner, with rose-colored "wing-like" projections, and a lovely golden center, the intellect guiding it appearing and shining forth like sunlight. Possibly a long, long time ago some clairvoyant observed this, giving rise to the expression that "thoughts have wings."

There is also what might be called "grasping animal affection," if this term makes any kind of sense, or such a feeling deserves the name of affection. It is a most unpleasant color, lurid with sensuality, and deadened with selfishness. The form is characteristic, having curving hooks protruding from it which are never seen except when there is a strong craving for personal possession. This type of thought- form usually does not throw itself out boldly, but projects halfheartedly from the astral body.

In devotion of prayer, self-renunciation may take the lovely form of a beautiful and strangely-shaped "flower." The "flowers" produced do not take the form of flowers we would see on the physical plane, those to which we are accustomed, but this is the best term we can think of to describe them. The "petals" seem to unfold with a beautiful living light. There are also beautiful cone or spire-shaped forms, which rush by quickly – the outrush into manifestation of a grand emotion which is rooted deep in the knowledge of fact. The person who feels such devotion as this is one who knows in whom he has believed, and who has taught himself how to think. They are usually a pure blue color, filled with the living light. It is possible to see also the result of such a thought – the response of the Logos to the appeal made to him, the truth which underlies the highest and best part of the persistent belief in an answer to prayer. This is usually seen (when it is seen at all) as a pouring down, or "coming in" of beautifully colored rays of light. On each plane of His solar system our Logos pours forth His light, His power and His life, and naturally it is on the higher planes that this outpouring of divine strength can be given most fully.

The descent from each plane to that next below it means almost paralyzing limitation – a limitation entirely incomprehensible except to those who have experienced the higher possibilities of human consciousness. Thus, the divine life flows forth with incomparably greater fullness on the mental plane than on the astral – and even its glory at the mental level is indescribably transcended by that of the Buddhic plane. Normally, each of these mighty waves of influence spreads about its appropriate plane horizontally, so to speak, but it does not pass into the obscuration of a plane lower than that for which it was intended originally. There are, though, conditions under which the grace and strength peculiar to a higher plane may in a measure be brought down to a lower one, and may spread abroad there with a wonderful effect. This seems possible only when a special channel is for the moment opened; and that work must be done from below, and by the effort of man.

In other words, it has been explained that whenever man's thought or feeling is selfish, the energy which it produces moves in a close curve, and inevitably returns and expends itself on its own level – but when the thought or feeling is absolutely unselfish, its energy rushes forth in an open curve, and does not return in the ordinary sense, but pierces through into the plane above – because only in that higher condition, with its additional dimension, can it find room for its expansion. But in thus breaking through, such a thought or feeling holds open a door (symbolically speaking) of dimension equivalent to its own diameter, and thus furnishes the channel through which the divine force appropriate to the higher plane can pour itself into the lower with marvelous results, not only for the thinker, but for others.

The result of the descent of divine life is a very great strengthening and uplifting of the maker of the channel, and the spreading all about him of a most powerful and beneficent influence. This effort has often been called an answer to a prayer, and has been attributed by devout religious people (who have had religion "pounded" into them) to what they call a "special interposition of Almighty Providence," instead of to the unerring action of the great and immutable Law.

A significant fact is that some very complex thought-forms can be exactly imitated by the action of certain mechanical forces. With our present knowledge it would be unwise to attempt a solution of the fascinating problem presented by these remarkable resemblances; however we are now obtaining a glimpse across the threshold of a mighty mystery – for we begin to realize that if by certain thoughts we produce a form which has been duplicated by the processes of nature, we have at least a presumption that these forces of nature work along lines somewhat similar to the action of those thoughts. And, since the universe itself is a mighty thought-form, called into existence by Deity, it may begin to be more clear to us now that tiny parts of it are also the thought-forms of minor entities engaged in the same work, and thus we approach a comprehension of what is meant by the three hundred and thirty million Devas of the Hindus.

Intellect is indicated by the shades of yellow, and of course there are many types. Vague intellectual pleasure would be shown by a cloud, and can be mixed with other colors, of course. If the objects are selfish, it is a deeper and duller tint, when the intellect is directed chiefly into lower channels. In the astral or mental body of the average man in business, it would show itself as yellow ochre, while pure intellect devoted to the study of philosophy or mathematics appears frequently to be golden, and this rises gradually to a beautiful clear and luminous lemon or primrose yellow when a powerful intellect is being employed absolutely unselfishly for the benefit of humanity. Most yellow thought-forms are clearly outlined, and a vague cloud of yellow is rare. It indicates intellectual pleasure; the appreciation of the result of ingenuity, or the delight felt in clever workmanship. It can arise from the pleasure an ordinary man derives from the contemplation of a picture which has been painted, or from delight in hearing music which especially appeals to him.

The determination to solve a problem – the intention to know, and understand, shows itself as somewhat of a serpentine form. These are often seen during an argument, or especially when intelligent questions are asked at a lecture. When the answers are not satisfactory to the inquirer, who may feel that his problem is being evaded by the lecturer, his resolution to obtain a full and thorough answer to his question often results in somewhat of a cork-screw shape in the thought-form. Forms similar to these are constantly created by ordinary and idle, frivolous curiosity, but as there is no intellect involved, in that case the color is no longer yellow, but usually closely resembles that of decaying meat.

Another manifestation of desire is the ambition for place, or power. The ambitious quality is shown by a rich, deep orange color, and the desire, of course, is shown by hooks or claws. If the thought is a good and a pure one of its kind, it is clear orange – if it were base or selfish, there would be a darkening of the clear orange by dull reds, browns, or greys. Now of course a man who wishes place or power, not for his own sake, but from the conviction that he could do the work well and truly, and to the advantage of his fellow-men, would present a very pleasing and beautifully colored, although somewhat explosive, thought-form. In the case of purely selfish ambition, the thought-form could have a definite outline, but would, of course, be colored with a large stain of the brown-grey. Many are what we might call "floating" forms, and would be strongly indicative of general acquisitiveness -- the ambition to grasp for the self everything that is in sight. There could also be forms of the same general color, but the shape, such as a projectile with grasping claws, would indicate that the thought is rising steadily towards a definite object.

Murderous rage and sustained anger are shown in various forms, of course. They are an ugly brown and grey, mixed with lurid red. Jealous anger will show some green; a dash or two of orange would imply that someone's pride has been wounded. A thought of steady anger, intense and desiring vengeance, will show sharp, stiletto-pointed darts of red. In a less violent anger there may still be seen, coming from the cloud, definite flashes of anger ready to strike at those by whom the creator fancies himself to be injured.

An unpleasant thought-form is indicated by the dull brownish- green color of jealousy. They often take a snake-like form, with what would appear to be the head of the snake raised, indicating the eagerness with which the creator is watching the object of his jealousy. This remarkable resemblance to the snake with raised head symbolizes the fatuous attitude of the jealous person, keenly alert to discover signs of that which he, least of all, wishes to see. The moment he sees it, the form will change into the far more common one of the ugly cloud, where jealousy is mingled with anger.

Vague sympathy would be shown by a vague, of course, green cloud, but of a higher and purer shade of green. This would be, especially with an indistinct outline, the type which shows a general feeling of commiseration as might come over a man who read an account of a sad accident, or stood at the door of a hospital room looking in upon a very ill and suffering patient. This person is usually thinking, "how sad!", while a sharp and clearly definite disc of green is formed by the thought of the man who sees an accident and rushes over to see whether he can be of help to someone – in other words, active sympathy. The thought-forms of a highly developed person, especially those who actually direct them to those they love or wish to help, are so exceedingly beautiful that they defy any description, usually being pure sparks from one soul to another, and the colors, when they take color, are pure, vibrant, and electric. Their forms are difficult to be seen, since they vibrate so fast, and appear more as simply the brilliant darts of pure, living Light.

THE VERMIN OF OBSCENE THOUGHTS

Then there is still another kind of thought creations of men, which become embodied soon after they are born. These are the licentious, obscene thoughts of both sexes, which become the creeping, crawling bugs and vermin which infest untidy homes, low class hotels, and public houses. Then there are the biting, stinging thoughts, which embody themselves as flies, wasps and mosquitoes; and the poisonous thoughts, which become spiders and reptiles. These miserable creatures, born of man's lower mind, cannot use the atoms of a higher rate for vibration for their bodies, but must use those atoms with which they vibrate harmoniously. They gather up to the diseased atoms, the dirty atoms – those atoms which can no longer be used by men or beasts, and through those forms they express themselves upon the material plane. And thus man himself creates the destructive things of Earth which turn and wage war against him; for "God saw everything that He had made, and behold it was very good."

When an entity has attained a sufficient density within the subjective realm to be ready for embodiment, it has come to a point where it can have a direct influence upon human life, and then it reacts upon its creator according to the nature that was given it. When these elementals separate from the photosphere in which they were created, they often leave their creator, and impinge upon the auras of other persons. Sometimes they are utilized in magic, particularly in that form known as ceremonial magic, and students of occultism sometimes use them for the purpose of producing psychic phenomena. The transfer of material substances from one room to another, through closed doors and solid walls, or the disintegration and reintegration of so-called solid things is performed through utilizing these elemental forces of nature. Then there are the minds of animals, or animal souls, which have been embodied, excarnated, and have passed on to the subjective side of nature to await another opportunity to become re-embodied. These subjective entities still possess all of their animal propensities, but have no physical means of expressing them, and they belong to the vast multitude of dwellers on the threshold.

In Catholicism, this "threshold" is known as Purgatory; in Protestantism it is Hades, or the place for departed spirits. It is the sidereal realm of the medieval mystic; it is the astral, or psychic plane of the modern mystic and theosophist, and it is the first plane of the spiritualist, the plane for earth-bound souls. It is here, interpenetrating this physical world of ours. This threshold is the first of the subjective planes, and is called the threshold because it is the crossing over point from objective life into subjective life, and it is the doorway through which egos re-enter life. All souls must pass through it, but the more highly developed ones stay there but a very short time, and never a moment after they are liberated from their physical bodies. This is one of the reasons why occultists advance cremation of the physical body, because by this process the man in a few moments is free to go to the plane where he belongs, instead of being chained to his body on the threshold for weeks, months, or years, as the case may be. Souls are magnetically bound to their bodies, and until the "silver cord is loosened", they cannot be free.

As man's vibrations are raised, he necessarily contacts with this first subjective realm; and the influence of the four classes of entities, previously mentioned and popularly known as the psychic forces of nature, are exerted upon him. The unconscious sensitive is always susceptible to influences which produce moods that other persons do not have. At times he feels great depressions, fears impending calamities, and is influenced in various ways by the denizens of the next plane. And when an excarnated objective mind which has lost its higher mind finds a sensitive person whom it can control in mind and body, it immediately commences to manage his affairs. It enjoys by proxy, as it were, the intoxicating liquors that it forces its victim to drink. It gratifies its lust by controlling its victim, and compelling him to sin. It revenges itself, through its ignorant victim, upon persons whom it hates.

The denizens of the next plane, and especially the excarnated minds of depraved men and women, and the detached objective minds, utilize mankind for the purpose of vicarious enjoyment. A drunkard does not lose his love for liquor when he leaves his physical body.

There is nothing in the process of the change called "death" which changes character. It is natural that a drunkard should wish to enjoy what he considers the pleasure of his drinking, and so he selects a subject that he can influence. This sensitive, whose will is not yet strong enough to resist this strange influence which is thrown upon him, yields to the temptation and is overpowered. He indulges what he believes to be his own appetite for liquor, and the more he drinks the more he wants. When he is overcome with the fumes of liquor he is crowded out of his body by the controlling entity, who takes possession of it and enjoys a vicarious drunk at the expense of his sensitive victim. A love for gambling, intense sex desire, civic wrongs, and all kinds of crime are often traceable to what used to be referred to as "spirit control". When we read of a horrible murder or crime being committed by some man who declares that "God spoke" and told him to do it, we may be sure that the real cause was just behind the scenes, and the crime was instigated by a dweller on the threshold. *Life magazine* carried an article on the UFO mystery, including a story and "cartoon" showing "beings" floating around, invisible in space, as described by a psychic.

Since this first subjective plane interpenetrates this physical world of ours, it is at first incredible to the student who develops clairvoyant sight that there can be such throngs and crowds of beings upon that plane, while incarnated souls are moving about them utterly unconscious of their existence. When studied with clairvoyant sight, there appear to be thousands of beings, jostling and pushing each other about; some playing pranks, some quarreling. And the souls of animals run about, following both incarnated and excarnated beings, and each other – large and small dogs, kittens, cats and rats, and often monkeys, who evidently had been someone's pets. In the country the souls of cows and horses and sheep may be seen mingling with the incarnated herds or flocks of their kind, and it seems that the first subjective plane is as greatly crowded with the souls of animals as with human souls.

In the fields it may be noticed that the female animals are the greatest centers of attraction for the disembodied animal souls of their kind; and the cause of this is the possibility of rebirth or reincarnation for the animals who are being drawn again into physical life. They are attracted to the female animals more than to the males because it is through them, as mothers, that they may again be able to gain physical expression. And what is true with the animals is also true with humans. Some women, especially those who are at an age and in a condition where motherhood is possible are surrounded by disembodied egos who are ready for rebirth.

THE REALM OF DENSE SHADOWS

There are places that for unknown reasons, seem to attract the lower vibrations of lust, greed, and narcissistic thoughts. These places are the realms of dense shadows, which darken some places to what resembles twilight, even though it is broad daylight. The mental atmosphere in those places vibrates at a rate of which the clairvoyant is conscious of as shadows. These places create mental cesspools or vortices of gross vibrations which draw into them, by their attracting power, such disembodied entities or souls that not only prefer darkness rather than light, but they actually create darkness by the density of their thought vibrations.

In every home, rich and poor alike, there is much suffering, but there is happiness too. In every class there are individuals who are positively good, who live up to their highest ideals and their homes are filled with bright and uplifting vibrations, and around such incarnated souls are the disembodied entities who are suggesting beautiful and inspirational thoughts to assist them in their work for themselves and others. In other homes, often where there is wealth and social prestige, there is degeneracy and drunkenness, and this condition applies equally well to each of the two extremes of society. Persons who have nothing to do, and those who would do nothing, are surrounded by disembodied entities of a like or worse nature than themselves, who suggest demoralizing thoughts which are accepted and acted upon. Nearly all of these disembodied entities are what are known as "earth-bound," and cannot pass to higher planes than the first subjective because their love for material things is greater than for spiritual qualities. They stay with the sensual because they love sensuality; and will eventually either reincarnate or sink lower because of their grossness.

There are semiconscious sensitives who are influenced by the denizens of the next plane. By semi-conscious sensitives we mean persons who have reached a point in their development where they are conscious of the existence of a psychic plane, but do not know the nature of it. They are conscious of psychic force, but do not know the nature of this force. Most persons, when they reach this point in their development, begin to investigate psychic phenomena immediately. A student of occultism who is a conscious sensitive is required to develop upon the mental plane before he is permitted to study the psychic realm.

He must first attain the proper poise and development by learning to think clearly. Then he is taught how to use Cosmic Forces, and to surround himself with protecting currents, before he is taught how to function upon the psychic plane. After this has been accomplished, he can look down upon the psychic realm, and can penetrate into it without fear of attracting to himself unpleasant companions, or getting into unfortunate or compromising situations.

THE DANGERS OF THE PSYCHIC REALM

It is impossible for ignorant or semi-ignorant persons to investigate the psychic realm without being more or less influenced by it and perhaps it will be well for us to examine the various classes of investigators and see something of the dangers to which they are subjected. The investigators of spiritualistic phenomena or spiritualism may be grouped in the first class. Spiritualism is necromancy, revamped and is a practice that has been inveighed against by those who knew the dangers attending it, and by those who wrote the sacred books, since mankind came upon this Earth. Its six chief aspects are automatic writing, inspirational writing, inspirational speaking, trance mediumship, independent slate writing, and materializing mediumship, all of which will be discussed in a later chapter. In all of these, passivity is the sine qua non of success, because mediumship is the end in view, and passivity is the means by which it is to be attained.

And after mediumship is attained, it simply means that this person has become an instrument through whom these excarnated, unattached objective minds and other denizens of the psychic plane may speak or write, or perform like clowns in a circus. These entities, many of them, have become detached from their own higher principle, and must live on someone in order that their existence may be prolonged. Because without its subjective, the objective mind slowly deteriorates, and after a time fades out. These ignorant or malicious lower minds impersonate our departed friends, and glibly give us instructions about our domestic and business matters. They advise us when and where to buy and sell stocks; they give us long lectures on religion, and advise us about the training of our children. Think, if you can, of someone such as Jack the Ripper giving a lecture on morality.

Sometimes these "angel guides," as they like to be called, aspire to fame and pose as Lincoln, Shakespeare, or Napoleon – forgetting that at the moment, at a dozen places in different cities of the world, alleged Lincolns, Shakespeares and Napoleons are doing the same thing. They urge sensitives to become mediums, and to organize "developing circles," in order that they may attach themselves to more and more people. And all the time we are studying under them and are worshipping at their séances, they are absorbing our magnetism and are ruining mentally, morally, physically – and often financially -- those persons who become their mediums. For mediumship soon becomes either possession or obsession, and both of these conditions lead to insanity. Hereafter the term "obsession" will be used to designate all cases where a human body is wholly or in part controlled by a disembodied entity.

An investigator of the psychic plane, of the first class, must either become a medium himself or use a medium for the purpose of studying that plane. In either case he is subjected to imposition relative to the cause of the phenomena obtained. It is a well-known fact that a large percentage of the communications received from so-called spirits are untrue, or of a nature one would not expect from the inhabitants of that plane. Mediumship usually leads eventually to insanity, or to the premature death of the medium. Even when there seems to be a controlling entity of a comparatively higher order than is usually found on that plane, there is necessarily a constant diminution of the medium's forces. And as the vital forces of the medium diminish, he becomes unreliable, and frequently has to resort to fraud and pretense in order to continue his exhibitions.

Anyone who knows anything about this subject is aware that there are sometimes genuine phenomena, but more often they are simulated. This will also be taken up with the discussion of "true" mediumship – the mediumship of those who work under the guidance of, and directly with, the Cosmic Masters rather than the so-called "spirits" or dwellers of the psychic realm. It is admitted by unprejudiced investigators that the majority of "spirit controls" are of a "low order." But this is explained by them in their statement that "like attracts like," and that mediums and investigators attract "spirits" of a nature kindred to themselves, which is not saying too much for the mediums and investigators.

The second class of investigators may be known as passive clairvoyants, or those persons who cultivate passive mediumship for the purpose of functioning upon the subjective plane. Such a clairvoyant permits an entity to enfold or envelope his body while it impresses a mental picture upon his mind, and then the medium describes the picture he sees. This is not true clairvoyance, because the entity that impresses the medium is responsible for the picture, and it may be nothing but a fanciful creation of its own. The medium has not seen a reality, but has looked at the mental creations of another – and when we consider the character of most controlling entities, we feel safe in saying that possibly their pictures may not be altogether reliable.

The third class of investigators may be called artificial clairvoyants, and this class is composed of crystal gazers, magic-mirror gazers, etc., who by these practices throw themselves into a self-induced semi-hypnosis. In this state or condition they become susceptible to psychical influences, and mentally impressed pictures are the result. Vanity, or the desire for money-making, is usually the cause for this kind of practice, rather than a desire for growth or development, and the dangers from psychic influences are fully as great as in the classes before mentioned.

But there is a true clairvoyance or seer-ship which depends upon two things – a well-developed subjective mind that rules its objective mind, and a peculiar physiological condition. Close to the center of the brain of every human being is situated a tiny organ called the pineal gland, and this is the chief center through which the mind must function, in order that he may possess the X-ray vision that enables him to look beyond the material plane, upon the inner or subjective planes of consciousness. This gland can be attuned to finer vibrations than register in any of our other senses, and these vibrations relate us to the inner worlds, or planes. The further study of the pineal gland, and of true clairvoyance itself, will be taken up in future chapters; however, we will state here that the student of occultism, at a certain point in his progress, is taught how to direct special cosmic currents of force into this gland, to enlarge and raise its vibrations. When this has been accomplished, the student can function upon the subjective plane by an effort of his will as easily and well as he can see on the objective plane by opening his physical eyes. With this class of clairvoyants there is no passivity or trance condition, but there is a conscious shifting of the consciousness from one plane to another; and it is according to the development of the man whether or not he is able to function upon many or few of the subjective planes of being.

The unattached student of Occultism is one without a Master or Teacher. He is one who knows of occult powers and forces, and longs to possess them, and he courageously faces the dangers without assistance. This great desire for growth leads him to seek quick development, which is natural. The great majority of people, when they first hear of occultism, and occult teachers, immediately want a teacher. Then they begin to think that they are developing rapidly in occultism, and when certain subjective influences come about and they feel their peculiar vibrations, they immediately conclude that a Master has come to teach and help them. And there is a fact concerning the Masters which it is absolutely necessary to clear up at this point, regardless of the effect it may have upon some of our readers.

The Masters have been grossly misrepresented by some who claim to be students of the Masters, to work with them, and even to be their representatives. They have been represented by some as constantly tapping all and sundry upon the shoulder, begging to teach them. They have been represented by others as playing practical jokes, quarrelling among themselves, and various other employments utterly unbecoming to a Master of Wisdom, and, we are sorry to say, they have been represented by some as fools.

We feel that it is necessary to state at this point that until a man has become, in heart and spirit, a Disciple, he has no existence for those who are Teachers of Disciples. And he becomes this by one method only – the surrender of his personal humanity. The Masters definitely do not beg people, good or bad, to be permitted to teach them-in fact, it is quite the reverse. A Disciple is recognized by a Master, after a long and arduous journey on the Path, in one way only– by his Light; the pure light of his soul shining from within him.

The subjective entities, wishing to gain control of ambitious students, impress them with the thought they love to entertain, and soon these students of occultism are under the influence, and perhaps under the absolute control, of the dwellers upon the threshold. No teacher of occultism will ever try to control you in mind or body. You are divine because you are a part of Deity, and therefore your body and your life are yours. A teacher has no more right to control your mind than he has to violate your body, and no student, teacher, or Master of occultism will ever attempt it. When you feel peculiar influences around you, or if you hear voices saying, "We have come to help you; you are progressing rapidly," you may know it is the dwellers of the threshold who are talking to you. All students of occultism, whether attached or unattached, are helped by the Great Ones, but only when they are earnestly trying to help themselves. They are never touched, or coerced, or worked upon subjectively.

The student who is studying sincerely along these deeper lines is always watched and will be helped when he deserves help. The student who declares that he is going to work out his own salvation; that he is going to develop, and uses the knowledge he has gained to live according to his ideal, is a Probationer. If he persists in this course for a period of seven years, he will draw to himself a teacher in physical form. That teacher may be a Master, an Adept, or an advanced student-but the teacher who is best suited to him in his development at that time. And during the seven years of probation, help will be given to him in various ways.

"When the student is ready, the Master will appear" – but it does not follow that everyone who thinks he is ready for the higher occult teachings is really prepared for them. A very great many students struggle on for a while, but are so badly beset by their old habits, and by the subjective entities that are aroused by the new order of things, and who immediately set about trying to drag these students back into their old habits of living, that the student finally gives up the struggle. Let those who desire to push on in their evolution take the attitude that they will not study the psychic forces at all, and they will not look for a Master in that realm of being; that they will begin work by building up character, and by practicing what has been taught, for the psychic realm can offer absolutely nothing of value. It is the higher and better knowledge that you can utilize that you should desire – the true occultism which teaches the laws of being.

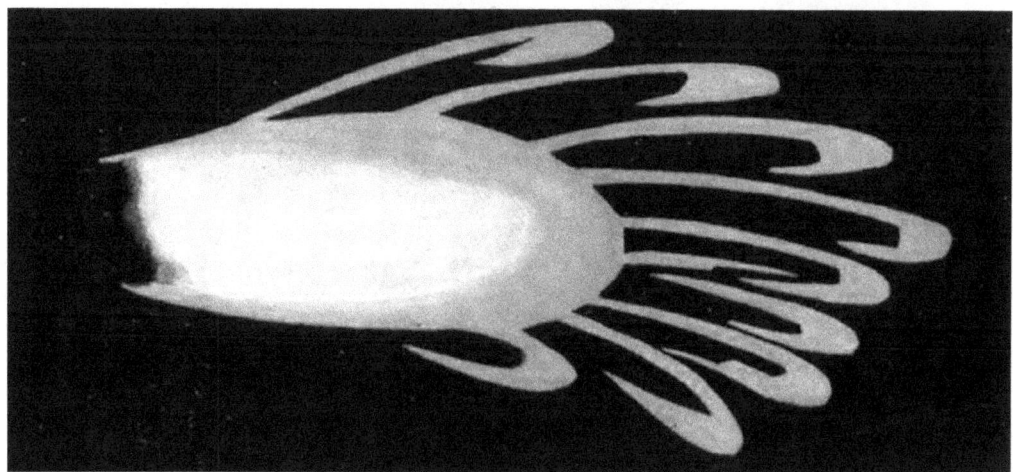

This Thought-Form is of desire—the ambition for place or power. From the 1901 book "*Thought-Forms*" **by Annie Besant and C.W. Leadbeater.**

It is not the physical body which visits the other planes, nor is it the objective mind; it is the Higher Self, the real person within, the subjective mind.

8

THE SELF – ITS RELATION TO SPACE AND MATTER

This chapter will be of a special interest to those people interested in the UFO mystery or what might be termed "outer space contact." This will explain the experiences of such writers and lecturers as Orfeo Angelucci, Howard Menger, and "Marla Baxter," who have had the experience of what might be termed "bi-location." We do not wish to go into the argumentative aspects of their experiences, but merely wish to show that Orfeo Angelucci, as an example, has experienced this "zombie-like" condition and has honestly reported it in his book, *"The Secret of the Saucers."*

The phenomenon of being able to distinguish between subjective and objective experiences is not uncommon with many of the so-called "space contactees." We sincerely hope that this chapter will help vindicate many of the people who have been subject not only to public ridicule, but also threats to their personal safety, by those who believe they should be committed to institutions for their mental health. In closing, we may state that it would be well if every practicing psychiatrist could read this entire book before passing judgment upon those whom he does not completely understand, for, as it says in the Bible, "Judge not, that ye be not judged."

As we have stated before, in occultism and in the attainment of Adeptship there are no shortcuts. The conditions which are described here must be fulfilled, because real knowledge of the higher worlds will not be revealed otherwise. Those who will not go through the spiritual training and learn the foundations of the science may develop certain psychic powers-but they are likely to perceive the spiritual world inaccurately and untruly.

The one great handicap in developing the power of perception is impatience. If you do not go through step by step, you are likely to develop the spiritual organs wrongly. No one with defective eyes can depend upon his sight- and no one with defective spiritual perception can depend on his perceptions. The spiritual organs must be built on a sound foundation. To immoral persons the spiritual vision is always confused and clouded; their perceptions will never be clear, and will never be of much value, so it is really just a waste of time for such persons to try to develop true seership. The only good it would do them would be that they would eventually realize that their actions and deeds were interfering with their development, and in time they would correct them.

Right living and right thinking will be very beneficial. The human thought, if used energetically with inner force, can comprehend more than is generally supposed to be possible. The reason for this is that in thought there is an inner essence which is in connection with the supersensible world. Most people are not conscious of this connection, because they know nothing of the "sixth sense". They receive knowledge from the supersensible world without knowing it – and they would deny the possibility of knowledge coming from the supersensible world. Of course, what is communicated to them is not understood as it would be by those who are spiritually trained, and consequently they cannot make good use of it.

The student of occultism gradually develops to a state of thought which is not derived from sense-observation, and then learns to realize how, within the soul, thought contacts thought, when even the connection of ideas is not occasioned by any power of sense-observation. He becomes conscious that thought possesses an inner life and that, while engaged in thought, he is in the realms of a supersensible, living power – that there is something real which flows in upon this inner life, just as the outer objects make an impression on his senses, when he observes them.

The people who will believe only what they can see will not, of course, be able to believe that they are affected from within as well as from without. Before one can realize this, he must have the inner experience. In time, though, he will be able to distinguish between the thought created by his own volition and those experienced without any voluntary exercise of his own will. He has then reached an advanced stage wherein, instead of relying on the impressions derived from the external world of the senses, he has received contemplation from within.

After he has commenced to receive advice from within, instead of depending entirely on the senses, he is training the higher organs of cognition, and these new organs provide a new world, wherein man learns to know himself as a new ego. These new organs of perception will soon make their appearance known by their activity. The eyes and ears are passive, being affected by light and sound, while the perceptive organs of the soul and spirit are in a continuous state of activity. But it requires a systematic course of training before these organs reach the point of perfection that the student may be able to use them for observing things in the higher world. When this takes place he has reached the Cosmic Consciousness state. Before he will reach this state, however, he must not only control his actions, but his thoughts, for "as a man thinketh, so is he." He must pass beyond that stage where he is affected by the sense organs.

From the beginning of the modern UFO era, there have been those who claim to be in contact with "extraterrestrial beings."

The spiritual training requires a very great deal of patience; naturally there is preparatory work to do, and no one can say how long it will take. Those who are impatient to wait cannot experience anything, as they have not yet acquired the proper attitude toward the higher worlds. Long before the student is able to see, he becomes conscious of his own soul and spirit, and things are experienced which are very different from those of the external world.

The astral body that he becomes aware of is not only of a different substance, but is of an entirely different world; one of which heretofore he knew nothing. Our "helpers" on the other side work upon the astral body in much the same way in which the world of the physical senses works upon the physical body, and we can be wonderfully helped through our astral body, providing that we do not shut out this influence. We do this often without knowing it, by saying or thinking, "I am aware of nothing" – as is very often the case when we have formed our own ideas as to how these perceptions should present themselves to our vision, and we do not see anything as we had supposed it should appear. If one says, "I can see nothing," one is forgetting that these experiences are fundamentally different from those of the external world.

It is very important that the student form the right attitude of mind during the training and practice. This is vital. He will become conscious that he is standing upon the threshold of the world of soul and spirit, and he will wait with patience, so that this wonderful knowledge is revealed to him when he is ready for it. He will no longer have any doubts, but will have become conscious, and say, "I will practice all of the exercises which are suitable for me, for I know that during the time thus spent all of the things that are of importance to me will come to me; I do not ask for them impatiently, yet I prepare myself to receive them."

AWAKEN THE INNER SELF

There is no training as satisfactory as that which gains the perception of the higher worlds; and to know that one is traveling the correct road toward gaining knowledge. The meaning of birth and death is then finally made clear, and the awareness that that which is released from the human physical body at death passes on through many states in the future.

The seeker becomes aware of that which is within him – that which moves onward within him from incarnation to incarnation. The great tendency of most students, and those who are learning the advantage of contemplation, is to want to withdraw from the outer world, but this is a serious mistake, and will dwarf and wither the inner life. The student must continue to do his duty to the world in which he lives. Rather than to be always receptive to the impressions of the outer world, what he strives for is the power to draw from his inner self when he so chooses.

Simply because he is taking up the higher work, he must not forget his ordinary duties, for until they are done he is not free for other service. He should undertake no new worldly duties; but those which he has already taken upon himself must be perfectly fulfilled. By this we mean, of course, all clear and reasonable duties which he, himself, recognizes, and not the imaginary duties which others would try to impose upon him.

The waves of outward life affect the inner man from all sides, and instead of controlling the outward life, he is controlled by it. The outer forces cannot develop the inner man; it can be developed only by the inner calm of the soul. Outer circumstances can affect only the outer life; they never can develop the spiritual man. One must awaken the new and higher man, the subjective mind, from within. Once the inner self is awakened it becomes the "Ruler," the "Master Within," and directs the circumstances of the outer man with sure guidance. As long as the inner self is unawakened, one's power cannot be developed.

If another than yourself has the power to make you angry, then you are not the master of yourself. This means, of course, that you have not found the Ruler within you. You must develop the power within, and then let the impressions of the outer world approach you as you choose, for only after striving for and attaining this power can you reach the desired state. You must learn control of temper, so that you feel no anger or impatience. You must learn control of the mind itself, so that the thought may always be calm and unruffled; and (through the mind) you must learn control of the nerves, so that they may be as little irritated as possible.

This last is very difficult, because when you try to prepare yourself to follow the Path; you cannot help making yourself and your body more sensitive, so that its nerves are easily disturbed by a sound or a shock, and feel any pressure acutely. The calm mind also means courage, so that you may face without fear the trials and difficulties of the Path you have chosen; it means steadiness, so that you may make light of the troubles which come into everyone's life, and avoid the incessant worry over little things, with which many people spend most of their time.

It must not matter to you what happens to you from the outside; sorrows, troubles, sicknesses, losses – all of these must be as nothing to you, and must not be allowed to affect the calmness of your mind. They are the results of past actions, and when they come you must bear them cheerfully, remembering that they are transitory. They belong to your previous lives, although some are directly traceable in this life, and you cannot alter them; therefore think rather of what you are doing now, which will make the events of this life and the next life, for that you can alter, and also mitigate the present, if handled correctly.

It will require a good deal of practice to possess always the inward calm, but the greater the effort needed, the more important the achievement. Everything depends upon the inward truthfulness and sincerity with which we think of ourselves and the actions of others. But after the Higher Being is awakened, something else is still needed. If a man thinks of himself as a stranger, it is only himself that he contemplates; he looks at his experiences, to which his mode of life subjects him, and he must rise above them and aspire to a purely impartial point of view, no longer connected with his own individual circumstances.

He must think of those things which concern him as concerning another person, although he himself may dwell in entirely different conditions and circumstances. By doing this, he rises above the personal point of view and becomes objective about himself. His attention is directed to higher worlds than those he knows in his everyday life. Then he begins to long for those higher worlds, about which his senses and his daily occupation tell him nothing.

In this way he becomes more conscious of the inner part of his nature. He learns to listen to the voices within him, which speak when all is calm; and inwardly he is able to converse with the spiritual world. During this time of meditation he is, for the time being, withdrawn from the everyday world, and no longer hears its voices. All around him is silence. His entire soul is filled with inward calm and contemplation, and converses with the purely spiritual world. This calm contemplation is necessary – he must develop an earnest desire for such calm thinking.

Many highly developed students state that they are unable to communicate with higher Beings, or to converse with the spiritual world, and we would remind them of Jesus' words, "unless ye become as little children ye cannot enter the Kingdom of Heaven" – and His explanation –"...for the Kingdom of Heaven is within you." Some intellectual students, we fear, feel that all they need do is arm themselves with several books, adjust their glasses, and sit and wait – and the Beings of other planes, thus notified, will enter the room and introduce themselves.

The first thing to remember here is that you cannot confine the Beings from the spiritual plane to your methods. To begin with, you are not working in your accustomed medium; you are working in a higher creative form that you do not know how to use – except unconsciously. Do not strain to make a contact – keep the body relaxed, but free, and stimulate the emotions to respond.

Let your spirits rise – let your heart dominate, and abandon yourself to its impulses. Learn to evoke your own inner vitality.

You must expand in spirit, and not intellectually. Of course it is almost like learning another language, so that you can communicate with the other planes of being with understanding-but otherwise communication is hopeless. The brain is the executive, and not the originating branch of our personal government. There is no substance in pure intellect; it is just a very line shadow. Pure intellect is aloof and unrelated; whatever the brain is incapable of handling, it denies. Imagination is the very gateway of reality – it is the one thing you possess that connects you with the next substance.

Imagination is the transmuting chemical – the only way to get outside yourself. How else could you function beyond your fleshy limitations? Use your imagination masterfully, not as an onlooker. The whole trouble is in using too little, for a little imagination has no strength; instead of freeing you, it is captured. A mere passive willingness cannot help you – you must understand that communication with the higher Beings must be done by your own "heart desire," and not "mind desire." It is useless for any student to simply sit with only mental preparation. You must have soul preparation. And when you do not succeed, seek the reason within yourself. If there is no growth or corresponding demand from within, you are not truly seeking; you are apathetically making an appeal which has no power behind it.

By all means we do not wish to be misinterpreted as stating that it takes intense concentration, for a bodily or mental vacuum is unnatural and impossible. To check the flow of normal physical impulses is also unnatural.

Whole living implies the simultaneous functioning of all of the parts of yourself. Only the sharp focus of your attention is shifted as desired to that portion of your being where it is important that it should function for the business of the moment. It is just as serious a mistake to concentrate wholly in the superconscious as it is in the brain-mind or the body. Give to each its balanced due of yourself, for that balancing is the art of life.

Naturally in order to visit another plane of consciousness it is necessary to free yourself from your body. Actually, it is simply a matter of withdrawing attention from one thing and giving it full-strength to another. The more you can relax the body, the more power you possess, and the more you can use the spiritual in conjunction with the physical. Ignore the body, except for its necessary functions. The first point is to keep it in perfect health, so that it can be the more easily ignored.

Many students at first report that they freed their consciousness from the physical body and found themselves upon another plane of being, but being "afraid" suddenly that they would not be able to return to the physical body, the fear-thought plunged them into the physical body immediately and they suffered a shock to the entire nervous system. We also feel that another warning is important here, and that is to those who lose the balance between the planes of being.

Naturally the place for such meditation and concentration is in the absolute privacy of your room, where you will not be disturbed. After you have advanced to a very high state of development you will have learned to be "two places at once" – and sometimes even three planes of being at one time. But we would warn students to seek privacy for two reasons. One is that a sudden noise or disturbance can result in a severe shock to the nervous system. Another is that when students become too interested in the spiritual plane, and ignore anything on the physical or mental planes, they become out-of-balance. Sometimes they wish people to see how "spiritual" they have become, and begin walking about in public as though semiconscious, staring into space with a rapt smile upon their lips. It is this type of thing which gives occultism a bad name among those who do not understand it.

It is not the physical body which visits the other planes, nor is it the objective mind; it is the Higher Self, the real person within, the subjective mind. It is entirely possible, at a higher stage of development, to be physically occupied with the objective mind doing its normal work, while the subjective mind is elsewhere, as we explained. The main thing is to "sweep" back and forth, so that the dividing line between the two worlds does not show. "Commute" all the time; it is easy if you keep in practice. Learn to get outside of the physical body, and train yourself to be at home outside it. This is to develop a habitual consciousness. The most danger is not in getting out of the body, but in returning to it.

When you wish to rest, merely transfer your center of consciousness. The distance to the other consciousness is not a distance of space; it is simply a slowness in penetrating. It is only the lack of the right combination which makes it seem distant, and it is very near when you clear the intervening denseness which is not space. When you are in a dark room and a bright light is turned on, the darkness and light occupy the same area. One overcomes the other, and reveals what the other did not. Instead of being in the one dark substance of consciousness, you are in the brighter, revealing one. Density is gone. You are in the same place you were, actually, but with greater vision, for All is One-here and now.

YOUR KINSHIP WITH ALL CREATION

Space is only an imaginary boundary, and not a definite reality. There really isn't any such thing as "space" as we understand it. It is only relative to the plane of awareness, or consciousness. We are all occupying the same "space" or consciousness, and it is not a case of distance at all – it depends solely upon who is experiencing it. Learn, and remember, that space is not distance – space is degrees of perception. Distance is only slowness in getting there. Leaving the body is merely a complete withdrawal of attention from the body and a transfer of being into a different center of the same consciousness – an expansion of consciousness, such as dreaming. The physical may be in bed while the conscious being may be walking in "space."

Sensitiveness capable of absorbing wisdom through direct impression suffers enormously from the world of combat, and as awareness increases so does suffering. Because of this, unfortunately, the spiritual aspirant often prefers to seek a sheltered life and become a bystander. Such a person may have an exquisitely sensitized vision, but he is absolutely sterile because of lack of human contact. The bystander probably regards his reaction as one of fastidiousness, but it is really inertia-atrophied force, and loss of productiveness.

Any sensitive person is useless in employing the force of the higher consciousness if he is always vulnerable to the return blows of the world. Suppose he is trying to accomplish something and he becomes subject to irrelevant personal attacks; obstructions of all kinds. The minute he becomes susceptible to that, he is automatically shut off from the power-current which was going to help him accomplish. He must learn to protect himself against a lower element which is superior in quantity, and learn to protect his mind against the darts and arrows which poison resolution.

Each time you meet a person you may learn something from him. You will by no means consider it right to excuse everything in those with whom you come in contact, nor to ignore every wrong action and see only the good qualities. We do not learn by condemning a fault, but by realizing that it is a fault. There will be obstructions, and a necessary resistance – but how else can one rise? How does an airplane rise, but through the resistance of the air? There will be no dearth of stress points – but that is life; and life, in the last analysis, is people. It is in one's dealings with people, one's relations with people, that one meets the deeper resistance by which the consciousness may rise. This is life, and this is the nature of its substance.

There will always be unreceptive people, and you must learn to protect yourself from getting into their zone of action. In other words, you must first learn to insulate yourself. Insulation is not unsympathetic – it is merely the precaution the doctor takes against infection. Insulation is not isolation. Learn to keep yourself whole – the strategy of war is to divide the enemy, and you must recognize instantly when you are being divided. Do not be discouraged, even when failure turns into actual defeat. You decide, as a Master should, how things should be – and you make them so. You must dominate your materials, instead of being dominated, and because of your strength of perception you are able to look beyond inevitable failure to inevitable success.

Of all the qualifications necessary, Love is the most important, for if it is strong enough in a man, it forces him to acquire all the rest – and all the rest without it would never be sufficient. There is a dignity and reserve and depth to the real thing. It is a quiet feeling, a silent feeling of kinship and sympathetic response, instead of the usual indifference. Remember your kinship to all created things. The sympathetic contact makes it possible to contain the whole world within yourself, expanding to contain them all. But it is not a merging of individualities, for they are distinct – it is the merging of the substance possessed by all of them.

Stop shrinking from being misunderstood – accept it, for you always will be. Search, instead, for the constant inner citadel, the inner fortress, and consciously establish it. You will not find it in your brain – look for it in the region of the heart, or, more accurately, in the intangible sensations that have no organic position. This is the great security – the foundation of any superstructure of effort you may want to build. There is nothing more important than creating this abode of emotional security, spiritual order, and demonstrable strength. As long as you have this inner power, you needn't mind what is battering against you, nor what tools or dynamite are used. Such can only be a surface nuisance. The shell may be scarred, but you have withdrawn the part of you that can be hurt.

A certain resignation should pervade the soul. In order for this to come about, it is necessary that the soul be the Master over the expression of joy and sorrow, pleasure and pain. Some are afraid of becoming dull and unsympathetic if they do not rejoice and weep when others do, but this is not so. Whatever is pleasurable the soul enjoys – and whatever causes pain and sorrow, the soul feels. But what the soul must learn is control over the signs of joy and sorrow. Instead of becoming dull and unsympathetic, you become more susceptible to all joy and sorrow around you, and you must see that you indulge in the pain and pleasure to the full – yet without giving yourself up to it so as to outwardly show it. Justifiable sorrow should not be suppressed, but involuntary weeping should be restrained. Indignation at something you know to be wrong is not condemned, but the passion of anger is.

You must pick out the proper "wave length" and travel on it, in order to reach people. The sympathetic assumption of kinship empowers you with the attributes of higher consciousness. You are no longer restricted by the limitations of position, in the geometrical sense, because anything you love you turn your attention to ardently – and you become one with the object of your attention in this Greater Entity. This Greater Entity gives you the ability to broadcast yourself, to travel on it sympathetically, as it were. The Greater Entity, or Kinship, is the wave length to which one tunes in order to communicate with fellow beings.

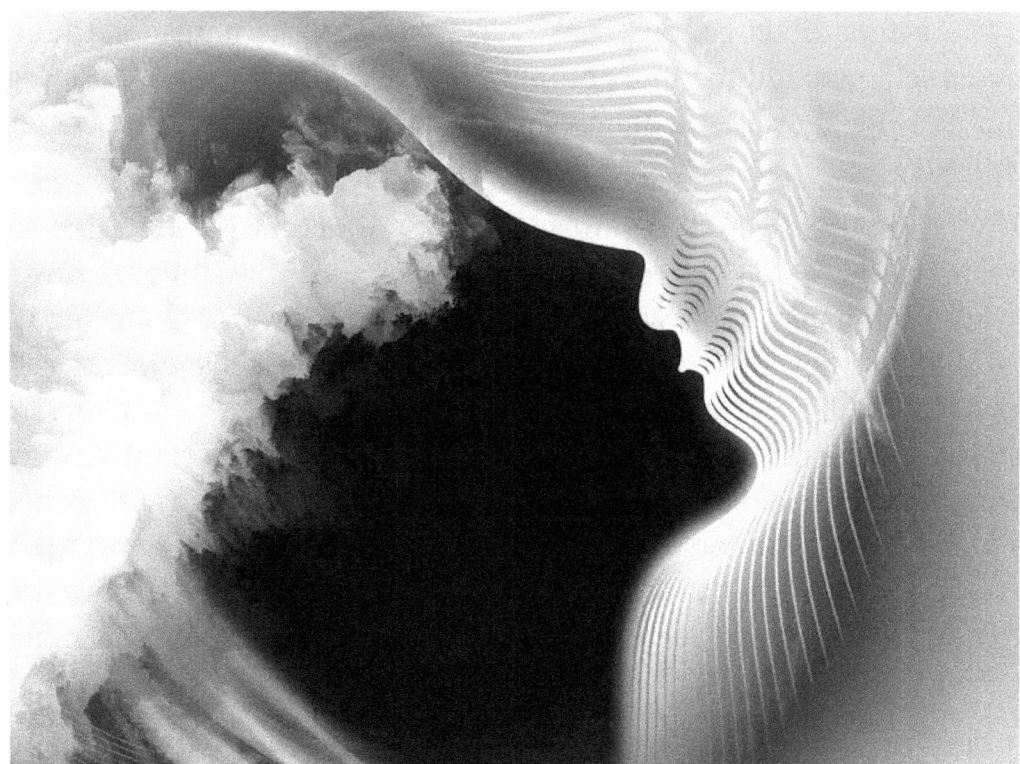

Your thoughts literally create your reality and this has direct influence on your finances, success, health and general well being.

You send out to others a radiation of your own Inner Flame-the Light. No words exist which can exactly express this Inner Flame – it is one of the most silently apparent of possessions. It travels from heart to heart in its own channel of expression and exchange. You always sense it -- even those sense it who do not acknowledge it with anything better than mental sophistication. It is a unique and unmistakable thing, the kindly radiation of one who conducts, even though unconsciously, the current of Universal Force. This radiation is the one thing which does not work in alternate rhythm of activity and rest.

Radiance should not wax and wane in power depending upon the earth's recognition of it. It is continually existent under all conditions, whether others see it or not. This is your own bit of frequency, which you alone can manipulate. Therein is happiness secure – the control of destiny is in the steady maintenance of a course satisfactory to your highest apex of perception; radiance is the reward of permanence of heart. There is always an expanded and a contracted form of everything. Will-power is the contracted form of the higher force. Think of it, rather, as desire-power, for will-power is doing something in spite of your desires. Never look upon anything as impossible. Some of your demands can be fulfilled only after you have first educated yourself up to a desire for that which is possible, and have, in so doing, arrived at being able by means of your strong "willing" to treat the impossible in such a manner that, through the will, it becomes transformed into the possible. One of the most powerful forces is the belief in your power to do it. That, combined with the effort to be successful, will accomplish almost anything. Without it you sink into your own limitations, and consider them almost impossible to overcome. But if you get the belief that it can be done, and back it up, nothing is impossible.

THOUGHTS ARE REAL THINGS

The student will soon realize that this new world which he contemplates is just as real as everything that surrounds him. He begins to consider thoughts which come to him as real things. In time he will realize that revelations of his quiet thinking seem much higher, and more real, than the things existing in space. He realizes that thoughts are not mere phantoms, but speak to him through Beings who were hidden from him before. Then he hears the voices through the silence, speaking to him. Before this, his ear was the only organ of hearing – now he hears with his soul, and an inner language and an inner voice are revealed to him.

It is a period of great delight when this experience comes to him. An inner light floods his whole world. Through him passes a current from a divine world, bringing with it divine bliss; thus, through meditation, he gains super-sensual knowledge. However, he must always be careful not to let thoughts of an unrefined nature take possession of his soul. This would prevent him from attaining true spiritual knowledge. All thoughts must be carefully defined, and he will find it a great help if he does not let the thoughts which spring up within him lead him astray.

New conceptions of reality will be formed, but it is by no means necessary for you to withdraw from the world in which you live, nor to abandon your duties. You must realize, however, that the most insignificant actions and experiences are shaping your future. When once this fact is revealed to you in your moments of contemplation, you then become endowed with fresher and fuller power for your daily duties, for then you know that there is a reason for your suffering. Thus instead of weariness you have happiness, and are full of strength. No matter what may happen, you will go forward erect. In the past you did not know why you worked and suffered; now you know. Those who rise by meditation so that they are able to be united with the spirit are bringing life within them – the eternal element which is limited by neither birth nor death. Their meditation becomes the means by which they also attain the recognition and contemplation of their eternal, indestructible, essential being. *Ancient religions all tell of this communication. Modern man was unprepared philosophically to accept the sudden contacts with "space beings" as described by UFO contactees. Although confusion exists, the subject has received publicity through books, TV and radio, as well as private publications of or by "Saucer Clubs."

It is often asked why man knows nothing of those experiences which lie beyond the borders of birth and death. He can open the path to this knowledge by proper meditation – this alone can penetrate beyond the borders of birth and death. Everyone can attain this knowledge, for in each of us is the faculty of recognizing and contemplating for ourselves the truths of occultism – all we have to do is to use the right means. You could not perceive tones, nor see colors, if you did not have eyes and ears. Nor can the eye see if there is not light to make things visible. Occultism develops spiritual eyes and ears.

The natures of people being so different, it is obvious that for particular individuals special methods of training become necessary. There are many paths which may be followed, and many roads to attainment, and it is not necessary for you to follow all of the roads or to follow one after another, for they will all lead to the same goal. As to the length of time in meditation, we must remind you again that the greater the length of time during which you can meditate uninterruptedly, the stronger will be the effect called forth. Every excess in these matters, however, may become injurious, and in time you will be able to determine the proper length of time you should meditate.

The path which we call "imaginative knowledge" is the first step toward the higher knowledge. Cognizance dependent on sense perceptions and on the working up of such perception by reason (which is sense-bound) is known as objective cognition. There are other stages beyond this. By imagination we do not mean conceptions which lack reality, but rather that kind of perception which is called into being by the soul in its state of higher consciousness. The things perceived in this state of consciousness are spiritual facts and spiritual Beings, to which the senses have no access, and since this condition of the soul is caused by meditating, or "imagination," the sphere to which this condition of higher consciousness belongs may be termed the imaginative world, and the knowledge relating to it, imaginative knowledge. You see that imagination, in the occult world, is very different from the imagination of the sense world, for in one it means the lack of reality, and in the other, actuality. *Lack of discrimination on the subject of subjective imagination has led many astray. It eventually caused Howard Menger to doubt his own experiences.

At the beginning, the soul of the student is weak in all that appertans to a perception of the world of soul and spirit, and he will therefore need all of the inner energy he can muster in order that, while meditating, he may retain a firm impression of the suggestion before him. If you wish and feel that you are ready to attain genuine contemplation of the higher world, you will not only have to maintain your hold on these, but you must also be able to continue in a condition in which not only the influences of the outer world of sense cannot affect the soul, but in which also the imaginary presentiments above mentioned shall have been effaced from your consciousness. Then only will there enter on the plane of your consciousness that which has previously formed by means of meditation. It is a matter of great importance that there should be a sufficient amount of soul power at your disposal, so that what has been formed can be spiritually discerned, and will not escape the attention, for this is necessary where the inward energies are as yet little developed.

The disturbing influences of the outer world of sense, no matter how hard we may try to exclude them, are nevertheless great. It is not the disturbances which we ordinarily control, but those which in ordinary life escape the attention. Owing to man's nature, a certain condition of transition has, in this particular, made possible that which the soul in its waking state was powerless to affect, owing to the disturbances of the physical world, things it is capable of achieving during sleep. The one who meditates seriously will, if sufficiently attentive, become aware of a certain aspect wherein his sleep is affected. When you have reached this state you will feel that while sleeping you are not asleep, but that the soul has periods in which it is active in a certain way during sleep. Under such conditions these natural processes have a deterrent effect upon the influence of the external world, which the soul is not strong enough to ward off. But when you are able to really meditate, the soul releases itself during sleep from the condition of objective consciousness, and realizes that it is in a world of soul and spirit.

There are two ways in which this can take place. The person may while asleep, become aware that he is in another world; or he may, after awakening, remember that he has been in a different world. The former feeling requires a greater amount of energy, and for this reason the second is more common. Gradually, however, he reaches that state in which he becomes aware of having been in the other world during the entire time of his sleep, only emerging there from when he awakes. When he reaches this state, his memory of Beings and facts connected with the other world will become ever more and more distinct, and he has then reached the stage known as the continuity of consciousness during sleep.

THE CONTINUITY OF CONSCIOUSNESS

A great step will have been taken when you have attained the continuity of consciousness during the ordinary sleep, even if you have only certain periods during the sleeping hours when you are conscious of being in the other world of soul and spirit; or if you still retain the memory after awakening. This condition is only a transition state. We do not wish you to think that in this state you receive any conclusive views of the soul and spirit world, for in this condition the soul is very uncertain and unable as yet to rely on its experiences. But it is through such experiences that the soul ever gathers strength enabling it during the waking hours to ward off the disturbing influences of the internal and external world, and to attain a state of consciousness as to the spirit and the soul into which no impressions of the senses will intrude. All of these previous states are but a preparatory means for spiritual vision.

There are two soul experiences which are of importance. The first is when you say to yourself, "...while disregarding everything the external world may yield to me in the way of impressions, yet I, when turning my gaze inward, do not see a Being whose activity has been entirely extinguished. On the contrary, I behold one that is self-conscious in a world of which I know nothing so long as I permit myself to be only impressed by the sensations from the outside." When this happens, the soul will have the feeling of having given birth to a new Being; this new-born ego will have qualities of quite a different kind from those which were formerly in the soul. * Dante expresses this condition in his lines in the first canto in *"The Divine Comedy."* "In the midway of this, our mortal life, I found me in a dark wood astray."

The second experience consists of becoming aware of that former self, henceforth detached, as it were, and being at one's side in the guise of a second entity. That which has been imprisoned previously now develops into something which we are able to confront and in this state we feel at times exterior or apart from that which we have previously regarded as our personality. It is now as if we were two different egos -- one which we have known, and the other a new Being, much superior to the first. We realize, however, that the first ego acquires a certain independence in its relationship to the second.

This is of great importance to know; for by it you come to know what it means to live in that world which it has been your endeavor to reach by means of training. It is by means of the second ego that we come in cognizance of the spiritual world, and it can be developed into that which has as much significance for the spiritual world as our sense organs have for the physical world of the senses. If your development has proceeded along the correct lines, the student will not only be aware of himself as a new-born ego, but he will be able to recognize the spiritual fact and the entities that surround him, as they will seem to be just as real as those of the physical world through the action of his physical senses, so this is a very important experience.

You must be able to let that which is really present in the world around you affect you without disturbing the influences of your own personality. You will also have to adapt yourself to the spiritual world around you in the right way, for you become a citizen of the spiritual world as well as this world. Your thoughts must be guided according to the eternal laws of truth – the laws of the "spirit-land," otherwise you will not be able to understand what comes from that land.

He who directs his inner life in such a way steps upward from stage to stage and the supersensible world unfolds to this spiritual perception. He will then learn the real meaning of the truth communicated about this world, and he will come in contact with Beings who can, for the first time, make things clear to him. These are those Beings known as the "Great Guides of the Human Race," and they will be present to assist him as soon as he is ready for their assistance.

Then your initiation takes place. What then occurs cannot all be given here, but we will indicate that you perceive a new dwelling place, and become a conscious dweller in the supersensible world. Wisdom now flows to you from the higher sources, and your knowledge hereafter does not come from without. You become merged in the Light; the problems of the world are then solved, and you no longer hold converse with the things which are shaped through the spirit, but with the shaping spirit itself. You are then able to hold intercourse with the Spirit itself, and able to recognize each false form in which you had imagined the Spirit appeared before. By "false form," we mean that which man ascribes to the spirit, in his ignorant conception, is superstition. You will be above superstition, because you will then know what the true form of the Spirit is.

Those who have not experienced the manifestation referred to are likely to ask, "How can anyone know that, while thinking he perceives spiritual manifestations, one is dealing with actualities and not mere imaginings, visions, or hallucinations?" This is not a very difficult matter to determine, as anyone who has trained to reach this state can easily tell the difference between his own presentiment and a spiritual reality. The difference is just as real as the difference between thinking your hand is touching a hot bar of steel, and actually touching one. You learn to know the difference by experience. Just as you know that the mere thinking of the hot steel will not bum you, so does the Disciple know whether he is experiencing a spiritual fact or whether his awakened spiritual organs of perception are under the impression of actual facts or entities.

We will endeavor to write some rules which will show you how not to fall the victim of delusions. When the new-born consciousness commences, the soul has reached a very definite condition. It is due to this condition that you become the ruler of your sensations, conceptions and feelings; of your passions, impulses and desires. Observations and conceptions cannot be left in the soul to follow their own way; they must be controlled according to the law of thought. It is the ego that now takes charge of these thoughts, or laws.

Desires and passions follow the same law. Their forces should be guided by certain ethical laws, and by reason. The moral judgments made by the ego either mislead the soul or guide it safely to its natural estate. Meditation brings a form of mental "detachment" whereby the ego is able to detach itself from the lower, concrete mind, and thus gives birth to a state of being which has been loosely termed, "The Higher Ego."

The student finds himself in a peculiar condition of dwelling in two states of consciousness at the same time. This is the danger point. Psychiatry designates these two conditions of mind as being very dangerous, for at this juncture a person may find himself unable by an act of will to maintain his balance in these two states of consciousness at once. He is then known as a schizophrenic.

To avoid this schizophrenic state of mind, one must realize that man is a natural animal, as well as being a potential god or spiritual being. Resolving the conflict between his lower nature and his higher ideals is the whole purpose of psychiatry; namely, the removal of the "guilt" complex.

The ego having the ability to give birth to the spiritual self by evolution creates this duality of self. This duality, commonly called the "higher" and "lower" self, is the battlefield. To win one must accept this: situation and learn to reconcile one with the other. If one dwells too much in the abstract world and has not the developed mental strength to feed the lower mind and compensate, he becomes a daydreamer; the one who walks out among traffic and gets killed. Emotional states create havoc. The aspirant becomes ascetic, may be celibate, and injures the physical vehicle, whereas a sane, moderate approach will naturally and gradually bring him to a normal moral state. If this new birth has been normal and natural, and he is sufficiently developed in his "lower" self, and has attained that firmness in the matter of ethical judgment, stability of character and thoroughness in the matter of his conscience, he will then be ready to have all of these virtues within the first ego when the birth of the second comes about.

It will be seen from the above that the first meditations; should be on non-harmlessness, unselfish love, and right motivation, for to "take the Gates of Heaven by storm" is dangerous without proper training. Philo means love; Sophia means wisdom. From philosophy is born wisdom. Kwannon is the oriental equivalent of love and wisdom; symbolically she gives birth to the "new man." This is shown in a painting by Kano Hogai in the Imperial Collection in the Imperial Museum, Japan.

The person with the firm determination of doing all in his power to follow the first meditations will give confidence to the first ego in the execution of that which it has to fulfill, and he need never fear when the second ego becomes detached as the result of spiritual training. He must remember, though, that the power of self-delusion is very great, and may lead him into the wrong belief that he has now reached the desired stage.

While the spiritual training is going on, the student develops his thought life to such an extent that he is not exposed to the dangers which are often thought to be connected with this training. This cultivation of thought also brings about all the inner experiences which are necessary, but this is done in such a way that the soul does not suffer from any injurious shocks. If it were not for the development of thought, these experiences might produce a feeling of great uncertainty in the soul. The method outlined brings all of the experiences into play in such a way that he gains the effects, but it does not cause serious shock. By paying strict attention to his thoughts, the student becomes like a spectator of the experience of his inner life, whereas, without such thought-development, he is in the very midst of the experience, and is shaken by all the shocks incidental to it.

Before the real Adeptship can be developed, there are certain qualities which have to be developed by systematic training. The following are very important. The soul must control the thoughts, the will, and the feelings. This is done by acquiring firmness, reliance, and balance, so that these will not leave after the birth of the second ego. This acts in a dual capacity, as it also provides the new ego with strength and inner fortitude.

One of the first lessons to be learned is that your thinking power be confined to facts only. In the physical world of the senses, life is a great teacher of the human ego, without regard to reality. If the soul were disposed to wander aimlessly about it would soon be corrected, unless it were willing to enter into combat, – for the soul must conform its thoughts to the facts of life. When you think of things away from the world of the physical senses, you miss the corrective influence of the latter. If this thought is not able to be its counselor, it will be very unsteady and uncertain. Therefore, the student's thoughts must be controlled so that their course and object may be self-determined. You must cultivate an inner firmness; a capacity to concentrate strictly oil one subject. For this reason, the examples used for meditation should not be complicated, nor too foreign to daily life, but it is best to use something that is simple and familiar.

Anyone who is able to fix his mind for five minutes of each day during a period of five months on such ordinary objects as a pin or a lead pencil, excluding for the time being all other thoughts not connected with the object under contemplation, will have progressed very favorably. You can select a new article each day, or the same one can be used for several days. By fixing your attention for a time on a familiar object, you may be sure that you are thinking in accordance with facts, and anyone asking himself the following questions, "what are the constituent parts of a pencil?," "how were these materials prepared?," "how were they afterward put together?" and "when were pencils invented?," or anything else he may think of in this connection, will be adapting his conception more to realities than he who meditates upon the descent of man, or attempts to determine what life is.

The simplest objects of meditation prepare us more for an accurate conception of the world and its various stages of development than those of a learned and complicated nature, for the most important thing is not only to think, but to think accurately, by means of the inner force. Once you have been trained to accuracy, there will be a desire instilled in you to think in conformity with facts, which will become habitual, even when thought is not feeling itself under the control of the physical sense – world and its laws. Thus do we free ourselves from the tendency to let our thoughts drift about aimlessly. *According to press reports, astronauts are given many severe tests, both physical and mental, to ensure that a stabilized "mind" will operate outer – space vehicles. The Russians have considerable physical "know-how," so it is not strange that they should investigate Yoga. On March 17, 1959, a United Press International report stated that Russian scientists were investigating an Indian farmer named Ramanada who, by practicing Pranayama Yoga, could stop his pulse and respiratory functions. This was verified by the Andhra Medical College.

In the same way in which it governs the world of thought, so the soul should hold control in the realm of will. In the physical sense – world, man is urged on by this or that necessity, and the will feels that it has to satisfy these wants. But when man reaches the higher state, he must accustom himself to obey his own commands; though when he once acquires this habit he will feel less and less inclined to desire that which is of no consequence. All of the discontent and instability in life come from the desire for things, the actuality of which we never consider. Discontent such as this might, when the higher ego is desirous of leaving the soul, cause that person's whole inner life to be thrown into confusion. It is good training to give yourself some command to be carried out daily for a couple of months, as for instance, "today, at some particular time, I will do a certain thing." By such an exercise we arrive in time at a stage where, by ordering the time at which a thing is to be done, and the manner in which it is to be done, it will be accomplished just as arranged.

Only by this exercise can the student gain the inner quietude requisite to his soul, in order that at the birth of the higher ego the soul may not find itself as a kind of double-dealing entity, leading a second and unhealthy life alongside the higher self. Some may be of the opinion that they have reached a stage of development where they do not need these exercises, but from experience we have found that these are just the ones who do need them. It is quite possible that you are able to keep your composure in the ordinary affairs of life; but, when ascending into the higher world, to maintain equanimity is more difficult.

It must be understood that before you can develop Adeptship you must show that you are capable of using the power wisely for yourself and for others. You may fool yourself as to what you may think you possess; but you cannot fool the Powers who know, for they know what you need. Our life may have trained us in certain things, but the qualities we must possess to become Adepts require a special training. If our life has made us become excitable, this must be removed. If we have not the control over ourselves which we should have, we must train ourselves to overcome this condition, so that we may be capable of responding to the impressions we receive. The man who is unable to laugh when he wants to, where there is anything to laugh over or not, has just as little control over his laughter as one who is perpetually laughing at everything.

Error, vice and ugliness prevent the soul from seeing truth, goodness, and beauty. If we look for the bad, the false and the inferior, that is all we will see. He who looks carefully will always find something beautiful, something to admire. Aim to keep an unbiased mind, regardless of any experience you may have had. Never be guilty of saying, "I have never heard of that before; therefore I do not believe it!" We should be ready to hear anything new, and we can learn a great deal from watching a young child, or a flower-bud, or a leaf on a tree. We must judge our present experiences by our past ones, but it must be remembered that the new experiences may contradict the old.

FIVE QUALITIES OF THE SOUL

There are five qualities of the soul which the Disciple must develop and by training make his own: controlling the trend of his thoughts; controlling the impulses of the will; equanimity in the matter of sorrow and joy; positiveness in his judgment of the world, and impartiality in his view of life. After he has devoted a certain length of time to acquiring these qualities, he must devote the necessary time towards blending them into one harmonious whole within the soul, and in order to do this he will have to practice the exercises together, until he brings them into harmony, as desired.

You will find these exercises very helpful in giving yourself knowledge of the higher worlds. They will make you aware of your failings and the means necessary to give strength and security to the intellect. Everyone will need these exercises, although, necessarily, each one will need different kinds, depending upon the capacities, temperament, and character of the student. These exercises will present themselves to you, and in time you will receive a great deal more good than you at first supposed you would. For example, if a person has but little self-confidence, he will realize this, and in the course of time he will, by persistent practice, gain the needed confidence – and it will be the same with any other quality of the soul.

The student of occultism learns how important it is to be capable of raising these capabilities to a higher power, and to be able to control his thoughts and feelings so that the soul will have the power to maintain complete inner quietude for the time desired-periods when the student can keep at a distance from his mind and heart those things which in any way deal with the ordinary everyday life; its pleasures, joys, cares, sorrows, and distress. During these periods he should not permit anything to intrude excepting that which the soul itself admits. Those who do not know may think that it is not right to withdraw from the world at any time, but you will find that you are the gainer thereby if you will withdraw in heart and spirit from life and its duties for a certain length of time each day. By giving yourself up to the inner quietude you will be better able to perform your outer duties.

You should aim, during these periods, to detach yourself entirely from thoughts of your own personal affairs, and train yourself to think of what would benefit mankind in general. Discipleship makes it possible to fill the soul with messages from another, spiritual, world, and if they have the power of enthralling the soul to as intense a degree as any personal concern or care, then you will have gathered knowledge of great value.

Those who train themselves so that they control their soul-life will possibly reach such a point of development as will permit their reviewing their own personal affairs with the same objectivity as those of others; it is excellent training for Adeptship to review one's own experiences as if they were those of others. Thus, in time, you must be able to control your day's actions so that at night you will be able to review every act you performed during the day – and if you did anything you should not have done, it is called forcibly to your mind; and the next time you will probably not do it. Do not overlook the great value of looking at yourself every day as if you were reviewing someone else.

It is well to start at first with just trying to control your actions for a portion of the day. When you succeed in doing this, then increase the period. You will soon become aware of how your every act is impressed on the brain. To be forewarned is to be forearmed. When you have your mistakes brought consciously before you, you will be able to overcome them, and in time you will assume a fearless attitude with regard to the events of life which confront you, and you will be aware of them and meet them with absolute beliefs and the inner confidence that they will not affect you. This training will be found very valuable, and there will soon be a great change in the nature of your thoughts and feelings.

Of course it is much easier to talk about self-control than it is to practice it, but nevertheless there are certain ways whereby we can, in a measure, exert self-control. There are persons who, if they read in the Scriptures that certain things should be done, will do them simply because the Scriptures command that they be done. And there are persons who will do things because their parents, or someone they love or honor, says such a thing should be done. In such cases the effort is but a perfunctory one, unless a reason for so acting be given, and very little good comes of the obedience to the command under either of these circumstances.

No one can be truly great who has not the power of self-control. It does not matter how many virtues a man may have; if he allows himself to give way to paroxysms of anger and loses his self-control at critical moments, his greatness becomes largely diminished; neither can he become really successful in any chosen field or line of work unless he has first developed self-control. Imagine, if you can, a statesman who has not developed this art of self-control, and you will find that at the moment he needs self-mastery most it utterly deserts him. Imagine one of the great financiers of this country not having sufficient control over his tongue to be able to keep his plans secret-how long would he be a factor in the world of finance?

In the case of physical health, unless there is an approximate control of the emotions there will never be permanent good health, because there cannot be perfect health without perfect self-control. The reactions which naturally follow outbursts of emotions bring about physical disorders; if not immediately, then in the course of time. And above all, there can be no progress made in occultism until there is self-control, and that which really determines the growth of a student is his power to control himself. Without this power, intuition cannot be fully awakened; clairvoyance and clairaudience cannot manifest, and his development is otherwise greatly retarded. A student cannot make use of the higher forces of nature unless he becomes self-controlled first. A mental healer cannot assist or relieve a patient so long as he is in a perturbed condition of mind himself. A student cannot dominate his own body unless his mind is poised and undisturbed; he cannot concentrate upon a person at a distance and pick up his thoughts, unless he has the power to make his own objective mind quiescent while the power of concentration is put into action.

THE IMPORTANCE OF SELF-CONTROL

Every time you lose your self-control, your aura, or magnetic field, becomes so actively inharmonious that all of the creations you wish to draw to yourself are repelled. You cannot be a successful creator upon the spiritual, mental or physical planes unless you are able to control your emotions sufficiently to enable that which you have created to come to you. One can never escape from pain until self-control is reached – and one can never reach the place of Peace until the conquest of self has been made.

Self-control is the control of the objective mind by the subjective mind. Another way of expressing the same thing is to say that self-control is the control of the emotions by the Higher Self. Sensations and emotions are the manifestations of the objective mind of man, as we have seen. One complete conquest of the objective mind by the subjective mind is sufficient to establish self-mastery; in other words, we do not have a new objective mind to conquer in each natural incarnation.

To illustrate this, let us take hydrogen to represent the objective mind, and oxygen to represent the subjective mind. Now the time for the union of the two minds has come, and the oxygen blends with the hydrogen, making a drop of water. The union of these two in the drop of water corresponds to the union which makes the real inner man. This drop of water may at one time be in a clay jar, at another time in a copper kettle – it may be another day in a crockery bowl, and then in a china cup – but it is the same drop of water, no matter what its environment may be. During all of your different incarnations there is but one entity, the psychic man, who is composed of these two minds incarnating together in various different physical bodies; and if you once conquer your objective mind you will be its ruler throughout eternity. Looked at in this light it does not really seem such a hard thing to do, when you consider that you have only one conquest to make. But while there may be but one conquest, there will be many battles to fight, and it is during these battles that victory is constantly shifting, sometimes being made on one side and sometimes on the other. But finally the conquest must be made by the subjective mind. *This is the story of the dark and light Angels of the Kabbalah, Job and the Angel wrestling, and the Hindu version of Krishna's battles.

In the early part of our evolution the pleasures of physical and animal man seem to be greater than the pain and consequently the subjective mind, in order that it might receive the pleasures of sensation, permits the objective mind to have absolute dominion. But any force grows with use, and the objective mind, as it manifests itself more and more, becomes so strong that finally the reactions that follow pleasure bring more pain than pleasure, and the subjective mind awakens to the situation and begins to demand a way out of pain. We have been indulging in these sensual pleasures during all the ages past; life after life we have given way to the objective mind, and have allowed it absolute sway and dominion, because we have thought there was more pleasure to be had out of life in that way. But reactions came and pain taught us that there is a better way to live. Pain is the evidence that the objective, mind has not been fully conquered.

The subjective mind is the "I am I" of man; it is the self-consciousness, or that part of him which studies the states of his unconscious, and modes of mind. It is the center of consciousness in him, and until it has been awakened there can be no self-control. Emotions will not control themselves, and, as the term implies, there must be a Self which can control them; there are two aspects of these minds, the positive and the negative. In the subjective mind the negative side is the intellectual, and the positive side is the will. But at this period in our history the intellectual side of our nature is awakened and the will is not. The objective mind also has two aspects; the negative – or reasoning side, and the positive side, or desire. These two aspects in the objective mind are blended to a large extent, and because they are thus united, that mind is strong.

Our first great object should be to awaken the will portion, or force aspect, of the subjective mind, in order that the will and the intellect, united, may control the objective mind. There is force enough in the positive side of this subjective mind to accomplish anything it desires, and therefore it is in our interest to awaken this latent but tremendous force in ourselves. As an example of how it works, I say I wish to do something. This is the desire, or the positive side of my objective mind expressing itself. But another aspect of my mind replies: "No, you must not do that, because it is not right." Here are certain aspects of my two minds in activity, the desire or positive portion of my objective mind, and the intellectual or negative portion of my subjective mind; and if my will, or the positive portion of my subjective mind is not awakened, it will be more than likely that the positive side of my objective mind will win the battle. But if the positive side of my objective mind says that I want to do something, and my will, or the positive side of my subjective, says, "you do not want to do anything of the kind, and you shall not do it," then there is put into action a greater force than desire, and the desire is overcome by the higher, or positive side of my subjective mind- the will.

At a higher conscious level, we are truly creating our experience from our higher selves.

The emotions are natural forces on their proper plane; and because they are natural, many persons think it unnecessary to control them; and many who would like to control them do not know how, because they do not understand their own natures. Simply because a thing is natural is no reason why it should not be controlled. Electricity is a natural force. Used properly for illuminating purposes it is a very good thing – but it is a natural force and can be used to destroy human bodies, and valuable property – so there may be a perversion of natural forces through the misuse of them, since they seem to make up the greater portion of ourselves. In appearance they are many, and yet, on close analysis, we find only four basic ones, and the battle will not seem so hard if we can realize this.

The emotion which causes us the most needless suffering is Fear. Together with Sensuousness, animal Sex Desire, and the most subtle of all, Vanity, these are the basic elements of the emotional nature. You cannot conceive of any emotion that has not its origin in one or more of these four basic ones. Let us briefly examine the nature of each of these emotions, since the larger part of the actions of mankind are directly attributable to one or more of them.

Fear is the cause of most anger, most jealousy, most murder, failure, theft, doubt, discouragement, despondency – and many of the lesser inharmonious conditions. Analyze any one of these states of mind and you will find that fear is the father of it. Eliminate fear and you have destroyed the root, or basis, for many of the emotions which lead men astray. Begin your fight directly upon fear, and not the many phases of it, and a tremendous amount of force will be saved, for it must be conquered before very much will be accomplished, in life. You will remember that you were told that the mind is magnetic, and draws to itself whatever it frequently thinks about. When you are constantly fearing something, you are drawing toward you the very thing you fear, and the reason that humanity has not been swept from this planet long ago is because it has shifted its fears from one object to another so often that it has never held to one thing long enough to destroy itself.

To accomplish rapidly the destruction of this great enemy, it is well to begin by controlling some of its grosser forms, such as physical cowardice. Great numbers of men and women are inwardly the most wretched cowards and yet suppress the external expression of their fears because they are ashamed of them. Here is where the fear of public opinion is greater than the fear of something else, and the emotion is not conquered, but shifted. Try to conquer your cowardice, because it is an enemy to you and will retard your development. There are very few persons, actually, who do not fear someone. You may not be conscious of the fact, but if you stop to think you will see that it is true. You dread to meet Mr. Jones because you do not know what he will think of you – or because he is wealthy and you are not, and you are afraid that you cannot make as great a display as he can. Or perhaps you have heard that Mr. Smith is a great statesman, and you are in awe of statesmen; so you stammer and grow red, and wish you were a thousand miles away when you are introduced to him. The first thing to do toward overcoming this fear of persons is to declare, "I am not afraid of Mr. Jones, or of anyone else." Then calling to mind the image of Mr. Jones, or Mr, Smith, say to it as if he were there in person, "Mr. Jones, you do not have the power to make me uncomfortable, and I am not afraid of you" – and continue to repeat this assertion until your perturbation has subsided and you feel that you could face him without a tremor of fear or embarrassment.

Many women are afraid of mice. To people of this class we would suggest that they think about the many small boys who have made pets of tiny mice, and love them; and if a child is not afraid of a mouse, there is surely nothing about them for an adult to fear. A child loves his pet mouse, and we do not fear the thing we love. They are small centers of consciousness, and we are only larger centers in the same consciousness. The same life principle that sustains them sustains us; and after we have come to a realizing sense of our relative positions our fears will fade away, never to return, for we realize that all is one.

When you have eliminated the grosser forms of fear, then attack the finer forms, such as fear of the unseen, or the unknown. Many persons' lives are made utterly wretched because of their fear of the future. They are continually expecting things that never happen. Others are afraid of the criticism of the world, and a common question on their lips is, "what will people think?" You must remember that the world always criticizes and condemns everything and everybody that it does not understand. You must declare, therefore, that you are not afraid of the criticism of any individual, nor of the public at large; that you are not dependent upon anyone for your health, wealth or happiness; and that the approval and disapproval of other persons, whether collective or individual, are alike to you. If you declare this earnestly and often, you will overcome all fear of criticism.

PERVERSION OF NATURAL FORCES

Fear being eliminated, we next turn our attention to sensuousness, which is the result of a perversion of natural forces. The animal indulges in his senses in order that he may live; but man indulges his senses not only that he may live, but also to get pleasure from his indulgences; and it is the over-indulgence that constitutes the perversion of this natural force. Negative reaction seldom follows the natural indulgence of the senses for the purpose of living. If a creature eats because it is hungry, and stops when the hunger is appeased, there will be no adverse reaction; but when the senses are indulged more for pleasure than from necessity, and there has been an over-stimulation, a negative reaction always follows the indulgence.

Asceticism is one of the moral reactions from sensuousness. In many places in the Orient, especially in India, asceticism is taught as the proper method of living. Many schools of philosophy in America have adopted this Eastern teaching. This is the other extreme, and, like most extreme views, is not productive of the best results; hence the Western School of occultists does not coincide with the Eastern School on this point, which, after all, is but a question of the method of development. Suppression of the senses, for the West, is not the best plan, and Western occultists have found that better results are gained from regulation of the senses. By regulation is meant a moderate indulgence in all that pertains to the normal use of the senses; but never an over-indulgence. In this manner you may have all of the pleasures of life without the penalty that comes from excess.

Sackcloth and ashes do not indicate that the wearer of them has become spiritual. To deny the body its natural functions, or to whip or torture it, does not make a person wise and good; there is no more reason in trying to gain spirituality through asceticism than there is through over-indulgence. Use your senses properly, and enjoy all of the harmless things of life – and let the mind, not the desire, determine the extent of the use of the senses. This is regulation, the teaching of Western occultism.

The third and great basic emotion that mankind has to learn to control is sex desire. This, too, is a natural force, and is a part of the force of life and love; it is a part of the force of magnetic attraction, manifested in the Absolute, and manifesting in every part of it according to the nature of its vehicle. In the minerals it is chemical affinity; in the animals it manifests as the desire for procreation. In man this force, like sensuousness, should be regulated. Here again Western occultism differs from the Eastern schools, where asceticism is taught.

In man this emotion should be so well regulated that it should become a creative force, instead of an animal desire for procreation or an expression of lust. We do not mean that this force should be only transmuted into mental power, but that it should be used consciously to create bodies, unmarred by passion or lust, for the use of egos who desire to reincarnate, rather than uncontrolled passion and lust.

Use this natural force by all means, but do not abuse it; regulate it, but do not eradicate it. The normal condition of man requires that absolutely no part of his body should become atrophied or useless, but that every part of him, whether spiritual, mental, or physical, shall be in perfect condition. Pity the person who tells you that sex is "wrong," or "bad," for they have much to learn. Adepts, and even Masters who re-embody, marry and have children, and lead perfectly happy and normal wedded lives. Giving something up, rather than using it in its proper perspective is merely an indication that you are afraid of it, and no negation of any kind interacts favorably upon the higher centers.

In man's progress and search for happiness on Earth, he seems to find it necessary to investigate and explore all the by-ways which lead from the highway of life. It is a much narrower path, and more difficult to follow, and it is called celibacy. It is never found nor tried by anyone until after that one has lived through a few lives of sexual over indulgence, with their attending miseries. Then, with the soul filled with loathing, or fear of the consequences of sexual excesses, the celibate often rushes to the opposite extreme, and enters into a life of sexual repression.

If he becomes fanatical on the subject, he shuts himself away from the world and refuses to see or to speak to those of the opposite sex. Perhaps he finds a few others who are smarting under similar afflictions, and he prevails upon them to join him in forming a society or brotherhood, which they agree to call a "holy" order – and perhaps the remainder of that life will be spent where they cannot be reached by their former temptations. In their desire to live apart from the world, they sometimes retire to the mountains and build such barriers between them and their fellow-men as will guard them from what they believe to be their greatest enemy, women, and there they undertake to do God's will.

Since all kinds of experiences are necessary to the development of an ego, this kind of life, from an evolutionary standpoint, is a sort of resting place, where man stops in his career while he reviews his past experiences, and assimilates the good that is to be gained from them. The life of the celibate is a long step in advance of the life of sexual overindulgence, and there can be no doubt that in his new position he gains an advantage. But – if he has become a celibate because of his hatred for women, or because he fears that he is not strong enough to meet and overcome the temptations that the world holds for him, then he has not conquered his passions, and the Divine Law will force him back into the world in some future life, to finish fighting the battles from which he has fled.

If a man becomes a celibate because he is afraid of the consequences of living a life where his desires for sex are too strong within him, then the continued and enforced repression of the physical expression of those desires will produce a congested condition of his generative organs, and also other organs which are sympathetically connected with them, and with the consequent physical and emotional ills and imbalances. He has not escaped from the consequences of his desires for sexual union, nor from the result of the physical repression of those desires.

The true principle of celibacy is represented by the person who lives the life of chastity because he loves chastity, and not because he fears consequences or future punishment. And when that point has been reached in his evolution, he has no fear of becoming either a lunatic or a fool, and his life will not be spent hiding within the walls of a monastery.

The last great emotion that must be conquered before perfect self-control is acquired is vanity. This emotion is so subtle that at times it almost baffles us. The peculiarity of this fault is that the victim does not recognize his defect of character. You can seldom convince a vain person that he is vain; and because of its subtlety, it is the hardest and the very last emotion we have to conquer. The first aspect of this fault is the grosser or physical vanity which pertains to admiration for its own particular attractiveness of feature, form or face. It is the feeling which prompts a woman to wear a particular style of dress, not because the dress is beautiful and she loves beautiful things, but because she believes others will admire her in it. This grosser form of vanity we can conquer if we wish to, because occasionally it is revealed to us by our friends or enemies, and when it is discovered it can be eradicated. But this is only the beginning of the battle, because next beyond, and still more subtle, is another phase of vanity which is mental, and this is still harder to recognize in ourselves.

Mental vanity expresses itself in all mental forms. If a man discovers that he is in a small degree superior to his fellow men he feels it, and often looks with contempt upon his weaker brothers. He tries to dominate those whom he believes are his inferiors in intellect, forgetting the fact that he himself is but an infant as compared with the souls who have passed in evolution beyond him. And it sometimes requires many incarnations and many sad experiences to eradicate this defect of character, which really limits his evolution.

Then comes spiritual vanity, and this is the force which actuates all reformers. This is the vanity which makes men say, "All is wrong with the world." It is another way of saying the Supreme Consciousness is wrong in its management of terrestrial things – and "...I must go forth into the world and right it. God has made mistakes, but I shall correct them. I know the answers; therefore everyone must be made to think as I think; I shall lift up all humanity to my plane, and help all mankind to my great level." Spiritual vanity comes in such a subtle guise that one does not recognize the motive that lies behind one's efforts – and yet the time comes in the evolution of that particular individual when his spiritual vanity must pass away, as it usually does, in martyrdom.

There comes a time in the soul's career when that spiritual vanity is burned out of his nature, and he becomes a perfected, self-conscious center in the Universal Consciousness, impersonally working for the raising up of the whole of mankind, according to the Divine Plan. Here is the true At-One-Ment, where your saviors pass away from the adulation and worship of men, and become the unseen and generally unknown workers for humanity – the Silent Brotherhood, who teach, inspire, and raise humanity as fast as it can receive-unknown and unrecognized except by very few; with never a word of praise, never a word of recognition, and never a word of thanks or of appreciation from the world for their sacrifices and their efforts. Spiritual vanity must pass away before perfection is reached.

CONTOL THE BASIC EMOTIONS

In order to control these basic emotions we must learn to exercise our wills. There are two very good rules by which, if persistently followed, self-control can be attained. The first is, never speak until you have thought with your subjective mind. It will be impossible for you to speak before you have thought at all, because you cannot have a material manifestation of speech until there has been some mental action. But do not let the emotions of the objective mind become expressed in words before you have thought with the subjective mind.

The second rule is, never act until after you have thought with your subjective mind. Acting only upon emotion usually leads to regret, and is always followed by a reaction. Action motivated by love without wisdom can be more damaging than helpful. Joy without restraint can lead to accidents. When these two rules are put into practice even occasionally, they will help you; but if you practice them constantly you will be surprised to see how soon you will begin to dominate the four cardinal emotions; and after they are destroyed, all others must disappear, because they are but branches of these four basic emotions.

There are certain aids which will assist you to carry out these rules. First, you should realize that all uncontrolled emotions are the result of ignorance or undevelopment, and this knowledge will rob them of their power over you. You will know that you are at the emotional point in your evolution, which is an indication of ignorance of your own power of self-control. Then you will begin to see the need of development, and will set about correcting the fault. A child fears the dark because he does not know its nature or its cause. If he is carried into a dark room and the light is turned on, and he sees nothing there to injure him, his fear is immediately dissipated. His fear was banished when his ignorance was destroyed. If you can show a person that there is no "bad luck" except that which he has created, and that the "evil" he fears he builds for himself, immediately you destroy the power he has given to these conceptions. If a man is vain of his knowledge, and he can be made to see that the field of knowledge is unlimited, and that his vanity over the small amount that he possesses is but an indication of his great ignorance, immediately his vanity disappears. So it is by enlightenment that any or all of our emotions are controlled or eliminated from us.

The second great aid is this: if we understand what habit is, and know the law which underlies it, and if we know that much of our yielding to our lower natures and lack of self-control is a matter of habit, we shall be able to destroy habits much sooner than if we do not understand them. There are two elements which enter into the formation of a habit. The first is what might be called the law of periodicity, or periodical return, and the second is the initial impulse. The law of periodicity causes a thought or an act to be repeated within a determinate time.

The intensity with which the thought was projected, or the act performed, determines the time in which the tendency to repeat itself will manifest.

Every thought, every feeling and every tendency will repeat itself at given periods of time according to the intensity of the initial impulse that gave it birth. Recognizing this law, if you will remember the exact time your habits repeat themselves, you will be prepared to overcome them with greater success. What is called the association of ideas is a good illustration of the working of the law of periodicity. For example, if we go to our room, or to any place where we can be alone, and send out an intense thought at nine o'clock in the morning, or at any special hour, we will find on the following day at the same hour that we will be inclined to repeat the thought. If we yield to our inclination each day, at the end of the week the habit will be formed, and it will require some effort to resist the temptation to repeat the practice we have begun. This is the way habits are formed through the cyclic law, bringing back to us the thoughts and things we ourselves have created.

The same law which helped you form the habit will help you overcome it if you but reverse the rule in this way – when the mental picture recurs, destroy it by denying that it can materialize. For example, if you have been holding the picture of a loss, declare that you cannot lose anything that belongs to you, and when your picture of loss comes up, refuse to look at it and put into its place a picture of something you want. If you have a habit of thinking of yourself as an invalid, destroy that habit of thought by picturing yourself in the possession of perfect health. If you have created the habit of picturing death for yourself or for a loved one, reverse the picture, and see him and yourself well and happy; and the law of periodicity will bring your new pictures along with the old ones, since they are associated together. Each time the two pictures appear, look at the new and refuse to see the old, and soon the old picture will fade out and disappear and a new order of things will be established.

Another great aid in conquering the emotions is through the power of suggestion. Heretofore the objective mind has been making most of the suggestions, which the subjective mind has passively received. For example, you feel a draft of cold air, and immediately your objective mind suggests to your subjective mind, which is really you, that you will have a cold. You accept the suggestion and reply that you know this is true; by sitting in the draft you are certain to have a cold. Immediately you commence to see the picture of yourself with a cold, for you have accepted the suggestion and claimed the creation of the objective mind for your own, and there is nothing that will prevent the picture from materializing for you. But if you will use the same amount of force in refusing to accept the suggestion of your objective mind that you do in fighting the cold after it has materialized, you will not let it materialize at all.

If you desire to conquer the emotion sensuousness, and your objective mind insists upon gratifying its appetite for the pleasure of eating, you should take the position that you do not want any more food, and should suggest to your objective mind that it does not want any more. Speak to it as if it were another person, or a child. If you have the habit of drinking, or smoking, and you wish to overcome these habits, suggest to your objective mind that it does not want to drink or smoke; that there is no real pleasure to be derived from the gratification of these tastes and appetites, and besides, there is a great deal of money wasted by the indulgence in them, and you will soon see, if you persist in this use of suggestion, that your desires will change and you will conquer sensuousness without a great deal of inconvenience or annoyance.

There are certain declarations and suggestions that most persons who work along this line find extremely beneficial, and we will give you a few of them. Suggest to your objective mind, "I am your master, and you are my servant, my instrument, and you must obey me." If you persist in making your objective mind pay attention to this declaration, you will soon begin to feel that you are master, and your objective mind must accept it as the truth; and as soon as both minds recognize the truth of that declaration from that moment self-control and self-mastery are assured.

Another way to take from the objective mind its power over the subjective mind is to declare, "You cannot control me," or "you cannot disturb or make me uncomfortable." The word, "cannot" always expresses limitation, and, used in the proper place, it destroys wrong creations; used improperly, it limits one's power to progress. It is useless to argue with the objective mind, because it is a waste of force; one might just as well argue with an animal and expect to convince it of the error of its ways. The only way to be successful in conquering it is to command and compel it to obey, and when it attempts to argue with you, command it to be silent. Tell it to be still, and let that be your answer to all its protests and arguments; and the greater the vehemence with which you speak these words, the sooner the objective mind will obey you.

Replace desire thoughts with positive statements of rejection of the habit – crowd out the "wanting" thoughts – leave no room for them, and do not allow the objective self to insist that it is the "real" self. This is a type of salesmanship. You convince yourself, by constant repetition, until you regard your desire mind as completely separate from the real you. The only danger here is in emotional self-hypnosis. Discrimination is required to avoid mistakes.

Separate yourself from your objective mind in thought, and for convenience while learning to master it, identify it with your body. Realize that you are separate from, and superior to it, treat it as if it were a child entrusted to your care by Deity to enlighten and educate. And while you are putting into practice these suggestions, demand daily from the Supreme Power the highest wisdom of which you are capable of receiving, for "...all things whatsoever ye shall ask in prayer, believing, ye shall receive."

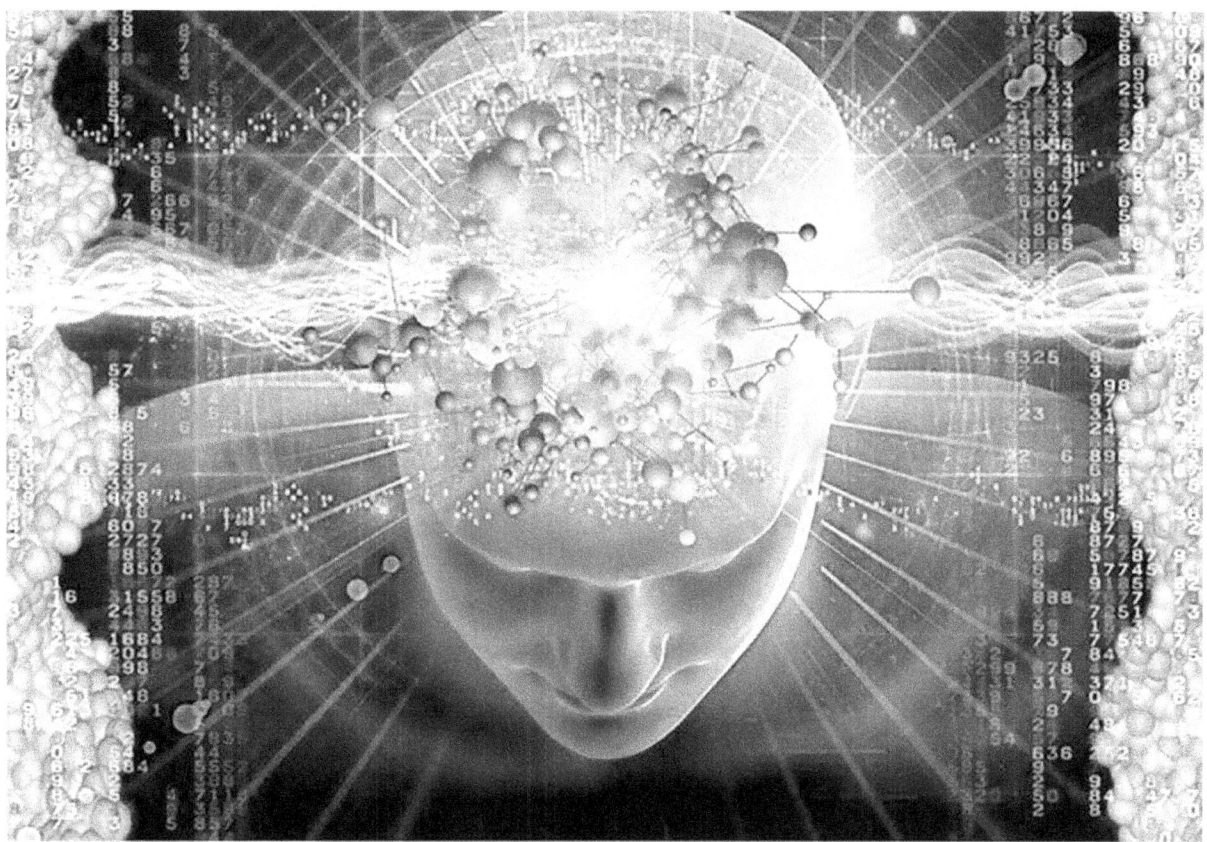

Your subjective mind holds the key to a life of excellence. The Universal mind is also subjective in nature because it too creates what is impressed upon it through your thinking.

Dr. Robert Lanza, an adjunct professor at Wake Forest University Medical School, suggests that death is an illusion because the living consciousness of a person is energy which exists across the infinity of multiverses.

9

THE REALITY AND ILLUSION OF DEATH

The following chapter will explain the *"Egyptian Book of the Dead,"* the "Limbo" of the Christian, and the "Bardo" of the Tibetans. For the Theosophists it is the Kama-Loka, Rupa-Loka of Deva-chan. In the Sanskrit it is Avatamsaka-Sutra, guarded by a Tathdgata, or Dyhan Chohan.

With all due respect to Egyptologists, there seems to be a great deal of confusion with respect to the periods or kingdoms in Egypt. We find by studying the wall paintings and art work of Egyptian times, to which this generation fortunately has access, that most of the kings of Egypt were in constant egoic battle with each other to impress history that they were the greatest. This has resulted in the establishment of records during their reigns of which they had little or no understanding. To clarify this, it should be understood that with the Egyptians, as with most of us, tradition and legend are not easily disposed of in the public mind; therefore when a King depicted some supernatural event he wished to be associated with it. One may confirm this statement by examining the records of all of these periods.

The persistent legend that runs through all of these dynasties is to the effect that the God-King, who in ancient days was married to his sister, or Twin Ray, and might even be incarnate as one person, would always return "home" in a solar boat. The solar boat, of course, in modern times, could be interpreted as a space ship. Modern researchers are still puzzled as to the actual function of the great Pyramid of Giza. Its ancient function was destroyed long before the advent of the subsequent pyramid builders. The fabulous kings of Egyptian history had fallen into a materialistic state whereby the corpse and its materialistic necessities were paramount. Therefore a study of the hieroglyphics of Egypt will reveal nothing more than a tradition rather than a way of life, as the Egyptians failed to understand the ancient teachings; consequently, their empire disappeared.

Each proud civilization has had the opportunity of studying and understanding this ancient wisdom. Failure to do so has always made it possible for an opposing philosophy, exemplified by brute force, to destroy them. Today we face the same situation.

THE FEAR OF DEATH

From the very beginning of the time that the objective, or animal, mind was created upon the Earth, it has always been afraid of the transition we call death. This is due in part to its intense desire for life, and also to the fact that it is oblivious to all of its past states of consciousness, and is entirely unconscious of a continued state of existence upon any other plane than the material, for the seat of the memory of past incarnations is in the subjective mind. To the objective mind, physical form is life, and it believes that in order to maintain life the material, physical form must be preserved. Since its desire for life is greater than all of its other desires, the disintegration of the form, for the animal or objective mind, is the greatest misfortune that can happen to it. And until each subjective mind is eventually able to impress upon its objective mind the truth that life is really God, and is therefore eternal, and that its physical existence is not dependent upon physical form, humans will continue to fear death and the disintegration of the form more than anything else in the world.

Men formerly believed that immortality could be gained only through the preservation of the material form, and, because they wished to meet again those whom they had loved and lost through "death," they used every available means they could think of in order to preserve as intact as possible the deserted physical shells, with the hope and belief that at some future time those same bodies would be re-animated and be restored to the bereaved who were left behind. Therefore, it was really the objective man's desire for perpetuity that caused men to have their own and their friends' physical bodies preserved after the egos had left them for other realms. Some races thought that "death" was really a form of suspended animation, and that, by means of it, the life principle or the soul was locked into the body, and would remain there until some great Being should come to earth and could arouse and restore it to activity, "the graves shall be opened up and the dead come forth." To the persons who believed this, the destruction or loss of the physical body caused even greater sorrow than the actual "death," since such a loss, to their way of thinking, would have prevented any possibility of resurrection, and of consequent immortality.

There were other people who believed that the ego of a man was not locked inside his body after "death," but was bound to it by invisible fetters which permitted it to go only a few feet from the body. And the followers of this faith believed that it was a sacred duty to daily place food and drink at the head or feet of the corpse, or somewhere within its reach, so that the "life principle" could consume them, and thus be kept strong and able to use the body when the time came for it to be restored to activity. To these persons, the failure to provide food and drink for an excarnated ego was a much greater crime than murder, and was punished by slow torture, such as starvation, or some terrible affliction which was believed to be equal to what the souls suffered in consequence of the neglect of the ones who had failed to provide the food and drink.

To the occultist there is no "death," according to the common acceptance of this term. The condition we call death is a complete demagnetization of the atoms which compose a material form. Complete demagnetization of a form produces the entire disintegration of that form, and since the atoms of which a form is composed are held together only by the magnetic attraction that exists between them, disintegration cannot become complete until all of the magnetism has been withdrawn from the form which the atoms combined to compose. Therefore a physical body cannot really be called "dead" until it is entirely disintegrated, and any artificial means which might be used upon it to prevent it from disintegrating will only retard the demagnetization.

We have already discussed vibrations, and the magnetic attractions and repulsions of the atoms. We will now continue a little further with the subject of vampirization, since vampirization is usually the beginning of disintegration, or "death." The demagnetization of a physical body is produced by the constant expenditure of its magnetism in greater quantities than it is received, and this condition may be produced in various ways. The generation of force, which is always magnetic, is entirely dependent upon the rotary motion of the atoms composing a center. And since the expression, or giving out, of force, is dependent upon the elliptical motion of a center, we can easily understand why the physical body of a man or an animal generates the most force when it is resting or sleeping. In other words, natural sleep, which is absolute rest to a physical body or center, is the greatest generator of magnetic force of any condition into which that body can enter.

Everything that has form, whether it is so called inanimate, or animate, is created subject to cyclic law; and during the first half of its daily, weekly, monthly, or yearly cycles it possesses much more magnetic force than it does during the latter half of those cycles. This is because the magnetic force is constantly flowing and ebbing through material forms, whether they are suns, worlds, or men. And this flowing and ebbing may be regarded as action and reaction, or life and "death." When a world is created and given its orbit, one half of the time it travels towards the sun, and the other half of the time it travels away from it. When it is going toward the sun, it is becoming magnetized, and then it is generating more force than it is giving. But when it is going away from the sun, then it is giving more magnetism than it is receiving, and all of the inhabited worlds are alike in this respect. As conditions are now, the Earth is gradually giving more magnetism than it receives, and the time will eventually come when it must either rest or disintegrate.

This is because as the Earth grows older, its responsibilities increase rather than diminish, for as men and beasts multiply, more demands are made upon the earth for their maintenance, and its natural resources are consumed in greater quantities. In addition, every year it is robbed more and more of its minerals, which when in their natural states serve as repositories for the magnetic force it receives from the sun during the Earth's flood tides. But the Divine Law provides periods of rest for the worlds and suns, just as opportunities for rest are provided for men and beasts that live upon these worlds, and these Cosmic rests are taken by the planets to the full limit of the time given to them. Because of taking these rests, their lives and their usefulness are prolonged.

In the life of a world there are seven great periods of inactivity, each lasting as long as the periods of activity, and in this way each world is able to regain some of the magnetism of which it has been robbed. But it never fully regains all of it, for if that were possible, it would continue in the form in which it began to exist until the end of the Cosmic Day in which it was created. This would not be desirable, because in order that evolution may not be limited or delayed by old forms, all forms must be made to give way to new ones when their period of usefulness is ended. For it is the same with worlds as it is with men; they live and revolve about their central suns until their material forces have been spent, and they become physically demagnetized and unfit for further use. Then their time of rest comes on. The throbbing life force is either suspended or withdrawn, and their consciousness is then changed from action to inaction.

For as long as humans have had consciousness there has been the awareness of death. With this also comes the belief that our soul is infinite, a part of the Universal Consciousness.

DEATH - THE SECOND BIRTH

There comes a time when the disintegration or "death" of the physical body or material form must come, and, because of the breaking of family ties and familiar associations, this is often a very sad occasion. To the evolving, developing ego that becomes disembodied, "death" is really a second birth into a higher realm or plane of consciousness and it is through this transition that it becomes relieved of all physical pains and discomforts. But, because of its love for the friends it must leave, who mourn and grieve because of its absence, it is sometimes made to suffer great mental depression and sadness, and is thus prevented from entering fully into the joys of the mental and spiritual states of being. This is because the sorrow and grief of its earthly friends attract and hold it to earth. By their wishing or demanding that it shall return to them, it is drawn back by the magnetic attraction of love, and is sometimes deprived of mental or spiritual happiness for years because, of the mourning of its friends.

And this is really a very selfish attitude for us to take when we have become separated from a loved one through transition. For if we were to honestly search ourselves for the cause of our grief, we would find that it is really self-pity which motivates it. We are really sorry for ourselves, that we must be separated from our loved one. We will no longer feel the loving touch, we will not hear the voice we loved – we will no longer be able to enjoy the association, and the pleasure of the company of that dear friend, and we weep from sheer frustration, for we know that we are powerless to bring back the soul of the one who has gone. If the person had suffered from a disease, and every hour spent upon the earth plane was one of torture, and we truly loved that person, we surely would not want to hold him here with us, but should be glad to see his release from that painful condition. But many will say, "What of the one who is struck down in perfect health? This should not have had to happen." But if we truly loved that person we would not want to hold back his development and evolution. We must remember that there is a Divine Design for each of us, and many of us do not know the Plan for our own evolution, let alone that of another person.

When the time has come for an ego to leave its earthly vehicle, the real process of death is as natural as was the process of its birth into the world, and is very similar. As the head of the human child is born first and afterwards the body, in just this manner the head of the ego emerges and rises above the physical head. Then slowly the shoulders, and then the body, appear, and finally the limbs and feet. There are always disembodied egos waiting to receive and assist the passing soul, and, if the shock of its separation from the physical body has been so great that it is unconscious for a time, as is often the case, these disembodied friends support and strengthen it, until it has regained consciousness and enough magnetic strength that it can support itself. We are never idle after transition, for there are many things to be done in order to prepare ourselves for a return to the earth plane in another body. There are many who are employed, when they are not otherwise learning and assisting in various works, in guiding the souls who have just passed through transition to their new homes, and giving them every possible care and assistance.

For the first few hours after its disembodiment, an ego is never so strong as afterward, because so much of its magnetic force is still left in its deserted physical body. But as the body grows cold, because of the continuous lowering of the rate of vibrations of the atoms composing it, the magnetic force is drawn into the ego that has just left it. With this added magnetism, the disembodied ego gains strength and greater consciousness, and if the physical body should be cremated, and not embalmed or entombed, the ego is liberated from its material body as soon as its physical atoms are dispersed. For there is a magnetic cord that binds the ego to its body until complete disintegration has taken place, the same as the umbilical cord unites the infant to its prenatal envelope, and it is as great a kindness to sever the magnetic cord and liberate the ego by cremation as it is to cut the umbilical cord of the newly born infant, and set it free from its own encumbrances.

Man's body is of such design that no use of it will be denied him after he reaches the spiritual realms. Here on earth there are beings that can fly, who can walk, can swim, drift, float-beings who can go swiftly or slowly. No one can do all of them combined. Each one has his own particular limitations, but eventually, after transition, the collective powers appear in everyone. We do not have physical bodies in the higher realms, because there is really no physical substance there, as we understand it here. In order that you may more readily understand this, it is necessary to recall that Universal Consciousness passed through a series of stages and changes in order to make matter out of light. Our bodies there will be composed, not of the chemical elements as here, but simply of the substance that preceded the stage of such elements. In other words, it is merely the taking of the development as far as it had gone prior to the creation of actual matter, as we call it, and molding that mass into form.

From this it would seem that the creations, after death, go backward, but this is not so. It is merely the putting aside of the material burdens of the form, and clearing itself of the debris out of which it was born. What we look upon as material and "substantial" is really only a dream, for all matter is unstable, transitory, and soon goes back to its composite conditions. The body of the soul is a part of Universal Thought, advanced beyond the stage of light, but not as far as the stage of chemical elements. There is no change when the elements are not used. The infinite Soul is composed of no elements; therefore it does not change, as nothing can affect it. The intelligence in the tree is not the tree itself. The mind in man is not the "man" himself. He can have his legs cut off, and his arms; yet his mind does not suffer any loss. That part which can leave the body while the latter is asleep, and visit distant parts of the globe, is not the body, nor the mind, but the soul-consciousness. *The *Shrimad Bhagavata* explains that this is the stage that one experiences in the reality of the arch-formulae, "Thou art That" (tat-tvamasi); "All this is but the Principle, the Brahman" (sarvam Khalu-idam Brahma). All is one.

Many cannot understand how we will be able to recognize our relatives and friends on the "other side" if they do not have their physical bodies. They do not realize that the identity is wholly in the mind, but it is not in the physical mind. All of our experiences, enjoyments, and happiness are stored away in the subconscious mind. After death, subconscious mind comes into its own estate. It is the power that feels, that knows, and that enjoys the scenes. The individual Being exists in its mental activity, and there is a spiritual body created out of the new birth, so that the Creator may have around him immortal companions, for both His and their happiness. The love for companionship is a very strong emotion.

LIFE IN THE HIGHER REALMS

If you can imagine what a life in the higher realms will mean – with a body as described, and a mind of the keenest appreciation, with a sense of perpetual endurance and strength, then you will realize how worthwhile it would be for you to try to free yourself from the dream world, or earthly existence. When you arrive in the new world, there is a feeling, which will take possession of you, of the limitlessness of this new world. You do not arrive at the border, and you do not know which way leads to the center. Every direction in which you look you see the vast dominions stretch out. And if you were to fly over that infinite world, you would seek the end in vain, for there are broad, level fields for thousands and thousands of miles, to use an "Earth" term.

The soul leaves the body in much the same way in all cases. The physical body grows negative and cold as the elements of the spiritual body grow warm and positive. The feet first begin to grow cold. Over the head there is a magnetic halo, an ethereal emanation, which is golden in appearance, and throbbing as though conscious. By the time the body is cold up to the knees and elbows, the emanation has ascended higher into the air. The legs are now cold to the hips, and the arms to the shoulders, and although the emanation has not risen any higher in the room, it appears larger. The death coldness steals over the breast. If the person has been suffering great pain, there are signs of agony, the head and body tossing from side to side. Then, just before death, all feeling of pain is lost, and the body becomes perfectly calm as though going to sleep.

"The Soul Hovering over the Body Reluctantly Parting with Life." Engraving for the 1808 deluxe edition of "The Grave," a poem by Robert Blair.

It has ceased to breathe, and the pulse has stopped; the emanation is elongated, and looks like a human form. It is still connected with the brain, however. The head of the person is internally throbbing; a slow deep throb – not painful, but more like the beat of the sea. The thinking faculties remain retained, while nearly every part of the person is dead. Often a dying person, even at the last feeble pulse beat, will arise impulsively in bed to speak to a friend, but will fall back dead. The brain is the last to yield up the life principle; the soul, or what is called the emanation, which usually extends about half way between the body and the ceiling, is connected with the brain by a very fine thread which is invisible to the ordinary eye, but can be plainly seen by the clairvoyant. The emanation now ascends, and there appears something white and shining, which looks like a human head; in a few moments the faint outline of the face appears, then the neck and shoulders, and then, in rapid succession, the other parts of the body.

It is a trifle smaller than the physical body, but is a perfect duplicate, minus all of its disfigurements. The thread connecting with the brain within the physical body can still be seen. Then there is a withdrawal of the electric principle. The thread snaps, and the spiritual body is free and ready to start on its journey. Then it is able to pass through what we call solid substance, which really is not solid at all. When one has developed himself so that he can see the spiritual body leaving, all of the horror of death which is possessed by people who cannot see anything of the beautiful process of the interior is lost to him. If they could only see the newly risen spiritual body move off toward a ray of magnetic light which has penetrated the room, they would know that they had no cause for weeping – they would know that the departed soul is indeed not "dead," but merely separated from its physical body, and that they themselves will pass through the same experience in a few years.

Around the head of the spiritual body there is a golden shaft of Celestial Light, which is sent from above as a guiding power. The spiritual being is still asleep, like a newborn babe; the eyes are closed, and there is no consciousness as yet, for this is an unconscious slumber. Sometimes the sleep is long, and at other times very short. The guiding power sent from above now starts the spiritual body on its journey. Sometimes it passes through a solid wall, and at other times its guiding power will suggest to someone about the body to open a door, or a window. This person, of course, is not aware of the fact of having received the impression to open the door or window for a few minutes. The spiritual body then silently leaves the house. The celestial attractions soon draw it to its new plane. There it is surrounded by a beautiful assemblage of guardian friends. They throw their loving arms around the sleeping one and on they speed to the World of Light. This is a true vision, and nearly all true clairvoyants know it to be so, for many have experienced the celestial flights of the soul.

That the soul passes out of the body, then, we know, for we have seen it. This spiritual body has an existence and a position somewhere in space; it must follow the laws of space, including time, and have a relative, as well as an absolute, consciousness. In the case of a man who is killed suddenly or violently, he loses all sensation; existence seems nothing. In cases of sudden death by accident, individuality usually returns in a few days, after he reaches the "Summerland." He is guided by some, brother and tenderly cared for until he can realize the change, for often in these cases people wake up on the other side and cannot realize that they have really died. When the proper time approaches for the spirit's awakening, he hears celestial music, or the murmuring melody of distant streams. Then sensation gradually returns, and he is made to realize where he is.

There are people to whom we are very much attached; their outward appearance may not appeal to us, but we have an invisible manifestation emanating from them, or coming from them. You have met people for whom you have felt a strong liking. You never stopped to think of the cause for this attachment. It was not the clothes they wore, nor their beauty, for you have seen others more beautiful and better dressed for whom you did not have the same feeling. All beauty except that which comes from within is perishable. Among the animals there are none more beautiful than a panther, a lion, or a tiger, providing they are securely locked in a cage. But if we should meet them in the woods, when they are hungry, they would become horrible. It is the same with people; we do not care so much for the clothes they wear, nor the beauty of the person, as we do for the spirit which they manifest.

That which we love is within. We do not see it, but it is there. When so-called death comes, and we are separated from our loved ones, and they are no longer able to manifest through their bodies as before, we do not find the corpse interesting; in fact, many cannot bear to look at a dead body. All that has endeared it to you has gone. That which you loved was within, and manifested outwardly; that invisible something which we did not see manifested through that body. Death is necessary in order that new life may arise. There could be no life without death, and so there could be no real knowledge of the visible world without insight into the invisible, and to understand the visible we must explore the invisible. Without this knowledge, life would become feeble. With it we are strengthened, and it renews our freshness and health.

CONNECTION WITH THE PHYSICAL WORLD

Even after death man does not sever all connection with the physical world. He usually has unsatisfied desires that still sustain the connection. These desires and wishes spring from his three lower bodies, and can manifest only in the external. For instance, hunger is caused by the external body; just as soon as the external body is no longer connected with the ego, hunger ceases. If the ego had no further desires than those springing from its own spiritual nature, it could, at death, draw satisfaction from the spiritual world into which it has been transplanted. But it still has other desires. Life has kindled a longing for pleasures that can only be enjoyed by means of physical organs, although these pleasures do not originate in these organs. It is not only the three bodies which demand gratification from the physical world, but the ego also finds pleasure in that world of which there is no like enjoyment in the spiritual world.

During life there are two kinds of desires of the ego; those which come from the bodies and must be gratified within them, but which come to an end when the disintegration takes place, and those which come from the spiritual nature of the ego. When the ego lives in the body, those cravings are satisfied by means of bodily organs. The hidden spiritual element is at work during the bodily manifestations of the body organs and senses. The spiritual element is also at work after death, although in a different form. Those spiritual longings of the ego it still possesses after death. It can still enjoy, while even the senses are no longer the medium through which the spiritual rays pass.

The first after-death experience differs in many ways from those of our present life. When man is passing through the purification stage, he lives backwards. He goes over his whole life since birth, starting not at birth, but at those events immediately preceding his death, and passes through them all backwards to his birth. He sees with spiritually enlightened eyes all of those things which were not of a spiritual nature, and he knows that they were not. For example, if a man dies at fifty, as he reviews his life backwards he finds that at forty he became very angry at someone, and did him an injury. Now, in going over the experience, he does not feel the satisfaction that his attack gave him, but, instead, he experiences the pain he inflicted upon the other. This pain which he feels in the afterlife experiences is caused by a desire of the ego arising only from the outer physical world. Therefore, in doing wrong to another, you not only injure him, but also yourself, although the injury to yourself is not always apparent during life. After death, however, all of the wrongs which you have done to others become visible to the ego, and have to be destroyed in the "consuming fire" in the same way in which they were created.

When, in going through your past life, you finally come to your birth, all of your desires have been purged in "purifying flames," and there is nothing then to interfere with your devoting yourself entirely to the spiritual world. It takes a period of time equal to one-third of the time that one has lived, to cast off the astral corpse and purify it after death. After passing through the purification, the ego is ready for an entirely new state of consciousness. Before death, images of some kind had to be brought before it, before the light of consciousness would fall on it; but now everything is seen from within. The ego lives upon the earth plane between birth and death, but it depends upon the manifestation of the senses. It is only when the ego becomes freed from all ties of sense that it can see with its true innermost nature, which the senses had obscured.

When you develop your clairvoyant observation, and are able to visit the place of purging fire, you will see sights which will horrify you. It will be a painful vision, the pleasure of which seems to consist in destruction, and passions impel the dwellers there to evil doing of such a description that the evil of the physical world would seem insignificant in comparison. But it must be remembered that what may seem horrible to us is looked upon as good by these beings. The beings going through the purification are not visible to the physical sight, but to clairvoyant sight only – but their effects are clear and apparent. When man passes through the purification, he finds himself in the spiritual world where everything is of a spiritual nature, and his longings can only be satisfied by spiritual things.

After the purification period, then everything pouring in upon the ego from the spiritual world is not only a reforming, but a reorganizing force. After a certain period the ego gathers around it an astral body, which will again be able to inhabit an etheric and physical body like man possesses while on this earth between birth and death. The man will once more be born to renew his earthly existence, with which, however, will be incorporated the results of his former life. Until the rebuilding of his astral body, the man sees this construction going on. The powers of the spiritual world are not manifested through the external organs, but from within. He is able to observe that manifestation as long as his attention is not turned to an outer world of perception. When the astral body is reconstituted, his attention is then turned outward. The astral body then longs for an etheric and a physical body. It is thereby turned away from its inner revelations, and this is why there is an intermediate state, during which man is immersed in consciousness, for consciousness can emerge again in the physical world only when the necessary organs for physical perception are formed. When this period commences, the consciousness illuminated by inner perception ceases, the new etheric body begins to link itself to the astral, and man can once again enter a physical body.

THE LAW OF KARMA

Before the attachment of the etheric body takes place, there is something of very great importance which takes place before the man enters into another physical existence. During his former life he created disturbing forces which he saw after death. For instance, by losing his temper he imagined that something said to him justified him in striking another person, and causing him pain. After death it was shown how he was made to suffer for the pain, and how it prolonged his purification process. Before he again reenters into physical life, these hindrances to his evolution confront the ego anew. Just as on the threshold of death, he again sees a memory-picture of his past life, and all of its mistakes. He also sees a vision of the approaching life. He sees before him all of the obstacles which will beset his path, all that he must overcome before he will be ready to advance in his evolution. The picture that is still impressed upon him, of having caused another man pain, influences him in entering life again to make amends, for that pain caused by him in his previous life has a determining effect upon the new. His present life will, to a great extent, be controlled by his former life, for this is the Law of Destiny, or the Law of Karma (Cause and Effect.)

Since we have discussed the re-embodiment of man by the term popularly known as reincarnation, we must now take up the matter of what becomes of him between his embodiments, or incarnations, after the purification process has been completed. And just as there are different states of matter in our physical world, such as gases, liquids, and solids, so are there different states of matter in the subjective world, and these different grades do not lie separate and distinct from each other. On the physical plane we have many conditions where substances interblend, and where each substance actually occupies the same space, while lying within the other. We also have the solid earth, with certain waters both within and on the earth. And outside the earth we have water or vapor in clouds, and yet within both the earth and the clouds is air, or gases, which extend further out into space.

On the subjective side of life there are finer forms of matter, which interpenetrate our earth, water, and gas. Around the earth there are belts or zones, composed of finer matter very much like the rings around Saturn, and the densest of these rings interpenetrates the earth, while each of the other rings extends further and further out into space, according to its rarity and size. These rings are material, but each is of a different tenuity of matter, which is caused by its different rate of vibration. It is to these several belts, or zones, that man goes between his incarnations, and it is to the first belt, the one which interpenetrates the earth, that the souls or minds of the animals go.

According to a man's rate of vibration, or specific "soul" gravity, he is drawn into one or another of those inner belts or spheres which corresponds to his own vibrations. The subjective belts or spheres are not for the growth or development of man, but are places of rest, where he reviews the experiences and assimilates the knowledge gained on earth. It is impossible for man to pass beyond the photosphere of this earth and incarnate upon other planets until his vibrations, which control his specific gravity, have become so high and so god-like that the law of gravity operating here can no longer confine him to the earth or the subjective planes which surround it.

A man's thoughts are the cause of his vibrations, and therefore a man who is material, sensuous and sensual is by harmonious vibration drawn to the first subjective plane, and becomes earthbound. He cannot rise higher than any other animal, and so he remains in this first belt which surrounds and interpenetrates the material world, until he is ready to reincarnate. But as a man's mentality overcomes his emotions, in his course of evolution, and as his subjective mind finally learns to control his objective mind, he becomes more spiritual. His rates of vibration become higher, and then, when the time comes to rest between incarnations, he is drawn to the belt which is of a higher rate of vibration, and goes further away from the earth. So you see, there are actually several "Heavens."

And now comes a very important point in the mental aspect of this law of re-embodiment, which is the practical side of it. Man is not only a center of consciousness, but he is also a center of self-consciousness. He has free will, within certain great latitudes, and he has freedom of choice, and this fact holds him to a great responsibility; for man, by his own choice, or thinking, determines not only his heaven, but also his earth life. In other words, he directs both the time of his incarnation, or re-embodiment, and the environment of his re-embodiment. The less developed an ego, the more rest it requires between earth lives; this is a general rule, and applies to every living thing. You could not expect a child to work as hard, or as continuously, as a man, and you would not expect as much of an undeveloped man along any line as you would of a developed man; and so we see that the thought or development of a man determines the length of time which must elapse between his re-embodiments. Weak, tired, and disappointed souls, who are ignorant of the laws of life, require a long time between incarnations. The average period between incarnations is approximately one hundred and forty years for the great mass of men but according to the strength of an ego, and its desire to evolve, and therefore its desire to have a vehicle through which to evolve, does the period of time between incarnations lessen or lengthen, and among progressive egos the time between incarnations averages much less.

We can readily see that the shorter the time between re-embodiments, the more experience must be gained, and the more knowledge carried over from one embodiment to another, the more rapid is our progress on our evolutionary journey. It is advantageous for a soul to keep his body for a very long time, or, in other words, to prolong each of his incarnations to as great a length as it is possible to do. It is a great mistake to cast aside a body before it has become so old and worn that it is no longer of any use as a vehicle.

Every moment of our lives we change our bodies, and make them better or worse by our thoughts. We also create our environment, either liberating or enslaving ourselves according to the quality of our thoughts and emotions. We create ties between ourselves and other souls through hating as much as through loving, because whatever our minds dwell upon we draw to ourselves. If you think of someone you love, immediately there is a vibration in the ether between you and that person. If you continue to think of that person, the vibration becomes intensified until a blue magnetic cord becomes established between you, a mental telegraph wire, so to speak, over which your thoughts pass to each other. This connection is visible to the clairvoyant, but not to the physical eye, and can only be destroyed by disuse for a greater or shorter lapse of time, according to its size and strength.

If you hate a person, you are constantly sending hateful thoughts to that person, and by doing this you are keeping a constant vibration of the ether between you. After a time this vibration becomes a real pathway for your thoughts to travel upon and it actually binds you to the object of your hatred with an invisible bond; yet this bond is harder to break than a bond of steel. This is the reason that groups of egos come back to earth and incarnate in certain families and communities. Those who love each other are drawn again and again into closer relationships of life, not because "blood is thicker than water," but because of the ties they formed in past lives.

And then there is the great law of equilibrium, or the Law of Justice, which we are constantly putting into action by our thoughts. This law modifies our evolution, and limits our scope of free will under certain conditions. There is a law of absolute justice, and it is only man's own unjust thoughts which lead him to believe otherwise. Perfect love is synonymous with absolute justice, and God is Love. If balance were not maintained on all planes, chaos would reign supreme. On the physical plane we can see the manifestation of equilibrium everywhere if we look for it. For instance, if you throw a stone into a pool of water, you will see how the disturbance caused by displacing the water at a certain point is adjusted by the movement on the surface of the water from that point to the; extreme edge of the pool, and back again to the point of the disturbance below the surface. This is the law of equilibrium working to adjust the water of the pool to the new condition. It is through equilibrium that the great law of justice brings back to man exactly what he has sent forth, and this is why he often finds in his everyday life that he must readjust himself. "For whatsoever a man soweth, that also shall he reap."

If a person is born and reared under favorable circumstances, it is because the character of his thoughts brought him into that environment. He was attached by the Great Law to the parents who were able and willing to give him the advantages he received. We could save ourselves much misdirected or wasted force and sympathy if we would only recognize the fact that "nothing ever happens by accident" in this world, but that everything is governed by Law. We do not say that we should leave unfortunate souls where we find them, but we should not attempt to quarrel with the law which is giving to them exactly what they have asked for at some time in their past. However, if you see a soul who wants help, then by all means help it; but do not weep over those who are enjoying the fruits of their own thought labors, and do not be dissatisfied or criticize God because some souls have placed themselves in certain unpleasant walks of life or have brought upon themselves unhappy conditions.

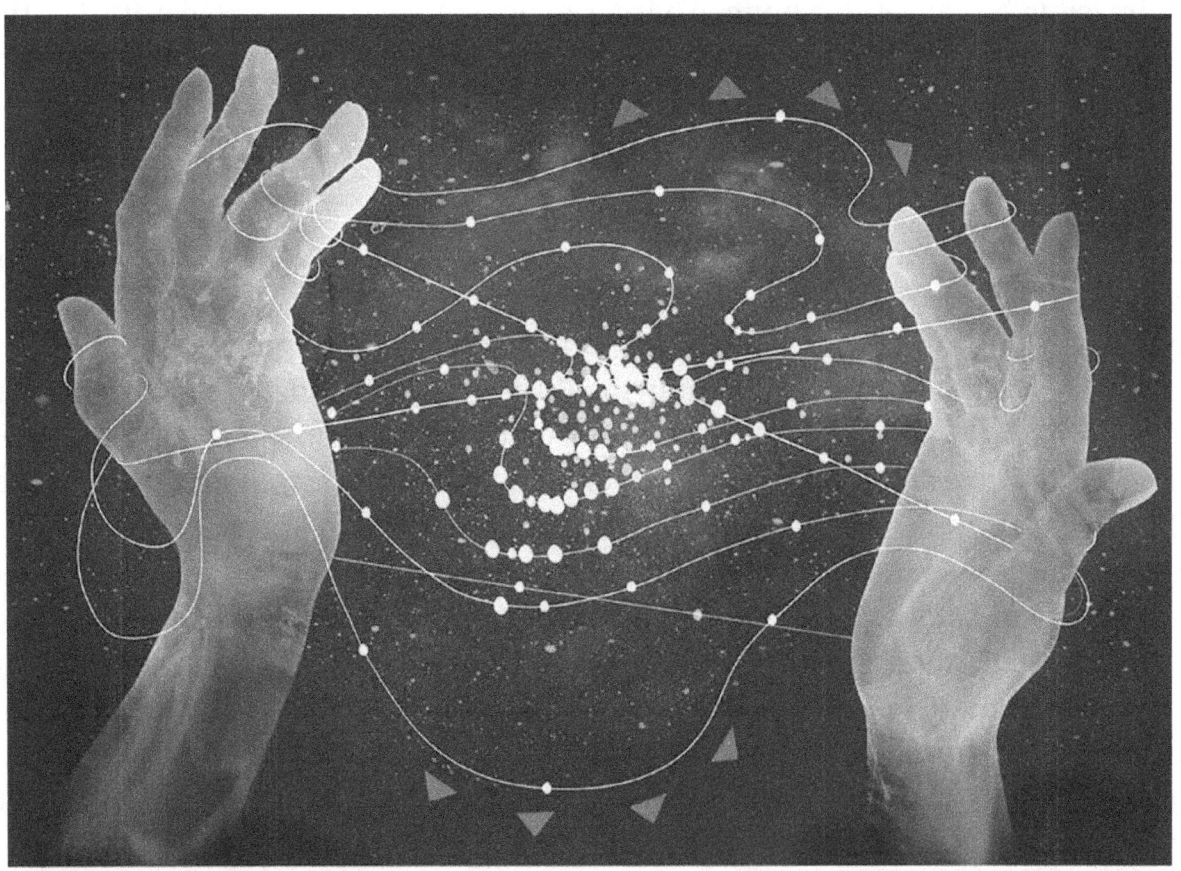

The law of karma refers to the law of cause and effect. Every conscious act brings about a certain result. If we act motivated by greed, hatred, or delusion, we are planting the seed of suffering; when our acts are motivated by generosity, love, or wisdom, then we are creating the karmic conditions for abundance and happiness.

Man not only determines his birth and the quality of his body at birth, but he modifies his body every moment of his life. *The Law of Karma (Cause and Effect) operates also in those bodies his parents supply; i.e., Mendel's Law still holds good (the hereditary theory), but few see the all inclusive laws operating.

The dissipated, sensuous, and sensual criminal, thinking only of that which pertains to the external side of life, excarnates and after a time is brought back to earth into an environment where he is prenatally marked with the very characteristics that his own mind indicates. He takes the type of body which is the best expression for him. It is most unusual for such a soul to succeed in getting out of that environment in just one life, because its body and brain express so strongly those particular characteristics. It is possible, however, for it to do one of two things; either to indulge in its criminal acts until the depths of degradation have been reached, and it learns that the price is entirely too great to pay for such pleasures and decides to reform, or it may commence to fight for self-control from the beginning, and gradually change its body and environment by changing its thought.

In the sense of making his own character, then, man is his own maker. He has the free will to think, and every thought is a tendency in a given direction. One thought does not make a character, of course, but one thought is a tendency toward a character, since once the initial impulse is given it has a tendency to repeat itself until a habit is formed, and habits make character. Therefore, every thought a man thinks has its effect upon his destiny, not only in shaping his present life, but also his future incarnations.

CREATING A FEAR OF HELL

In the beginning of the Christian era, the followers of Jesus began teaching and healing humanity, according to the manner in which he had taught and healed before them. Later they decided, after many sad experiences, that it was necessary to teach something besides the doctrine of Love to the cruel, animal men of their day. So instead of following in the footsteps of Jesus and continuing to teach, as he had, that God is a loving Father, and is ready to receive and to help all of His children, they digressed from the path of true Christianity, and began to use hell and eternal damnation as a club with which to beat men into submission, and to force them to worship according to their dictates. In the same manner that some parents believe it is necessary to frighten their children into submission and obedience by threatening that a "bogie man" will get them, so the early Church fathers succeeded in frightening men into obedience and submission by threats of the devil and a future punishment. When they found that men could be influenced through their fears more readily than through Love, they intensified their teachings by painting terrible pictures of a future state of existence.

Believing, as so many of the Church fathers did, that the Christian Church was the only doorway to salvation, and that every soul who did not enter it was doomed to destruction, they did not hesitate to give their wildest flights of fancy to inspired truths, which they felt would serve to bring souls into that institution, and since a story never loses details by being repeated, as the years went by the stories of hell, as given by the early fathers, lost nothing by their constant repetition. And when they saw how well their schemes had worked toward increasing the membership and consequent support of the Church, they redoubled their efforts and their falsehoods. After a time, forgetting – or ignoring – the fact that Jesus had said, "Suffer little children, and forbid them not to come unto Me, for of such is the kingdom of heaven," they invented new hell horrors by including unbaptized and stillborn infants along with the sinning adults on their lists of candidates for that terrible place.

However, like all other destructive things, by reason of their own natures these deceptions finally returned upon and destroyed themselves. The unreasonableness and injustice of such a thing as infant damnation finally rose like a great wall between the faces of the bereaved parents and their God, until it came to pass that either God or the creed must go out of their hearts. To some persons these teachings brought materialism, while many women and men became infidels, and repudiated God altogether. Then there were a few who were brave and strong enough to repudiate the belief in hell, and banded themselves together into a society called Universalists, declaring that hell was upon earth, and that man received his punishment as he went through life, and not hereafter.

It was formerly a habit of all teachers to wear cowls and skirts, and while dressed in this manner they demanded and received a reverence from the people which greatly aided them in controlling their worshippers. This was because the teachers so nearly resembled the pictures of the heavenly saints whom they professed to represent on earth. However, gradually, as the more modem clergymen commenced to adopt a style of dress less saintly and more fashionable, much of the halo of sanctity was removed from their personalities, and it became quite difficult for the mass of men who had so blindly worshipped signs and symbols, as interpreted by the teachers clad in vestments, to accept as Divine Truth anything given to them by men dressed in trousers and waistcoats. And, notwithstanding the terrible threats of eternal damnation so generously bestowed upon them, many evolving souls revolted from the tyranny of the Church, and adopted newer and easier forms of worship.

This religious reaction, of course, was in perfect accord with Divine Law, which always brings reaction to follow action along any line of thinking and doing. It was natural that there should be a reaction and a relaxation from the established forms of worship, even to the extent of disbelief in a future punishment, or even regarding a future state of existence. It could not be otherwise after the peoples' long submission to the ironclad creeds and dogmas of a Church which depended for its cornerstone upon hell and damnation instead of Divine Love.

When mankind had reached a point where it really wanted to know the truth, there occasionally appeared an individual with intellectual strength and mental poise sufficient to enable him to rise and denounce all man-made creeds, and to declare that there is no anthropomorphic God, but that this is a universe of law, in which all men have the right to a freedom of thought and a freedom of speech. When these intellectual giants first appeared before the people and repudiated the teachings of the Church, the fear enslaved souls fully expected that God, in His vengeance, would pour out His wrath upon those men, and that they would speedily meet with some terrible physical or mental affliction. But when it was seen that those heroes of the times were still permitted to live and to speak what they believed, many who had become surfeited with the old orthodox teachings, and who really desired freedom of thought and action, accepted their words as expressed truth.

Since dire future punishment for terrible crimes is no longer predicted, people have become lulled into a false sense of security. They have swung to the other extreme, and believe they have nothing to fear as a punishment except perhaps public opinion, which is sometimes very gently expressed concerning society's favorites. And because of this belief, a large portion of the human family has again entered into indulgences and transgressions against Divine Law which it dared not enter while bound by the fear of hell. The individuals who believed themselves to be God-fearing were mistaken; they were only hell-fearing, and now that hell has been almost wiped off the religious map, they are neither the one nor the other.

As sad as "death," or the disintegration of a physical body, is to those who love and lose it, it is not to be compared with the sadness which comes to the beings who, by their missions, are sometimes compelled to witness the "second death," or disintegration of another soul or ego. This is a dreadful fate, and it may be a small comfort to know that it comes to the minority instead of the majority of disembodied entities who pass to the subjective planes or realms. Diametrically opposed to the spiritual plane of consciousness, called Nirvana by the Eastern students of occultism, is another plane which the same students call Avitchi. In our scriptures it is called Hell, and represents the very lowest depths of degradation into which an entity can fall. Nothing but conscious, persistent, and unceasing transgression of the Divine Law can bring a soul to this fearful place, and a true knowledge of the existence of it is never given to students until they are far enough advanced to be able to bear that first-hand knowledge without it dangerously affecting them.

The "second death" happens more often to objective, or animal, minds, which, because of their persistent wickedness, have been deserted by their subjective minds. But there are instances where a Son of God goes downward, instead of upward; where it continues to yield to the suggestions of its animal mind until it comes to a point where it deliberately and consciously chooses the left-hand path, instead of the right-hand path, and then it goes down into the nether world instead of up into the higher spiritual realms.

REALMS OF LOWER SPIRITUAL VIBRATIONS

Second death is produced in much the same manner as physical death, or disintegration. The vibrations of a dying soul grow slower and slower, and its specific gravity grows denser and denser until it can no longer remain upon what is called the first subjective plane, or purgatory, but is drawn by the law of attraction, which is also gravic force, down to a lower plane, to continue there its wretched existence with others of its kind. When disintegration really commences, like the old demagnetized physical body it has left it begins to grow darker and darker as its density increases, until it becomes as black as the realms into which it has descended, for there is not one ray of light that penetrates the greatest depths of the awful darkness of that place. Then the form of the dying soul commences to change in shape, and begins to disintegrate, and this disintegration, or second death, continues for centuries.

But before the form of the dying soul begins to disintegrate or be dismembered there is always a hope that it may be saved from that fearful fate, and be raised to a higher plane of consciousness. There are strong and beautiful egos that voluntarily go down into those depths to try to help and save the denizens of that nether world. If, as sometimes occurs, one half of a soul has gone wrong and has sunken into "hell," while the other half has evolved to a point of development where it is able to undertake the work of trying to save its half from annihilation, or "second death," then it descends and approaches as near to it as its vibration will permit; and whispers words of encouragement and consolation to the sinful sufferer, and offers help if it will only try to rise again.

To an incarnated ego it would seem that any soul who had sunk into that place would need only an opportunity for escape to consent to liberation, but such is not the case. In Avitchi, or Hell, a soul becomes so depressed with its wretchedness, so discouraged, and so pessimistic, that it often refuses to make the least effort to change its mode of thinking in order to rise out of its condition. This is because, by its many lives of perversity of thought and action, it has brought itself into a mental condition which holds it as firmly as prison walls and iron bars hold a prisoner. It is a sad picture to see a beautiful ego pleading with its unhappy half, and attempting to raise or lead it to where it may catch a glimpse of a higher and better plane of consciousness which may be gained if it will only make an effort for itself.

No soul has either the power or the right to save another against its will; and it does not matter how far it may have advanced in its development, it cannot bring another into happiness without that other's cooperation and conscious effort in its own behalf. Sometimes these unhappy beings are convinced and persuaded to retrace their steps, and thus rise out of their wretchedness. But more often they will neither respond nor listen to those who would help them. Then they gradually sink lower and lower while becoming more and more wretched, until at last complete disintegration or re-absorbment into the lowest or black cosmic current obliterates them forever from the Universe as individuals.

Because there are advanced egos upon Earth who wish to know the truth, whether it corresponds with their preconceived notions or not, it is possible for many to profit by the results of the investigations and experiences of students with clairvoyant sight; therefore we will attempt to describe the state, or plane, of Avitchi. In its upper portion it vibrates red, while the lower portion vibrates black. The red cosmic current not only surrounds and penetrates the surface of the earth, but it also permeates it, becoming black towards its center. Its darkest, deadliest shades are as destructive and as disintegrating to a dying soul and ego as corrosive acid is destructive to a material body. It eats, consumes, or absorbs the soul atom by atom, until it is entirely disintegrated. Let it be understood that souls and egos are not lost or destroyed through the vindictiveness of an angry God, but through their own willful sinning, and in no other way.

Only very strong and advanced egos are able to visit this plane, and then in the company of another equally strong and advanced soul, since an inexperienced ego, if left to itself, is sometimes caught between two entities, denizens of the lower plane, and is detained and demagnetized by vampirization until the magnetic cord between the physical body and their victim becomes absorbed, and dissolution of the physical body ensues. After descending for several hundred feet into the earth one discovers that there are a number of caverns opening into each other. Subterranean streams of water pour forth from great holes in the rocky walls, flowing through the caverns from end to end and disappearing with a roar over the edge of an abyss in the last cavern. The walls glisten with minerals, and there are veins of ore among the rocks. Great quantities of gold may be seen in the bottoms of shallow streams, which have been washed by the running water until they glitter and shine.

Here groups of entities may be observed who look more like apes than men...with distorted features, grinning mouths, and bulging eyeballs, they make a wretched picture. Their legs are crooked and withered, their arms covered with knots or lumps, and their hands and fingers look like claws. These are animal souls, or objective minds, which were too strong for their subjective minds to control, and who were deserted and left to their fate. When they first passed from physical life they lingered for a time in Purgatory, or upon the first subjective plane of being, casting their diabolical influence upon the minds of such men as they could control until, weakened by their unwise expenditure of magnetic force, and thus losing their power, they were swept from the first plane by the law of evolution or adjustment, which places every individual where it belongs. By reason of their density, these creatures settle here and remain in this plane, or condition, until another cyclic change or movement of the law. Then they are destined to descend still lower, since, being only objective minds, there is no hope of their ever being raised from this condition.

One may see many types of entities also; unfortunate beings who had neglected their opportunities for progression, and are now taking the consequences. Some look frightened, others sad and despairing, but many are rebellious and bitter. They are of many shades of darkness, and, having nothing else to do, they meditate upon their mistakes, or dispute or quarrel among themselves. After passing under many miles of sea, and then down deep into what seems to be almost the center of the earth, one comes into the greatest of all the caverns. This is the place which first gave rise to the Bible legend of hell, or the lake which is supposed to burn forever and forever with unquenchable fire, for that, like nearly all of the old legends, was founded upon fragments of truth. This cavern seems to be a center of attraction toward which many of the vital fluids and gases of the earth are drawn. There are monstrous holes in the walls and roof which look as if they had at some time been vents and served as chimneys to the place. Everywhere are seen heaps of rocks, looking as though they had been heated and tossed into the cavern by some tremendous force, and left to harden in their present grotesque shapes. There are deep, dark pools of water and streams which gush and trickle, according to their size, from among the rocks and crevices. Here and there may be seen hiding and dodging among the shadows the ugly, misshapen forms of some of the inhabitants of that plane. *The stories of Richard Shaver and the Deros are based on these facts.

After traveling about a mile or two, the floors begin a gradual descent, and the further one goes the sharper becomes the decline. Everywhere around are heaps and piles of rock. A glimmer of light appears, glowing from the fiery lake. Looking down, at perhaps a distance of a thousand feet, one sees what seems to be a huge caldron of liquid rock, seething and bubbling, and spurting high toward the roof of the cavern as if it were forced upward by numerous fountains. There is a constant and terrific roaring sound, and a sickening stench arising from the gaseous and sulphurous fumes. This condition is the result of a meeting at that point within the earth of such of the fluids and gases as are combustible by coming into contact. The combination of sulphur, gases and oils, with the different chemicals which are there in great quantities, produces the combustion, and the continuous flow of oil and gas into the center supplies the fuel to keep it burning. This is the largest of the several lakes now existing within the center of the earth, which supply the different volcanoes with their fires.

The entities one sees here are coal black, and they glitter in the firelight as though covered with scales. They are all deformed; some with huge heads and broad shoulders, with legs and arms that seem like sticks. Others have large bodies and small heads, and eyes that look like living coals of fire. All have monstrous mouths and huge ears, and all are hideous. There are even greater depths than this and a place even worse than this, where not even the Masters go. This is where all forms become slowly absorbed, except for their heads, which remain conscious and continue to float about upon a black sea of cosmic consciousness – and finally, after many centuries, the heads, too, become absorbed and drawn back to help swell the great torrent of destructive cosmic force, the upper portion of which is red and is constantly sweeping around and through the earth, and which is ever ready to supply animal man with material for his passions and lower emotions. * *"Dante's Inferno"* is accurate.

Ancient teachers knew the truth, since many were clairvoyant and were conscious of all of the states and grades of happiness or degradation into which souls can come. But because this is the lowest extreme of an abnormal condition of which they were conscious, they used it to frighten men into good behavior. It was not prepared for "lost souls" or egos, but they sank into it themselves, by reason of their sinning, and by the same law of attraction, egos may rise by reason of their goodness and wisdom to great spiritual heights.

THE ASCENDING SUBJECTIVE PLANES

As we have mentioned, Avitchi is the very lowest plane, and next comes Purgatory, or the first subjective plane. The second subjective plane, or first "heaven," which surrounds the earth outside the first plane, is the temporary abode for disembodied egos who have struggled through and have overcome many of the temptations of earth, and have gained a point of such development where they desire to progress instead of retrogress. For such egos, this is a resting place between earth lives, where they may digest, so to speak, their late experiences, and assimilate the good to be had from each. When an ego has reached the second subjective plane, then it is not likely to fall into Avitchi; however, that is not impossible. And should such a fate befall it, then it is due to the fact that it was more negatively than positively good, and fell through lack of strength to resist some great temptation upon earth. After such an ego has been permitted to suffer for a time the consequences of its mistakes, a stronger one goes down and attempts to encourage it, and to assist it to rise out of its unhappy condition. That angel of mercy is usually the other half of itself; however, instances such as these are very rare, although they do sometimes occur.

Passing through the atmosphere of the next higher plane, the third subjective plane, one finds a lovely, peaceful heaven of rest. There are no shadowy places, no darkness, and no gloom here. One sees everywhere trees and flowers, mossy banks, and flowering shrubs. There are beautiful homes, and large, magnificent buildings like amphitheatres, erected for assembly halls. Everything seems to be as tangible and firm as the Earth seems to our physical bodies, and the Beings one meets upon this plane are radiant and beautiful. It is upon this plane that the great temples of art, literature, music, etc., are found, and the beings resting upon this plane have every opportunity to study and learn whatever interests them, while waiting to reincarnate. A silvery light shines everywhere, and there is restfulness in the atmosphere, and a feeling of serenity and peace. *Monsignor Benson's book, "*Life in the World Unseen,*" by Anthony Borgia.

At the boundary between the third and fourth planes of being, the silvery light begins to change into a golden yellow light. There are beings upon that plane that shine as brightly as the sun, and the colors which radiate from them are more beautiful than those of a rainbow, because they are living colors. There is soft music in the air which seems to come from every direction, and a wonderful fragrance which is the essence, or souls, of the beautiful flowers with which this plane is filled. The beauty and glory of this plane is almost impossible to describe, and one who is still in physical embodiment cannot do more than stand at the boundary and look for a short time, since the vibrations of that plane are so high that it is impossible to penetrate it unless certain designated Beings are sent to assist one, and this is very rare.

The golden light radiating everywhere intensifies the glory of the beautiful buildings seen in the distance, which send forth gleaming rays of diamond, amethyst, emerald, sapphire, and other precious stones from which they have been built. Upon this plane dwell the Lords of the Universe, the Cosmic Hierarchy, and the beloved Cosmic Christ.

But this is not the highest plane, the "heaven" referred to in the Bible, with streets of gold and pearly gates, is still beyond. That plane is what the Eastern students call Nirvana, and is where perfected souls go to rest forever and ever, as we reckon time. But individual bliss in Nirvana does not last forever, since all individual conditions must at some time change. The egos who enter Nirvana have reached Godhood, and before leaving the fourth plane they elect whether they will undertake the mission of assisting human souls onward in their development, or pass into Nirvanic bliss and finally fade out as individual souls, and become absorbed into the yellow cosmic current, becoming a part of the Universal spiritual force. Many choose to become one with that force, and forever lose their individuality, rather than return to earth and witness the error and suffering there. Others, after they have reached this plane and rested for a season, prefer to return to earth and assist those who are coming on behind. The ancient religious teachers selected the two extreme conditions or states of consciousness as Heaven and Hell, and omitted the intermediate planes of being, except the first subjective plane, which they call Purgatory, where the majority of disembodied souls go. By working upon man's fears and hopes they expected to prevent his sinning, and thus raise him to higher realms. They did what they thought best at the different periods of time in which they served humanity, but old forms and old systems of religion must give way to new, and man now needs greater truths and more freedom of thought than ever before during this period of evolution.

DEATH OF A PLANET

Having discussed the death and disintegration of the physical body, we turn to the death and destruction of a planet, or world, for as we have mentioned, worlds also die and disintegrate, and become re-absorbed in the Universal Consciousness, to be reborn again at a future time. The first thing one sees is a great brilliant light, which does not resemble a sun, or moon, or anything with which we are familiar. It appears to be rather oval, and gives out tremendous flashes of light, with streaks of vivid blue lightning coming from it, which end in forks of electric fire that detach and go hurtling out into space. Then this "center" draws its great light within itself and appears to be green, seeming to shrink to only half its former size and suggesting a huge coiled serpent ready to strike. In the center a dark flame of red burns. There are a great number of electric currents all focusing at the point of the light, creating a generating center of magnetic force, since this is a celestial dynamo; the heat caused by the intense radiations of the electric currents produces a radiation sufficient to ignite the gases, and combustion is the result of the focusing.

The electric currents come from a light some distance away, which is a group of seven suns, radiating orange, red, green, blue, and yellow. In the center of each of the suns is an orange spot of light, which melts into red, and then green, etc. In the red, near the center, is the force which sends the tremendous currents of light focusing at this point and producing the center. The vortex is evil-looking, and destructive. Finally a large, dark globe – the "dead" planet, floats closer and closer to the vortex. There is no longer anything on it; no life, not even any soil. Everything is black and crumbled and seared, and there is a deathly silence. The dead world begins moving in wide circles around the evil looking vortex, seemingly helpless, and caught by the attracting power. The sounds are terrible, with a shrieking and screaming as the planet comes closer to the center – sounds of thunder, explosions, and crushing and grinding. The horrible red center of light turns nearly black – and then there is the final crash. The eye suddenly blazes out with terrific power and seizes the helpless planet, grinding it into atoms. The flames begin to fade, and the atoms of the dead and useless planet are scattered through space.

The seven Elohim who, as a group, generated and sent their electric forces at the creation of a new planet, withdraw them when the corpse of an old planet is destroyed – and this lesson can be applied in removing rubbish from our own mundane paths in life. The power operating through great centers also operates through small ones; man, with his physical body, generates within himself the same type of power which operates constructively or destructively through space.

Like vibration, power cannot be described as either good or bad, but the manner in which it is expressed, and the centers through which it operates, determine the results of its action. The results are what determine whether it has been used or misused; a person is not possessed of "evil power," since it is impossible for the power itself to be evil. It is possible, however, for a person to produce temporarily a so-called evil as a result of the misuse of his power.

And thus does the world advance. Those who neglect their advancement will one day have the opportunity again, but they will have a long time to wait. By clairvoyance we are able to observe not only those changes in the future in which not only the earth takes part, but also those which take place in conjunction with the planets around it. The terrestrial and human evolutions which have advanced themselves far beyond the ordinary, so that they have had to detach themselves from the earth in order to have the others catch up to them, will, in some future time, unite with the earth, and the earth will become a Sacred planet, such as Venus.

In time, the moon will be united with the Earth again, and the reason for this is that there will be a sufficiently large number of human souls who will have the inner power which will make it possible for them to render the moon-forces fruitful for further development. This will take place at a time coincident with the high development which a sufficient number of human souls will have acquired. But there will be another group, which have chosen the path of evil; these latter souls will have committed so much evil and error, and the Karma will be so bad, that it will be necessary that they become separated from the rest, into the erring section of humanity which will oppose all that which is good. Those on the right side will acquire the power of using the moon-forces, and will be able to transform the evil section so that they will be able to keep up the advancing evolution, but as a separate kingdom.

Then there will be an intermediate period, and the Earth will be changed into a new condition in which there will be no mineral kingdom. The forces of what we now call the minerals will then be transformed into vegetable forces. The vegetable kingdom, however, will be quite different from the present one, and will appear in the next state as the lowest of the kingdoms. The next higher kingdom will be the animal, which also will be greatly transformed. Next is the human kingdom, the descendants of the evil community which previously inhabited the Earth. Then will appear the descendants of the good humanity of Earth, as a human kingdom on a higher level. Those who have reached the last kingdom will be the Guardians of the Threshold, and it will be their work to assist those souls who have fallen into evil ways, so that they may be able to gain admission into the true human kingdom.

By means of what we call our imagination, inspiration, and intuition of the higher regions of the spiritual world, we gradually ascend into those regions within which dwell the beings who have to do with human and Cosmic evolution. When we have developed such faculties, we can trace intelligently human evolution between death and a new birth in a way that will seem to us possible and comprehensible. There are here also higher regions of existence that we can only briefly indicate. When we have developed our intuition so that we can perceive supersensual knowledge, we live in the midst of a world of spiritual beings. Even that in which humanity is interested today extends upwards, in a certain sense, as far as the world of intuition.

The so called dead are all around us, for our subconscious mingles with all that does not die. And all around us also, are those who are merely sleeping, and must be awakened. Each of us has a duty and a responsibility to his brothers, and we must help them to awaken the sleeping Christ within. The Lords of Form are responsible for man having his independent ego, and this ego, in the future, will harmonize with the beings of Earth, of Jupiter, of Venus, and of Vulcan, through the force gained due to the existence of wisdom during the Earth life. This force is Love, which must be developed into a Cosmos of Love. There must be love in everything the ego unfolds. The germ of love is planted in the innermost core of human nature; it must penetrate through the whole of evolution.

There can be no higher development without love. Everything that man will achieve will be by the right sowing of seed, which will represent love. The greater the love, the greater will be the creative force of the future. From love will grow our spiritualization; the more spiritual knowledge that flows into human and terrestrial evolution, the more force will be stored up for the future. Spiritual knowledge is transformed, through its own nature, into love. Gradually what has been preparing as wisdom on Saturn, the Sun, and the Moon will become active in the physical, etheric, and astral bodies of man; it appears there as the Wisdom of the World, but within the ego it is intensified.

From the Earth period onward, the wisdom of the outer world becomes the inner wisdom, and, when this is concentrated, it becomes the germ of love. Wisdom leads to love, and love is the essence of wisdom, reborn in the ego. We cannot hope to more fitly close this chapter devoted to the presentation of the facts of the occult world and the world of spirit, than by stating that we sincerely hope it has helped you, in some small measure, to a greater understanding of the "unity of spirit," and the Brotherhood of Man, in the divine relationship wherein the greatest among us is the servant of all. The possession of great gifts is an added responsibility. We are only stewards of our powers on behalf of others, and our desire to gain knowledge and influence should be vitalized and dignified by the intention to use them to help, teach, and serve our fellows, and in such service shall we ourselves be blest.

Engraving of occultists John Dee and Edward Kelley "in the act of invoking the spirit of a deceased person." From "*Astrology*" (1806) by Ebenezer Sibly.

10

GHOSTS

This chapter, devoted to "ghosts," needs no explanation from us. The English-speaking peoples have an avid appetite for ghost stories, so, familiarity breeding contempt, we ask you not to pass over this chapter too lightly, although it may well be the most popular chapter in the book.

However, we should not like to pass over this chapter without drawing to your attention the fact that lunacy, as the word indicates, has a peculiar attachment to the moon phases. Police records show that emotional crimes are always increased at full moon. Very little scientific investigation has been done to study the relationship between the moon and man's lunar body. Dr. Kilosko, of Vienna, before World War II, had carried on interesting experiments showing that silver salts under controlled laboratory conditions would respond accurately on a graph to lunar phases. Professor Burr, of Harvard University, has also carried on extensive research into plant life and its relationship to lunar phases. However, most people dismiss the moon's influence on both the vegetable and animal kingdoms as something belonging to the "*Farmer's Almanac.*"

Our present interest in the moon is to establish a landing for military purposes, each competing nation excusing itself for spending billions of dollars of the taxpayers' money by claiming that this is necessary for self-protection.

Psychic development is soul growth, and is not a "special gift from God" to one individual any more than to another, but it is the result of the soul's environment and consequent ability to see or to be otherwise conscious on planes other than the material, while it still functions in a physical body. That "psychism" pertains to and is an attribute of the animal soul, or objective mind, and not of the spirit or subjective mind, is shown by the fact that many animals are psychic. There are many instances on record of horses that have been frightened by disembodied entities, and have refused to draw a vehicle containing the dead body of a man or beast. This was because they saw, or were conscious of, the disembodied soul of the corpse, which they feared. And dogs have been known to fear, or to follow and obey the will of, a disembodied ego that was invisible to persons not psychic – yet no one could possibly claim spirituality for the animals.

The cult which is called by its followers "Spiritualism" has had much to do with bringing confusion to the minds of investigators along this line of thought. Many persons believe themselves to be spiritualists because they have accepted as a truth the fact that there is eternal progression for the human soul, which belief is an entirely separate and distinct thing from a knowledge of spirit, or of things spiritual. Every living thing is animated by a soul, and this soul, whether it is of a plant, an animal, or a man is the evolutionary force within, which reincarnates again and again until sometime and somewhere it reaches the spiritual plane of development. Then, and not until then, can it properly be called spiritual.

The imprudent manner in which psychic power has been manifested is the chief cause of the disrepute from which psychism suffers at the present time. No thinking, intelligent person is apt to accept as true a thing that is told him by a wild eyed, long haired, pallid faced and oddly dressed person who poses before the public as a psychic. The woman who tells everybody she knows and everybody she meets that she is "so psychic," or that she "examines psychically everything and everybody she sees," is an unfortunate, misguided specimen of imprudent psychic development, and is therefore totally unreliable in her statements.

The material plane upon which man lives is interpenetrated by the first subjective plane, which is crowded with disembodied entities that cannot get away from the material stage whereon they acted their various parts in the drama of life. It is perfectly natural that their dispositions and desires should not be changed merely by the laying down of their bodies. And it is natural that if they can find embodied egos that they can influence or control they should try to do so, because it is the natural tendency of undeveloped natures to desire to manage other persons' affairs for them. There are hundreds of men and women in physical life who are ready to give advice to others about the most delicate and intricate matters pertaining to their private affairs, and then bitterly resent it if their advice is not followed. And these are the same types of egos upon the first psychic plane who offer themselves as "heavenly guides" to mortals.

The person who is psychic may permit his business, if he has any, to be conducted under the guidance of an entity who was an Indian warrior, and whose business during his last earthly experience was that of hunting and fishing, and taking scalps. If the psychic fails in business, he wonders what was the cause of his failure, since he followed faithfully the directions of his "Indian Guide." In his marital relationship he may be guided by an entity who in Earth life was a polygamist, and who still believes in a plurality of wives. If the psychic finds himself in prison for the crime of bigamy while acting under the guidance of this "control," he wonders how it could have happened.

WHAT ARE GHOSTS?

It is to the confounding of the words "spirit" and "ghost" that many mistakes are largely due. Ever since the story of the Witch of Endor was written, many have believed that all ghosts are spirits, and that an ego becomes a spirit as soon as its material body is laid aside. It is by mistaken analogy that men have founded the belief concerning persons; for example, as it is often said of a slender, pale faced, negatively good woman that she is "spiritual." Because a ghost is supposed to be tall, slender and white, it has become a general belief that height and pallor and a willowy form are spiritual requisites, and that without them it is impossible to be or to become spiritual. To clear up this misconception once and for all, let us take up briefly the subject of "ghosts." The ghosts of dead men are of three kinds; the physical ghost, the desire, or astral ghost, and the thought ghost. Then there are three combinations of these three. The physical, desire, and thought ghosts are parts of living men, who, upon the death of the physical bodies, depart to their respective worlds where they remain a while, then break up, dissipate, fade out, and in time are re-collected from the planetary reservoir and used again in the evolutionary process.

The physical body is the ground in which the astral, or form-body, is rooted. The astral or form-body of the physical body becomes the physical ghost after death. While in the physical body, or issuing from it, the form or physical ghost is in appearance somewhat like smoke, or carbonic acid gas; as to color, it is a greyish, reddish, yellowish, bluish, or silvery-violet hue. The physical body is heavy, but has little density; whereas the physical ghost has little weight, but exceeds the physical body in density. It weighs between one and four ounces. *The American psychic researcher, Hereward Carrington, made this test using a specially built scale.

Now the process of "dying" begins by the loosening of the moorings of the physical ghost from the cells, organic centers, and nerve centers of the physical body. This starts at the feet and works upwards. As soon as the ghost leaves a part of the body, the latter becomes cold, and numbness follows. Like smoke, the astral body curls and rolls itself upwards until it reaches the heart. There it gathers itself together into a globular mass. Then there is a pull at the heart, a gulp at the throat, and it lifts itself out through the mouth. This is generally how one "dies," and this is the usual exit from the body, although there are other exits.

Though the astral body is now out of the physical body, it is possible that death has not yet taken place. The globular mass may remain as it is for some time, over the physical body, or it may take on at once the form of the physical. Death does not take place until the magnetic cord is broken. The magnetic cord of life is made of four coiling strands within three sheaths. It appears to the clairvoyant as a silvery strand or slender cord of smoke between the physical and the form above it. As long as this cord is not broken, the body may be resuscitated. Just as soon as this cord is broken death takes place. It is then impossible for the astral form or physical ghost to reanimate the physical body.

The desire ghost and the thought ghost may separate from the physical ghost just at the time of death, and from each other just as soon as death takes place. Or, they may remain with the physical ghost for some time, or the desire ghost may remain with the physical ghost, and the thought ghost be separated from both. Just which is determined and depends upon what the person thought and did during the life of the physical body. Nothing occurs after death that regulates these matters. The conditions of the physical ghost after death, and the desire and thought ghosts in particular, have been determined by the activity or sluggishness of the mind and desire, by the application of, or neglect to apply, the knowledge possessed, and by motives which influenced the thought and the actions of the person during his physical life.

The concept of ghosts, and also ghost stories, dates far back into human history and has captivated and mystified the human race for generations.

If the mind and desire of the person were lazy and sluggish, and without aim or purpose during physical life, they may remain in a state of torpor for some time after death, before the separation occurs. But if the desire has been forceful, and the mind is very active during life, then, after death, the desire and the thought ghosts will generally not remain long with the physical ghost. In cremation, the fires burn the physical ghost when its physical counterpart is burned. When the physical body is burned up then there will be no physical ghost to manifest. Cremation, aside from its sanitary advantages, prevents the physical ghost from being used by its desire ghost—when the mind has left, to cause trouble or to draw force from living persons. When the globular mass has arisen from the physical body after death, it may take on one or many forms, but finally it will assume the form of what was its physical counterpart. Wherever the physical body goes, the physical ghost will follow; in other words, should the body be interred in a distant town, the physical ghost will remain with it.

When the desire and thought ghosts are separated from it, the physical ghost will not depart from its physical body unless it is attracted magnetically by a person passing near it, or unless magnetically summoned to a particular place by the presence of a person with whom it was concerned during life. The physical ghost may also be called away from its physical body by certain persons we call "mediums," and they are able to make it appear under certain conditions.

Another case of the ghost wandering from the physical body may take place when the body is buried in or near a house which the person had long frequented during life. Sometimes the ghost may wander to a section of the house where the living one did certain things, or where habitual acts were performed by him. Then the ghost may be seen visiting those places and going through the acts as it did them in the physical body.

It is easy to distinguish between the physical ghost of the dead, and that of the living man. The physical ghost of the dead has no animation, and drifts about without any special aim or purpose. When the physical body decays, the physical ghost loses cohesion of form. When the physical form commences to decay, the physical ghost clings to it, or moves around it like phosphorescence in the moisture of a decayed log which is seen in the dark, and the physical ghost disappears with the body as does the phosphorescence when the log crumbles to dust. The physical ghost is only a shadow, an automaton of the body, without purpose, and can harm no one of its own volition.

HOW TO SEE GHOSTS

One with clairvoyant sight is able to see ghosts most any evening in cemeteries where there are frequent funerals. There he will see physical ghosts in various stages, from the newly formed ghosts of a body recently buried, to the faint phosphorescence of remains in decay. Sometimes under favorable conditions, physical ghosts may be seen in burial grounds by people who apparently have no clairvoyant sight. Ghosts are seen sometimes stretched over a grave, or in reclining position, and often they arise gently and float into the air so as to keep away from you. They assume many different positions – sometimes their hands will be clasped behind the back and, with head inclined, they will walk up and down a certain distance, as they formerly did when thinking over a problem.

There are three factors that determine whether a ghost can be seen; namely, the physical body of the ghost, the prevailing magnetic influences, and the physiological organism of a physical dead body. The skin, flesh, blood, fat and marrow supply the physical condition, even if the physical body is in the last stages of decay. The proper magnetic condition takes place when the moon exerts a stronger influence on the physical body than does the earth. Any person who is psychically inclined at all, and who is sensitive to lunar and terrestrial influences, is able to see ghosts when conditions are right. Anyone who is easily affected by different atmospheres of places, and on whom the moon and moonlight make impressions, favorable or unfavorable is sensitive to terrestrial and lunar influences, and can see the physical ghost when the two other conditions are supplied.

The "family thought-ghost" is originated by one member of the family thinking over some certain feature, aim, trait, or misfortune of himself or someone of the family. By continually thinking a certain thought, it increases in force and body and becomes a complete thing, a definite entity of the original thought. When the idea of this thought-ghost is communicated to other members of the family, they will value some of its deeds, and be impressed with the beliefs that, when seen, it appears to give warning of some impending misfortune, all of which the originator of it believed. This is how the family ghost is born. The family ghost of misfortune is generally started by one member of the family feeling that something is going to happen. This feeling is communicated to other members of the family, and then, if something does happen, it becomes a fact. The theory is supported, and the thought-ghost becomes a reality in the minds of the family.

The thought-ghost will generally appear to them as a forewarning; they continually live in the apprehension that something is going to happen. That thought compels the things to happen. The family gives the ghost extra force by telling of the many warnings it has given of the disasters and tragedies in the family. These instances are generally much magnified by the family, and by this the ghost is nourished. The ghost furnishes the phenomena which stimulate the faith in the supernatural, and it will be likely to make the members of the family impressionable, and also is likely to awaken their astral senses of clairaudience and clairvoyance.

The death-ghost is generally born in a curse. The curse thrown at a person, or a suggestion about a person of his family, is impressed upon his mind and he builds up the mental spectre of death. When he passes beyond, or some one of the family does, the death is an established fact, and becomes a reality in the thoughts of the family, and is nourished by their continued thoughts, as are other family ghosts. The "death-ghost" becomes a fixed reality, or is expected to give warning when someone of the family is about to die. It may use as its manifestation the breaking of a mirror or other furniture, or the fall of something suspended from the wall, a bird flying into the room and dropping dead, or it may choose some other manifestation which the family recognizes as the warning of the ghost that death is near for someone of the family. These warnings are really of very little practical use, outside of showing that there are times when such things are known in advance before they actually take place.

All thought ghosts can be broken up by lack of nourishment. The family thought ghost will continue to exist as long as it is nourished by members of the family. People outside the family, who may know of the family ghost, may remind them of it, but only those of the family can nourish it. Just as soon as the family loses belief in the ghost, it dies from lack of nourishment. Or, sometimes it is destroyed by the strong will of some member of the family. To destroy the thought ghost, all that is necessary is to do something contrary to the nature of the ghost. This will have a dissipating effect upon the thought ghost, and it will also influence the minds of other members of the family, and stop them from supplying the nourishment which is necessary for the maintenance of the ghost. *The rite of exorcism is often successful due to faith.

PHYSICAL GHOSTS

The appearance of physical ghosts is controlled by natural law, as is everything else. Every living physical object has a form body within and around it. The physical body is composed of physical substance. The form of the physical body is composed of lunar matter from the moon, of which the average person knows very little. Physical and lunar matter are the same in kind; they differ in that the particles of lunar matter are finer and lie closer together than those of physical matter, and lunar and physical matter are to each other as two opposite magnetic poles. The moon is a magnet, and the Earth is another magnet. There are certain times when the Earth's attraction is stronger than the moon's, and at other times the moon's attraction is stronger than the Earth's. These periods are regular and certain, and these constant alternating magnetic attractions cause the phenomena which is called life and death. What is circulated in the lunar and physical matter are the life units from the sun. It is necessary, in order to build up a physical body, to have the life units of the sun, which are conveyed by the lunar matter into physical structure. After death and the dissolution takes place, the life units are returned by the lunar matter to the sun.

Every living object is affected by the magnetic attraction of the moon and earth. The Earth pulls on the physical body, and the moon pulls on the form within the physical body. These magnetic pulls are what cause inhalations and exhalations of animals, plants, and even rocks. During physical life and until the body has reached the mid-day of its power, the Earth pulls on its physical body, and the physical body holds its form body, and this draws from the moon. Then the tide changes; the moon pulls on its form body, and the form body draws from the physical. When death is to take place, the moon pulls the form body out of its physical, and death follows. The moon continues to pull on the physical ghost and the earth on the physical body until they have been resolved back into their respective elements. These magnetic pulls are what cause that which we call decay.

When the Earth pull is stronger than the moon pull, the physical ghost will be drawn close to the physical body under the ground, or in its tomb, and it is rarely seen by mere physical vision. When the moon pull is stronger than that of the Earth, then the physical ghost will be drawn away from its physical body. The pulsing or undulating movements of the physical ghost are generally the result of the magnetic action of the Earth and moon. Because of this magnetic action, a reclining ghost will generally be seen a little above the physical object. When a ghost is moving, it does not walk as if it were on solid ground. The moon's attraction is strongest when it is brightest; then physical ghosts are most likely to appear. But on a bright moonlight night they are not as likely to be seen by the eyes not used to seeing them, as they are very nearly the color of the moonlight. They are easiest to distinguish under the shadow of a tree, or in a room.

The ghost often appears as if in a favorite dress or suit. The costume it wears is the one that made the strongest impression on the physical ghost by the mind before death. One reason why physical ghosts so often used to appear as if in a shroud is that shrouds are the garments in which bodies formerly were last laid away, and the astral body or the physical ghost had been impressed with the thought of the shroud. The last century was full of ghost stories, and the ghosts were inevitably similarly dressed in long, formless, waving "robes," and in fact, on Halloween, children wishing to represent a ghost will drape themselves with a sheet. In accordance with changing times, the shroud having been practically abandoned, ghosts no longer appear in this manner, although the memory persists.

Ghosts have the unnerving ability to appear when least expected on photographs taken with cameras and cellphones.

The physical ghost will pay no attention to a living person unless the person attracts it. Then it may come toward the person, and may even put out its hand and touch, or take hold of, the person. What it does depends upon the thought and magnetism of the living person; in other words, if the unfortunate person has a horrible dread that the ghost which it sees may touch it, then in all probability it will. The touch of a physical ghost feels like a damp rubber glove, or like the feeling of water when you are out in a canoe and put your hand into the water. What the feeling from the touch of a physical ghost may be depends a good deal upon the state of preservation of its physical body.

A physical ghost cannot commit any acts of violence, cannot catch hold of anyone and hold him, nor can it make someone do something which he does not wish to do. The physical ghost is only an empty automaton, without will or motive. It cannot speak to one who attracts it, unless requested to speak, and then it will only speak in an echo of a faint whisper, unless the living person furnishes the ghost with enough of his magnetism to produce a louder sound. If the necessary magnetism is furnished by the living person, the physical ghost is able to speak in a whisper, but what it says will lack sense, as a rule; and undue importance should not be given to what it says. Ordinarily, the ghost's voice sounds hollow.

The odor of a physical ghost is that with which everyone is familiar who has been in a death chamber or with any dead body, or in vaults in which the dead have been laid away. The odor comes from the particles which are thrown off from the physical body and thrown off by the physical ghost. Every living body throws off physical particles, which affect the living beings according to their sensitiveness to smell. The reason the odor of a physical dead body and its ghost is disagreeable is because there is no coordinating entity in the dead body, and the particles thrown off are, by the living organism, sensed through smell to be opposed to its physical wellbeing. If you have ever noticed it, you will remember a certain unwholesomeness.

If you are unable to see a ghost near a dead body that is no reason to believe that it is not there. As a rule it can be seen only by a sensitive, but occasionally, when conditions are just right, it may be seen by a person who is not sensitive, or at least does not know he is sensitive, and who has not tried to develop his finer faculties. Those who have never seen ghosts may not believe in them, even though they may be almost touching them. When they are very near you, however, you will be likely to have a creeping feeling up your spine, or on your scalp. This feeling is caused a good deal by the fear, and picturing to yourself the possibility of the existence of that which you so far had denied to exist. Anyone who is determined to see a ghost, and who looks for one, will have eventually no difficulty in distinguishing between a ghost and his own apprehension or fancies of a ghost.

The physical ghost is without volition, and can do no intentional harm, but a ghost can harm a living person by an unwholesome atmosphere which its presence causes. Sometimes the presence of a physical ghost has caused a peculiar disease to a person living near where the physical body is buried. The diseases are not caused by the noxious gases which affect the physical body of the living, but by diseases which will affect the lunar or astral form body of the living. All living persons will not be affected in the same way, but only those whose own form body, with the physical, attracts the physical ghost, and still does not possess the positive magnetic force to repel the ghost – whether it is seen or not. In this case the physical ghost of the dead preys upon, and sucks the vital and magnetic qualities from the form body of the living person. When this takes place, the physical body does not contain enough vitality to perform its own physical functions, and, as a result, wastes and droops. Those who live near a burial ground and have wasting diseases, and are unable to secure relief from physicians, would do well to move to a more wholesome place, where they will soon note an improvement.

It is possible to make a ghost leave you by willing it to go away; but by this you cannot drive it very far from its physical body, nor can the physical ghost of the dead be broken up or dissipated and disposed of, as it is possible to dispose of the desire and thought ghosts. Everyone should understand what a physical ghost is, but: it is not wise to hunt for them or want to come into contact with one, unless it is one's duty, for there are some Adepts whose special work is with these ghosts.

Those who do not know what a physical ghost is have a dread of them, whether they believe that ghosts exist or not, but there are some that will take great satisfaction in hunting for ghosts. If anyone hunts ghosts, thinking that he will have a thrilling sensation, he will be likely to experience it, but it will probably be a different kind of sensation than he expected to get. If one starts out to prove that there is no such thing as a ghost, he will be surprised and perplexed if he puts forward the necessary effort in his search, though he may not see a ghost, he will be convinced in the end that he is unable to explain certain phenomena he has seen or heard. This might not have been caused by ghosts, yet it will leave him in suspense, and though he may still believe that there is no such thing as a ghost, he will be unable to prove that there is not.

A WARNING NOT TO COMMUNICATE WITH GHOSTS

We would not advise anyone who has not had a special occult training to try to communicate with the ghosts of the dead, as he would be running a great risk- unless he is prompted by a desire to assist in the cause, and not by a selfish motive, such as a wish for sensation. We mean by this that his researches and investigations, into the phenomena of ghosts must be undertaken with the idea of adding to the sum of human knowledge for the benefit of humanity, and not merely to satisfy a morbid curiosity, nor to create a reputation for being an authority on the occult. Neither should his motive be solely to communicate indiscriminately with the spirits of the dead, or with those who have passed beyond the border. His motive for dealing with ghosts should be serious, and in order to do an unselfish act for the greater knowledge and good of humanity; he will then be protected against unseen forces. But if his motive is contrary to this, he will be very likely to suffer from public opinion and/or psychic attack.

Scientists who have attempted to prove that there is no such thing as a ghost have acknowledged that they have failed in their investigations. They have come in contact with mysterious forces which they were unable to explain. Scientists have also tried to prove the immortality of the soul, but have not been successful; however, they have been able to prove that physical, desire, and thought ghosts exist, although this does not prove the immortality of the soul. It only proves to those who are ready to believe, that ghosts exist, but that physical, desire, and thought ghosts will, in a short time, be dissipated. A ghost will only endure for a certain time. Immortality is for man, and not for his ghosts, and from the foregoing, we might add, in closing this chapter, that the probability of anyone seeing the famous "great Caesar's ghost" is not likely.

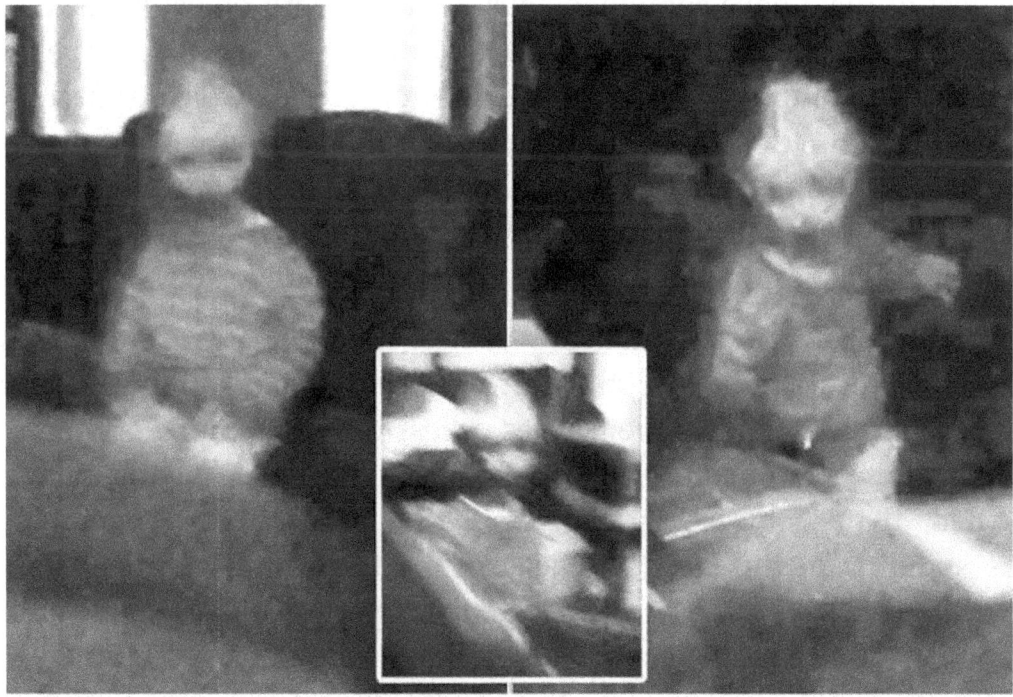

Adam Ellis, a cartoonist who lives in New York City, claims his apartment is haunted by the ghost of a child he calls "Dear David."

11

PROBLEMS OF ILLUSION

This chapter warns of superstition. From the middle ages, our culture has been bedeviled with superstition, and superstition, being a half-truth, has been very difficult to eradicate. Men of science have continually sought materialistic truths. The greatest of them have combined spiritual truth with objective fact. This has led us to our present day wonders. The greatest danger is that we believe that materialism is the ultimate objective of man's progression. This reflects itself in the battle between the two major planetary philosophies. We need only to examine our short Anglo-Saxon civilization to see quite clearly that superstition bred such horrors as the Spanish Inquisition, the Salem Witch Trials, and pseudo-occult societies ranging from the Witch's Sabbath to self-immolation.

Superstition is the acceptance of facts without proof. We sincerely hope that no one will evoke superstition with respect to this book, but check each step of the way from personal experience, regardless of the opinions of others. Much of the literature now on the market covering outer space, flying saucers, and unidentified flying objects is the result of superstition generated by a misunderstanding of the facts; also caused by the willful creative thinking of those wishing to "believe." The United States government has spent millions of dollars on various projects such as "Project Blue Book" and "Twinkle Star" to analyze this confused situation. Due to our present means of communication, the stories have passed rapidly around the world, making the analysis an almost hopeless job due to the unintentional confusion generated by well-meaning people.

As this chapter covers illusion also, we can do no better than quote Professor Carl Jung, for, as he states in his book, *"Flying Saucers; the Modern Myth,"* page 149, "the simultaneous visual and radar sightings would, in themselves, be a satisfactory proof of their reality. Unfortunately, well authenticated reports show that there are also cases where the eye sees something that does not appear on the radar screen, or where an object undoubtedly picked up by radar is not seen by the eye."

A Student of occultism is not permitted to use the knowledge he gains for his own selfish purposes. He has a certain, definite work to do. For instance, when he meets a man he is able to read him like a book; he sees his flaws. Had he known so much about him before beginning his studies, he would probably not have associated with him; but now he not only sees what a handicap these flaws are to the person, but he also sees his grander qualities. He will not think any the less of the person because he has the flaws, but he will have a great desire to help him.

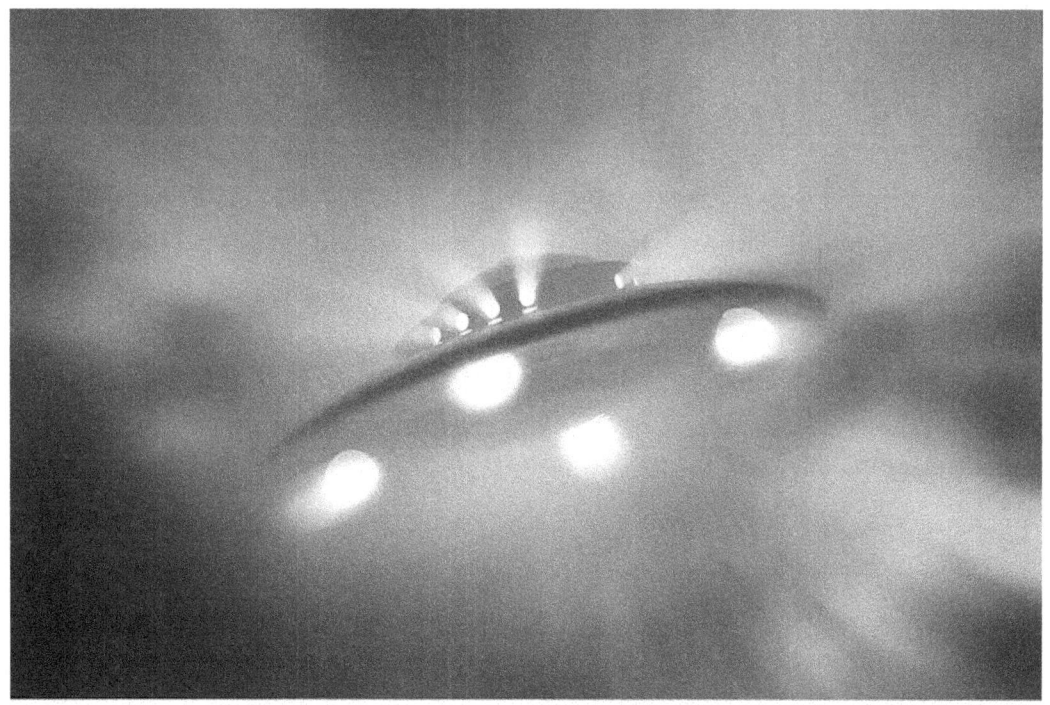

UFOs, at times, seem to straddle a place between reality and illusion.

SUPERSTITIONS

The more capable a man is of fixing his attention upon those events of life which do not primarily demand any measure of personal criticism, the greater will be the possibility of his providing himself with a foundation for growth in the higher worlds. For example, a man may start to do a certain thing, and something "within him" tells him not to do it. Perhaps the person will pay no attention to the warning, and will act according to his original intention. Or, it may be that the person heeds the inner prompting, and finds out later that he would have done wrong had he followed the dictates of his own reason. Experiences of this nature prove very valuable, and after he has been guided successfully a few times, he will begin to realize that "there is something within me that is a surer guide than is that measure of judgment of which I am at present possessed. I must, therefore, retain an open mind in respect to this inner "something," to the height of which my own capacity for judgment has not yet attained."

The soul is very much benefited by such occurrences. They show that premonitions are of value, and we can learn from them what we are unable to perceive through our regular channels. By giving conscious thought in this direction, you enlarge the life of the soul. It will be necessary for us to warn you here, so that you will not fall into a dangerous condition. If you were to stop to consider whether your judgment is right, or that "voice" that spoke to you, you would be at the mercy of every kind of impulse. Indeed, you would be likely to suffer from habitual indecision and superstition.

Superstition is disastrous to the student of occultism. It is necessary for the student to exclude all superstition, dreaming, and fantasy. He who has had experiences which have pleased him, that cannot be grasped by human reason, will not be likely to approach the spiritual world in the right way. No partiality for the "inexplicable" will ever make an Adept. It is well to understand that you must divest yourself of the idea that a Seer is one who presupposes the inexplicable and the unfathomable wherever and whenever he chooses.

The student should feel that everywhere there are hidden forces, and hidden beings, and also that the hitherto unfathomed forces are capable of being understood whenever the proper conditions and powers become available. There is at every stage of the development of the seer a change in disposition which is very important. This consists in not assuming, in his search for truths, an attitude such as renders him particularly anxious as to the way in which this or that question can be answered. It is very necessary that he should concentrate his energies on trying to develop as best as he can the faculties within him, and this he can do only by means of patient, inward labor; and after these faculties are developed he will find the answer to certain questions that he has longed to have answered.

This is the attitude of the soul which the student must cultivate, for it can help him to bring his nature to greater maturity, and will help him to resist wrong impulses. Whenever he is in doubt, if he will only wait a minute the correct answer will come to him, for within him is the power to solve the greatest problems in accordance with the measure of his powers; but here, also, balance and poise of the soul play a significant part. There are certain exercises which are very beneficial in acquiring intuition. The person should banish from his soul, for the time being, everything he has hitherto known, either by outer or inner experience. If, however, after rejecting the outer and inner experiences, nothing should remain within his inner consciousness; that is to say, should his consciousness disappear altogether and he drift into unconsciousness, then he will be able to recognize the fact that he was unfit to undertake the exercises leading up to seership at that time.

After he has reached the higher stage his consciousness will not any longer be void after throwing off those inner and outer experiences – but, instead, such rejection will still leave a certain residue which the student can use for inner meditation, just as he has been previously instructed to use the inner and outer impressions. This will be a new experience, as it is different from everything else he has ever experienced. When it takes place, he will recognize it as something absolutely new. It is a perception, and is just as real as the sound to our ear at present; but it can only be felt by inner consciousness through our intuition, just as the sound can only reach our consciousness through the ear. When conscious intuition is developed, the last remnants of the physical and sentient world are banished from man's impressions, whereas the spiritual world begins to loom up before the understanding in such a way that it has nothing in common with the characteristics of the world of physical senses.

Through the exercises used for attaining intuition, certain movements, formations and tendencies which were not there before will now appear in the human etheric or vital body. By these organs he learns to read the secret writing, and to understand what lies beyond that writing. After a person becomes clairvoyant, changes occur in the etheric body of the person in the following way: near the physical heart there is a new centre which develops into an etheric organ. From this organ there are currents which flow, in the most varied manner, to different parts of the body. Some of these finally radiate their light out into exterior space. The more highly developed the person is, the greater will be the projection of this light. The center near the heart is not, however, the one which, under correct training, first tends to evolve. There must be formed a provisional center first, in the head, which afterwards moves downward to the region of the larynx, and finally locates near the heart. If the proper training is not gone through, it is possible that this organ might develop near the heart first, in which case there would be danger that the student, thus trained, would develop only into a visionary dreamer, and not a practical seer.

The student finally evolves so that he can render these currents independently of his physical body; he then becomes capable of using them separately, and they serve him for the purpose of setting in motion his etheric body. Before this can take place, however, certain currents and radiations must come into action around his etheric body, which surround it like a fine network, thus enclosing it as if it were a separate entity. When this takes place, the movements and currents within the etheric body are able to put themselves in touch with the world of the soul and spirit outside them, uniting themselves with that world in such a manner that the affairs of the soul and spirit transpiring externally combine and mingle with the inward world and with that of the etheric body. When this has taken place he is able to consciously observe the world of inspiration. This occurs in a different manner than the cognizance of the physical sense-world, where we become aware of the world of our senses, and gather our perceptions and ideas, opinions, and conceptions. But the knowledge we receive through inspiration does not come in this way.

INTUITION

The answer to any problem that comes to the mind like a flash is an inspiration; there is no thinking after perception has taken place. The answer we receive from our physical sense cognition comes only after it has been translated into terms, and not as in the case of inspiration, which is simultaneous with the perception. If it were not for being surrounded by the fine network previously mentioned, there would be a danger of becoming entangled in the surrounding world of spirit and soul, with the probability of not being able to separate from it.

The exercises for attaining intuition, if practiced, not only affect the etheric body, but extend their influence to the supersensible forces of the physical body. These changes of the physical body cannot be noticed by the ordinary sense observation, and only the Disciple himself can notice them, as they have nothing to do with any external powers of perception. They are the result of a development consciousness, and these intuitional experiences will be of great assistance, even after having rejected all previous inner and outer experiences. Intuitional perceptions are of a delicate and subtle nature, with which the physical human body at its present stage of development is coarse in comparison, and therefore proves a detriment to the success of intuition. However, if the exercises are practiced with energy and perseverance and the required calmness, the hindrance of the physical body can be overcome. The student will become aware of this by degrees, as the actions of the physical body, which had before taken place without his own volition, now come under his control.

Every true intuition comes directly from the supersensible world. As the student progresses along the path that leads to knowledge of the higher worlds, he becomes conscious that the cohesion of the powers of his own individuality appears in different form from that which it possesses in the world of physical senses. In the latter, the ego causes a uniform cooperation of the powers of the soul to take place principally of thought, feeling, and will. These three soul powers, under normal conditions of life, are in perpetual relation to one another.

As we pass along the path to the higher cognition, we become aware that feeling, thinking and willing do actually assume a certain independence, as for instance, a certain thought no longer urges us, as though of itself, to a certain condition of feeling and willing. We perceive something correctly by means of thinking, of course, but yet, in order to feel that we are right, we must feel a certain independent impetus feeling coming from within. Thinking, feeling and willing no longer remain three powers, radiating from the ego as their common center, but become, instead, separate and independent entities, just as if they were three different personalities. For this reason the ego must be strengthened, for not only must there be order among the three powers, but the control of these three entities depends upon it.

This condition is known as the Cleavage of the Personality. It is advisable here to remind you how important it is to practice exercises that will make your judgment more firm and certain. If you are not firm and certain it will be seen at once how weak the ego is, and it will not have the necessary control over the powers of thought, feeling and will. In the presence of this weakness, the soul would be dragged by three different personalities in as many different directions, and there would be no inner privacy left. But if the development has proceeded along the right lines, this multiplication of itself would be the means of advancing forward, and it would become as a new ego, and be a strong ruler over the independent entities which now go to make up the soul.

As the student advances further along the path he will find that thought, now functioning independently, arouses the activities of a fourth distinct entity of the soul and spirit, one that is really a direct influx into the individual of a current which bears a resemblance to thoughts. The whole world then appears as a thought-structure confronting the man, just as the vegetable and animal worlds do in the domain of the physical senses. In the same way do feeling and will, which have become independent, stimulate two powers within the soul to work in it as separate entities. Then there is a seventh power and entity added, which is very much like the ego itself. And so you see, a man reaches a certain stage of development, he is composed of seven entities, all of which he has to guide and control.

This whole experience becomes associated with a further one. Before man enters the supersensible world, thinking, feeling and willing are known as merely soul experiences. But just as soon as he gains entrance to the supersensible world he becomes aware of things which express nothing of the nature of the physical world, but which belong solely to the soul and spirit. Behind the new world, he perceives Spiritual entities. These present themselves to him as an external world, as things in the domain of the physical senses, such as stones, plants, and animals, have been perceived by the senses. The student reaching this stage observes a great difference between the spiritual world unfolding itself before him and the world he has been accustomed to recognize before, by means of his physical senses. A bush in the sense-world remains a bush, no matter what the man's soul may think or feel about it. But this is not the case with images of the soul and spirit world, for these will change in accordance to man's own thoughts and feelings.

If a man has secret inclinations which are only waiting the chance to break through, those inclinations will show their effort in the soul and spirit world which is thus colored in a certain way by that person's entity, quite irrespective of how much he may, or may not, know of his own being. He may be able to keep these inclinations veiled from the outside world – but not from God. Therefore, in order to advance to the higher stages of development, a man must be what he really is, and not what he seems to be. He must eliminate all his imperfections. Before he can do this, he must know what he takes with him when leaving this world. In the world of physical senses, man devotes most of his time to developing his ego, his self-consciousness; and then this ego acts as a point of attraction for all that concerns man. In this ego are contained all of his personal sympathies, passions, propensities, opinions, and so on, and his ego also becomes a point of attraction for his personal karma, or the law of cause and effect. When we unveil the ego it is possible to see the destinies still awaiting it during this and future incarnations, according to how it may have lived during former incarnations, and had acquired this or that quality. It is encumbered by all of its past actions and deeds as it ascends into the world of soul and spirit. Thus, as man has lived, so is he judged by the law of the spiritual world.

CONTROL YOUR IMPULSES

Man recognizes that he has impulses, but he doesn't try to use these impulses to alter any of his undesirable qualities. If he did not give way to these impulses, but simply turned his attention away from his own self, remaining as he is, he would naturally deprive himself of even the possibility of knowing himself in regard to that particular matter. But if he looked at himself as he would look at a stranger, and examined his different qualities, he could either improve himself or not. His present condition in life will determine which course he will take. If he takes the former view, a feeling of shame will steal over his soul. The man who is prepared to stand before the Masters in the other world is the one who lives so that he has nothing to conceal, either outwardly or inwardly.

The ordinary man is not aware of this inward feeling which confronts the Disciple. He does not have revealed to him the secret feeling of shame in the soul, yet, to the Disciple, this feeling acts very much in the same way as the conscious feeling of shame in ordinary life. If this feeling were not present, man would see himself as he is in very truth. He would not only inwardly experience his thoughts, feelings, ideas and decisions, but he would perceive these as he now sees animals, stones and flowers. This feeling is what obscures man from himself, and hides him also from the entire spiritual world. Owing to the obscuration of man's inner self, he becomes unable to perceive those things by means of which he is to develop organs by which he could penetrate into the soul and spirit world, and he is unable to transform his own self so as to make it capable of developing these spiritual faculties.

The person who learns to understand the law of Karma in this world is not likely to be greatly disturbed when he sees his fate marked out for him. As stated before, after entering the soul and spirit world, the ego is the first picture that the human soul sees. This is man's double, which is bound by certain laws of the spiritual world to be the first impression he receives. It is easy to understand why this is so. In this physical world man is not only cognizant of what he feels by his physical senses, but this cognition is also inward, and thus a person is actually warned every time he does something he should not do. According to the development, these warnings will be heeded or not.

To the occult student, when doing something which he should not do, comes a feeling of "being ashamed" which is not felt so strongly by the ordinary person. The occult student learns to look at his physical body as if it were something entirely apart from him. He finds a great delight in being able to control his feelings, passions, etc. Any weakness is considered unworthy of the soul. If he will acquire the habit of considering everything that affects the physical senses as being connected with the physical body, which should be controlled by the soul, he will find it very beneficial. Just imagine that your desires, feelings, impulses, etc., are those of your double. If they are not beneficial, then control them.

The average person's actions close the door to the world of soul and spirit. If you take but one step to try to penetrate within the spiritual world, that feeling of shame comes before you, and automatically the door is closed and what was ready to be revealed to you, providing you had not had the feeling of shame – is concealed. Eventually you can unlock the door at any time you want to. All you have to do is to live so that you will have no hidden feeling of shame.

You will find it very helpful to look upon anything which you know you should not do as on something the impulses for doing which belong to your double, which you intend to control. Your double will represent your Karma, containing all of your past accumulated defects. You realize all this now. It has taken you a long time to find it out, as it has everyone else. But no one is permitted to gain knowledge of the higher worlds before understanding certain truths concerning it. The physical senses must first be brought under full control before there is really any desire to seek entrance into the super-sentient worlds.

Firmness and surety of judgment must be cultivated before the inner capacities can be developed. And then, when the student comes face to face with his double, he conquers himself, instead of being overwhelmed. This meeting cannot be avoided, and must take place before you can enter the supersensible world. And it can sometimes be a terrible experience, in which it seems that you are fighting for your very life. You must learn to distinguish between the appearance which things present to you through your own entity, and that which they really are – for you can find the difference only when you behold the image of your own entity, and have separated from your surroundings everything proceeding from your own inner being.

Before the man approaches the world of soul and spirit he has so lived that he no longer has the sense of shame, and finally this new world becomes visible to him. Then the double stands before him as a regenerated Guardian. However, if he has the sense of shame he is denied admission, as he is unfit. The double stands before the entrance as a Guardian, ready to deny admission to all who are as yet unfit, and thus his own double acts as his Guardian of the Threshold of the world of soul and spirit. In occult science this is referred to as the Lesser, or Outer, Guardian. The other Guardian will be spoken of later.

Besides meeting with your double upon entering the supersensible world, you also encounter the Guardian of the Threshold as you pass the portals of physical death, and it gradually reveals itself during that development of the soul and spirit which takes place between death and a new incarnation. But then the encounter does not overwhelm you, for now you know of the other worlds of which you were ignorant during the life between birth and death. Any person who has not encountered the Guardian of the Threshold upon entering the world of soul and spirit will be likely to fall prey to one delusion or another. He would not know the difference between that which he himself brings into that world, and that which really belongs to it. However, by the training that students go through, he learns the truth of what will inevitably take place sometime. This training everyone should have before they pass beyond the border, as it will guard them against deception and phantasm.

The student must be very careful not to degenerate into a visionary, liable to either suggestion or auto-suggestion. If the necessary precautions are taken, such deceptions are destroyed at their source. We will give you enough precaution here to put you on your guard. There are two sources from which illusions arise. Our own soul -- entity is likely to color reality. In this physical-sense world the danger arising from this source of deception is slim, for we have the external world ready to assert its own forms as they are, regardless of how we may wish them to appear. But, in the imaginative world, all the pictures are changed by such wishes and interests, and we have them actually before us – that which we ourselves have formed, or at least have helped to form.

The student, through his meeting with the Guardian of the Threshold, becomes aware of everything within him, and that which he takes with him into the spiritual world. Therefore he does not suffer from delusions, and the training which he received prior to leaving this world is in itself calculated to accustom him to exclude self – even in the things of the physical world, letting the matters and occurrences speak for themselves. Everyone who has made a study of this work will be able to await the meeting with the Guardian of the Threshold in all tranquility. When this meeting takes place, you will have to prove whether you are prepared to exclude your own entity when confronted by the soul and spirit world.

And there is another illusion which you must guard against. You must never place a wrong interpretation on an impression you receive. When you are riding in a fast train, the trees and objects appear to be moving, but they are not, you are moving in the train. Of course, you would not be mistaken in this case, but there are illusions occurring in the physical world which are not so easy to see through as the one mentioned. However, if you will always use sound judgment, you will be able to see through illusions.

THE WORLD OF ILLUSIONS

In the world of soul and spirit it is not so easy to distinguish which are illusions and which are not. In the world of sense, facts are not altered by human delusions concerning them; you can correct a delusion by examining the facts, but in the world of soul and spirit this is not immediately possible. If we study a supersensible problem from the wrong spirit of judgment, we then carry that wrong judgment over into the thing itself, and it becomes interwoven with the fact, the two becoming very difficult to distinguish. The error is no longer in the person, and the correct fact exterior to him, but the error will have become a component part of the exterior fact. You will see the extremely fertile source for illusion and deception that one would be liable to if he entered the supersensible world without the proper training.

The student becomes able to exclude delusions which might tinge the phenomena of the supersensible world with the color of his own entity, and he must also be able to acquire the further attribute of making the second source of such delusions ineffective. He is able to do away with what arises within himself after the meeting with his own double,* and he will also be able to eliminate the second source of delusion if he is able to develop the power for judging by the nature of a fact seen in the supersensible world – whether it be real or illusionary. If the delusions were exactly of the same appearance as the realities, differentiation would be almost impossible. But this is never the case; illusions seen in the supersensible world have their own peculiarities which makes it possible to distinguish them from realities, which shows the importance of knowing the qualities by which you can recognize the reality.

Plato believed a reality existed, but he seemed to doubt humans could discern what that truth looks like. Even the Bible suggests that the human ability to see truth is incomplete, akin to seeing "through a glass darkly."

Anyone who has never made a study of occultism would naturally come to the conclusion, after reading this chapter that one would have his hands full in guarding against delusions, since they are so numerous. He may also think that possibly all of the experiences of the supersensible world might be delusions. Anyone taking this view ignores the fact that all true occult training develops you so that you do not have to depend upon what someone else tells you, and you are taught how to proceed to remove the sources of delusion. In the first place, any occultist devoting the necessary time to the study of occultism to be worthy of being called an occultist will, during his preparation, have acquired enough knowledge about these matters so that he will be in a position to avoid delusion, and also self-delusion. His training will have made him level-headed, and capable of using right judgment at all times. His training will have taught him that it is never safe to rely on vague presentments and premonitions. His training has made him cautious – much more so than he would ordinarily have been and he has gained knowledge of the great cosmic events, and therefore he is fully prepared to tackle matters which necessitate the exertion of the judgment; a process by which this power is both refined and sharpened.

If it were possible for a person to jump over the preparatory work in the training of a seer, and be able to foretell the future, as so many would like to do, he would not possess the strengthening of that sound power of judgment which makes it possible to distinguish between illusions and reality. So you can see the necessity for understanding the groundwork on which occultism is built. This is so arranged that the consciousness of the student is enabled, during the time he is practicing inward meditation, to examine carefully all that passes within his soul.

Men, through higher educational development, have gained a kind of soul activity although they are not able to know the origin of such activity. The occult student, however, studies to remove his own soul-activity from his consciousness. He does not permit anything to enter that he cannot investigate, and of which he cannot learn the entire contents. Therefore, the student is able to see how pure reality within the soul and spirit world is constituted, and he will apply the test to everything that comes within his observation in the realm of spiritual realities. And there is no reason why he should not be able to distinguish delusions from realities. He should also be prepared to determine just as quickly the delusions in the spiritual world, such as psychic entities masquerading as higher Beings, as he is able to in the physical world, where he knows that the imaginary hot bar of steel cannot burn him.

This test, of course, only refers to our own experiences in the supersensible world – not to communications made to us that we have to apprehend by means of our physical understanding and our sense of truth. The student should do all he can to distinguish between what he learns from one kind of knowledge and that of another. He must be willing to accept communications made to him regarding the higher worlds, and should try to understand them by using his own observations; before he accepts them he must carefully test them to see whether they possess exactly the qualities which he has learned to be correct by his infallible intuition.

After meeting with the Guardian of the Threshold, the occult student will have other experiences to face, and one of the first things of which he will become conscious is the inner connection which exists between this Guardian of the Threshold and that soul-power we have already characterized by referring to it as the Cleavage of Personality – the seventh power to resolve itself into an independent entity. This seventh entity is, in regard to certain aspects, no other than the double, or Guardian of the Threshold itself, and it sets up a certain task before the student. His ordinary self, which now appears to him in an image, had to be directed by the new-born self, so that there arises a kind of antagonism against the double, which will do all it can to gain the upper hand. This is done so that the right relationship may be set up, in order that he may be prevented from doing anything but what may result from the influence of the newborn ego, and this is what develops the powers of firmness and vigor.

In the higher worlds, this self-cognition is a little different from that in the world of physical sense. In the latter, self-cognition takes place as an inner experience only; the newly-born ego becomes immediately discernable as an externally spiritualized vision. The reborn ego you see before you, but you cannot see it entirely, for whatever road you have taken to reach the supersensible worlds, there are no higher roads possible until you are able to perceive still clearer visions of your Higher Self. Therefore, it can only partially reveal itself to the student. There are certain temptations placed before man which are simply tremendous. Until you have passed through these tests you will have only a glimpse of the higher self, and you will be able to compare these only from the standpoint you have acquired by your physical senses. Some may think these tests too severe, but they are indeed very necessary if you are to develop in the right way.

We wish to call to your attention here what it is that appears as the double, or Guardian of the Threshold, so that you will be able to place it ever in front of the Higher Self, in order that it may be able to judge correctly the disparity between what it is at present, and what it is destined to become in the future. However, while considering the subject, the Guardian of the Threshold will assume quite a different aspect, for it will now disclose itself as a picture of all the obstacles which oppose the development of the higher ego, and then we come to know under how great a strain the ordinary ego is.

If by this time the student's training has not made him strong enough to say, "I will not remain at this point, but will persistently work my way upwards toward the higher ego," then the chances are that he will become weak and will shrink back, and be afraid of what yet lies ahead of him. He will give up trying to work his way farther, and he will have fallen captive to that image which, as Guardian of the Threshold, now confronts his soul. It is peculiar, though a fact, that the person who becomes a captive will not know it. On the other hand, he will think he is getting along all right and passing through another experience, for the image called forth by the Guardian of the Threshold may be of the kind that it will stir up in the soul of the person the feeling that it is the impression which normally appears to all at this stage of development. He has before him all possible worlds in their entirety, in other words – he has the impression of having attained to the heights of knowledge, and of, therefore, having nothing really higher to work for. So you can see that instead of feeling himself captive, he feels that he has gained all of the secrets of the universe. There is no reason why you should be surprised at this, for you must remember that by the time these experiences are felt, you are standing within the soul and spirit world, and the special peculiarity of this world is that it represents events in the reverse order to that in which they really happen.

The picture seen by the student at this point of development shows him in a different aspect from that in which the Guardian of the Threshold first revealed itself. If you remember, in the first vision were seen all those qualities which, as the result of the influence of Lucifer, are contained by the man of the ordinary ego, but, by the development another power has now, by Lucifer's influence, also invested the soul of man, this being the one known as the power of Ahriman, and during this physical life this power prevents man from becoming aware of those entities of the soul and spirit world which are behind the surface of the exterior world. The development of your soul may be plainly seen under the influence of this power. Those who have been sufficiently prepared for this experience will, when they experience it, have been able to determine its true meaning. And then another form will soon become visible – one referred to as the Greater Guardian of the Threshold.

This one will suggest to the student not to rest content with the grade to which he has attained, but to go on faithfully with his work. It will stir up within him the consciousness that the world he has conquered will only become a truth and not an illusion, if the work commenced is carried on to a successful conclusion. Those who have pursued a wrong system of training; that is, have started to develop mediumship instead of mastership, will be likely to face this experience unprepared, and will, when they meet the Greater Guardian of the Threshold, be very likely to be filled with feelings of boundless and immeasurable horror.

The meeting with the Lesser Guardian, you will remember, furnished you with the opportunity of judging whether or not you know the difference between delusions and reality, as would be likely to occur when you interweave your own personality with the supersensible world, and so you must pass the test and prove that you are able to withstand those illusions which are to be traced to their source when you meet the Greater Guardian of the Threshold. Should you be proof against the powerful illusions by which the world of images to which you have attained is falsely displayed to you as a rich possession, when in reality you are a captive, then you are guarded also against the danger is mistaking appearances for reality during the further course of your development.

The Guardian of the Threshold will appear in a different form in the case of each individual. The meeting with him corresponds exactly to the way in which the personal nature of supersensible observations is overcome. That is, to have the opportunity of entering a realm of experience which is free from any tinge of personality and every human being has this opportunity. When you have been able to pass the two tests, you are then able to distinguish in the spiritual world between what you, yourself, are, and what is exterior to you, and you will then know why it is absolutely necessary that you should understand the cosmic occurrences mentioned in this work, in order that you may understand humanity itself, and the life process. The fact is, you do not understand the physical body at all until you understand how it has been built up.

The same is true of the etheric body, the sentient body, and the sentient soul. Man is the development of the entire world surrounding him, and everything about him corresponds to some process, to some entity in the external world. When a certain stage of development is reached, the student comes to know the connections of his own identity with the Cosmos, and this is known in occultism as becoming aware of the relationship of the little world, the microcosm, that is, man himself, to the greater world, the macrocosm.

BECOMING ONE WITH THE UNIVERSE

When the student has gone this far, he becomes aware of another experience; he feels that he has grown together with the entire world structure, although he remains fully conscious of his own independence. This is known as the merging with the universe, becoming "At One" with it, but not losing the personal identity. In occultism we speak of this stage as the "becoming one with the macrocosm," and it is very important that this condition must not be imagined by anyone in whom the separate consciousness ceases, the human entity flowing forth into the All, for such a thought would be but the expression of an opinion which is the result of untrained reasoning.

The whole evolution of the human spirit is a progressive at-one-ment. In the at-one-ment between the Ego and the personality lies the mystery of the Christian doctrine of the Atonement. One unification takes place at the moment of individualization, when man becomes a conscious, rational entity, and as evolution proceeds, successive at-one-ments occur.

At-one-ment on all levels; emotional, intuitional, spiritual, and Divine, consists in conscious, continuous functioning. In all cases it is preceded by a burning, through the medium of the inner fire, and by the destruction, through sacrifice, of all that separates. When the webbing that separates the etheric body and the emotional body has been burned away by the inner fire, the communication between the bodies of the personality becomes continuous and complete. There is a somewhat analogous situation on the higher levels; the intuition corresponds to the emotional, and the four higher levels of the mental plane to the etheric. In the destruction of the causal body there is a process analogous to the burning of the web that leads to the unification of the bodies of the personality. The disintegration that is a part of the arhat initiation leads to unity between the Ego and the Monad, and is the perfect at-one-ment.

The "chitta" is the mind, or mind-substance, the mental body; the faculty of thought and of thought-form making – or the sum total of the mental processes; it is the material governed by the ego or soul out of which thought-forms are made. The "psychic nature" is the emotional or astral body, tinged faintly with mind, and is the material clothing all of our desires and feelings, whereby they are expressed.

These two types of substance have their own line of evolution to follow, and they do so. Under the Logoic plan, the spirits or divine sparks are imprisoned by them, being first attracted to them through the mutual interplay of spirit and matter. By the control of these substances and the restraint of their instinctual activities, these spirits gain experience and eventually liberation, and may be clearly seen by one with clairvoyant sight. Thus the union with the soul is brought about; a union which is known and experienced in the physical body upon the plane of densest manifestation, through the conscious, intelligent control of the lower nature.

The next state is known as "Beatitude," and it will not be necessary to describe this stage, for we have no language to express man's experience at this time, and it can only be said that any conceptions of this state can only be acquired by means of such thought-power as would no longer be dependent upon the instrument of the brain. In order that you may understand the separate stages better, we wish to mention that they do not necessarily have to follow each other consecutively, for the course of training may be taken up very differently by some people. In everything there is a certain individuality which must be taken into consideration. One unfolds much faster than another. The student may be taking one stage, and another stage partially, at the same time. He may be practicing exercises which lead him on to inspiration, intuition, or cognition, between the microcosm and the macrocosm into the sphere of his own experiences.

When the student becomes more conscious of intuition, he not only comes to know the pictures of the spiritual world, but he is able to read their secret script, and he also acquires knowledge of those Beings to whose cooperation is due the creation of the world to which man himself belongs; he now knows himself in his true form which he possesses as a spiritual being in the soul and spirit world. By his efforts he has gained the knowledge of the higher ego, and in so doing, will have become aware of how to act in order that he may overcome his double, the Guardian of the Threshold. A little further on he will meet the Greater Guardian, who appears before him, instructing him to continue in his unfoldment. The Greater Guardian is now the one held up before him, and the one he is to try to resemble.

This is a very important stage of development, and when he has risen thus far, he will be in a position to recognize who it is that is really standing before him as the "Greater Guardian." Then, in the student's consciousness, the Guardian is gradually transformed into the figure of the Christ. In this way, the student, through his intuition, will have become initiated into the sublime mystery which is linked with the name of Christ – the Cosmic Christ is now revealed as the "Great Example" for humanity.

This is how, by intuition, the Christ becomes recognized in the world of the Spirit. Then, too, does it become possible for the student to understand those events which took place historically during the Atlantean period, and how it came to pass that at that time the Great Sun-Spirit, the Christ-Being, took part in the world's development, and how He still continues to guide its evolution. The student learns this from personal experience, and it is then, through intuition, that the meaning of evolution is fully disclosed.

Everyone can gain knowledge of the supersensible worlds, and in time all must learn it. It matters not what your position may be; you must, in time, strive for knowledge and truth. For this earth passes through a certain development, and you must keep up with it. The longer you put off your starting point, the more difficult will be your Path. Life in all forms is continually changing, and evolution is leading humanity on to a higher state continually.

12

OMNISCIENCE, OMIPOTENCE AND OMNIPRESENCE

This chapter on Adeptship is the time of trial. It is symbolized by the drama depicted in the Gospel of St. Luke, Chapter 4, verses 1-24. We find that this Arcana clearly defines what these temptations are and also the rewards of being able to "run the gauntlet" of fire. Organized religion seems determined that the mass of men shall be kept in ignorance of these facts. The Church has simplified the Arcanum into the simple composition of "good" Angels and an evil Satan, Lucifer, or Mephistopheles. If you doubt that Magic is known by the Church and Church Authorities, you have only to examine the Rite of Exorcism as established by the Roman Catholic Church and the Anglican Church.

A manuscript was printed in 1501 under the authority of Pope Alexander VI, entitled, *"Spiriti-Commando"* This paper tabulates the angels, devas, or spirits that can be summoned for the purposes of good. A similar paper was published in 1686 by one Andrew Luppius, a licensed book seller of Wesal, Duipsburg, and Frankfurt, Germany. All of these papers are translations from the Hebrew Kaballah. Ancient Hebrew scholars were very familiar with the powers and attributes of qualified Adepts. For this reason the works of a Rabbi such as Jesus caused no great commotion at the time of his demonstrations. It is small wonder that a great portion of the Hebrew world accepted him as a Rabbi but not as a Messiah.

Should anyone care to study these manuscripts, it should be done with full awareness that the Holy Roman Catholic Church has with wisdom suppressed this knowledge which is contained therein. In summation we may state that this is the balancing of the scales between good and evil, or man's temptation to use magic for selfish purposes. From Adeptship man goes to Mastership, should he survive this trial by fire. This trial is depicted in the Egyptian Judgment of the Dead, wherein a man's heart is put on the scales as a balance against his soul. These judgments are experienced daily by the average man when, due to some circumstance, either natural or unnatural, he must make a decision to do either what he knows is right, or to act in his own selfish interests. He then becomes his own fudge and jury.

This is the development of conscience, which is Divine Love, the ability to realize that there are invisible pressures for good and evil. Daily economic pressures blind men to this responsibility. This affects all degrees of society.

THE THREE ATTRIBUTES OF SPIRITUALITY

Spirituality is composed of three attributes; Omniscience, Omnipotence, and Omnipresence, and unless an ego has acquired to a greater or lesser degree, something of the first two, he cannot claim to be a spiritual soul.

The first attribute to be gained is Omniscience, which means to have gained all knowledge. An ego must know how to act before it can act wisely; and in order to gain and possess something of this spiritual attribute, man's power of concentration must be increased until he can place his thoughts on something besides himself, and hold them there until he has mentally absorbed the knowledge he desired concerning that thing. How can a man be or become in any degree Omniscient when his power of concentration is so weak that he cannot hold his thoughts for five consecutive minutes on a single subject?

Omnipotence is the next higher attribute of spirituality, and means to have all power. To gain or possess Omnipotence, in any degree, a man must at least be able to concentrate upon and use the spiritual cosmic forces, and he must have evolved to a point of development where he can demonstrate over disease and disharmony in his mind and body, and also, at least temporarily, remove it from the bodies and minds of others. He must possess enough Omnipotence to give him power over his own lower nature, and power to control his own environment.

And after he has gained this attribute in ever so small a degree he will never again become a victim of circumstances nor an object of charity.

Omnipresence means to be everywhere present at the same time, and this is the last aspect of spirituality. It can also be gained only through mental development and spiritual power. To become capable of being everywhere present, a mind must be untrammeled by form, and must become one with Divine Mind. It must have lost its desire for individuality, and become absorbed by the Universal Principle. To the Western occultist this aspect of spirituality is not a desirable ultimate to be attained, and since higher and greater individualization is the goal to which he aspires, he never demands Omnipresence. To the students of the Eastern school of occultism, to gain Nirvana and Omnipresence is to reach the highest condition of spiritual happiness that can be attained in the Universe; and some demand and receive it.

For the utterly tired soul who feels that to be reabsorbed and thus be able to rest forever in the bosom of the Infinite, without an individual care or responsibility, Omnipresence is the necessary spiritual attribute to demand in order to reach that state. But it is never well to make that demand until an ego has gained Omniscience, in order that it may know all things, and Omnipotence, in order that it may have all power, and thus be able to decide its fate without prejudice or passion.

GOING INTO SILENCE

We wish to bring to your attention at this point a subject which is of great interest to everyone, as there are only a few who have a clear idea as to what is meant by "Going into the Silence." Going into the silence is nothing new; the oldest oriental writings speak of it. It is written in Sanskrit that "He who would hear the voice of silence (or the voice of Spiritual Sound) has to learn the nature of the intense and perfect concentration of the mind upon some inferior object, accompanied by complete abstraction from everything pertaining to the external universe, or the world of the senses."

When the pupil has ceased to hear the many, he may discern the one, the inner sound which kills the outer. Before the soul can see, harmony within must be attained. Then only, and not until then, shall he forsake the religion of the false, and come into the realm of the true.

We can discover the joy of living when we grasp the present moment, and this will give us a delightful sense of peace, tranquility, and love.

The student invariably asks why it is necessary to go into the silence. There are various reasons for this, but one in particular is so that he may come into contact with the source of all life power. Not everyone is ready to come into contact with the great world of spirit. There are many who would become very much alarmed if, by any miracle, they suddenly found themselves in the world of silence – separated completely from the world of outer motion. Most people are even afraid to be alone in the outer silence; they could not endure it to be alone for a month of solitude, and those who feel this way should never try, at the present time, to enter the silence, although in time they will be able to enter it.

Everyone receives more or less stimulus from nature's sublime forces, but only up to a certain point. The individual can become the center of a power himself, capable of acting from within, and impressing his thoughts on the outer world instead of only receiving those of other persons. It may be said that there are two grades of people; the ones who receive only from the outside, and those who are creating power within themselves. Those of the one class drift along; those of the other class control themselves, and stand alone, constantly receiving help from within. There will come a time when the individual who has been merely drifting along with the tide, with no thought of whither or why, will make an effort to step aside from the multitude. He will be casting around for some place where he can stand firmly. He will want to get his bearings, and consider what this whole world is about. It is then that he is ready to enter the silence.

Whenever there is a real desire to enter the silence, the individual has reached a certain period in his evolution. It is not possible at first for a person to enter the silence, for he cannot expect to do it in the same way that he would sit down to have his photograph taken; but the fact that one desires to do it is proof that it is time, at least, for him to start to try. And one of the first things he learns by going into the silence is that he must live to benefit mankind.

"The selfish devotee lives to no purpose. The man who does not go through his appointed work in life has lived in vain. Believe thou not that sitting in dark forests, in proud seclusion and apart from men will lead thee to the goal of final liberation. Shalt thou abstain from action? Not so shall thy soul gain freedom. One must reach self-knowledge, and self-knowledge is of loving deeds of the child." These sayings were written thousands of years ago, but they are just as true now as they were then.

By this time you have no doubt come to the conclusion that you want to progress, and there must be a complete renunciation of the lower self if you want to evolve your spiritual powers. If you want to be godlike, you must be spiritually evolved. But the majority of students wish to be able to use their super-human powers before they have learned the laws that govern these powers. You must become a real man or woman, however, in every sense, before you can become godlike. There should be no doubt in your mind by this time as to your belief in Seership, though you are likely to doubt your personal ability to develop your powers so that they will be of conscious value. But once you become conscious of the working of your inner nature, a mighty sense of peace will cast its veil over you, and you will then begin to understand how Adepts and Masters assist in controlling the world, though unknown. The fact that you have been attracted by the subject is proof that your psychic or soul force is awakening, as it is proof that you are semi-consciously en rapport with the sphere of spiritual influence.

We have often been asked if it is not necessary to study under a Master. When we say no, students seem quite surprised, but the truth is that every great Master, and every Adept, has developed alone, by himself. Of course you may gain something by visiting and conversing with others who have developed themselves, but if you will study the lives of any of the occult masters you will find that they had no earthly teachers, but were assisted by their Guardian on the Threshold. Yours is there to help you – just the same as theirs helped them. So never, ever hold yourself back from beginning a study of occultism simply because you do not know any person who will teach you.

We find many self-styled masters masquerading as Occult Masters. They make it a point to inform aspiring souls that it is dangerous to study occultism without the aid of an Adept or Master, and even go so far as to tell them of the dangers from which they will suffer if this is not done, and that "you are bound to fail," claiming that you can achieve nothing without the aid of a teacher. And we would give another warning at this point – you will find many "advanced students" (at least in their own opinions) who will be more than willing to force upon you a garbled conglomeration of "knowledge" which will utterly confuse you and hold you back considerably. A person may have studied for years, yet have learned very little indeed. Age has nothing to do with development, for a very young person who is sincere and pure in heart may develop quite rapidly and be far in advance of the self-righteous individual who, because he has made a half-hearted study of the subject for fifteen or twenty years, feels that he "knows everything."

There is a very, very old rule which we wish to give at this time, and this is in very simple words, "To will, to dare, to do, and to be silent!" And this last is indeed the hardest of all. Many students who are just beginning may find that they have a rapid development in some phase of occult teachings, which is, of course, the result of hard work in this and other lives, and not "luck," or a "gift from God." When we have a beautiful spiritual experience, or when we converse for the first time with a spiritual being or a Master, it is natural for a joyous heart to want to share the experience with friends. And the joy of the wonderful experience has often been abruptly taken from the student by the reaction of the "friends," for many who talk the most about these things have never really had the experiences.

And so we find jealousy in some cases, or, "I am more highly advanced than you, and I cannot understand why you have had such an experience, and I have not." We meet with doubt in many cases and, worst of all, sometimes we are shocked to find a friend who will accuse us of having actually "invented" the experience in order to have something to "brag" about. And since we become much more sensitive to such things as we progress, it is far better to begin practicing immediately to "be silent," no matter how much you wish to share your experience, in order to avoid this sort of thing.

It is true, of course, that if you could come into contact with a Master, his developed soul could not help but have a psychically and spiritually uplifting influence over you, but the person who sets his heart on gaining spiritual knowledge becomes an atom of living desire and aspiration, and attracts to himself what he needs to further his development. He will be advised to secure certain books. Unconsciously he becomes in rapport with men and women who are working along the same line of thought, and whose minds are vibrating in the same key. He attracts them, and they attract him; and the right environment is thereby created and all are mutually benefited. This is the result of sympathetic vibration.

Each time you have a strong wish, you start a magnetic center which places your mind in conscious, semiconscious and subconscious touch with the finer forces and unseen intelligences of nature, and this is the way in which you are assisted in your spiritual development. You do not have to have a teacher, as you can train yourself; therefore, it is not necessary for you to long for a teacher, but be determined to develop yourself as best you can. Keep your heart sincere and true, cultivate and manifest the right desires, and hold to them firmly. If you will do this you will start into operation the law of attraction which will draw whatever you need to further your development. And if, at the end of seven years, you have been able to live in this manner, and you have held fast to your ideals, then, when you are ready, your Master will appear.

PURE MEDITATION

We will give some very brief instructions for going into the silence, or pure meditation, for if they are studied and understood and you earnestly desire to do so, the way will be opened for you. Select some place where you will be just as free from all interruptions as possible. Sit in an easy position, with the neck, chest and head in a straight line. Your room at first should be darkened. Close your eyes and thoroughly relax; become as limp as you can, having no tension on the nerves. Now practice a few rhythmical breathing exercises.

Sit perfectly quiet, and see what thoughts come to you. You are likely to be quite surprised at the thoughts that will chase one another in your brain. You cannot imagine how restless your mind really is, until you try to quiet it. Eventually it will quiet down, however, and look to you for orders. Now think of yourself as something separate from your body. Consider it the temple where you dwell; think of yourself as existing outside of it. Think of pleasure, hunger, thirst, and the painful sensations of the body, and all of the other cravings, and consider them but as events of the past or present processes of human evolution, to be discarded as the sight becomes perfected and reaches the spiritual heights of evolution. In time, you know, the ego is clad in a "body of pure energy," and neither food nor drink is needed to sustain life.

Your emotions, such as fear, greed, selfishness, anger, infatuation, and hate, are not really you, because you can stand aside and analyze them. If you have allowed yourself to be identified with them, you have been made to suffer. Realize that you are above being affected by the grosser emotions, and cultivate the finer ones. Now study your intellect, and see how you are independent of it. A little study will reveal to you how the complex processes of intellect have been thoroughly analyzed and made amenable to control. You and your mind are not the same; even while you are engaged in the deepest state of concentrated thought action you can stand aside and watch the play of thought. You are able to think how you are immortal, invulnerable, and that you are part of the very essence of Divinity.

We now come to an important stage. Shut out all external and internal thoughts, and think only of that which leaves the body at the time of "death." Focus all of your mental energy inwardly upon your soul, and as you begin to realize this more and more, a veritable blaze of illumination will rise within you. This is a wonderful experience – this bathing in the great ocean of soul-force, and it will develop startling powers in anyone. It is capable of charging your being with powerful energy; it will brighten your intellect, lighten your physical weight, and may even give the power of rising in the air (levitation, or astral liberation); and it will develop a kind of clairvoyant power, and open up your vision on the subtle planes; you will be a transformed being.

The way has been pointed out for you. The task is solemn and sacred; never talk of it – simply try to put the teachings into practice; live them and think them. If you do, you will gain the power of externalizing spiritual strength in thought, word and action. But above all, never debase the science; if you do, it would be far better if you had never heard of it. Live up to it, and make it a part of your life. Be perfectly honest and sincere, and you will have nothing to fear, as your Guardian of the Threshold will guide you.

REACHING THE HEIGHTS OF THE SPIRIT

There are many who are ready to attain marvelous development, if they would only train themselves. Remember, a strict integrity to one's highest light is essential to development. Humility and purity should be the aim of everyone capable of communicating with the higher worlds. If we do not develop within ourselves the knowledge that there is something within us higher than ourselves, we shall never realize that there is something higher. The Adept acquires the power of leading his intellect to the heights of knowledge by guiding his heart to the depths of veneration and devotion.

The heights of the spirit are reached by passing through the portals of humility. You acquire right knowledge when you learn to desire it; you have the right to see reality, but you must first demonstrate by your actions that you have earned the right. There are certain laws of the spiritual, as well as the physical, world. If you rub a glass rod with the appropriate material it will become electric, and it will possess the power of attracting small bodies. This shows how natural law works. Every feeling of true devotion which comes from the soul develops a power which may, sooner or later, lead to the development of seership, or Adeptship. This is one of the laws.

It is necessary that you possess within you this feeling of devotion before you can gain entrance to the higher knowledge. If you do not possess it, it will be necessary for you to acquire it, which can be done by vigorous self-education which will create the devotional mood within you. Full importance must be given to this. In the present state of civilization we are only too ready to criticize, expressing our opinions, etc., rather than having devotion and selfless veneration. Even children criticize far more than they worship. Every judgment, every sharp criticism, frustrates the powers of the soul for the attainment of the higher knowledge, and in the same way all heartfelt devotion develops it. He who wishes to gain the higher development must create it within himself; he himself must instill it in his soul.

He who wishes to become an Adept must assiduously cultivate the devotional mood. He must look for that which demands of him admiration and homage. He should not criticize, or pass judgment. If you look down upon a man because he is weak, you rob yourself of the power to gain higher knowledge; but if you try to enter lovingly into his spirit, you gather much power. Train yourself along these lines; it is necessary for you to learn to search for the good in all things, and to withhold all carping criticism. Not only must this be your external action, but also your innermost action of the soul. Become a perfect being, and transform yourself completely, but this transformation must take place in your innermost life, in the mental life. It is not sufficient that you express your outward bearing toward a person; you must also have this respect in your soul. Before you can become an Adept it will be necessary for you to banish from your consciousness all thought of disrespect and criticism, and to cultivate thoughts of devotion.

Everything which you do that helps you to banish from your consciousness whatever has remained of a disparaging, suspicious judgment of your fellow men brings you closer to becoming an adept. When once you fill your consciousness with thoughts which evoke in you admiration, respect and veneration for everything, you rise rapidly in your development. Those who have gone through this stage know that in these moments powers are awakened which otherwise would remain dormant. This is the way the spiritual eyes are opened. You begin to see new and interesting things around you, and realize that heretofore you have seen only a small part of the world around you. Your fellow man now appears in quite a different aspect from what he did before. You will not yet be able to see the human aura, as a still higher training is necessary for this, but you can reach this training after going through a thorough training in devotion. *The system of Yoga covers this emotional state in what is called Bhakti Yoga. The Christian, by devotion and prayer to the various Saints and by emulating the desirable qualities of each, follows the same path.

The Adept does not appear any different than an ordinary person. You may live in close friendship with him, yet he will not impart any knowledge, because he knows you are not ready to receive it. He will only impart to you his secrets when you are ready for them. Nothing will make him divulge to you anything which he knows, should not be disclosed, and thus he goes on unnoticed by the outer world. There is really no reason why anyone should notice any particular difference in the seer or Adept. His duties are attended to as before, and his appearance is the same, more or less, as that of others. It is only the inner part of the soul that is transformed, that which is hidden from outward sight.

Think of yourself as something separate from your body. This is the way your spiritual eyes are opened to the true reality around us.

In the beginning of the change, the entire soul-life of the man feels the devotion for everything venerable. Those who are inexperienced will find it difficult to believe that feelings like reverence and respect have anything to do with their perception. This is because they imagine that perception is a faculty within itself, and stands in no relation to what otherwise concerns the soul, but remember, it is the soul which perceives. Feelings affect the soul just as food affects the body. Feed the body on crushed stone, and activity will soon cease. The same is true of the soul. It needs homage, veneration and devotion, which are the ingredients that make it healthy and strong, and especially strong for the action of perception, while, on the other hand, antipathy, disrespect and underestimation cause the starvation and withering of its activity.

The Adept can see all these things in the aura. The soul which harbors the feelings of devotion and reverence brings a change in the aura, for as the feelings change, so does the color of the aura. At this time the organ of perception opens, and is now ready to receive information of which it heretofore had no knowledge. Reverence awakens a sympathetic power in the soul, and through this we attract similar qualities in others around us. Our power will become more effective with others help. Gradually we learn to give ourselves less to the impressions of the outer world, and instead to develop a vivid inward life. It would be useless to try to develop Adeptship if you are changing from one impression of the outer world to another constantly, and with the entire attention on dissipations.

On the other hand, the Adept must not shut himself out of the outer world. Once the inner life is realized, it will point out the direction in which he ought to lead his impressions. The man with a depth of soul and richness of emotion feels much different from the man with few emotions. What we can experience within ourselves is what opens up the beauties of the outer world. To acquire intimate knowledge of even the outer world we must learn to control our feelings and ideas. All phenomena of the outer world are full of divine splendor, but we must discover the divine within ourselves before we can hope to discover it without.

The disciple must necessarily pass through a host of temptations, the purpose of each of which is to test the ego and to imprison it within itself. It is quite necessary that you should seek enjoyment, for in this way only can you prove that you are above temptation. If you mingle with the outer world and withstand the temptations, you are the better for it, if you are afraid of doing this, then it proves that you fear the temptation. There are many sanctimonious, self-righteous individuals who will tell you that you must "give up" practically everything except breathing – give up smoking, drinking, sex, coffee; give up pleasure. They will tell you that practically everything you do is "wrong." Because these individuals are afraid of these things, and have never overcome and conquered their own attitude toward them, they often are convinced that what applies to them applies to the whole world.

Of course there are many people who do not drink nor smoke, simply for the reason that they have no special desire to do so, and there are many who have overindulged and have overcome the temptation to the extent that they no longer indulge in that particular pleasure at all. But these are not the people who will preach the evils of indulgence to you. You will find people who consider anything and everything to be evil and wrong; while the Catholic Church has dances for young people, and card parties, as a means of amusement and sociability, we find (even though it is difficult for some to believe) that there are still religious groups who look upon dancing as a "sin," and the sure road to hell; while they are convinced that he who would sit down to a friendly game of cards has already reached the doorway of his wicked destination.

If you stop at the enjoyment, you will be the gainer by the contact with the outer world. While you live in this world, you must be of it, and not dead to it. The Adept considers enjoyment only as a means of ennobling himself to the world. He does not acquire great learning for himself alone, but that he may be of service to the world. One cannot be of service even to himself, let alone the world, if he takes the attitude that now he is pure and spotless, and must therefore hide himself from contact and contamination with mere humanity.

There is one important law which must never be transgressed, which is as follows: Every branch of knowledge which you seek only to enrich your own learning, and only to accumulate treasure for yourself, leads you away from the path; but all knowledge which you seek for working in the service of humanity, and for the lighting of the world, brings you forward. This law must always be followed, and no one will be an Adept until he has adopted it as a guide for his whole life. Never let anyone tamper with your individual freedom. Adeptship teaches that you should respect and cherish human individuality. Keep watch over each of your actions, and each of your words, so that you may not hinder the free will of any human being. There is no need for anyone to sacrifice his independence in order to become an Adept.

13

SOUND AND SILENCE

In our consideration of animal magnetism, we have only to consider that the medical profession, until very recently, has termed Anton Mesmer a "quack "At present there are bitter legislative fights in various states of the Union to place hypnosis under medical control Dr. Baird had as much trouble in establishing his theories on hypnosis as Pasteur did with his theories on pasteurization. Both of these techniques, sterilization and hypnosis, are accepted medical techniques. The rapid advancement of the radio and television industries was made possible by the vast amounts of money spent by commercial enterprises on advertising, or repetition, which is a subtle form of hypnosis. Subliminal advertising, admittedly effective, has been criticized as an unethical intrusion of the public mind.

Due to the mental laziness of most of us, an educational book such as this would normally find little response with the general public. We are encouraged only by the fact that shows like Rod Serling's "The Twilight Zone," and reality shows such as "Expedition Unknown" with Josh Gates, have had far more success than was anticipated by the television industry. These types of shows have brought in a new generation of people who had never heard of the paranormal, UFOs, and cryptozoology. This interest has led many to other aspects of esoteric knowledge, awakening that desire to know more about the nature of reality beyond what is apparent in their daily lives.

ANIMAL MAGNETISM

There is an emanation of certain particles called "animal magnetism" from one person who affects the will and nervous system of another. This was the basis of Mesmerism; however, Mesmer really taught two systems in one; first, that there is a flow of magnetic force, which he designated as animal magnetism, and that this emanating force is curative in its nature; and, second, that there definitely can be coercion of mind by mind. He practiced the first, and warned his students against practicing the other. The world, of course, confused his teachings, as it usually confuses anything of an occult nature, and remembered the second system without his caution.

Mesmer taught that there is a Cosmic Force which is a part of the Law of Love, or the Law of Attraction, and that it flows through man and may be directed by his will, as an emanation from him to another person. He showed that the force flowing from his hands was a force that he could draw into himself and then give to another. He also showed that he could get approximately the same effects by using large magnets, thus proving that this is a general, and not a personal, force, which he used.

The law of gravitation is a part of this magnetic force, and so is love in all of its gradations, whether it is human love, animal love, or passion. The law of attraction manifesting through an animal body we now designate as animal magnetism. This Cosmic Force, passing through an animal, is nothing more nor less than the Universal Life Principle, or the orange vibration which we will discuss in another chapter. Passing through man as human-animal magnetism, it manifests itself as that peculiar vibration or force which his development permits. There is, however, a physiological condition necessary to a body in order to make it magnetic, just as there is a physical condition necessary to make any mass magnetic. For example, glass is not magnetic, as compared with iron or steel. The rate of vibration of glass is so different from that of magnetism that it does not make a good conductor for that force as it flows over it. The condition necessary to make a proper basis for the animal or human magnetism to manifest is the excess, above the normal, of the number of red blood corpuscles in the body; and these red corpuscles must vibrate at a high rate.

With these two conditions there is established the physiological basis which enables the Cosmic Force to manifest; and having the proper physiological basis, a person, either consciously or unconsciously, draws within himself this

Cosmic Force through the left side of the body, and passes it out through the right side, the left being the negative and the right the positive side of the body. Animal magnetism can be utilized by man through the blending of his aura with that of another, or through transmission of physical contact, laying on of hands, etc. Most persons, such as faith healers, use this magnetic force without understanding the law which underlies it.

If an occultist desires to transmit this force to another person, he places his right hand on that other person's; then, after drawing into himself the force, he permits it to flow through him into the other. This force can be used advantageously for all nervous troubles, because it is the nerve fluid, or life force, which restores depletion; it is also helpful in cases of the consumption of any of the physical organs of the body, and if properly directed will build up diseased cells and restore wasted tissues. Many persons possess this magnetic force to a great degree, but do not know how to use it, while others perform cures unconscious of the power they possess, and without the action of their own will. A person who makes a practice of using his animal magnetism or life force for the treating of disease must become greatly depleted at times, since the natural inflow of life force is never so great as the outflow. If the natural inflow of the life force were as great as the outflow, our bodies would last forever, because this would make an even exchange of atoms, and no robbery could be perpetrated.

There is an actual emanation from one person to another, and this emanation causes an exchange of physical atoms. We are not speaking of the higher Cosmic Forces, which can be used for healing purposes without depleting the healer, which we shall learn how to use a little later on, but we are referring to the natural life force within the physical body which can be used as a curative agency, as Mesmer used it. Sometimes the healer absorbs the old, diseased atoms from his patients, through the manipulating with both hands at the same time, which carries from him his best atoms and returns the cast-off ones from his patients. It is not conducive to the good health of the magnetic healer to use both hands while treating the sick; but in case it should be done, immediately afterward both hands and arms should be bathed in hot water, rubbing the hands and arms from the elbow downward to the tips of the fingers. In this way it is possible to remove, by aid of the hot water, many of the low vibrating atoms which have been taken into the system.

Mental healing involves the transfer of healing energy; in other words, the energy is not from the healer, but the healer links with "Universal" or Divine energy to channel healing for the mind, body and spirit.

When a Mental healer begins to lose his force, or power to heal, the reason is first that his brain has become tired by continuous concentration, and its material atoms have taken a slower rate of vibration, because the outflow of magnetic force has been much greater than the inflow. Through his intense interest in his cases, perhaps his sympathies have gone out to his patients with his treatments – and here was an expenditure of emotional force. Without understanding the reason for his waning power, he tries to go on with the work of healing when he should rest and sleep, and in this manner bring back to himself the life force he has given away. After a time he finds himself depleted, and is compelled to retire from service, humiliated and hurt because of the unkind criticisms he has received from those he has tried to serve.

There is a better way to treat the sick than by the magnetic force which made Mesmer famous, and that is to remain in a positive condition of mind, control your sympathies, and thus hold your own magnetic force as a basis over which you may draw the higher Cosmic Forces and pass them on to others without depleting yourself. If you can control your sympathies and remain positive, then you can treat without depletion as many persons for whom you have time.

DIVINE MYSTICISM

Among all the phenomena of mysticism, the highest form both relative to range, power, scope, and Allegoric wisdom, is that which is known as Divine Mysticism, or Divine Miracles – the expression of esoteric magical occurrences as revealed by Deity to his chosen few. Jesus taught this Divine Mysticism but had to teach it in parables, for reasons which we have previously explained. "Magic," actually, is apparent every day, although it is not named as such. The so called miracles of science are really only one form of this. Much of the esoteric wisdom has been revealed to mankind through tradition and legendary lore. By dividing the sources of this revelation, it becomes apparent that to the Bible, tradition has ascribed "force" or "power" far greater than the power of the mere words represented there. However, there is contained within the Bible an esoteric occult significance of deep and tremendous magical import – the words of the Commandments and Psalms, and certain other passages, are definite magical formulas, each sufficient to a purpose.

Jesus said, "All this can ye do—and more, because God willed it so." God, not the old man with the beard, upon the shining throne, but the "Solar Intelligence," Deity-the Universal Principle. We were cast in the "image of God," we are God-like, and our God-like spirit is everlasting and enduring. The Great Solar Intelligence willed that we all should understand and become empowered with the expression of "divine power."

When Jesus healed, he asked the blind, "Believe ye that I am able to do this?" Then, after they said, "Yea, Lord," he touched their eyes and said, "According to your faith be it unto you" – and their eyes were opened. And so it is apparent that he made sure that the necessary element of the law of suggestion was present, before he healed them. He made sure of faith and belief, and then he made the suggestion. When the ten lepers called out to him, he simply instructed them to show themselves unto the high priests, and they were cleansed. He knew that if they did as he told them, they must have faith. And when one of the ten was grateful enough to return and thank him, the man was rewarded for this gratitude by being told the secret..."Go thy way-thy faith hath made thee whole." Jesus said, "Seek and ye shall find" – and behind this phrase lies one of the basic esoteric doctrines. Moses first learned this in his contact with the magicians of ancient Egypt. Jesus learned it through his wanderings in Tibet and India and Egypt. The principle of searching for the truth is part of our Eastern philosophy;

the Oriental doctrine of mastering the Mysteries by seeking for enlightenment through unfoldment has been an everlasting fact through its entire history. Knowledge gained in this way is all enduring, and so it is with the mysteries of everyday life, which have always been open before us. It is merely necessary to penetrate deeply, searching and seeking always, and we cannot fail to receive the answer.

Jesus left the power to heal as a heritage to all who should come after him possessing the required faith; he knew that the testimony of his disciples concerning the works he had performed would be compared with later exhibitions of the same power. He formulated the exact conditions necessary and indispensable to the exercise of the power to heal the sick by psychic methods, the same conditions which are necessary today. The condition which he declared to be essential, not only in the patient, but in the healer, was faith – the essential element, incidentally, of success in every field of human endeavor. He taught the disciples his methods of healing and sent them into the world to imitate his example. When they failed, as they occasionally did, he reproved them for neglecting his teachings, and upbraided them for their lack of faith. When he healed the blind men, he asked them first if they believed that he was able to heal them. He wasn't in the habit of uttering idle words; everything he said was important. He wouldn't have questioned those men about their faith in his powers, if it hadn't been important.

When he raised Jairus' daughter from the dead he required faith, the faith of the subjective mind, or soul. The belief of the objective mind has actually only a limited control, governed by circumstances. When Jesus raised a person from the dead the conditions were, in one sense, the best possible to enable him to obtain complete mastery of the soul of the deceased, by the power of suggestion. The objective senses were in complete abeyance, and the body was dead, so there was no objective auto-suggestion of doubt possible. He commanded the soul of the deceased to return; he may not have employed objective language when he gave the command, but his soul, in perfect telepathic communion with that of the dead girl, and dominating it as only he could dominate the souls of men, issued his mental demand to the departing soul, and it obeyed.

No law of nature was violated, on the contrary, he understood the law perfectly, and applied it. He understood the importance of securing for his patient a favorable mental environment. He tried to quiet the fears of the father, and to impress upon him the necessity of holding in his mind the attitude of faith and confidence. The father was in telepathic rapport with the daughter, and it was important for him not to impress his own doubts and fears upon her departing soul. Jesus also understood the value of a positive mental force, in harmony with his own force and purpose. So he selected three of the most powerful of his disciples, Peter, James, and John, to be present, and kept the multitude of unbelievers as far away as possible. He said, "She is not dead, but sleepeth." He had to quiet their fears and stop the lamentations of the friends and relatives, since their hopeless wailing had a strong adverse suggestive effect upon the soul of the girl. And the only way in which he could do this was to assure them that she was not dead. Also, he was filling the departing soul with the subjective faith necessary to enable him to command it to return to the body.

The Bible then states, "and he charged them that no man should know it, and commanded that something be given her to eat." If Jesus insisted after each healing demonstration that "no man should know it," he must have had a very good reason, and the reason is that when a person is suddenly healed by mental processes, skeptical persons are apt to either dispute the fact entirely, or else ridicule the idea. This is an unfavorable mental suggestion, and often causes the person to look for the return of the disease. And the disease, therefore, usually does return. "He commanded that something be given her to eat," which shows that he definitely did not rely on "magic" and that ordinary means of imparting vigor were not ignored. He never hesitated to apply material remedies in connection with, or in addition to, his occult power.

There may be a divergence of cause and effect between the powers of Moses and Solomon and the "magical art" of Jesus, but all of them have their roots in the Divine Force of God. The miracles of Moses and of Solomon were based upon Kabbalistic formulas as; revealed by God to His chosen few at that time. The underlying, principles of the Kabbalistic forces of the invisible world are ruled by means of esoteric formulas, which, in turn, effect and command powerfully, the spirits governing the several houses of Astral Magic. The miraculous power of Jesus lies in the union between the God Within and the Almighty God of the Universe. There is a magical formula controlling this phenomenon, and that is the power of Belief and Faith which, while governing separate entities when bound together, exercise tremendous impulses for good or for bad. Subjective faith may be acquired in direct contradiction to objective faith or belief; but after an experimental demonstration of the power of subjective faith, objective belief no longer sets up an auto-suggestion against it. It then becomes knowledge, and in that sense it ceases to be faith.

HYPNOTISM – ARTIFICIAL SLEEP

And now we return again to the particular aspect of the subject known as hypnotism, which is an artificial sleep which may be produced upon one's self or upon another; and it may be produced by the power of will, by mechanical processes, or by the will supplemented by mechanical processes. The mechanisms that are used to produce hypnosis are mirrors, bright lights, or anything which will serve to excite the optic nerves and raise them to a rate of vibration which will enable the subject to pass into hypnosis, or sleep. Unnatural stimulation of the nerves of the eyes, or of the nerves at the base of the brain or by focusing the sight at an angle of forty-five degrees and then gradually raising it until the pupils are turned upward above the upper lids, will produce an abnormal nervous excitation, and while the subject is in this condition he readily accepts the mental suggestion of sleep, and passes into hypnosis.

In this way the subject is literally "forced" out of his physical body; and is under the control of the operator's mind, and is also exposed to any or all influences upon the subjective plane which he has abnormally invaded. If the hypnosis is complete, then both minds of the subject are under the control of the operator; but if the hypnosis is only partial, then nothing but the objective, or lower, mind of the subject is controlled. But while in this condition, and passive to the will of another, the subject must accept as true everything suggested to him by that controlling mind; and whatever posthypnotic command is given to him in sleep he will obey when he awakens, without knowing why. From the first moment the subject yields his will to another, he becomes that other's slave, if that person should desire to make him so. So long as the operator lives in this world, so long could he be able to control that subject.

It is contended by modern hypnotists that the mind of the subject is not dominated to the extent of coercion, or beyond the power of the subject to act independently; or, in other words, that he cannot be compelled to do a wrong against his will. Cases have been cited where subjects refused to stab a man when the operators gave them a real dagger and commanded them to do so. Other cases have been cited where the same subjects were given paper daggers and were told to strike designated persons. This command was obeyed instantly, and because they obeyed in the second instance, and refused in the first, it was generally concluded that they could not be coerced to commit a crime against their wills. This actually proves only that both minds of the subject were not under the control of the operator, and that if they had been, the subject would have obeyed in the first instance as quickly as in the second. Nothing can prevent a hypnotized subject from obeying the commands of the operator, or controlling mind, when once the subject is fully under his influence. If a person consents to be hypnotized, it is because he does not know of the dangers he incurs by consenting, and his ignorance should not be taken advantage of by one who knows better.

There is another phase of hypnosis, however, which has produced extraordinary results, but it must be made clear that these results have been produced by skilled physicians, surgeons, and psychiatrists, and not by the person who regards it as a "hobby," or another means by which to "liven up the party." And of course hypnosis in medicine is used by a skilled and thoroughly trained operator who is employing it for the benefit of mankind. It has been used successfully in place of an anesthetic during operations. It has also been used with amazing results in cases of severe pain and suffering, particularly in cases of very severe burns where skin grafts were necessary, and exercise of the hands and arms was imperative. Where the slightest movement caused untold agony to the patient, hypnosis was used and the patient not only was able to exercise the hand or arm at the suggested intervals, but was found to be going through the motions of the exercise even during sleep. Therefore, anyone who is truly interested in hypnotism, and is absolutely sincere about it, should definitely consider this phase of it – and by pursuing his interest may at the same time contribute much toward alleviating a very great deal of pain and suffering of mankind.

MENTAL DOMINION

There is another phase of mind control which is more subtle and dangerous than that of mechanical hypnotism, because it can be used without the knowledge of the subject, and without the immediate presence of the operator. This branch is called by the occultists, "mental dominion." Hypnotism by mental dominion is produced by mental suggestion alone. It makes no difference whether the subject is present, is in the next room, or even in the same state with the operator, for he can be reached equally as well at any time or place. Investigators have discovered that putting the subject to sleep is not essential, and that just as effective work can be done by repeated suggestions until the subject should accept and act upon them, believing them to be his own thoughts.

Unless you have made a study of this practice of mental dominion, you have no idea of the extent to which this subtle power is being used in the world today. It is openly taught in magazines and the internet with alluring ads which offer to teach *"Personal Magnetism," "Hypnotism," "The Secret of Power,"* etc., and, under various names, each of these teachers, professors, or "doctors," offers, for a monetary consideration, naturally, to teach anyone at all how to dominate his fellow men, how to enslave another, and how to "positively enable any intelligent person to exercise a marvelous influence over anyone whom he may wish to control." There is no limit to the power of mind, nor to the field of operation through suggestion.

In the beginning of the use of occult forces, suggestion is one of the most powerful of the mind's instruments which the student learns to use. It should not be identified with hypnotism, although it can be used to produce hypnosis. Like any other force, it can be used for good or for evil, and the line that lies between the right and wrong use of it is as narrow as the edge of a razor, and just as sharp. In the practice of magic, these two ways diverge and we find what are known as White and Black Magic. The first is a straight and narrow path, which leads to the mountain top of power and wisdom, and to reach it is salvation. The other is the broad road which leads to pitfalls and to destruction, and many souls are enticed to travel upon it. It was the wrong use of this power of suggestion which destroyed us as Atlanteans, and from present indications it would surely seem that we did not learn through that experience that we do not have the right to enslave the mind of another person.

Mind must be reached by thought, and if the thought is constantly repeated, nothing can prevent a suggestion from reaching its destination, because telepathy is based upon Law. But whether the suggestion shall be accepted and acted upon depends upon the recipient; and it is upon the acceptance or the rejection of suggestion that the freedom or the enslavement of a mind is determined. There are different kinds of suggestion, two of which are known as audible and silent. Audible suggestion is something in which we constantly indulge, whether we are aware of it or not, and it is something that we should learn to control, because it may be either constructive or destructive, and if it is the latter we may do much harm to others.

Hypnosis is an extremely powerful process. Anything powerful can be used to do harm as well as good. Careless use of hypnosis can interfere with a person's psychological and spiritual development.

Parents and teachers are constantly making audible suggestions to children which have a great effect upon them. If a teacher calls his pupils dunces and dolts, and tells them how stupid they are, he is pretty sure to find in them just what he suggests. However, if the teacher was to tell them that they are bright and intelligent children, and should therefore have no trouble in learning their lessons, the suggestions would be constructive, and the child would respond by having a desire awakened in him to learn, since the mind of a child is plastic, and is easily impressed by audible suggestion. The objective mind is always ready to see the dark side of life, and will readily accept any audible suggestion of a destructive nature; and since there are constructive suggestions which can be made to help others, we should not be continually hindering rather than helping our friends.

Silent suggestion is of two kinds, hetero, and auto, the former meaning suggestion to another, and the latter meaning suggestion to one's self. There is greater power in silent suggestion, whether it is used for right or wrong, than there is in audible suggestion, because the silent thought sent to another is subtle, and the recipient, knowing nothing of its source, is often unable to combat it, thinking it originated in his own mind. Silent suggestion can be used for the benefit of another so long as it is suggestion, and is not carried to the extent of coercion. For example, if you have a friend who is likely to give way to temptation to do wrong, you would have a right to say to him, "you are good and true; you can resist that temptation because your own Divine nature has asserted itself," and your friend will come through his struggle victorious.

You may always suggest mentally to a person what you have a right to say to him audibly and often it is inexpedient for you to say audibly what you have a moral right to say, for rudeness is inexcusable. If someone calls and is taking up more of your time than you can spare, you have a moral right to say mentally, "why don't you go?" You have a right to protect yourself from intrusion upon your work. Or, if someone has borrowed money from you, and you do not like to ask him to return it, even though you need the money, it would be perfectly legitimate for you to say mentally, "return the money you borrowed." You have a right to help yourself through life when it is not at the expense of another person; and you have no conception of the number of obstructions this silent power will remove from your path, or how much good you can accomplish with it. Like all other forces, this power grows with use, and you can use silent suggestion as a moral stimulus.

Silent suggestion can also be used as a defense. When you are conscious that a person is trying to influence you, refuse to accept his suggestions, and declare that he cannot accomplish his purpose. This will turn his force back upon himself, and render him impotent to affect you. If you know that someone is trying to take advantage of you, commence to work on his moral nature, until you bring forth into action all the good there is in him. In this manner you are doing a double good; you are working for yourself, and are also bringing out the best in another. But you have no right to coerce another person under any circumstances. You may suggest strongly, and forcefully, but not to the extent of coercion, not even to develop the moral nature of another. You may suggest to another person who owes you, "give me the money you owe me," but you have no right to say, "You shall return the money; you shall never sleep again until you have paid me."

When you are suggesting to another to do something for you, speak of yourself as a third person, and you will have much better results. For instance, if you wish to say mentally to the person who owes you the money, "you want to repay the money," he might not know which money was referred to. However, if you include your name; for instance, "Pay Mr. Smith the money you owe him," your suggestion will be understood and very likely will be acted upon. Also, when you make a mental suggestion, suggest doubly. In other words, make one suggestion to the subjective mind, telling it the truth. When you suggest to the objective mind, advice it along the lines of personal interest. In other words, you might say to the objective mind, "It is to your interest to pay Mr. Smith the money you owe him, for if you do not, there may be another time when you need his help and friendship and it will not be forthcoming." To the subjective mind you might say, "You are an honest person, and will be glad to repay to Mr. Smith the money which you rightfully owe him."

Auto-suggestion is suggesting to yourself, and you should always let the auto-suggestion be made by your higher mind to your lower self. Let the subjective mind give, and the objective receive, the suggestion. Suppose you wish to break a habit; then you would say to your objective mind, "you cannot do this thing again." Sometimes the objective mind will answer, "Why can't I?" Then you must reply, "Because it is not to your interest to do it, and you do not want to; you have no desire to do it, for all your desire is gone." And the objective mind will begin to wonder where the desire has gone, and at that moment accepts the suggestion made. In this manner you can break any habit, if you will persist in making the suggestions.

Deity does not coerce its children, and no child of God has a right to coerce another, because it is morally wrong to do so. Whatever exists on the mental plane must become embodied on the material plane sooner or later, and a man's body is a limited expression of his mental traits, as are also the tendencies and habits of his body. Suppose a woman comes to you and begs, "Save my husband from becoming an alcoholic!" and you undertake the task of stopping the man from drinking. You make your mental suggestions and say, "you shall not drink anymore; you shall suffer an agony of fear, and excruciating pains, every time you attempt to take a drink." You may prevent the man from drinking, but you have not destroyed his love for it, and you have really only delayed his evolution, since he will have to come back to face the same conditions at another time; if not in the same body, then in another one, in a future life – or whenever your will has ceased to control him.

A LITTLE KNOWLEDGE IS A DANGEROUS THING

There is something here which must also be brought to your attention, and it is not very pleasant. However, it is all too true that when people begin studying, and have learned one or two Laws, they are sometimes misled into believing that they now know everything, and are authorized to go about mentally "saving" all of their friends, and feeling quite proud of themselves in the thought that they are doing a great work. However, a "little knowledge is a dangerous thing," and before one can take it upon himself to change a person's thoughts and character to what he believes it should be, he must first know the truth concerning the other person's character. Many times we "suppose" that we are doing right, but none of our friends are what they should be. And, sad to relate, usually the imaginary "fault" we see in another person is but the reflection of that very fault which we have in ourselves. The objective mind constantly misjudges other people. Often heard is the very old expression, "Don't judge others by yourself," which is rather a difficult habit to break.

It should not be forgotten that hypnotic influence has a reactionary influence upon the operator. For example, suppose a person attempts to throw his hypnotic influence upon you, and you are so positive, or your vibrations are so high, that his influence fails to affect you; then as a natural operation of Law, that force which he sent out, not reaching its intended destination, returns to the sender. If it be a malignant force, it will do for the sender what it was intended to do for the victim. The greatest crime known to the Great Law is the coercion of an individual center or mind to do evil. No one ever coerced another, or used suggestion to the detriment of another, and no one ever brought disease or misfortune upon another, that he did not eventually have to drink to the dregs the cup he held to that other's lips. He may escape punishment from the human law, but it will be impossible for him to escape from the Divine Law.

In order to send malignant influences to another, the sender must hold in his mind the picture of the disaster he wishes to create for that other. It is impossible to do this without creating a matrix in his own aura, and this matrix will draw back to the sender just what he has created, for the Great Law works automatically and impartially, and irrespective of the fact of whether or not he has succeeded in bringing down disaster upon his victim.

You can make yourself immune from this malignant force, first, by being mentally positive, so that you are not what the hypnotist calls "suggestible." A person who is suggestible is in a passive condition of mind, and receives suggestion easily. If you make a practice of concentrating your thoughts upon whatever you are doing, your mind is active and positive, and thoughts foreign to you cannot find lodging within you. Few operators are persistent enough to continue their suggestions when they fail to reach the subject after a considerable length of time. Second, it is accepting the suggestion which enslaves. You cannot prevent the suggestion from coming to you if the operator is persistent, but you need not accept it; and, third, be on your guard against all suggestions, and examine critically all thoughts that come to you.

There is no one strong enough to make a suggestion to you and accomplish his purpose immediately. The effort must be repeatedly made before he can succeed. If you examine the thoughts which come to you and find them undesirable, then repudiate them and declare that you cannot be influenced by them. Fourth, do not entertain visiting thoughts until you know their character any more readily than you would entertain persons about whose character you know nothing. Select only the thoughts you want, and reject the suggestions you do not desire. Few people are able to do this, but instead are constantly being swayed by the influence of those with whom they associate. Other people's manners, words, and thoughts mold our lives to a much greater extent than we imagine, and this is because we do not think for ourselves; we do not generate our own thoughts, but accept whatever comes floating along to us.

Remember that no person can retain possession of anything which has been gained through Black Art or by dishonest methods. A thief may seem to prosper, but eventually the Great Law will make the proper adjustment, and his ill gotten gains will be swept from him, because Divine Justice does rule the Universe.

In the category of Nature's finer forces must be included that class of manifestations which are generally known as Telepathy, Thought Transference, Thought Force, etc., all of which are based upon the fact that there is present in all such mental states as thought, emotion, desire, etc., a certain rate of vibratory motion, which motion is capable of being radiated from the mind of the person manifesting these vibrations in such power and force that they may be registered with more or less distinctness upon the minds of other persons. In the more common forms of its manifestation, such mental force or power is known as Thought Force, Mental Influence, etc., and in its more pronounced and less common phases it is known as Telepathy and Thought Transference – but the basic principle is precisely the same in all of such cases, simple or complex though the manifestation may be.

We may state here, however, that the advanced occultists regard this class of phenomena as comparatively simple and elementary, and therefore not fully entitled to be included in the same category with the higher phases of Nature's finer forces, such as, for instance, Clairvoyance, Psychometry, Communication with the Higher Planes, etc. Notwithstanding this, we are of the opinion that any and every one of the finer forces of nature which are over and above the plane upon which the ordinary senses of man, normally developed, ordinarily function and operate, should be placed in one general category of the Higher Forces of Nature, particularly in a book of this type designed for the instruction of the general public upon these important subjects. Accordingly, these lesser manifestations of the finer forces in. the natural world shall be carefully considered, so that the reader may become acquainted with the scientific principles upon which they are based, and may be enabled to develop the power of manifesting such powers should he choose to do so, and also that he may understand the nature of such forces and powers when they are manifested by others.

CHITTA

The Hindu Teachings hold that the thing which we call "Mind" is not an intangible something different from anything else in Nature, but that, on the contrary, it forms a part of Nature's general manifestation, and is a substantial thing. The Hindus have given to this Mind Substance the name of Chitta. Without going into metaphysical discussion, or entering into technical details concerning this "Mind Stuff" or Chitta, we may say that the Hindus believe it to be one phase of the great Manifestation which we call Nature—just as that which we call Matter is another phase of manifestation. Like Matter, Chitta has its own particular kind of force or energy, its own rates of vibrations, and its own attribute of radiating its vibratory force or energy over space. Chitta manifests its activity in creating thought, emotions, etc., and also in receiving impressions from the outside world, which it translates into perceptions and ideals. Chitta, or Mind Substance, is not regarded by the Hindus as being identical with the Soul, or the Ego; but, on the contrary, they regard it as being an instrument for the expression of the activity of the Ego, or Soul, just as the Body is another kind of instrument. Both Body and Mind are regarded as being intended for the use of the Ego or Soul, and not to be identified with either of the latter. *Chitta could be likened unto the carrier beam of a radio station that utilizes the beam by modulation.

There are probably many to whom this conception of the vibration energy of Chitta, or Mind Substance, may seem strange. But such persons will be still more surprised, perhaps, when they are told that modern science has practically admitted the general truth contained in the Hindu Teachings concerning this, though modern science seems to cloak the facts of the case in technical terms. In layman's terms, every living being is a dynamic focus. A dynamic focus tends ever to propagate the motion that is a condition of it. Propagated motion becomes transformed according to the medium it traverses. Motion always tends to propagate itself; therefore, when we see work of any kind, mechanical, electrical, nervic, or psychic, disappear without visible effort, then one of two things has happened; either a transmission or a transformation.

And now we must determine just where the first ends, and where the second begins. In an identical medium there is only transmission, but in a different medium there is transformation. You send an electric current through a thick wire. You have the current, but you do not perceive any other force. However, cut the thick wire and connect the ends by means of a fine wire, and this fine wire will grow hot; there will be a transformation of a part of the current into heat. Take a fairly strong current and interpose a wire still more resistant, or perhaps a thin carbon rod, and the carbon will emit light. A part of the current, then, is transformed into heat and light. The light acts in every direction round about it; first visibly, as light, and then invisibly, as heat and electric current. Now hold a magnet near it, and if the magnet is weak and movable, in the form of a magnetic needle, the beam of light will cause it to deviate. If it is strong and immovable, it will in turn cause the beam of light to deviate; and all of this may be done from a distance, without contact, and without special conductors.

A process that is at once chemical, physical, and psychical, goes on in the brain. A complex action of this kind is propagated through the gray brain matter, as waves are propagated in water. Regarded on its physiological side, an idea is only a vibration, a vibration that is propagated, yet which does not pass out of the medium in which it can exist as such. It is propagated only as far as other vibrations allow. It is propagated more widely if it assumes the character which subjectively we call emotion. But it cannot go beyond without being transformed. Nevertheless, like force in general, neither can it remain in isolation, but manages to escape in disguise.

Thought stays at home, so to speak, as the chemical action of a battery remains in the battery; it is represented by its dynamic correlate, which in the case of the battery is called a "current." A force that is transmitted meets other forces, and if it is transformed only little by little, it usually limits itself to modifying other force at its own cost, though without suffering materially thereby. This is the case particularly with forces that are persistent, concentrated, and well seconded by their medium. It is also the case with the psychological equilibrium, nervic force, psychic force, ideas, emotions and tendencies, all of which modify environing forces without themselves disappearing. They are imperceptible when transformed, and if the next man is of a nature exceptionally well adapted to them, they gain in inductive action. *This demonstrates the futility of medical research on brain centers in animals by present methods. The public may not be aware of the extent to which cats, dogs, and such animals are used in such painful experiments.

So much for the conceptions of modern western science, which agree with those of the ancient Oriental occultists, although of course different names and terms are employed. However, we think it well worth your while to call to your attention the fact that the western scientists have not paid enough attention to the significant presence of a peculiar organ in the human body, which is regarded as the most important in its functions and offices by the Oriental teachers and the better mystic and occult schools in America, and which has a very close connection to the subject just discussed. We refer to that strange organ which we mentioned in another chapter, which is known to western science as the Pineal Gland, and now we shall see just exactly what this is.

The Pineal Gland is a mass of nervous substance which is found located in the human brain in a position near the middle of the skull, almost directly above the extreme top of the spinal column. It is shaped like a small cone, and is of a reddish-gray color. It lies in front of the cerebellum, and is attached to the third ventricle of the brain. It contains a small quantity of peculiar particles of a gritty, sand-like substance, which is commonly known as brain-sand, and derives its scientific name from its shape, which resembles a pine cone. Western scientists and physiologists still have not agreed regarding the function and office of this interesting organ, or gland, and the textbooks generally content themselves with stating that "the functions of the Pineal Gland are not understood." The Asian occultists, on the other hand, claim that the Pineal Gland, with its peculiar arrangement of nerve-cell corpuscles, and its tiny grains of "brain-sand" is intimately associated with certain forms of the transmission and reception of waves of mental vibrations. Western students of occultism have been struck with the remarkable resemblance between the Pineal Gland and a certain part of the receiving apparatus employed in wireless telegraphy, the latter also containing small particles which bear a close resemblance to the "brain-sand" of the Pineal Gland; and this fact is often urged by them to substantiate the theory of the Oriental occultists concerning the function and office of this interesting organ of the human body which is located in the brain of man.

THOUGHT-WAVES

One of the things which seem to greatly puzzle the average student of the subject of mental vibrations and thought-transference is that which may be called "thought-waves." The student is unable to conceive of a wave of "thought" being projected into the air and then traveling along until it reaches the mind of another person. The difficulty, upon analysis, is seen to consist of the inability to conceive of thought as being material substance, capable of traveling in "waves." It is no wonder that the student finds this conception difficult, for there actually is no such thing as "thought" traveling in this manner. The phenomenon of thought-transference is accounted for scientifically in quite another manner, as we shall see in a moment. The student is advised to note carefully this distinction, for upon its understanding depends greatly the intelligent comprehension of the entire subject of thought vibrations and thought-transference.

Perhaps this matter may be best explained by means of illustrations of the operation of electricity and light or electric vibrations and light vibrations. In both cases, the secret of the transmissions of the vibrations or waves of vibratory energy may be summed up in the word "transformation." For instance, when we transmit electric vibrations over a fine wire or thread of carbon, the electric vibrations are transformed into light vibrations, and manifest as "electric light." In another form of transmission, the electric vibrations are transformed into "electric heat." But this is merely one phase of the transformation; consider carefully the more complex phases. We speak into the receiver of a telephone, and the sound vibrations produced by our voice are transformed into electrical vibrations, and in that form travel over the telephone wire. Arriving at the other end of the wire, these electrical vibrations enter into the receiver and are there transformed into sound vibrations, and as such are heard by the person holding the receiver. Now note this – the sound vibrations do not travel at all; instead, they are transformed into electric waves, which in turn are transformed at the receiving end of the line into sound vibrations once more. And unless the receiving apparatus is present, and properly adjusted, there is no second transformation at all; and in such cases the electric vibrations simply remain as such.

Likewise, in the case of the wireless telegraphy, the electric energy produced by the sending instrument is transformed into subtle and finer etheric waves, which travel to the receiving instrument, and there are transformed into electric waves, the latter producing physical changes in the receiving apparatus which enable them to be read by the observer. In the case of wireless telephony, there is still a more complex process of transformation; the speaker conveys sound vibrations into the instrument; these are transformed into electrical vibrations, and the latter into the etheric vibrations which travel through space to the receiver. Reaching the receiver, the etheric vibrations are transformed into ordinary electric vibrations, and these in turn into sound waves capable of being sensed by the listener.

The same process is detected in the transmission of what we call light waves. The activities manifested by the substance of the sun set up certain vibrations which we call "light vibrations." These are communicated to the ether in the form of so called "light waves," but which are merely etheric waves of a certain rate of vibration. These waves travel through space and are transformed into "light" only when they reach some material substance capable of receiving and reflecting their vibrations. Science tells us that empty "space" is perfectly dark, and that light manifests only when the etheric light vibrations come into contact with material substance, and there are transformed into "light." Light, as "light," does not travel from the sun, what we know as "light" is simply the result of the transformation of certain etheric waves into "light" by reason of their contact with material substances.

And now for the analogy...mental vibrations are so only when they remain in their own uninterrupted medium, or channel of activity – that is, the brain and the nervous system of the individual. Many claim that they are able to leap over the barrier of flesh separating two persons, when such persons are in immediate physical contact and the conditions are of a certain kind, but as a rule they do not do so. But, as all investigators know, mental vibrations are capable of being transformed into some subtle form of etheric vibrations, and the latter when coming into contact with the nervous system of other persons may be again transformed, this time into mental vibrations which produced thoughts, feelings, and mental images in the minds of the second person or persons, corresponding with these mental states in the first person. Thinking this over carefully, you will be able to grasp the idea fully.

And here we find another startling correspondence between the phenomena of wireless telegraphy and that of thought transference or transmission of mental vibrations. We allude to the fact that while a wireless telegraphic sending instrument may be sending forth vibrations of the strongest power, its messages are capable of being received or "picked up" only by those instruments which are "in tune" with the sending instrument to at least a certain degree; to all other instruments, those which are not "in tune" with the sending instrument, there is no message perception. Precisely this same state of affairs is found to prevail in the realm of mental vibrations and thought transmissions. The individual receives only such messages as emanate from instruments with which he is "in tune" to all the rest he is deaf and unconscious. But once "in tune" with the higher vibrations of the mental realm, he will receive every message traveling on that particular plane at that particular time, unless he deliberately shuts them out. We shall see how this works out in ordinary life, as we consider the general subject of clairvoyance and thought transference in the next chapter. *Under proper amplification, grass can be heard to grow (it squeaks!) and spiders can be heard to roar as they pounce upon flies. Normally we do not know such things exist.

However, in connection with the above statement of the "in tune" Law, or rule of manifestation, we wish to again call to the attention of the student the important fact that this identical Law prevails in the case of communications from the higher planes of existence, the messages from the "Space People," the so called "spirit communications," and other messages of this kind reaching individuals on our own plane of existence. It is only when the individual on the

"Earth Plane" becomes "in tune" with the sending mental instrument of the entity abiding on a higher plane of existence that it is able to "pick up" the message being sent to Earth. Even the same individual is often unable to "catch" the messages at one time, while at other times he experiences no difficulty whatsoever.

An understanding of this fact, this Law or rule of manifestation, will throw a great light over many dark places of misunderstanding and perplexity concerning certain phases of occult and psychic phenomena. This feature of such phenomena will be considered in detail further on in the book; however, in concluding our consideration of the "just how" of the transmission of thoughts, messages, and "psychograms" between two minds, be they both of the Earth Plane, or one of the two on a higher plane, we would remind the student to remember always the two key words which are Transformation and Attunement. These two keywords will enable you to unlock many doors of thought on these subjects, doors which would otherwise remain closed to you.

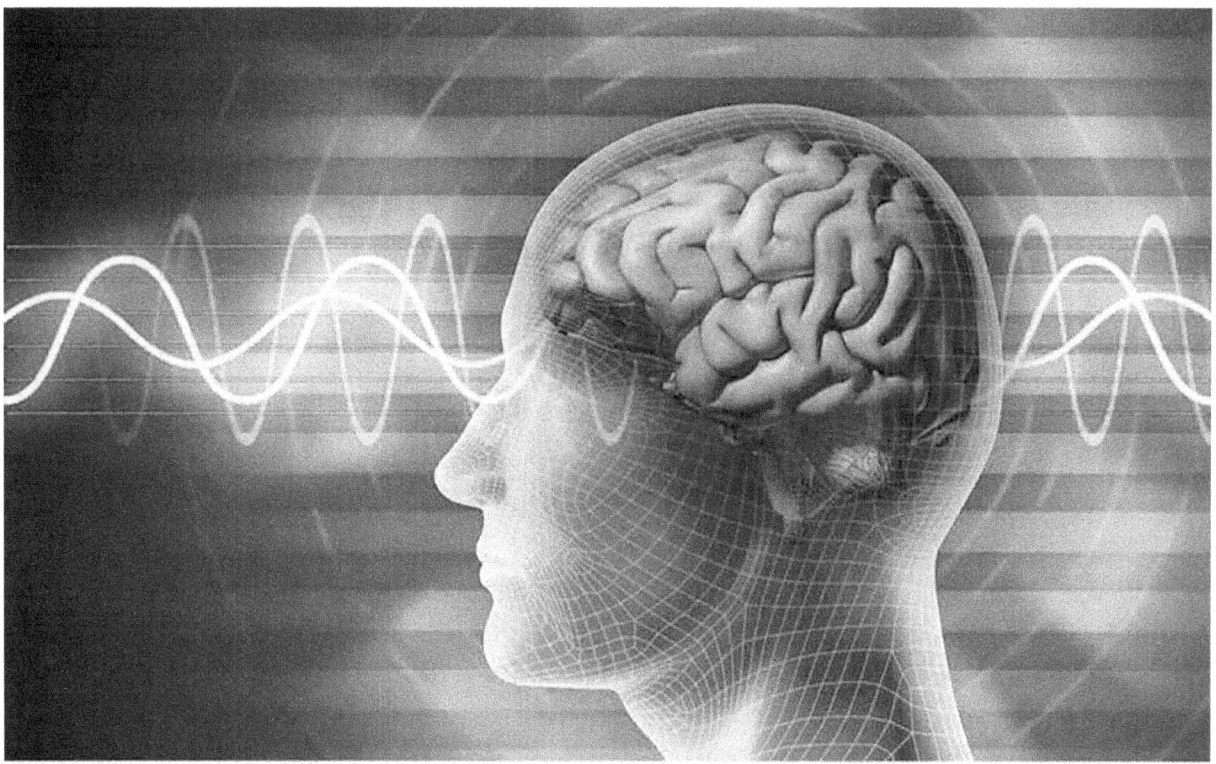

A thought is a force, a manifestation of energy, a vibration sent through time and space—and is as real and as intangible as the vibrations manifesting light, heat, electricity, magnetism.

14

PSYCHIC PHENOMENA AND THE UFO MYSTERY

In considering the chapter on psychic phenomena with its specialized branches of clairvoyance, psychometry, crystal gazing, etc., we must not assume that this is of interest only to gypsies and such unfortunate psychics who have had to scrounge a living from the gullible. It should be of interest also to the respectable Psychical Research Societies established all over the world, but in examining the lives and experiences of these unfortunate members of society many a learned scientist and professor has found it a lucrative hobby to write enormous tomes which come to absolutely no definite conclusions.

We might say that their efforts could well be designated by Erasmus' title: *"In Praise of Folly."* Many investigators disregard what they cannot prove, and what they can prove, they do not understand. This they freely admit. With utmost contempt for the academic opinions, mankind as a whole has indulged itself in palmistry, crystal gazing, teacup reading and sand writing from time immemorial. For the most part this has been indulged in as a pastime for pleasure because the financial returns have not warranted any serious consideration by the more intellectual groups in society. The Tarot cards have developed into the universal pastime of playing cards. Gambling for money is considered by most people as something more than "luck," and they attempt to pit their intuitive powers, or psychic faculties, against the turn of the wheel or card, as the case may be.

Clairvoyance is when someone seems to have special insight into future, past, or present events when they have no previous experience or knowledge base to fall back on.

It has always been disconcerting for the gambling man, be he a follower of the stock market or the race tracks, to find that after his many careful mathematical calculations, more often than not the "little woman's" intuition will sometimes bear greater results than his own efforts.

In closing our comments on clairvoyance, we wish to draw attention to two clairvoyants who have exerted a great influence on the minds of men. One is Swedenborg, who demonstrated such irrefutable evidence of his ability as a clairvoyant able to record actual happenings taking place at a distance, that he was able to establish a religion. The other, of course, is the famous Nostradamus. The students of his quatrains have established to their satisfaction that many historical events were forecast by this Seer. Henry James Forman published an excellent book, *"The Story of Prophecy in the Life of Mankind "* and in it we find that Saint Malachi, born in Ireland in 1094, in the town of Armagh, Ulster

County, was the author of what is termed, "The Papal Prophecy," which predicts that after Pius XI there will reign only seven more Popes and then the end.

According to the Church itself, one of the conditions of his Sainthood was "That God conferred upon him the dual gift of miracle and prophecy" In view of the fact that Nostradamus predicted that the City of Paris would be destroyed from the air, perhaps we should lend an ear to our present day clairvoyants who claim contact with space people who continuously warn that unless we change our entire moral concept and attitude toward each other, as men under the Fatherhood of God on this planet, we are headed for inevitable self-destruction with the use of atomic weapons.

CLAIRVOYANCE

A large and interesting class of occult or psychic phenomena is that known under the very general classification of "Clairvoyance," which term we have thought it advisable to employ in this sense in this book, notwithstanding the technical objections urged by some against such a general usage. The term "clairvoyance" means "clear seeing," or "clear sight," but its special meaning, established by long usage, is "a power of discerning objects not perceptible to the normal senses." When it comes to the technical use of the term by students and teachers of psychic research and occultism, however, there is found a confused meaning of the term, some employing it in one sense and others in another one. Accordingly, it is perhaps as well to explain the particular usage adopted and followed in this book.

The English Society for Psychical Research, in its glossary, defines the term as follows: "The faculty or act of perceiving, as though visually, with some coincidental truth, some distant scene; it is used sometimes, but hardly properly, for transcendental vision, or the perception of Beings regarded as on another Plane of existence." A distinguished investigator of psychic phenomena, in one of her reports to the English Society for Psychical Research, has given the following definition of this term, as employed by her in her reports: "The word 'clairvoyant' is often used very loosely, and with widely different meanings. I denote by it a faculty of acquiring supernormally – but not by reading the minds of persons present – a knowledge of facts such as we normally acquire by the use of our senses. I do not limit it to knowledge that would normally be acquired by the sense of sight, nor do I limit it to knowledge of present facts. A similar knowledge of the past, and, if necessary, of future events, may be included. On the other hand, I exclude the mere faculty of seeing apparitions, which is sometimes called clairvoyance."

The term "clairvoyance" is used here in the particular sense indicated by such definition, as last quoted. The student of this book, therefore, is asked to distinguish clairvoyance, on the one hand, from the phenomena of telepathy, or thought transference, and, on the other hand, from the phenomena of communication with Beings or entities on other planes of existence, including the perception of apparitions. The phenomena of clairvoyance may be subdivided according to methods employed, and also according to general distinctions.

The classification of clairvoyant phenomena according to the method employed would include, first, Psychometry, in which the clairvoyant becomes en rapport through the medium of some physical object connected with the person or scene which is the object of his psychometry. The second method employed is Crystal Gazing, etc., in which the rapport is established by means of a crystal ball or "magic" mirror, into which the clairvoyant gazes. The third is Direct Clairvoyance, in which the clairvoyant directly establishes the rapport by means of raising his or her psychic vibrations so as to become "in tune" with the finer vibrations of Nature, without the aid of physical objects.

The classification according to general distinctions includes, first, Present Clairvoyance, in which the objects perceived by the clairvoyant are present now in space and time, although invisible to physical sight; second, what is known as Space Clairvoyance, in which the clairvoyant vision includes physical objects and scenes removed in space from the immediate normal perception of the clairvoyant and, third, Time Clairvoyance, in which the clairvoyant perceives objects or scenes removed from him in past time or future time. In order that the student may obtain a comprehensive understanding of the phenomena of clairvoyance, we are presenting here a brief general outline of the particular phenomena fitting into these several classes, and will give also a general idea of the principal methods employed to obtain the phenomenal manifestations in question. We begin by calling your attention to the three general classes of methods employed to obtain the manifestation of clairvoyant phenomena; namely, Psychometry, Crystal Gazing, and Clairvoyant Psychic states, respectively.

In psychometry, the clairvoyant establishes the rapport with objects, persons, or scenes, removed in space or in time, by means of some physical object associated with the distant object, person, or scene. The physical object may be a piece of clothing, a bit of stone, a coin, a piece of jewelry, etc., which has been closely associated with that which the clairvoyant desires to sense psychically. The distinctive feature of this class of clairvoyant phenomena is this connecting link of physical objects, and one writer has compared this connecting link with the bit of clothing which the keen-scented bloodhound is given to sniff in order that he may then discover by scent the person sought, the latter having previously worn the bit of clothing presented to the dog's sense of smell.

Occultists have elaborated a technical theory to account for the phenomena of psychometry, or rather to account for the action of the "connecting link" of the physical object employed between the clairvoyant and the distant object, person or scene; however we do not think it advisable to enter into a discussion of these elaborate technical theories, which are apt to confuse the beginner and to distract his attention from the important facts. We believe it is sufficient to say that the "connecting link," or physical object seems to carry along with it, in its inner substance, or nature, the vibrations of its past environment; and that the clairvoyant, coming into receptive contact with such vibrations, is enabled with comparative ease to follow up the psychic "scent" until he establishes clairvoyant rapport with the distant object, person, or scene associated with the physical object. When it is remembered that the physical "scent" of anything is merely a matter of the detection of certain vibrations, the illustration is seen to be not so very far out of the way after all.

The untrained clairvoyant usually cannot find a particular astral picture when it is wanted, without some special link to put him en rapport with the subject required. Psychometry is an instance in point. It seems as though there were a sort of magnetic attachment or affinity between any particle of matter and the record which contains its history-an affinity which enables it to act as a kind of conductor between that record and the faculties of anyone who can read it. One of the most familiar instances of the production of clairvoyant phenomena by means of Psychometry is the production of the rapport or affinity with distant scenes by means of the connecting link of some small object which had at some time in the past been located at that point. In such cases the psychometrist usually presses the small object up to his or her head, and then induces a passive, receptive psychical condition; then, sooner or later, the clairvoyant experiences a "sensation" or "dream picture" of the scene in question.

Often, once the picture of the scene is obtained, the clairvoyant may manifest more marked past-time clairvoyance in the direction of running back over the history of the scene itself. There are cases on record in which the clairvoyant has been able to give the history of certain places in ancient Egypt, from the connecting link of a piece of mummy cloth, or else to give a picture of certain events in antediluvian times, from the connecting link of a bit of fossil substance. The history of Psychometry is filled with remarkable instances of this kind. Bullets gathered from battlefields also serve very effectively as such psychometric connecting links. Old furniture, old pictures, and old jewelry are also common objects serving to produce wonderful phenomena of this kind. In fact, any physical object having past-time or far distant space connections may be employed effectively in such experiments.

Psychometry is frequently employed to describe underground, or "mine" conditions existing at the present time at the particular place from which a particular piece of ore or mineral has been taken, which ore or mineral has been handed to the psychometrist to be used as a connecting link. As many practical miners know from actual experience, many valuable coal, zinc, lead, silver and gold mines have been successfully located in this way. In such cases the psychometrist has been able to follow up the psychic "scent" given by the piece of mineral, and thus to describe the strata or veins of the minerals lying underground and unopened by the pick or drill.

There are no special directions to be given to the student in psychometry. All that can be done is to suggest that each person should try the experiments for himself, in order to find out whether he has, or has not, the psychometric power in some degree of development. He may be able to develop his psychometric powers by the general methods given for psychic development; but, in any event, he will find that actual practice and experiment will do much for him. Let the student take strange objects and, sitting in a quiet room with the object held to his forehead, endeavor to shut all thoughts out completely, from the outside world, and forget all his personal affairs. In a short time, if the conditions are right, he will begin to see, mentally, flashes of scenes associated with the history of the object in question. At first these impressions may be somewhat disconnected and more or less confused, but before long there will be noticed a clearing away of the scene, and the mental picture should become quite plain. Practice will develop the power. The student should practice only when alone or when in the presence of some sympathetic friend or friends. He should always avoid discordant or inharmonious company while practicing to develop his psychic power. Many of the best psychometrists keep their physical eyes closed when practicing this power, thus allowing the inner senses to function without distraction from the outer senses.

Letters, clothes, hair, coins, ornaments or jewels-in fact, almost any article which has belonged to, or has been worn by, its possessor for any length of time, will suffice to enable the psychometrist to relate himself to, and glimpse impressions of, the personal sphere of that individual. Some psychometrists succeed better with certain kinds of objects than with others. Metals and minerals are not good "conductors," if we may use that term, to some operators; while they are very satisfactory to others. In the same way, some psychometrists are very good character readers, others are very successful in the diagnosis of diseases, some can read the book of Nature, while to others it is a sealed book, or nearly so, but they are able to gauge the mental qualifications of their visitors, while others realize their moral and spiritual states. Again, some read the past and enter into the present states or conditions of their clients, while others are successful in exercising prophetical prevision. These differences may be modified, and the boundaries of the perceptive power may be extended by self-study, experiment and culture; but every psychic has his qualifications and his limitations; one will succeed where another person may fail; therefore it is well for each one to discover what he can do best, and what sphere he can best occupy, and then endeavor to fill it.

CRYSTAL GAZING

The second of the three general classes of the methods employed to obtain the manifestations of clairvoyant phenomena is that known as Crystal Gazing. In this class of methods the clairvoyant establishes the rapport by means of a crystal, magic mirror, or similar object, which serves principally to concentrate the psychic visual powers to a focus, and thus to enable the psychic to raise his or her psychic vibrations at that concentrated focused point.

The use of crystal balls and other bright objects for this purpose has been common to occultists and psychics at all times, past and present, and at all places, oriental or occidental. The earlier races employed shining pieces of quartz or other clear crystal rock for this purpose. Later, polished metals were used in the same way. Shamans of various cultures employ clear water, glowing embers, or sparks for this purpose. In some places, the soothsayers hold drops of blood in the hollow of their hands for divining purposes. Others bore a hole in the ground, fill it with water, and then gaze into it. Some tribes use dark polished stones. Ink blots, bowls of water, ponds, a highly polished surface, in fact, almost every object capable of presenting a polished surface has been employed at some time as an aid to psychic vision. In Europe and America in the present day, quartz or good glass crystals are so used; but others obtain quite satisfactory results from the use of watch crystals laid over a black cloth, preferably a piece of black velvet. Some use highly polished bits of silver, while others have cups painted black on the inside, into which is poured water.

There is no particular virtue in any particular object used for this purpose, as such objects merely act to focus the psychic power of the person, as we have already mentioned. And certainly the student should not fall into the error of supposing that the crystal, or similar object, has any miraculous or supernatural power whatsoever; it is simply an instrument, like the microscope or the telescope, nothing more or less. However, at the same time, it must be admitted that there is much truth in the claim of certain crystal gazers to the effect that the use of a particular crystal seems to have the effect of polarizing its molecules so as to render it a more effective instrument in time. In fact, the phenomenon seems to bear a close relation to the well known case of the long used violin becoming a more perfect instrument, and giving forth richer and fuller notes than a new instrument. Experts in crystal gazing insist that the crystal gazer should keep his own crystal for his own particular use, and not allow it to be used indiscriminately, particularly in the case of strangers or of persons not sympathetic with psychic subjects. They claim that each crystal becomes polarized according to the individual character and needs of the person habitually using it, and that it is unwise to allow others to disturb this quality in it.

All experiments with crystal gazing should be conducted in a serious, earnest manner, and all frivolity or trifling should be avoided for the best results. This, of course, is true concerning all phases of psychic investigation, as all students of the subject know. Authorities agree that the crystal gazer should sit with his back to the light, and should never have it in front of him. And, while an earnest, steady gaze is desirable, there should be no straining of the eyes. Do not try to avoid blinking the eyes, however; there is a difference between "gazing" and "staring."

While some experimenters obtain results from the time of the first trial, others find that it requires a number of sittings before they begin to obtain even faint results. The psychic picture in the crystal usually begins by the appearance of a cloudy, "milky" mist, succeeding the former transparent appearance of the crystal. The milky cloud becomes more dense, and finally there appears in its midst a faint form, outline, face or scene of some kind. Some have compared this gradual emergence of the picture to the gradual development of the photographic plate when the latter is subjected to the action of the developing fluid.

Each and every form of clairvoyant picturing is possible in crystal gazing, for crystal gazing is merely one particular form or method of inducing clairvoyant or psychic vision, and is not a distinct branch of psychic phenomena in itself. The results can be classified as follows:

Crystal gazing is one of the oldest forms of clairvoyance. Practitioners not only use the traditional crystal ball, but can also use mirrors, candles, glasses of water, etc. Any reflective surface can be used.

1. Images of something unconsciously observed. New reproductions, voluntary or spontaneous, and bringing no fresh knowledge to the mind.

2. Images of ideas unconsciously acquired from others. Some memory or imaginative effort, which does not come from the gazer's objective self. Revivals of Memory. Illustrations of thought.

3. Images, clairvoyant or prophetic. Pictures giving information as to something past, present or future, which the gazer has no other way of knowing.

What is desired through the regular use of the translucent crystal is to cultivate a personal degree of clairvoyant power, so that visions of things or events, either past, present or future, may appear clearly in the interior vision, or eye of the soul. In the pursuit of this effort only, the crystal becomes a beautiful, interesting and harmless channel for pleasure and instruction, shorn of dangers, and rendered conducive to mental development. Those who employ it for purely "parlor games," to try to find out those things which should not concern them, or for monetary gain with no desire to help those who wish to have a reading, will find themselves trapped hopelessly on the Astral plane. There is a Royal Road to crystal vision, but it opens only to the combined password of Calmness, Patience, and Perseverance. If one fails upon the first attempt to ride a bicycle, it is obvious that the only way to learn is to pay attention to the necessary rules, and to persevere daily until the ability to ride comes naturally, and thus it is with the would-be Seer. Persevere in accordance with these simple directions, and success will sooner or later crown your efforts.

Two principle classes of visions will present themselves to the sitter, and these are the symbolic, indicated by the appearance of such symbols as a flag, boat, knife, gold, etc., and the actual, which is scenes and people, in action or otherwise. Persons of a positive type, the more active, excitable, but decided type, are most likely to perceive symbolically, or allegorically, while those of a passive nature usually receive direct or literal revelations. Both classes will find it necessary to cultivate carefully discrimination, truthfulness, unselfishness, gratitude for what is shown, and absolute confidence in the love, wisdom, and guidance of God Himself.

Different manifestations of clairvoyant vision may be classified according to the distinction of Time and Space. Clairvoyant vision may disclose objects, scenes or persons either nearby in space, or far off in space; either existing in the present time, past time, or in future time. In as much as the visions of crystal gazing are merely particular forms of clairvoyant vision, it follows that all of the several above named distinctive forms of vision are manifested in crystal gazing. The vision shown in the crystal may be that of something very near in space, or perhaps very far off in space, or removed in space only at a moderate distance. Likewise, such vision may be based upon things existing at the present time, or at some period of past time, or at some period of future time. Each or all of the manifestations of visions of past, present or future things, events, persons and scenes are possible to the clairvoyant vision of the crystal gazer, and pictured in the reflecting surface of the crystal or other shining surface employed by him in his experiments.

DIRECT CLAIRVOYANCE

The third of the three general classes of the methods employed to obtain the manifestation of clairvoyant phenomena is that known as Direct Clairvoyance. In this class the clairvoyant directly establishes the rapport with the past or present, near or distant, objects, persons, scenes or events by means of raising his or her psychic vibrations so as to become "in tune" with the finer vibrations of Nature, without the aid of the physical objects required in the methods of psychometry and crystal gazing.

Some clairvoyants, manifesting their powers by means of the methods of direct clairvoyance, produce in themselves the condition of a trance, or semi-trance condition. Many students believe that these conditions are absolutely necessary for this kind of phenomena, but they neglect, or are actually unaware of, the fact that many of the highest forms of this class of clairvoyant phenomena are manifested by clairvoyants who are no more in a trance condition, or that of semi-trance, than those following the methods of psychometry or crystal gazing. Actually, all that is required is that the clairvoyant maintain a quiescent mental attitude, shutting out the sounds, sights and thoughts of the outside world, and concentrating the full attention upon the clairvoyant work before him or her. Some, it is true, pass easily into the semi-trance, or even the full trance condition, but this is not necessary. The state of clairvoyant reverie may be safely and effectively induced by the practice of mental concentration alone. All that is needed is that the consciousness be focused to a single point—become "one-pointed," as the Hindu teachers tell us. The intelligent practice of concentration accomplishes this without the necessity of any artificial means of development, or the production of abnormal psychic states.

You are easily able to concentrate your full attention when you witness an interesting play, or listen to a beautiful rendition of some great masterpiece of musical composition, or gaze at some miracle of pictured or sculptured art. In these cases your attention is completely occupied with the interesting thing before you, so that you have almost completely shut out the outer world of sound, sight and thought-but you are, nevertheless, perfectly wide awake and conscious. The same thing is true when you read a very interesting book, the world is shut out from your consciousness, and you are oblivious to the sights and sounds around you. We frequently witness the sight of two lovers to whom the outside world is non-existent for the time being, and to whom there is nothing in the world except themselves. Again, persons often fall into a "brown study." or "daydream," in which all consciousness of the outside world seems to be shut out, yet the person is fully conscious and wide awake. These mental states are very much akin to that of the trained clairvoyant, and is the state which should be sought after by all clairvoyants, whether they are following the methods of psychometry, crystal gazing, or that of clairvoyance, for the principal is one and the same in all such methods.

Occasional flashes of clairvoyance sometimes come to the highly cultured and spiritually-minded man, even though he may never have heard of the possibility of training such a faculty. In his case, such glimpses usually signify that he is approaching that stage in his evolution when these powers will naturally begin to manifest themselves. Their appearance should serve as an additional stimulus to him to strive to maintain that high standard of moral purity and mental balance without which clairvoyance is a curse, and not a blessing, to its possessor.

Between those who are entirely unimpressionable and those who are in full possession of clairvoyant power, there are many intermediate stages. Students often ask how this clairvoyant faculty will be first manifested in themselves, or how they may know when they have reached the stage at which its first faint foreshadowing are beginning to be visible. Cases differ so widely that it is impossible to give this question any kind of answer that will be universally applicable. Some people begin by a plunge, as it were, and under some unusual stimulus become able just for once to see some striking vision; and very often in such a case, because the experience does not repeat itself, the seer comes in time to believe that on that particular occasion he must have been the victim of a hallucination. Others begin by becoming intermittently conscious of the brilliant colors and vibrations of the human aura; yet others find themselves with increasing frequency seeing and hearing something to which those around them are blind and deaf. Some see faces, landscapes, or colored clouds floating before their eyes in the dark before they sink into sleep; while perhaps the most common experience of all is the beginning of the recollection, with greater and greater clearness, of what has been seen and heard on other planes during sleep.

As we have said, in our consideration of the general subject of clairvoyance, there is possible a general classification of clairvoyant phenomena according to general distinctions; the present clairvoyance, in which the objects perceived by the clairvoyant are present in time and space, although invisible to normal sight; Space Clairvoyance, in which the clairvoyant vision includes objects and scenes removed in space from the normal perception of the clairvoyant, and Time Clairvoyance, in which the clairvoyant perceives objects or scenes removed from him in past time, or future time. While the general methods of manifesting these various forms of clairvoyant power are practically the same, yet the nature of these several forms of phenomena vary considerably; this is particularly true in the case of the distinction between past-time clairvoyant phenomena and future-time phenomena, the difference between the perception of what has been and that which has not yet been.

In what is called Present Time clairvoyance, the objects seen by the clairvoyant are present in time and in space, at the moment and place of the perception, although invisible to normal sight. It is seen at once that if the object seen clairvoyantly is present in time and space to the clairvoyant, and yet is incapable of being perceived by the normal sight of the clairvoyant, then that object must be capable of being perceived only through vibrations above the normal range of the human senses. Perhaps the precise nature of this class of clairvoyant perceptions will be better understood by a more detailed description of the objects actually perceived by clairvoyant present-time vision.

Into each center of consciousness flows the magnetic force called the life principle, and by reason of that inflow into all forms there is a constant pushing out of old atoms, and a replacement of them with new elements. And this is true, whether the form be on the subjective side or objective side of nature. This passing in and out of the atomic life force makes a fluidic sphere; around each man and around everything. In electricity we call this fluidic sphere the electric field; in the sun we call it the photosphere, and around a magnet we call it the magnetic field, or field of attraction. This is one reason for the law of physics which says that no two masses can approach each other without being mutually affected, because, being brought into juxtaposition, there is an attraction and repulsion due to the flow of the life forces, and the exchange of atoms which is constantly taking place, between them. There is essentially nothing in inert matter to attract, but the inflowing of the life force, and the throwing off of old particles makes a change of atoms between masses that are near each other, and they attract or repel according to their similarity or dissimilarity of vibration.

It is the existence of the magnetic field of an animal or a man which enables a dog to follow the scent of either. As a physical, animal body passes over the ground, it throws off from itself particles or atoms with each effort or emotion. A certain quantity of these particles is left imprinted upon the earth; and since every individualized consciousness possesses its own distinct odor or perfume, due to its condition of development or rate of vibration, it is not at all difficult for the dog to keep the scent of the creature he is following. The atoms left upon the earth are impregnated with the odor of that person or thing which the dog is able to distinguish from any other.

When we come to the higher centers of consciousness, as in man, we not only have the life force as an element which builds, but we also have a thought force which is constantly manifesting, and by its vibratory flow is modifying the life force. Each person discards from himself not only the physical atoms which he has used, and which have his vibration, but also the finer forms of matter which go out with his thought force; and therefore there is a continuous stream flowing out from each individual to other centers, and these streams leave their impression upon everything the person thinks about or touches. A sensitive coming in contact with a part of the outflow from a man can read his character as well as a scientist by taking up a piece of coal can tell you its chemical constituency or its probable age and formation.

In ancient times, the sphere surrounding man was called the aureola when it encircled his whole body; when it radiated only from his head and shoulders, it was called the nimbus, or halo. Later, this magnetic field in either respect was called the Aura by western occultists, while in the East it was called the Sacred

Auric Egg. The ancient masters of art always represented their saints with a nimbus about their heads, and were accustomed to paint their most divine characters as surrounded by an aureola. In the pictures of Christ there is a radiation from the entire body, while in those of his disciples there is usually only the nimbus to be seen. And these old painters were right in their conceptions; they were sensitives, and saw that according to the development of the ego was the extent of its emanations. In the ordinary man this radiation extends from two to six inches from the body; but as man develops in thought, power and capacity to draw into himself cosmic forces, his radiations expand until they may extend six inches to several feet outward.

THE HUMAN ENERGY FIELD

This aura is one of the chief causes for the unaccountable likes and dislikes we have for persons whom we meet; for, if one is at all sensitive, one can feel very distinctly the auras with which one comes in contact. If we meet a person whose vibrations are very much higher than our own, we will be likely to either revere that person, or else dislike him intensely for being so far in advance of us. We will be greatly disturbed by the higher vibrations proceeding from him, which will very likely call forth all the good in us, or bring all the sediment in our nature to the surface; in other words, the aura of a highly advanced ego will bring out the best or the worst in those who come into contact with it. Knowing this, and being sensitive to these sudden likes and dislikes for persons, you may save yourself much discomfort by keeping a safe distance between yourself and those who disturb you. A distance of three or four feet will be sufficient to prevent you from feeling so plainly the vibratory force of another under usual conditions.

This aura also accounts for the great depletion that many persons feel when they come in contact with other persons, for it is all too true that there are human sponges who, unconsciously perhaps, maintain their own lives by drawing all the magnetic force of life they can get from others, and you will recall this was previously discussed under the name of vampirization.

We will now give a description of the human aura, for many students find that they have been seeing this clairvoyantly for some time, but did not know just what it was that they saw. And if you have not seen it as yet, the description will help you to recognize what it is when the time comes that you do see it. We shall also divide the aura into two classes for this particular explanation; the Human aura and the Prana aura.

This mode of clairvoyant vision discloses the interesting phenomena concerned with the human aura, or psychic atmosphere which surrounds the human body for a space of several feet, assuming an egg-shaped form. The trained clairvoyant vision sees the human aura as a nebulous, hazy substance, like a luminous cloud, surrounding the person for two or three feet on each side of his body, becoming denser near the body, and gradually becoming less dense as it extends away from the body. It has a phosphorescent appearance, with a peculiar tremulous motion manifesting through its substance. The clairvoyant sees the human aura as composed of all the colors of the spectrum, the combination shifting with the changing mental and emotional states of the person.

But in a general way, it may be said that each person has his or her distinctive astral auric colors, depending upon his or her general character and/or personality. Each mental state, or emotional manifestation, has its own particular shade or combination of shades of auric coloring. This beautiful kaleidoscopic spectacle has its own meaning to the occultist with clairvoyant vision, for he is thus able to read the character and general mental state of the person by means of studying his auric colors.

The human aura is not in a state of calm phosphorescence, however. On the contrary, it sometimes manifests great flames, like those of a fiery furnace, which shoot forth great tongues, and dart forth suddenly in certain directions towards the objects attracting them. Under great emotional excitement the auric flames move around in swift, circling whirlpools, or else swirl away from a center. Again, it seems to throw forth tiny glistening sparks of psychic vibrations, some of which travel for a great distance.

The clairvoyant vision is also able to discern what is called the "Prana" aura of a person. By this term is indicated that peculiar emanation of vital force which surrounds the physical body of each and every person. In fact, many persons of but slight clairvoyant power, who cannot sense the auric colors, are able to perceive this prana aura without trouble. It is sometimes called the "health aura," or "physical aura." It is colorless, or rather about the shade of clear glass, diamond or water. It is streaked with very minute, bristle-like lines. In a state of good health we find these lines are quite fine and rather stiff like toothbrush bristles; while in the case of poor health these lines droop, curl and present a furlike appearance. The prana aura is sometimes filled with minute, sparkling particles, like tiny diamonds in vibratory motion.

To the clairvoyant vision, the prana aura appears like the vibrating heated air arising from a fire, or a stove, or from the heated earth in summertime. If the student will close his eyes partially and peer through narrowed eyelids, he will in all probability be able to perceive this prana aura surrounding the body of some healthy, vigorous person, particularly if that person be standing in a dim light. Looking closely, he will see the peculiar vibratory motion, like heated air, at a distance of about two inches from the body of the person. It requires a little practice in order to acquire the knack of perceiving these vibrations, a little experimenting in order to get just the right light on the person, but practice will bring success, and you will be repaid for your trouble. In the same way, the student may by practice acquire the faculty of perceiving his own prana aura. The simplest way to obtain this result is to place your fingers, spread out into a fan-shape, against a black background, in a dim light. Then gaze at the fingers through narrowed eyelids, and half-closed eyes. After a little practice, you will see a fine thin line surrounding your fingers on all sides, a semi-luminous border of prana aura. In most cases this border of aura is colorless, but sometimes a very pale yellowish hue is perceived. The stronger the vital force of the person the stronger and brighter will this border of prana aura appear. The aura surrounding the fingers will appear very much like the semi-lustrous radiance of a candle flame, which is familiar to everyone.

All of the world's great teachers have taught substantially the same rules for conduct and morality. "Ethics" is not founded on police regulations or the sentiments of moralists, but is established on the immutable laws of nature. "Love your enemies" was one of the precepts taught by Jesus, and it has puzzled many of his followers to find the reason for this teaching. This precept has a purely scientific basis. Love is not an indefinite sentiment, but is something real; it is the highest and greatest dynamic force on this planet, and is one that manifests on all planes. And since it is a force, it is something we can feel on this plane of effects, and see on the mental plane, if we are able to function on that plane.

When pure love is sent forth from the subjective mind, it manifests as a constructive force, having its own particular golden yellow rate of vibration.

Anger, being an emotion, and proceeding from the objective mind of man, vibrates at a lower rate, which is red. A person who hates you, an enemy, sends a red current of thought toward you; but if you send loving thoughts in return, you are projecting a yellow rate of vibration which is infinitely higher and more forceful than the red, and the yellow vibration deflects the lower vibration so that it never reaches you. The higher rates of vibration will protect you from harm, and if you live according to ethnical principles, a high quality of thought or vibration is attained.

To continue now with our discussion of clairvoyant phenomena, another phase of this particular class is the perception of "thought-forms," which we have covered in a previous chapter. As we have mentioned, a strong thought or emotion manifests a certain high vibratory motion and takes upon itself a vibratory "form," which is plainly perceptible to the trained clairvoyant vision. These thought-forms manifest a great variety in appearance and character, and these have been previously described.

There is a phase of clairvoyant phenomena which may be called the X-ray Sense, for indeed it enables the clairvoyant to see through a brick wall, or some other material obstacle, or through a sealed letter, etc. The higher psychic vibrations easily pass through the most solid object, just as do X-rays, and consequently the clairvoyant is able to see what is happening on the other side of a brick wall, or inside the walls of a house. Likewise, the clairvoyant vision is able to pierce through the dense earth, and to perceive veins of mineral or metal lying concealed beneath the earth.

Another phase of clairvoyant power of this general class, but not one so nearly common as those above, mentioned, is that in which the clairvoyant may find himself in possession of the faculty of magnifying at will the minute physical particles to any desired size, as through a microscope, though no microscope yet made possesses even a thousandth part of this psychic magnifying power. By its means the molecule and atom become visible and living realities to the occult student, and upon this closer examination he finds them to be much more complex in their structure than the scientific man has yet realized them to be. It also enables him to follow with the closest attention and the liveliest interest all kinds of electrical, magnetic, and other etheric action; and when some of the specialists in these branches of science are able to develop the power to see these things whereof they speak facilely, some very wonderful and beautiful revelations may be expected.

In what is called Space clairvoyance, the objects, persons, scenes or events perceived by the clairvoyant are removed in space from him, often being located at points in space thousands of miles distant. The pages of works on occultism, and those devoted to the recording of proved instances gathered by the societies for psychical research, are filled with the most interesting cases of this form of clairvoyant vision. Instances are recorded, upon the very best possible authority, in which persons with clairvoyant powers have been perfectly cognizant of events occurring on the other side of the world, or across the Atlantic or Pacific oceans. In fact, it would seem that distance and space are practically wiped out in this form of clairvoyant phenomena, and that it is just as easy to see clairvoyantly over the space of a thousand miles as over that of a hundred feet – the principle involved being precisely the same.

In the theory of vibratory forces, as set forth earlier, we have the only scientific explanation of the phenomena of distant clairvoyance. Modern science, in its teachings regarding the radioactivity of physical objects, has thrown much additional light on this subject, and has corroborated the ancient occult teachings on the subject. These rays of higher vibratory power are like the rays of light or heat, though much higher in their rate of intensity and vibratory motion, and though the most delicate scientific instruments are able to register some of these, it is still admitted by science that the highest of these radioactive vibrations are beyond the scope and field of even the most sensitive instrument known to science. This is saying much, when we remember that some of the delicate instruments of science are so sensitive that they are able to register the heat waves of a candle at the distance of one mile; while others are able to record the presence of certain chemical elements in the most distant of visible stars, by means of the light waves carrying certain forms of vibration.

Under the radioactive theory it is quite reasonable to conceive of the clairvoyant sense being able to register and interpret these higher vibrations which are beyond the power of even the most delicate instruments of science. It must be admitted (the existence of such vibrations being granted, and science tacitly admits their presence) that ordinary distances on Earth would be no barrier at all to the action of clairvoyant vision capable of registering them. Moreover, in such cases all intervening objects would be penetrated by these waves, and they would be able to cross one another to infinity in all directions without entanglement, precisely as the vibrations of ordinary light do. Physical science and psychic science .at last seem to have arrived at a common ground of understanding, and many of the most advanced scientists do not hesitate to admit this fact.

Their view of a distant scene obtained by clairvoyance is in many ways not unlike that seen through a telescope. Human figures usually appear very small, like those upon a distant stage, but in spite of their diminutive size they are as clear as though they were close by. Sometimes it is possible by this means to hear what is said as well as to see what is done; but as in the majority of cases this does not happen, we must consider it as rather the manifestation of a separate power than as a necessary inherent quality of the faculty of sight. It will be observed that in cases of this kind the clairvoyant does not actually leave his physical body at all; he simply manufactures for himself, and uses, a kind of psychic telescope. Consequently he has the use of his physical powers while he is examining the distant scene; for example, his voice usually describes what he sees, even while he is in the act of making the observation.

In what is called Time clairvoyance, the clairvoyant is able to perceive objects, persons, scenes and events removed from him in past time or future time. That is to say, the clairvoyant perceives things which have existed in the physical world in times long past, which things have long since vanished from physical existence; or, on the other hand, he perceives things which belong to a future existence, things which have never as yet been in physical existence. The careful student will see at once that the principle of manifestation governing these two respective phases of clairvoyance must be quite different; and, accordingly, the two respective phases must be considered separately and apart from each other.

In what is known as Past Time clairvoyance, there is the manifestation of clairvoyant vision of scenes and occurrences of the past. Here, the clairvoyant perceives the events and scenes of past time just as clearly and plainly as if such were present before him in time and space. Just as in Distant clairvoyance, it is as easy for the clairvoyant to see things at a great distance as those at a short distance, so in Past Time clairvoyance it is just as easy for the clairvoyant to see things and events occurring five thousand years ago as it is to see things occurring one year ago, or one week ago. The principle involved is the same in either case.

To persons investigating the phenomena of clairvoyance for the first time, there seems to be a much greater mystery attached to the phenomena of Past clairvoyance than in the case of Distant clairvoyance. To such persons it seems that while the perception of distant objects, scenes and events is wonderful and mysterious, it is merely the perception of something now actually in existence-merely the extension of one's normal powers of vision, beyond the range of ordinary vision. The idea of the telescope enables the mind to grasp the naturalness of this kind of phenomena. But when it comes to the perception of things, scenes, and events which are no longer in existence, things which have passed entirely out of existence, the mystery seems to be increased, and incredulity becomes more insistent. But to the occultist there is really no more mystery in the one case than in the other, both sets of phenomena are seen to be perfectly reasonable and within the realms of nature. Let us see how and why the occultists view the matter in this light.

We may find many correspondences on the physical plane to serve as illustrations of the phenomena of Past Time clairvoyance, if we will but look for them. For instance, when we withdraw a heated stove from a room, the heat remains in the room. Likewise, though a woman bearing the odor of a certain perfume on her clothing may have passed from a house, the odor still lingers there. The wake of an ocean liner is often visible for hours after the ship has passed from sight. As modern science expresses it, "causes continue to exist in their effects." But we have a much more striking illustration and correspondence in the case of the transmission of light from the distant stars, which we will do well to carefully consider. Light "travels" at the rate of 186,000 miles per second. A "light-year," as known to astronomers, means the distance traversed by a light wave (at the stated rate of travel) during the period of one of our Earth years. Some of the distant stars are estimated to be fully one thousand light-years distant from us. Or, in other words, the light we now perceive as coming from them really is the light that left them one thousand years ago. If one of these stars were to be destroyed, observers on this Earth would not become aware of it for a thousand years.

The star whose light we may now perceive may actually have been destroyed nearly one thousand years ago. Other stars are only one hundred light years removed from us in space; others only a few years and others only a few hours. But the principle is just the same in all cases; namely, that we see the stars not as they are at the present moment, but as they were when the light left them many years ago. Thus, as you see, we may actually perceive events long after their happening. *The reader should obtain Daniel Fry's *Stairway to the Stars* for a lengthy explanation of this proposition. Mr. Fry claims contact with spacemen. The University of Edinburgh gave him his doctorate for this book.

This however, is but an illustration of the correspondence on the ordinary physical plane of certain things on a higher plane of Nature. Past Time clairvoyance is not dependent upon light-waves or any other of the lesser phases of vibratory activity. Instead, it depends entirely upon the phenomena and facts of a higher plane of nature – a plane which occultists have called the Akashic Plane. Some occultists prefer the general term, "The Astral Plane," but the former term is a closer and more definite one.

The Akashic Plane, as known to occultists, contains the impressions, or "records," of all events that have happened on the earth plane during the present cycle of earth manifestation. The very subtle and tenuous substance of the Akashic Plane, the term "etheric" may best describe the nature of this substance, contains traces and impressions of all of the happenings of the past of this earth, and such impressions may be read and seen by the clairvoyant who has developed sufficiently high powers of vision. These Akashic Records have well been called "the substantial memory of the Earth." Upon the subtle etheric substance of the Akashic Plane are registered the records of every event, thing, object, happening, or activity of the Earth which has existed or been manifested from the very beginning of the present cycle of the earth's existence. These records will persist until the final ending of the present Earth cycle, in the Planetary Aura.

SOURCING THE AKASHIC RECORDS

The clairvoyant whose powers of Past Time clairvoyance have been developed sufficiently, and who has mastered the art of concentration of his psychic attention manages to come into more or less perfect rapport or contact with these Akashic Records, and is thus enabled to read from them what he sees there. To him it actually seems as if he were seeing the actions of things in present existence, and many excellent clairvoyants are ignorant of the existence of the

Akashic Records, though they habitually read the contents of them. These clairvoyants simply know that they see these past happenings; they have not the faintest conception of how they are able to see them. This is no stranger than would be the case of a man who witnessed a motion picture for the first time, and who was ignorant of the mechanism involved in the showing of the picture, the existence of the film, etc. Such a man would know only that he "saw" the things, and he might even believe that he was gazing upon an actual scene in real life.

There are, of course, many degrees of power and development among clairvoyants of this class; and as a result we have many varying degrees of correctness in their readings. Some have merely a glimpse, as through dim glasses; and some obtain merely distorted reflections similar to those of a scene reflected in the troubled waters of a lake. Others see far more clearly; but it is reserved for the trained occultist to read the records as he would read the scene before him on the physical plane. The clairvoyant does not become infallible by reason of the faint awakening of his clairvoyant vision, he is not suddenly gifted with omniscience, as some seem to suppose. There are elements of error or imperfect visioning and interpretation, except among the advanced Adepts of the occult world. Comparatively few accounts of persons possessing this faculty of looking into the past are to be found in the literature on the subject, and it might therefore be supposed to be much less common than prevision, or future-time clairvoyance. However, the truth is that it is much less commonly experienced. It may happen that a person sees a picture of the past without recognizing it as such, unless there happens to be something in it which attracts special attention, such as a figure in armor, or in antique costume. It is probable that such occasional glimpses of these reflections of the Akashic Records are commoner than the published accounts would lead us to believe. As usual, we find examples of all degrees of the power to see into this "memory of Nature," from the trained man who can consult the records for himself at will, to the person who gets nothing but occasional vague glimpses, or has had only one such glimpse.

The psychometrist, who needs an object physically connected with the past in order to bring it all into life again around him; and the crystal gazer, who can sometimes direct his less certain astral telescope to some historic scene of long ago, may both derive the greatest enjoyment from the exercise of their respective gifts, even though they may not always understand exactly how their results are produced, and may not have them fully under control under all circumstances. In many cases of the lower manifestation of these powers, we find that they are exercised unconsciously.

Many a crystal gazer watches scenes from the past without ever realizing that he is, in effect, psychometrizing the various objects around him as he happens to touch them or stand near them. It would be well for all students to bear in mind that occultism is the apotheosis of common sense, and that every vision that comes to them is not necessarily a picture from the Akashic Records, nor every experience a revelation from on high. It is far better to err on the side of healthy skepticism than that of over-credulity, and it is an admirable rule never to hunt for an occult explanation of anything when an obvious physical one is available. Our duty is to keep our balance always, and never to lose our self-control, but to take a reasonable, common-sense view of whatever may happen to us.

In what is known technically as Future Time clairvoyance, we have the manifestation of the clairvoyant vision in the direction of scenes and events of the future. In this phase of clairvoyance the seer perceives the events and scenes of future time just as if they were present before him at that very moment. This phase of clairvoyance is far rarer and more uncommon than any of the other phases. In fact, it is so seldom met with in its perfection that its manifestation is a matter of greatest interest to those who make a study of the subject. It occasionally occurs in flashes and cannot be produced at will by the ordinary clairvoyant. Unfortunately, its very rarity and uncommonness cause it to be counterfeited and imitated by unprincipled persons, while actually only one in thousands is capable of manifesting absolutely true prophecy.

The student who reasons carefully and logically usually meets with what to him, at first, seems to be an insurmountable obstacle in the way of a rational explanation of Future Time clairvoyance. When it comes to an understanding of how anyone can expect to see, or can see, that which has never happened, he throws up his hands in despair. But, in this as in all the other phases of clairvoyant phenomena, there is found a reason and cause, although it requires some subtle thinking to find it, and to grasp it, even when it is found. Let us see what the highest teachings on this subject are.

There is a phase of prevision, or prophecy of coming events; however, that is not true clairvoyance at all, but simply the subconscious workings of the mind along the lines of a supernormal perception of the laws of cause and effect. Give the active subconscious mental faculties the perception of a strong existing cause, and it will often reason out the probable effect (the almost certain effect, in fact) of that cause, even though that effect lies in the mist of the future. The subconscious mind works upon the principle that "coming events cast their shadows before." But this, at the best, is not true clairvoyance, it is merely the statement of "probable" results, and effects of existing causes, wonderfully exact and clear though the deduction may be in some cases. But a thousand and one unforeseen things may arise to completely upset the prediction, or deduction, for it is never actually true until it occurs. We must look further for real instances of future clairvoyance.

FUTURE CLAIRVOYANCE

Time is but a relative mode of regarding things; we progress through phenomena at a certain definite pace, and this subjective advance we interpret in an objective manner, as if events moved necessarily in this .order, and at this precise rate. But this may be only one mode of regarding them. The events may be in some sort of existence always, both past and future, and it may be we who are arriving at them, not they which are happening. The analogy of a traveler in a train is useful; if he could never leave the train, nor alter its pace, he would probably consider the landscapes as necessarily successive, and be unable to conceive of their coexistence. We perceive, therefore, the fourth dimensional aspect regarding time, the inexorableness of whose flow is only a natural part of our present limitations. If we once grasp the idea that past and future may be actually existing at once, we can recognize that they may have a controlling influence on all present action, and that the two together constitute the "higher plane," or totality of things after which we are impelled to seek, in connection with the directing of form or determinism, and the action of human beings consciously directed to a definite and preconceived end. *The reader should obtain Ouspensky's *"Tertium Organum"* for more details.

The Hindus, as well as other oriental people, however, have a clearly defined and positive explanation of the phenomena of future-time clairvoyance, which must be included in our consideration of the subject, even though it does involve certain metaphysical or philosophical conceptions which are apart from our inquiry of the moment. The Asian theory is based upon that basic conception of the eastern philosophies which hold that the beginning, duration, and ending of any particular one of the infinite of successive universes created by the Supreme Being is to that Being but a single moment of time; or, as the celebrated Hindu proverb runs, "the creation, duration, and destruction of a universe is but the time of the twinkling of an eye to Brahman." In other words, that to the Supreme Being, all of the past, all the present, and all the future of the universe must be as but a single thought in a single moment of time, an instantaneous act of consciousness.

Those occultists and metaphysicians who have long thought, and deeply, upon the ultimate facts and nature of the universe, have dared to think that there must exist some absolute consciousness – some absolute mind – which must perceive the past, present and future of the universe as one happening; as simultaneously and actively present at one moment of absolute time. They reason that just as a man might see at one moment of his time some particular event which might appear as a year to some minute form of life and mind, the microscopic creatures in a drop of water, for instance, so that which seems as a year, or as a hundred years, to the mind of man, may appear as the happening of a single moment of a higher scale to some exalted being, or form of consciousness on a higher plane.

The daring flights of metaphysical fancy have resulted in the general acceptance on the part of advanced metaphysicians of the postulate of the existence of an Absolute Mind, independent of Time and Space, to which everything exists HERE and NOW. To such a mind, the entire sequence of events in the life, history of a universe would appear as a single unit of conscious experience, an infinitesimal point of time in eternity. The human imagination staggers at the idea, but logical thought finally accepts it as an inescapable conclusion of extended thought.

But it must not be supposed that the Asian occultists hold for a moment the theory that the clairvoyant actually obtains access to the Divine Mind, or Absolute Mind, when he experiences this vision of future events – their idea is very different from that. These occultists teach that the phenomena of each plane are reflected with more or less clearness upon the substance of the plane beneath it. This being so, it is readily seen that the seer who is able to contact any of the higher planes of being might thereupon see the reflection, more or less clear – or more or less distorted – of all that which is present in its completeness on the highest plane of all. This is a mere hint at the quite complicated occult teaching on this subject; but the capable thinker will be able to work out the full theory for himself in his own way.

The important fact is that future-time clairvoyance is a reality – that it is a matter of actual experience of the race, and one that has been authenticated by the investigations of learned bodies and societies for physical research in many different countries. Future-time clairvoyance, second sight, prevision, etc., are facts as fully accepted by such societies as are the facts of telepathy.

And before leaving the subject of clairvoyant phenomena there is something else to be brought to the attention of the student. We have endeavored to show that these phenomena do exist, and to give rational explanations for them, not only so that those to whom these subjects are entirely new may become acquainted with them, and interested enough to seriously begin occult study, but for another very important reason. With the coming of the Aquarian Age, our planet has moved into a new orbit, in which the vibrations are much more rapid. These more rapid vibrations affect every living person upon the planet, whether developed or not.

HIGHER VIBRATIONS AND CONTACTS WITH EXTRATERRESTRIALS

It is very difficult for many people to keep up with these higher vibrations, and their nervous systems are greatly affected by them. We suddenly have outbreaks of gun violence, or extremist political beliefs that cause families to break up. These are people who had been perfectly normal beings, going their own ways through life, who suddenly changed completely almost overnight. With the higher vibrations with which we have come into contact, everything is "stepped up" to a much greater degree; perhaps some of these people would have taken many years to bring out some of the darker sides of their natures and learn the lessons from their wrong doings. Now they are impelled to do everything more quickly, good or bad, in order to catch up, but now all of the destructive force in them is coming out more rapidly, along with constructive forces, rather than these actions being spread out over a period of years, as formerly.

We find many who are so thoroughly unable to cope with the changing times that their objective minds cannot stand the "shock" of the sudden change. Many have not heard of occultism, of clairvoyance, or of any of the faculties which we have discussed, and when one of these faculties, due to the more rapid progression and vibrations, manifests itself to them, they begin to think that they are mentally unbalanced, and are persuaded to go to a psychiatrist by their worried friends and families. Many of these people not only have not heard of such things, but would not be capable at the present time of believing them. Many people have come into contact with our friends from "Outer Space," beings who visit from Venus, Saturn, and other planets. Some who are more highly developed are capable of welcoming these beings, seeing and hearing them clearly, learning from them, writing books about their experiences with them, and giving lectures in order to prepare and help others for contact with them, for they are from higher planes of being than we on our planet, and their only purpose in coming here is to help us.

But others, in a flash of clairvoyance, or even physically, sometimes, see these beings and their minds translate the experience with so much confusion that they end up in mental institutions. *Reinhold O. Schmidt was institutionalized in Kearney, Nebraska, for his story, but was released after psychiatric examination. He claimed he boarded a "spaceship" at Kearney, Nebraska on November 5, 1957, and again at Elm Creek, Nebraska, February 5, 1958.

In addition, we must remember that some people do not attract the beings from Venus and other planets, but their states of development are such that they run screaming of the "little green men with purple ears and long red beards." Others say "well, they're crazy" but there is too much truth in these things to ignore the subject for the general public. One very good example of this is cases where people have described seeing someone from "Outer Space" with antennae protruding from his head. There is a basis for this also, since we all, at least those who have clairvoyant sight and are developed within lines of occult understanding, have the equivalent of these same antennae in the form of psychic centers on the sides of the head, at the temples. These psychic centers, called by oriental students "fan chakras," when in use send forth beams or rays of light which can be clearly seen with clairvoyant sight and may quite easily be mistaken for "antennae."

However, the main thing that we wish to bring out is that more and more people today are "seeing" and "hearing" things, and there are accounts on all sides of those who have seen spaceships and saucers, beings from "Space," etc, as well as many who are developing psychic abilities and do not know it; in fact, have never heard of these things. When they do have a psychic or clairvoyant experience, they come to the conclusion that they are losing their minds and often are either ashamed, or afraid to mention the experience to anyone, thus causing themselves prolonged mental anguish.

And when they do go to the psychiatrist, many times matters are made worse. This is not to say that some people do not need a psychiatrist, for this is not true; more people have emotional problems now than ever before, and the help of a trained psychiatrist is very necessary. However, this is not for that, type of person – what we say here is for those people who are afraid they are no longer "normal" because they have had an experience which they cannot explain, and therefore think they are losing their minds.

Many of these experiences have been thoroughly explained in this book, and they are signs of development, and not of insanity. However, the modern psychiatrists are not unfamiliar with them – but take a different view of the subject, with their own medical school explanations of what they do not understand. For instance, if you should find that you have been able to project your consciousness to another place, the psychiatrist would tell you that this is a "Fugue" state, or a state of automatism or somnambulism in which the patient takes a journey during this trance state as if he were awake. The faculty of magnifying objects on another plane is called "Macropsia," the faculty of telescopic sight, which we previously discussed, is called by the psychiatrist "Micropsia."

However, until humanity is better able to understand and appreciate these things, it is far better for your experiences to be kept to yourself, because if you do confide in family or friends you may suffer the embarrassment of being regarded as having "something the matter," since this is a well-known condition of those who "see things" and "hear voices." If you wish to discuss these things, by all means join an occult study group and make friends for yourself among those who do understand and who have had these experiences.

Planet Earth is entering into a new stage of spiritual evolution. With this comes the ability to "see" beings from other worlds who are here to help us. Art by Carol Ann Rodriquez.

15

PRACTICAL MEDIUMSHIP

In considering mediumship, we need only to examine the records of all ancient religions to find that mediumship is part and parcel of the doctrines. In Islam we find the whirling dervishes, very similar to the Shakers or Quakers who indulge in methods also used by Voodoo dancers; that is, to use a dance or rhythmic motion, to throw off the astral form so that the being may be possessed by some invisible spirit through which some form of prophecy or so called Divine information may be obtained.

The sad history of mediumship is the story of natural psychic functioning which, on being exploited, or becoming a necessity as a means of earning a living, causes most mediums, failing to produce the necessary phenomena when required, to resort to trickery or fraud. The fraud is sometimes unconsciously perpetrated, however. Dr. Nandor Fodor, a member of the New York Academy of Sciences, in his book, *"On the Trail of the Poltergeist,"* was unable to reach any positive conclusions, as he found that the subject of his investigations had unconsciously practiced fraud as well as producing inexplicable phenomena.

Most practicing psychiatrists, without full investigation, will come to the conclusion that the mediumistic man or woman entering into the first stages of mediumship is in need of medical help, if they are fortunate enough not to have been already institutionalized. According to Dr. Fodor, we read the strange admission, "...and also displayed his powers as a poltergeist, by making various articles in the room rattle on the furniture."

Due to the unfortunate necessity for deception by the vast majority of psychics roughly classed as mediums, we find that the honest and true medium suffers for the sins of his brothers. Under present economic conditions it is almost impossible for such people to follow the advice of Marcus Aurelius (121-180 A.D.), who stated, "Love the art, poor as it may be, which you have learned, and be content With it; and pass through the rest of your life like one who has with his whole soul entrusted to the gods all that he has; be neither tyrant nor slave to any man."

We classify mediumship as an art and not a science, because any art is dependent upon an emotional function rather than mechanical or mathematical repetition, as can be achieved in physical science. The failure to see this difference is the cause of so much failure in psychical research investigations.

The art of mediumship, both fraudulent and honest, has entered extensively into the problem of outer space activity, both from the standpoint of physical science and as a religious conception. Cults and societies have sprung up all over the world on the basis of religious interpretation of there being life in outer space. In April of 1958 the Pontifical Academy of Sciences in the Vatican appointed a commission of leading theologians to study the duties of the Church towards creatures in outer space. Apparently the position of the Roman Catholic Church is that there is a possibility of beings inhabiting outer space. However, Dr. Menzel, on January 22, 1958, on the "Alcoa CBS UFO" show, carefully censored by the U.S.A. Air Force, made this statement:

"We shall eventually go out into space, but nobody will ever come in."

This is a very dogmatic statement, and we find it opposed by another dogma recently established by the Roman Catholic Church to the effect that the Virgin Mary ascended bodily into heaven. Not all men of science agree with Dr. Menzel, however, for many men of science believe that Christ will return, and as he, too, ascended bodily into heaven, then we have at least two physically embodied beings in outer space who will eventually return as promised. Where does this leave Dr. Menzel?

Mediumship is as old as mankind. The practice of mediumship is recorded in all religious histories, under various names and disguises. When evolving mankind was dominated by religion, and not by science as it is today, the priestly caste was the medium between man and his God or gods. Communication between man and the unknown was achieved by specialists, who made it their business to see that the ordinary man was not distracted by either good or evil spirits. The priestly castes were generally individuals who had special abilities, and today we would classify them as "psychic."

Elaborate rituals were involved not only to aid the psychic in his work, but also to impress the customers.

MEDIUMSHIP THROUGH THE AGES

If we examine history we find that the most primitive cultures and the most advanced civilizations have existed side by side throughout time. The medium in primitive cultures has been the "witch doctor," the shaman, the medicine man, and the Voodoo "papaloi" and "mamaloi." The medium in civilized countries has always been the high priest or high priestess. Formalized religions in ancient times always supported their sanctuaries and oracles, and afforded them the greatest protection. Power, influence and kingship were often dependent upon the prophecies of the oracles.

With the destruction of so called pagan civilizations, the oracle or prophet has been replaced and the medium has become an outcast in society. In our western civilization the prophets of the Bible, who were the mediums of their time, are considered as being merely historians, or, at best, spinners of fairy tales. Christianity has frowned on mediumship, and we are admonished to have no intercourse with "spirits," evil or good. But, as we have mentioned before, both the Roman Catholic and the Episcopalian Church have rites of Exorcism.

If we examine the Nicene Creed we find this statement, "...I believe in the communion of saints..." Every professing Christian, therefore, is asked to believe that through prayer and/or intercession by a priest, it is possible to contact departed good souls who have been sanctified by the Church. Mediumship as a science is not practiced by any religious bodies today that have recognized apostolic succession. By this we mean Churches that are recognized by the Holy See of Rome. The Anglican Church, although not recognized by the Church of Rome since Cardinal Woolsey's time, claims it has the Rite or Ordination because St. Augustin had conferred on its Bishops the holy power, by the "laying on of hands." The fundamental belief of the Christian Churches is that St. Peter, having received direct power from Jesus the Christ, was able to transmit this power directly through the "laying on of hands." The "laying on of hands" gives the one endowed with power the ability to heal, to redeem from sin, and, if the recipient is ready, to bring illumination. This is the power of the "Holy Ghost."

THE RISE OF SPIRITUALISM

Present day mediums who have no authority from any religious body are attempting, through their own efforts, to achieve the above results. The public interest in mediums and mediumship in America has existed since the turn of the century as a result of the activities of the Fox Sisters, and the furor created by H. P. Blavatsky when she attempted to show that the popular form of mediumship, as practiced during her time, was a combination of both trickery and illusion. The illusions that she tried to dissipate was the fact, as pointed out in this book, that many mediums who were achieving true phenomena were not necessarily contacting departed "souls," but were more often than not raising astral shells or elemental forces and intelligences that had no relation to man as a spirit. She also tried to establish the fact that, with the aid of psychic forces or energy, it was possible to materialize thought forms or illusions.

Blavatsky found herself to be the target for anger from the practicing mediums known as "Spiritualists" and the condemnation of religious bodies who considered her to be no more than a medium herself. Since her time, mediumship or spiritualism has become so popular that we now have many organized and recognized Spiritualistic Churches. It is because of this situation that we have included this chapter on Mediumship. Around the medium has developed the séance room. For those who are not familiar with mediumship per se and the séance, we will enumerate the phenomena that take place as the result of the psychic power generated by the circle of "sitters" and expressed through the medium or transmitter.

The medium acts very much like a transistor in our radio systems of communications. He or she receives power from the invisible world that is transformed or made manifest into the power supplied by the living beings who compose the circle of sitters. The phenomena that have been well recorded and authenticated can be listed as follows:

1. Healing
2. Direct voice by possession of the medium's vocal organs

3. The moving of inanimate objects, such as tables, chairs, specially manufactured trumpets, etc.

4. The manifestation of lights, sounds and magnetic currents

5. Materialization of forms, human and otherwise

6. Levitation of the human body

7. Apports

8. Precipitation of written messages and pictures

Starting in the 19th century, a séance became a popular method to try and contact the spirit world.

Reference to any good book on mediumship will enable the reader to enlarge his knowledge of "Spiritualism" and its phenomena. We wish to draw to your attention that more of this type of phenomena has been faked than has actually been authentic. All magicians of the professional class claim they can reproduce these phenomena at will. This, however, does not mean that all phenomena are fraudulent. It is perfectly obvious to any logically thinking person that any masterpiece, such as an oil painting, which is original and authentic, can be counterfeited. However, it takes scientific examination to detect a counterfeit. This applies to money, works of art and psychic phenomena.

We now come to the heart of the problem. From the birth of modern science up to the present day, science has been concerned with the world of outer activity. Medicine has been chiefly concerned with curing man's ills in his physical body, and only recently has psychiatry turned its attention to the mental man. No science exists as yet for the study of the spiritual man. *One amazing exception is Wainwright House on Stuyvesant Ave., in the city of Rye, N. Y. It was the home of the late Col. J. M. Wainwright, cousin of the Gen. Wainwright who was a hero of Corregidor. It is now used by the Laymen's Movement to study spiritual values. It has a meditation room, the chairs of which came from the United Nations Meditation Room.

Religion and science, being divorced, have not joined hands to investigate the inner nature of man and his psychic functioning. Commercially it has not been profitable to exploit anything that is not of a material nature. The material world around us is man's field of development and naturally, under our economic system, this development is carried on for profit. Due to the great strides of science that are only possible from commercial pressures, science is now investigating the nature of energy and nature's finer forces. Unfortunately, man himself has been neglected as a Divine Being and all of our attention has been focused upon him as a commercial asset; and for this reason his health and welfare are part of the assets of a commercial civilization. Due to this situation, no academic method of study has been applied to his spiritual powers.

His spiritual welfare has been left solely with the religionists. Modern man in the Western world has drifted from religion, regarding it as a vague and nebulous method in a world of highly organized technical and scientific development that has brought him to the brink of annihilation by means of atomic warfare. Because religion has not been able to explain science and science as yet has not been able to explain religion, the average man realizes that he is on the horns of a dilemma; a dilemma that must be solved at all costs if We are to survive.

We suggest that if only a small portion of the billions of dollars spent on weapons were to be used for the scientific research into psychic phenomena, it would reveal the truths of occultism. This would enable us to achieve better health, better human relations, and establish the truth, once and for all, that we are immortal beings, and are not alone in the Universe.

Due to the disrepute in which mediumship is held in the public mind, it receives no recognition from science, religion or politics. These three bodies of society at present control the destiny and direction of human thinking. Occultism, as the dictionary will show, means "hidden" or unrevealed. Occultism is a science and its revelation can come about only by public demand. Premature revelations do more harm than good, or, at best, only arouse public ridicule. We have previously cited Leonardo daVinci and his inventions as a perfect example of genius being too far ahead of its time. We feel the time has come to make some attempt to justify the existence of the mediums. We hope to do this by showing their methods, their conclusions and their mistakes.

In this chapter on Mediumship we include all people who possess psychic power of some order or another, which makes it possible for them to be transmitters of knowledge of the hidden world. The world that science now calls "anti-matter" now exists within and beyond our material world. Due to our interest in outer space and the possibility of intelligent life existing on other worlds, the modern medium seems to have turned his attention from "heaven" to contacts with Space People.

CALLING ALL INTERPLANETARY CRAFT

The vast majority of mediums are mental, and as stated, the public interest is in outer space. It is natural or human for these people, the mediums, to "keep up with the times." As a result, contacts with Space People are the vogue. Let us list the phenomena associated with mental mediums:

1. Semi-trance or full consciousness
2. Possession and/or obsessions
3. The Poltergeist (moving of objects with no apparent physical contact)

4. Speaking in strange tongues, or intelligently about subjects unknown to the medium.

It will be seen from the above that the medium is not entranced. He or she does not create any objective or physical phenomena. As a poltergeist (a "throwing ghost") can be either conscious or unconscious, or with full knowledge of the action involved; that is, the moving of objects without contact, it is obvious that this mental phenomena is not in the same classification as moving objects by physical contact. By physical contact, of course, we mean the levitation of objects by magnetic induction. This is quite distinct from table-tipping, which could well be attributed to subconscious muscular movement.

The condition and phenomena created are varied and numerous. These were described in detail in the original manuscript on this chapter, but as the chapter itself would make a complete book it was decided, for brevity, to condense and rewrite the material. The field of mediumship has been investigated and recorded in papers, books and pamphlets, but little or no intense/academic study has been made; first, because of the scarcity of sensational mediums; that is, materializing mediums, and second, because science has only recently grown into the age of the invisible: i.e., the so-called electronic and atom age with all its vast potential for good and evil.

It depends upon man's mental and emotional growth as to what the results are to be. So it is with the medium, for after all, he or she is only a product of evolution; a human being endowed with faculties and powers above the normal. The vast majority of UFO publications carry messages purported to come from "Space People." These are the products of the mental medium.

At first glance this new phase of mediumship might seem ridiculous, and a product of wishful thinking (the "wish fulfillment" of the psychiatrist) unless we consider all departments of mediumship; physical, mental, and supersensual. Mediumship is physical, as has been tabulated, but the physical results depend on a combination of mental and emotional states. Two types of energy are required; the mental vibration, and the animal magnetic vibration. This is an over-simplification, of course, for convenience of discussion only.

These two energies within man animate him, but when directed outside of himself produce physical phenomena such as animation of inanimate objects by induction and supersensuous creations. For example, a living substance capable of being a vehicle or host for consciousness is a supersensuous creation. This has been designated as "ectoplasm," a word attempting to define the precipitation from living bodies of these dynamic energies in combination making substance.

Sir William Crookes experimented extensively with this phenomenon. He stated that it could become as hard as steel or as soft as an egg-white. This variation is caused by the degree of crystallization, such as in cooking egg-white. We must remember that with materializing mediums this is a living substance, attached by an "umbilical cord" to the particular force-field in operation in the medium at the time of precipitation.

The mental medium goes through the same psychological phases as does the materializing medium, but the major difference is that one or more force-fields may be operating but not those involved with ectoplasm. Because we are impressed by material objects continuously and have not learned yet to appreciate the invisible, we too lightly regard the abnormal mental phenomena produced by the mediumship under discussion. Students of occultism are continually being warned to be on guard about this type of mental development. In the early stages of Rajah Yoga, which includes a system of meditation and concentration, the same type of mental phenomena occur as experienced by the mental medium.

The difference, of course, is in the understanding of the process. The medium, hearing what is called the "Army of the Voice," is quite convinced that these are intelligent spirits speaking, and he repeats what he hears. Depending on the development of the student, he may sometimes hear words and conversations seeming to come from the center of his head. Another phase of these phenomena is that the medium becomes "overshadowed" by his Higher Self and, depending upon his spiritual evolution, may deliver messages or orations that the medium's friends consider to be of "angelic" origin.

To digress for the moment, we draw to your attention an experiment performed by a French surgeon, Dr. Andre D'Joume, in which a tiny coil, coated with plastic to prevent corrosion, was placed in a remnant of the auditory nerve in the brain of a deaf man. The man's hearing range was extended from the normal limit of 15,000 cycles to a high frequency of 40,000 cycles – ultrasonic vibrations that no human had ever before heard. From this it is obvious that the mind of man is capable of perceiving very high rates of vibration, and he is only limited by the organs of sense perception.

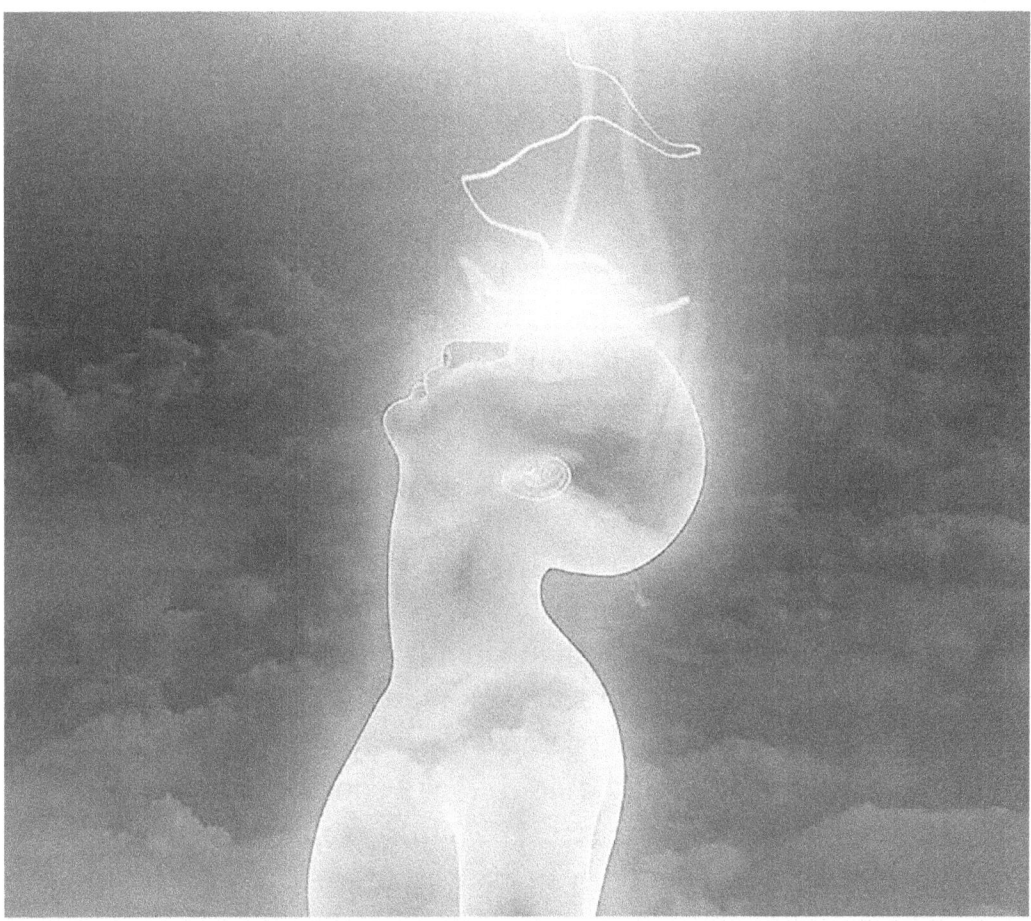

Channelers communicate with the deepest inner self, the divine, or the spirit world. Some even claim that their source comes from another planet or dimension and is not human.

Mediums obviously have untrained supersensuous organs of perception and this leads them to speculations that have become dogma in the world of spiritualism. The majority of beliefs subscribed to by the spiritualistic movement are based on the religious conceptions of the spiritualists. It is no wonder that they ascribe their phenomena to devils, angels, and saints from heaven or hell, whichever the case may be. With heaven being located vaguely somewhere in space, it is natural that they should assume that the phenomena manifesting as voices should originate from Beings visiting us from that locality.

Scientifically, at the present time, we are not sure whether our sister planets are inhabited or not. Most scientists, however, have come to the logical conclusion that we cannot be the only beings in the Universe. Any planet with similar conditions as exist on earth could, and should, support life as we know it.

The limitations we place upon ourselves, and the lack of understanding of our true spiritual, or inner, natures, makes it impossible for most of us to visualize life as existing in any other form but the physical.

A little reflection will make it clear that we are more than physical beings. We are mental beings. Without accepting the proposition that we are also spiritual beings, we can clearly demonstrate that the illusion of life can exist apart from the physical. This is easily done by considering an ordinary dream. Most people dream, and those who do not, or claim they do not, merely do not remember. A chance remark during the day often triggers the memory of a dream experienced the night before.

In the dream state we have physical bodies, experience physical surroundings, and, for all intents and purposes, might just as well be awake except for the fact that most dreams that do impress us do so because of some fantastic or abnormal circumstance that could not possibly take place in a normal manner in the physical world. In our dream bodies we apparently have no means of making ourselves apparent to those who are awake in the physical world. This problem of the dreamer not being able to make contact with the physical world will never be resolved unless some scientific effort is made to show that the brain and the mind can exist independently of each other.

Occultism teaches that this can be demonstrated. It cannot be assumed, but must be experienced by the student beyond all doubt, and become a rational method of operation. No amount of reading or speculation will bring true belief. Other chapters of this book indicate the methods to be used to achieve this knowledge. When the student proves to himself beyond doubt that he can exist separately or apart from his physical body, then he may, for the first time, realize that intelligence may exist on other planets, but not in the physical form which we expect.

If science should have the opportunity to spend its time in the development and study of the above proposition, our whole outlook towards space would be radically changed. With this first step, mediums would find themselves in the enviable position, for the first time in history, of being the most sought-after people for study and experimentation. Mediumship, as such, would disappear, along with the wild theories that have developed and, with time, a scientific explanation would be available. We have now reached a period in evolution where, by necessity, we must turn within and study man instead of launching monkeys into space.

We have stated before that there are genuine and fraudulent mediums. Many genuine mediums are experiencing contacts with what are termed, "Space People." The difficulty that the general public has in accepting this fact is that they can conceive of man as existing only as a physical entity. By referring to our chapter on force-fields and materialization, it will be quite plain that intelligence existing in space with super-knowledge can easily precipitate a mental creation, be it a physical body or a physical spaceship. Science, at the present moment, is wrestling with its time-space and relativity concepts that momentarily will "blow the lid" off our pot of preconceived ideas.

Mediumship, from the beginning of time, has remained an art, unassisted by science, and has demonstrated man's innate ability to produce "miracles." Few people have the self-discipline to study occultism so it is obvious that natural mediums, due to emotional bias and religious beliefs, have not availed themselves of the opportunity to develop their art into a science. The major philosophical block to their approach to occultism has been the subject of reincarnation. The subject of reincarnation became popular in the West through the instrumentality of the Theosophical Society. Needless to say, Madame Blavatsky's attempts to convert the spiritualists of her day to occultism met with great opposition from so-called "Christian Spiritualists," who could in no way accept or understand the "Eastern, pagan doctrine of reincarnation."

In conclusion, we may state that science, being above religious bias and intolerance, no matter what the individual scientist's faith may be, must be the mediums' hope and salvation if mediumship is not to remain a pseudo-science.

GROUP WORK

In the preceding section on mediumship it has been pointed out that certain illusions exist about the truth of these phenomena. This will not be acceptable to those people who are convinced that they are right and we are wrong, for, "as a man thinketh, so is he."

Investigators who are firmly convinced that psychic phenomena do not occur are unscientific in their approach. Mental phenomena, in most cases, are dependent upon belief, or at least the "open mind." We must be scientific, impersonal and objective to be able to evaluate subjective and emotional conditions that regulate the final result; namely, the phenomenon desired.

No one would expect a radio set, which is a product of science, and in no way subject to any type of emotional disturbance, to receive accurately or clearly when a transmitter on the same wavelength is jamming the signals. A skeptic can unconsciously jam a mental signal. It is for this reason that the student who develops his psychic abilities alone has a better opportunity to achieve success.

The traditional method of developing a potential "psychic" is to isolate him in the beginning until such time as he has achieved an inner confidence that skepticism will not shake. When this development has been reached his own inner seeking leads him to group work. This method is the essential difference between mediumship developed publicly and the occult method.

As a medium, a psychic is influenced by the ideas and beliefs of those people who form his "developing circle." The final result is that the medium falls victim to many and varied unseen agencies, for "like attracts like." Due to the fact that mediumship, in the majority of cases, develops into the "trance state," the medium has surrendered his consciousness to the will of the group or to unseen entities of which he has no personal knowledge.

The objective of occultism is to develop continuity of consciousness. This means the psychic at no time surrenders his will to any unknown agency. When the first step has been taken safely, by avoiding any condition that engenders obsession or possession, or hypnosis by any living being, the student will automatically come to the attention of someone on the physical plane who will be able to guide him further along the path. This may take the form of personal guidance or merely being directed to the proper books that already exist on specialized branches of this study.

We wish to call to the attention of the student and disciple the most important outcome of the work and study, and this is what is known as "group work." In other words, eventually the disciple finds himself no longer alone, but coming into contact with other disciples and working with them as a unit. All workers for the general good must finally unite. The disciple working alone will undoubtedly be powerful in his own place, and within a very limited sphere, but the impression of evidence needed of the truth declared, and demonstration achieved, must emanate from the strong and irresistible co-operative forces in discipleship. The seed has been sown in a former life, and in contacting others the strong vibration of their concerted efforts, working silently upon his life and thought, does as much as the work itself in his hands, in quickening latent growth and bringing him to a feeling of security in the group to which he belongs.

Directly the disciple links himself with others on the Path he comes more and more to feel the reactive influence of those others upon himself. Upon encountering such others, recognition from the interior aspect is almost instantaneous, since it is a matter of synchronous vibration and of dedicated purpose. Their work on the Path has often allied them closely through the medium of meditation and in periods of withdrawal, and where they belong objectively to some special group of aspirants, on the plane of the Ego they are one, and under the supervision of the Master, in other words, one of an esoteric group carrying out specialized work under the direction of a Master.

The greatest and most important inducement to group work is the fact of the corporate character of all sections of the Brotherhood of Masters to which the disciple has given his allegiance. As above, so below, and the disciple eventually comes to realize that the Masters are not interested in his personal development primarily for himself alone, but are interested in forming centers of esoteric force consisting of efficient units working in harmonious combination and alignment.

The one thing the disciple must do is to find that particular group of servers to which he belongs on the inner plane, to recognize them on the physical plane, and to unite them in service for the race. This recognition is based upon unity of aim, oneness of vibration, identity in group affiliation, karmic links of long standing, and the ability to work in harmonious relation. Superficially, this may appear to be easy, but in practice it is not. Mistakes are easily made, and the problem of working harmoniously in group alignment is not as simple as it appears. Egoic vibration and relationship may exist, yet the outer personalities may not harmonize, and in this case it is the work of the disciple to then strengthen the grip of his Ego upon his personality, so that the esoteric group relation may become possible on the physical plane. He must do this, however, by disciplining his own personality, and not by the correction of his brothers.

Peace and inner calm sometimes arise from the absence of experience, instead of from the knowledge and use of it. If the "material" offered has not reached maturity and strength, and has not versatility and responsiveness and fullness of experience and understanding upon the several planes of life, this does not signify defeat, it is not a cause for discouragement, and provides no basis for honest criticism. It simply means that all of these factors must be present in the inner man before the Master can avail himself of his services, and the disciple will be the first to realize and acknowledge this when the time comes to accept the responsibility and accomplish the work which falls to his lot.

We have listed the rules which must be followed by the disciple many times in this book; however, as in all cases, there may be exceptions to meet special conditions. There have been such exceptions where the disciple has been doubtful in points of character. There have been marked idiosyncrasies, erratic departures, and temperamental disturbances; manifest weaknesses from a normal observer's point of view. Nevertheless a kind of technique has been in evidence which is of such value that all deficiencies of a general nature have proved of little hindrance, except in the disciple's own personal adjustment in life, and the Master has used that technique with pronounced effect.

It should be noted here that in true "group work," the highest: phase of the work is that done between groups of disciples and groups of Devas, the groups of various Beings from the higher planes of existence. All is One – the Path is One, Truth is One, the Masters are, indeed, One in the Cosmic in perception and illumination; yet each with a perfected technique peculiarly adapted to the mental, psychic and spiritual constitutions of the Initiates who seek their aid. Service is the keynote of the group, and service on the Path means service because one wants to, and must, serve. The service, however, is not necessarily occult in character; the disciples of the Masters are just as likely to be found engaged in political, social and economic fields, as in spiritual and religious. The act of service on the Path releases the power of the soul. *One such group activity is the "Temple of Understanding" sponsored by all responsible heads of various governments. It started with one lone individual. The public will hear more of this project in the near future.

To explain Devas to the general public is a difficult problem. Suffice it to say that Devas are intelligent centers of energy taking many forms. The vast majority are invisible, though we see their work all around us in physical-plane existence. They are grouped into "armies," and are under the direction of agencies that have special evolutionary work to do in connection with our planet and this planet's humanity.

When the individual has acquired a certain quality of love, these Devas will cooperate with him. They respond only to love, not intellectual power. The healing Devas make possible so called miraculous cures. Their ranks are vast, and cover many areas of knowledge yet unknown to the average man. All physical matter is composed, of Deva substance, for example. Intelligence exists in everything. Atomic science will radically change when the secret of atomic fusion is found to replace atomic fission.

Man's destructive efforts will be replaced by constructive endeavors. For this reason we must awaken to the power of love, the belief in Deity, and belief in ourselves if we are to win against atheism. Science is a tool for good or evil. The battle between rank materialism of the mind and the soul of man is enjoined. Science is the weapon both sides find available, by study and application. We urge scientists of the West to study occultism with new eyes, and hearts filled with love, if not for the unknown, then for humanity itself.

16

ENERGIZING YOUR THOUGHTS INTO REALITY
By Tim R. Swartz

Like everyone else that has ever lived on planet Earth, you have undoubtedly wondered at one time or another about your life and why you are here. Religion was created in an attempt to answer this question, and science has tried to fill some of the gaps in knowledge as well. This is why you are now reading this book. You have questions about life, its meaning and how you fit into the whole scheme of things.

Perhaps someday we will have a better understanding on the true meaning of life. Perhaps there is no overreaching, ultimate, meaning, but instead it may be unique to each and every conscious being in this universe. Nevertheless, just because we are uncertain about the meaning of our lives does not mean that we are merely floundering about, slaves to fate and uncertainty.

A great many people go about their lives completely out of control. They live their lives like robots going about their preprogrammed directions, only superficially aware of what is going on around them. They are essentially asleep. They are missing out on just how wonderful and amazing life actually is.

Those that are awake live in a constant state of utter amazement and happiness. Think about a time in your life when you were filled with pure excitement and happiness...a trip to an amusement park...Christmas morning, etc.

Try and remember how alive you felt at that very moment, how clear and beautiful everything was. That is how we should be feeling each and every minute of our lives. Life, this life, your life is meant to be enjoyed. We are meant to feel good, to experience joy and happiness. We are meant to thrive, to create, and to receive all the good we can imagine.

How can this be possible? Life usually seems so erratic and uncertain. Often we find our happiest times are suddenly taken away from us by what appears to be the cruel hand of fate. However, is this really the case? Are we nothing more than pawns in the game of life? Or is it all simply a matter of perspective? When we look at others situations and circumstances that our worse than ours, we feel blessed. When we look at others that we feel have a better life, we feel envious – it seems as if the grass is always greener on the other side of the fence.

What you give out to the universe is ultimately what can return to your own life.

This seems to be true until you realize that you are not simply an observer of life, you are an active participant – you are THE active participant. We are all a part of creation. When this universe was created, you were there. Our universe would not exist without you. Our universe could not exist without you.

Since you are a part of creation, you also have the ability to create. Without realizing it, you create every minute, every second of your reality. What happens to you in your life is the result of your thoughts creating your existence from moment to moment. If you are happy and optimistic, your life will reflect your thoughts. It works the same if you are sad and depressed.

German physicist Max Planck, the Father of Quantum Theory, said that "all matter originates and exists only by virtue of a force which brings the particle of an atom to vibration and holds this most minute solar system of the atom together. We must assume behind this force the existence of a conscious and intelligent mind. This mind is the matrix of all matter."

What Planck was saying is that the substance of the universe is consciousness.

If a tree falls in the forest and nobody is there to hear it, does it make any noise? Would the universe exist if we, as conscious beings, weren't here to observe it? To take that one step further – would the universe exist if we were not here to create it from moment to moment?

On the subatomic level, reality behaves in accordance with the expectation of the observer. As everything in the universe is composed of subatomic particles, reality behaves in accordance to our beliefs and expectations. We are unconscious co-creators. The universe is made up of energy. We are masses of energy. Matter is an illusion. The world seems like a solid, fixed thing that we can see and touch. But this solidity is an illusion. All we have around us is energy vibrating at different frequencies. These frequencies can be modulated through our thoughts and emotions.

All form arises from this infinite energy field. Everything in existence is a part of this field, separation is an illusion. Nothing is outside the boundaries of inquiry, for everything is within the infinite field. All is connected, and interdependent with everything else. Time does not exist within the infinite field itself, and all that has ever occurred within the domain of form is recorded forever.

CREATION BY THOUGHT

How do you look at your world – your life? Do you make an effort to make your life what you want it to be – or do you just go about your days hoping for the best? What would you say if you were told that the things that happen in your life depend to a certain extent on your thoughts and actions? On that note, have you even bothered to think about the control you have over your life and your reality?

This process is known as the *Law of Attraction* and has gone by many other names over the centuries. Thomas Troward, who was a strong influence in the New Thought Movement, claimed that thought precedes physical form and that "the action of Mind plants that nucleus which, if allowed to grow undisturbed, will eventually attract to itself all the conditions necessary for its manifestation in outward visible form."

In 1906, William Walker Atkinson took Troward's ideas even further in his book *"Thought Vibration, or the Law of Attraction in the Thought World,"* stating that "like attracts like." The following year, Elizabeth Towne, the editor of The *"Nautilus Magazine,"* a Journal of New Thought, published Bruce MacLelland's prosperity theology book *"Prosperity Through Thought Force,"* in which he summarized the principle, stating: "You are what you think, not what you think you are."

The book *"The Science of Getting Rich,"* by Wallace D. Wattles espouses similar principles – that truly believing in the object of your desire and focusing onto it will lead to that object or goal being realized on the material plane (Wattles indicates in the preface and later chapters of this book that his premise stems from the monistic Hindu view that Brahman pervades everything and can deliver what we focus on). In addition, the book also indicates that negative thinking will manifest negative results. It should also be pointed out that there are many notions of God within Hinduism but two are most prominent. 1. Monism (advaita) – God is impersonal without qualities or form. 2. Inclusive monotheism (dvaita) God is personal, exhibiting qualities, displaying a form, and performing activities.

The main idea is that "like attracts like" and that by focusing on positive or negative thoughts, one can bring about positive or negative results. This belief is based upon the idea that people and their thoughts are both made from pure energy, and the belief that like energy attracts like energy. The Theosophical author Annie Besant in 1919 compared her version of the Law of Attraction to gravitation, and said that the law represented a form of Karma.

Israel Regardie published a number of books with the theme of Law of Attraction as one of the prevailing Universal Laws. His book *"The Art of True Healing,"* written in 1937 is fully titled *"The Art of True Healing, A Treatise on the Mechanism of Prayer and the Operation of the Law of Attraction in Nature."* The book teaches a focused meditation technique to help the mind to learn to heal itself on both a physical and spiritual level. Regardie explains that The Law of Attraction is not only a valid method for attracting good physical health but is applicable in the pursuit of any aspect of life you would like to see changed.

The underlying substance of the universe is energy, specifically Mind or Consciousness. All things are created by the activity of the Universal Mind. Therefore, when you think, Universal Mind thinks.

NOT THE ONLY GAME IN TOWN

There has been a lot of attention over the last few years given to The Law of Attraction. Books such as *"The Secret,"* which popularizes the idea that all your hopes and dreams can be manifested into reality with just a few simple manifestations of correct thinking, is one example of the rehashing of old ideas. However, there is a lot more to The Law of Attraction than has been publicized.

A lot of people end up becoming disillusioned with The Law of Attraction when nothing seems to work the way they thought it was going to. What most people don't know is that The Law of Attraction is just one of 12 "Laws of the Universe" that has been a part of esoteric knowledge for thousands of years. Each of the 12 Laws of the Universe teach you something unique about well-being, happiness, and success. In other words, the Laws of the Universe provide us with a roadmap for how we can live our best life.

There have been entire books written about the 12 Laws of the Universe, so we will just give you a synopsis of each one in this section.

1. The Law of Divine Oneness

This law states that: We are all connected to one source, made of the same thing. We are like an interconnected web of energy, and everything we do sends vibrations throughout the entire web, affecting the collective consciousness.

2. The Law of Vibration

This law states that: Everything in the universe is energy vibrating, from your body to your thoughts to your emotions. Love is of the highest vibration and hate is the most dense and base vibration.

3. The Law of Correspondence

This law states that: Your outer world is always a reflection of your inner world. As above, so below; as within, so without.

4. The Law of Attraction

This law states that: The level of your vibration attracts circumstances, experiences and people of a like vibration.

5. The Law of Inspired Action

This law states that: Action taken from an inspired, high-vibrational place will yield tremendous results compared to action taken from a place of struggle and low vibration.

6. The Law of Perpetual Transmutation of Energy

This law states that: All energy in motion eventually manifests into physical form and can manifest back into energy.

7. The Law of Cause and Effect

This law states that: Commonly known as the law of karma, what you put out comes back to you.

8. The Law of Compensation

This law states that: The law of cause and effect is applied to our abundance.

9. The Law of Relativity

This law states that: Nothing can be judged as good or bad until it has been experienced and compared to something else.

10. The Law of Polarity

This law states that: There are two sides to everything and everything has an opposite on the SAME spectrum.

11. The Law of Rhythm

This law states that: There are patterns and rhythms to everything. Everything ebbs and flows, swinging to the left and back to the right. Like every season, everything has a purpose and function in the grander scale of the universe.

12. The Law of Gender

This law states that: Everything has masculine and feminine principles within it and must be in balance.

As we can see, being able to manifest The Law of Attraction is meaningless unless the other 11 Laws of the Universe are also taken into consideration. For instance, the Law of Divine Oneness states that we live in a world where everything is connected to everything else. Therefore, everything you do, say, think, and believe has an effect on others and the world around you.

Another law, The Law of Inspired Action, states that in order to manifest, you must take action toward achieving your goals. If you want something and believe it is yours, but do not act on it, you probably won't get it. Every day you must take steps, even if they're small steps, to bring you closer to your goals.

It's important to understand that there are many forces at play in the Universe all at once. The Law of Attraction is only one part of the giant cosmic puzzle.

THOUGHT VIBRATIONS

In his 1902 book, *"Thought Vibration: Or, The Law of Attraction in the Thought World,"* William Walker Atkinson points out that thoughts are a force – a manifestation of energy – having a magnet-like power of attraction. When we think we send out vibrations of a fine ethereal substance, which are as real as the vibrations manifesting light, heat, electricity, magnetism.

That these vibrations are not evident to our five senses is no proof that they do not exist. When we understand the laws governing the production and transmission of these vibrations we will be able to use them in our daily life, just as we do other forms of energy.

We are sending out thoughts of greater or less intensity all the time, and we are reaping the results of such thoughts. Not only do our thought waves influence ourselves and others, but they have a drawing power – they attract to us the thoughts of others, things, circumstances, people, "luck," in accordance with the character of the dominate thought in our minds.

Like a stone thrown into the water, thought produces ripples and waves which spread out over the great ocean of consciousness. Thoughts of love will attract to us the love of others; circumstances and surroundings in accord with the thought; people who are of like thought.

Thoughts of anger, hate, envy, malice and jealousy will draw to us the kindred thoughts emanating from the minds of others. A strong thought or a thought long continued will make us the center of attraction for the corresponding thought waves of others...like attracts like in the thought world.

Your thoughts have the ability of reproducing themselves; just as a note of the violin will cause glass to vibrate and "sing," so will a strong thought tend to awaken similar vibrations in minds attuned to receive it. Many of the "stray thoughts" which come to us are reflections or answering vibrations to a strong thought sent out by another person. Nevertheless, unless your mind is attuned to receive it, the thought probably will not affect you.

If you are thinking high and great thoughts, your mind acquires a certain resonance corresponding to the character of the thoughts you have been thinking. Once this keynote has been established, you will be likely to catch the vibrations of other minds keyed to the same thought. On the other hand, if you get into the habit of thinking thoughts of an opposite character, you will soon be echoing the low order of thought being put out from the minds of the thousands thinking along the same lines.

None of us lives in a vacuum. We are all part of the same consciousness that permeates the universe. We are largely what we have thought ourselves into being, the balance being represented by the character of the suggestions and thought of others, which has reached us either directly by verbal suggestions or by means of thought vibrations. With that, we can better understand that not only do our thoughts determine how our reality unfolds before us, but that our thoughts can also directly influence others and how their reality comes into being.

If you are thinking on how to make your life better, consider how your positive or negative thought patterns may be influencing those around you. Everyone has the final say on what happens in their lives. So, it is nice knowing that your positive thoughts are having a subtle influence and helping create better lives for others.

Unfortunately, a lot of people try to use the Law of Attraction in an effort to bypass the healing work that has to be done. However, there is no shortcut to achieving your heart's desire. If past experiences have left you emotionally scarred you'll attract what you don't want and become increasingly frustrated causing things to get worse.

You cannot change your energy, or vibrational frequency, until you free yourself from the pain of your past. Your unhealed wounds will continue to weigh you down causing continued and prolonged pain in your life. The heart is the connection between you and your higher self. Therefore, you can manifest much more quickly when you acknowledge and honor what's in your heart. That's because the heart's electromagnetic field is so much stronger than the electromagnetic field of the brain.

The manifestations made at the heart level are purer manifestations and perfectly aligned to what your soul wants. When the heart leads and the mind follows, you will come into a state called coherence. As a result, your manifestations will be much more powerful.

Your future is created by a succession of now moments. The overall vibrational frequency of your energy depends largely on how you feel now. So, care deeply about how you feel in the present moment. As soon as you start focusing on the now, and truly enjoy each moment, you won't care as much about when the manifestations happen.

Remember, the Law of Attraction is working all the time. It's the governing Universal Law that applies to everyone at every moment, not just when you want it to. Therefore, in order to make positive life changes, you have to accept your current circumstances, embrace the lessons life is trying to teach you and follow the path that unfolds in front of you.

CREATIVE VISUALIZATION

An important part of the Law of Attraction is the ability to use visualization to add that extra bit of energy to jump start your manifestations. Visualizing, or mentally seeing things and conditions as you wish them to be keeps your mind in order, and attracts to you the things you need to make life more enjoyable in an orderly way.

We all possess more power and greater possibilities than we realize, and visualizing is one of the greatest of these powers. It brings other possibilities to our observation. Everything in your reality originates from thought energies and comes into existence in exactly the same manner. All are projected thoughts, solidified.

Visualization works because your subconscious mind cannot tell the difference between reality and your imagination. By saturating your mind with vivid representations of you living your dream life, you inescapably communicate the goal to your subconscious mind. Your feeling should be that whatever it is that you desire, is normal and natural, a part of yourself.

Your subconscious will start to work on your "target" within a few days of starting your visualization practice. The more you visualize, the quicker you will "attract" your goals. And the more your subconscious understands what you want, the more effortless the whole process will seem.

Visualization is necessary for the Law of Attraction because your mind works with images rather than words. You can repeat a phrase such as "I have $5,000" over and over, but unless you are able to picture yourself having that money, plus feeling in your heart the joy of having $5,000, the process simply will not work.

Visualization is a very powerful process and it can help you manifest your desires. However, the opposite is also true. For most people, their thoughts tend to gravitate towards events that they most often observe. So if they are always observing negative events, they tend to think about how unlucky they are. With that, their thoughts create more negative events in their life.

Repetition is the key to success in acquiring any new skills. You have to practice your visualization skills. The good news is the more real your visualization, the more effective you will achieve what you desire.

Imagine you are watching a movie in your mind. You are the lead actor or actress in this movie. You are viewing your life as a third person. The key here is when you visualize behind your eyes; your mind treats it as a memory. Memory gets programmed into your subconscious mind and you will begin to form a belief that this memory is true.

Whatever your dream, always and always feel what you are visualizing. Of course, the emotions you attached to your visualization must be positive vibration. Remember, thoughts alone cannot manifest your dream into reality. The key is thoughts plus positive emotions.

Don't allow negative thoughts to enter your head and tell you it isn't possible. Simply push those thoughts aside gently and know that if you can see it mentally, you can create it in your physical reality. It is difficult to completely eliminate negative thoughts, so, after you have recognized your negative thoughts, make a conscious effort to instead replace them with positive thoughts.

Ideally, you should make creative visualization a daily part of your life – schedule time regularly to think about your better future. When you focus on current reality, you are acutely aware of what you don't have. When you focus on what you want with the energy of "I wish," or "I want," you are focusing with the energy of absence – absence attracts more absence.

Most people find it useful to set aside a specific time for the visualization (such as a fifteen minute period before going to sleep), but the most important thing is that you maintain your ritual of visualizing your goal until you obtain what you want in your life.

Although creative visualization, along with the Law of Attraction, are incredibly powerful and can certainly play a huge role in allowing you to develop the life you've always wanted, you substantially increase your chances of success if you also make concrete steps towards your goals. Visualization, putting your positive thoughts out into the universe, etc. works only if you actually get out and take action...action is the key to getting things moving for you. Thinking or visualizing will not get you there alone. You have to answer your phone...you have to interact and talk to people. You have to pay attention to synchronicities and the messages the universe is sending you. You will need to take the action that's aligned with your feel-good intuitional hits.

Take every relevant opportunity you encounter, be brave, and believe in a happier, more fulfilling life.

CONCLUSION

In this study of man, his relation to Universal Mind, Space and Matter, much has been said about relative subjects that may have seemed abstruse. However, scientists of good repute the World over, on both sides of the so called Iron Curtain, have come to the conclusion, by pure logic and reason, that the Planet Earth could not possibly be the only inhabited place in the universe, and that there are "more strange things 'twixt heaven and earth than this world dreams of..."

This book has been an attempt to bring the realization that life does exist, not only in outer space, but also within all forms of physical matter, both visible and invisible. With a more complete understanding of the true nature of man, we should make as much effort to investigate "inner space" as we are doing with outer space.

The material presented here should encourage men everywhere to know that not only are the space people here in embodiment, but that they exist also in various forms on our sister planets that life extends throughout the entire universe. We can do no better than to quote Saint Paul as he states in Second Corinthians, 12:3 – "...AND I KNEW SUCH A MAN, (WHETHER IN THE BODY, OR OUT OF THE BODY, I CANNOT TELL: GOD KNOWETH)..."

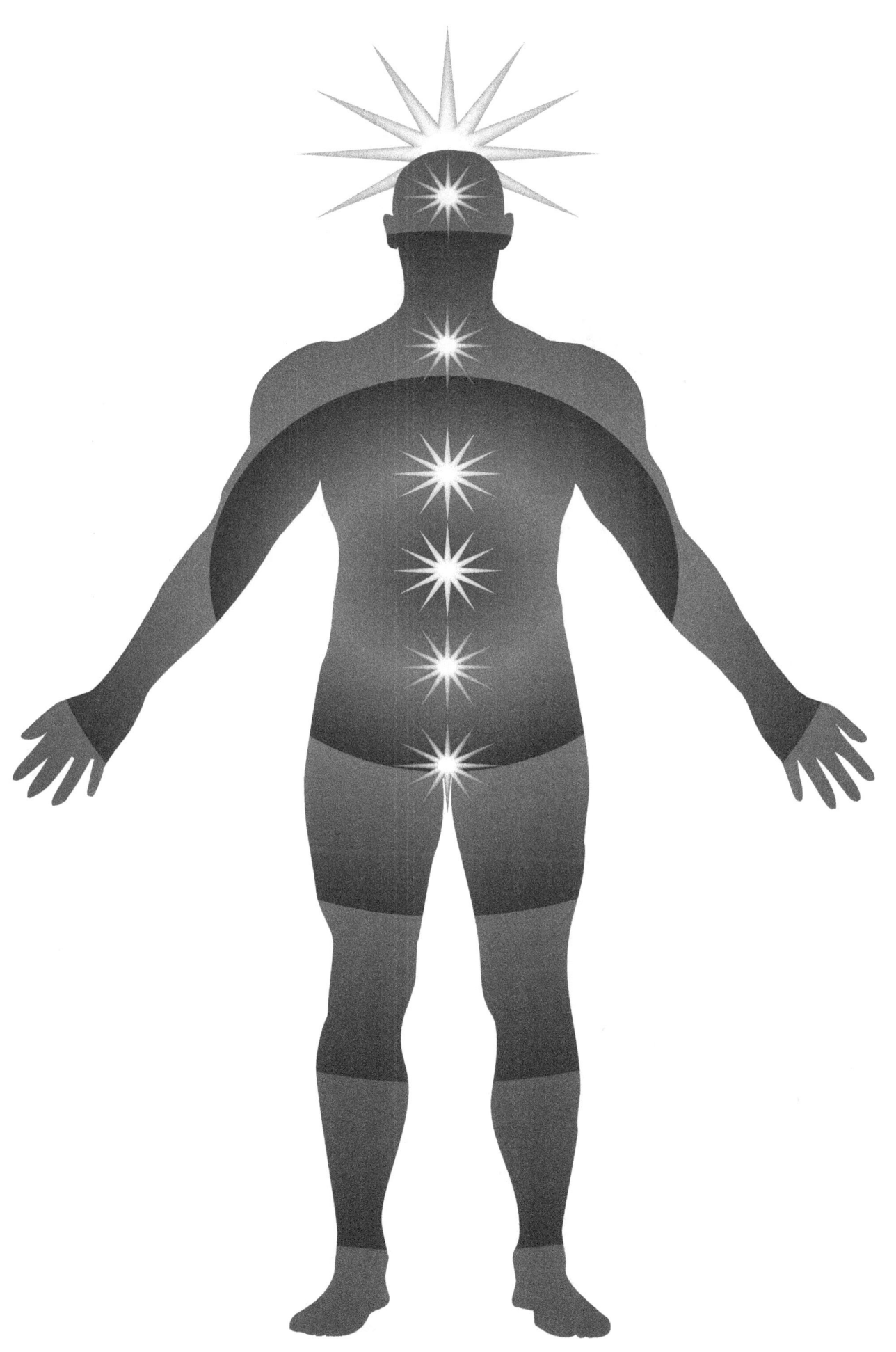

Our Dynamic Books Have Inspired Readers For Over Five Decades!

Maria D'Andrea
PSYCHIC AND SPIRITUAL COUNSELOR

631 559-1248 - mdanrea100@gmail.com

* * * * * * * * * * * * *

NOTE: Above information is for readings and counseling only. Books and kits this page to be ordered from the publisher (address below)

EXECUTE POSITIVE SPELLS AND UTILIZE MYSTIC POWERS

The following large format workbooks are based on the incredible occult knowledge and wisdom of Maria D' Andrea. Check off or list desired items.

- ☐ HEAVEN SENT MONEY SPELLS: DIVINELY INSPIRED FOR YOUR WEALTH
- ☐ OCCULT GRIMOIRE AND MAGICAL FORMULARY – A WORKBOOK FOR CREATING A POSITIVE LIFE
- ☐ POSITIVELY POSITIVE SPELL BOOK: VANQUISH ALL NEGATIVITY FROM YOUR LIFE
- ☐ SECRET MAGICAL ELIXIRS OF LIFE – LIVE LONGER, BE HAPPY, ATTRACT GOODNESS
- ☐ HOW TO ELIMINATE STRESS AND ANXIETY THROUGH THE OCCULT, CRYSTALS, GEMSTONES, MEDITATION, HERBS, OILS, MUSIC, INCENSE AND CANDLES
- ☐ SECRET OCCULT GALLERY AND SPELL CASTER. PLUS MARIA'S MOST POWERFUL SPELLS NEVER REVEALED PREVIOUSLY
- ☐ YOUR PERSONAL MEGA POWER SPELLS FOR LOVE, LUCK, PROSPERITY
- ☐ SIMPLE SPELLS USING AN ORDINARY DECK OF PLAYING CARDS
- ☐ CURSES AND THEIR REVERSALS: PLUS OMENS, SUPERSTITIONS AND REMOVAL OF THE EVIL EYE – Material by Maria and others.
- ☐ ANGEL SPELLS: ENOCHIAN OCCULT WORKBOOK OF CHARMS, SEALS, TALISMANS AND CIPHERS FOR CONTACTING ANGELS Material by Maria and others.

NOTE: Above books $20.00 each (add S/H)
☐ or all 10 just $179.00 + $12 S/H

EXPERIENCE THE AMAZING POWERS OF ALADDIN'S LAMP

MARIA D' ANDREA TEACHES YOU TO CALL UPON THE UNSEEN KINGDOM OF MAGICKAL BEINGS

Includes
1 Book by Maria
2 "Magic Lamp Incense Burner
3 Magickal Incense

Summon all you desire– as quickly as counting: One! Two! Three! For centuries the Aladdin's Lamp has been associated with power and success. King Solomon is said to have summoned and commanded the Genie to help construct Solomon's Temple. Beneficial Jinn can do your bidding. Lamp may differ from art.
☐ Send $35.00 + $5 S/H

THE COMPLETE SPIRITUAL AND OCCULT OILS WORKBOOK A-Z

☐ Here are over 1,000 magical powers of oils with easy to follow instructions for more than 1500 successful spells, recipes and rituals. Every conceivable formula and what purpose the oils are used for. $18.00

☐ Add kit of 5 spiritual oils Hex Breaking, Money Drawing, Commanding, etc. **Add $25 + $5 S/H**

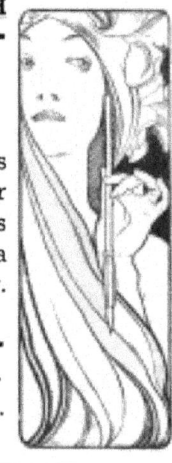

VIDEO WORKSHOPS

☐ Two Sets of DVDs, 6 mini workshops with instructions by Maria. Covers 25+ topics. Secret commands for Money. Power. Love. Spiritual Growth. Enjoy while you learn. **Both Sets $30.00 + $5 S/H**

MARIA'S "YES! YOU CAN " SERIES- $10 EACH
Easy to use reference manuals of various length (80-112 pages).
☐ "Sexy Medium's Love And Lust Spell Book."
☐ "Book Of Common Prayer."
☐ " Time Travel To Contact Beneficial Beings."
☐ "Supernatural Words Of Power"
☐ "Evocations To Evoke Summon Spirits."
☐ All 5 books $43.00 + $6 S/H

TIMOTHY BECKLEY, BOX 753, NEW BRUNSWICK, NJ 08903

TIMOTHY G. BECKLEY, PUBLISHER
Serving The Alternative Press And New Age Communities Since 1965

ISBN:9781606119747–$21.95   ISBN: 9781606110027–$21.95   ISBN9781606110539–$21.95   Timothy G. Beckley, Publisher

THE MOST POPULAR TITLES BY BEST-SELLING AUTHORS!
T. Lobsang Rampa • Brad Steiger • William Oribello • Nikola Tesla

ISBN: 978938294580–$21.95   ISBN: 9781606119839–$12.00   ISBN: 9781606112243–$19.95   ISBN: 9780938294917–$18.95

ISBN: 9781606111406–$19.95   ISBN: 978-1606111000–$19.95   ISBN: 9781606112120–$17.95   ISBN: 9781606111093–$21.95

Large, Easy-To-Read Formats • Fully Illustrated

For information about any of these books...contact Tim Beckley at

mrufo8@hotmail.com

Unsolved Mysteries! Hidden History! Unexplained Phenomena! Censored Events!

☐ **UFO REPEATERS—THE CAMERA DOESN'T LIE!— $24.00**

Here are the fantastic but true accounts of people from Turkey to New York City who claim repeated contact with Ultra-terrestrials. What makes their experiences so unique are the photos as evidence of their claims. Not blurry shots, but real hardware that came, they say, from space. Many have had numerous encounters, including Howard Menger, Marc Brinkerhoff, Ellen Crystal and Paul Villa.

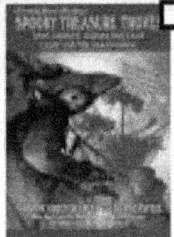

☐ **SPOOKY TREASURE TROVES: UFOS, GHOSTS, CURSED PIECES OF EIGHT AND THE SUPERNATURAL — $20.00**

From the Oak Island Knights Templar connection to the billion dollar Cocoas Island loot, paranormal manifestations have beckoned many to hidden treasures. Or these same spirits can lead you to an early grave to keep their secrets. Native American legends from AZ. Super Psychic Ted Owens in NM. Superstition Mountains. Kick ass book.
Over 300 large format pages.

☐ **T.LOBSANG RAMPA TRILOGY Famed Tibetan "Walk-In." 3 Best Sellers! - $29.00**

"The Hermit" — Secrets passed down by mysterious "Higher Order" who have protected and guided Earth since creation. *"Tibetan Sage"* — The Lama probes the history of our planet as he reenters the cave of the ancients and taken on a tour of the Hall of Records. *"Three Lives"* — Rampa delves deep into the magical realm of the human soul and immortality. Bonus Prayer-Meditation CD.

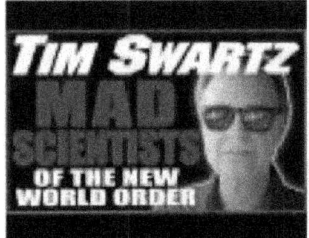

☐ **THE FINAL NAIL IN YOUR COFFIN! — $15.00**

A pox to all of mankind. Morgellons and Red Mercury Plagues may have been created in NWO Labs of "Mad Scientists." Emmy Award winning producer Tim Swartz delves into two modern conspiracies. Russians? Area 51?: Secret Order?

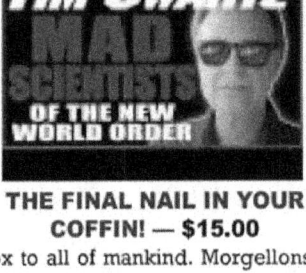

☐ **UFOS, TIME SLIPS, OTHER REALMS, THE SCIENCE OF FAIRIES — $15.00**

Here is your personal passport to the wonderland of Magonia. Another world awaits just beyond the realm of consciousness. A different explanation for the Saucer People. "Little Men" are NOT from Mars! "Banned" by "serious" researchers!

☐ Elfan Fairy Spell Pendant—**Add $20**

☐ **BIBLICAL UFO REVELATIONS and SEARCH FOR THE PALE PROPHET — $25.00**

Rev. Barry Downing says ET powers caused ancient miracles and both Testaments are manifestations of an alien intelligence. Was Jesus\sent from another planet? Sean Casteel asks: Who was the mysterious robe-clad healer who walked about the tribes of America 2000 years ago?
—**2 books.**

☐ **ANCIENT ASTRONAUTS 3 BOOK SET — $29.95**

By George Hunt Williamson. *"The Saucers Speak."* Calling all occupants of interplanetary craft. No need to set up huge telescopes or communicate via SETI. They can speak to you now! *"Other Tongues, Other Flesh."* The Wanderers, the Migrants, The Prophets, the Harvesters. The Agents are here! *"Traveling The Path Back To The Road In The Sky."* Strange saga of saucers, space brothers and secret agents.

☐ **ON THE EDGE OF REALITY: DREAM WEAVERS — MASTERS OF TIME AND SPACE — $15.00**

Brent Raynes says there are Ant People, Snake People, Blue People, Star People, Tricksters and "flying ghosts!"
Probe secret sites, and earthworks where strange energies and balls of intelligent light manifest. Learn how to wire the brain to process a paranormal-interdimensional experience.

☐ **OUT OF THE DARKNESS — $15.00**

Our planet is in great jeopardy! Psychics and Prophets offer shocking news about our future. Are we about to enter a new dimension of consciousness — or are we about to be blindsided by a series of unexplained, tragic, events? Is Planet X coming our way? Storms? Massive power failures? Can we avoid such frightening events?

☐ **SPECIAL — ALL ITEMS THIS AD JUST $148.00 + $15.00 S/H**
TIMOTHY BECKLEY, BOX 753, NEW BRUNSWICK, NJ 08903
24/7 Credit Cards 646 331-6777 (Private cell phone. Orders only. Leave all information (and your number).
mrufo8@hotmail.com for PayPal Invoices